PUBLIC VALUE AND
PUBLIC ADMINISTRATION

SELECT TITLES IN THE SERIES

Collaborative Governance Regimes
Kirk Emerson and Tina Nabatchi

Collaborating to Manage: A Primer for the Public Sector
Robert Agranoff

Crowdsourcing in the Public Sector
Daren C. Brabham

**The Dynamics of Performance Management:
Constructing Information and Reform**
Donald P. Moynihan

Federal Management Reform in a World of Contradictions
Beryl A. Radin

**Federal Service and the Constitution:
The Development of the Public Employment Relationship,
Second Edition**
David H. Rosenbloom

**The Future of Public Administration around the World:
The Minnowbrook Perspective**
Rosemary O'Leary, David Van Slyke, and Soonhee Kim, Editors

**How Information Matters:
Networks and Public Policy Innovation**
Kathleen Hale

**Implementing Innovation:
Fostering Enduring Change in Environmental and
Natural Resource Governance**
Toddi A. Steelman

**Managing within Networks:
Adding Value to Public Organizations**
Robert Agranoff

Managing Disasters through Public-Private Partnerships
Ami J. Abou-bakr

**Public Values and Public Interest:
Counterbalancing Economic Individualism**
Barry Bozeman

PUBLIC VALUE AND PUBLIC ADMINISTRATION

JOHN M. BRYSON
BARBARA C. CROSBY
AND
LAURA BLOOMBERG
EDITORS

Georgetown University Press
Washington, DC

Library of Congress Cataloging-in-Publication Data

Public value and public administration / John M. Bryson, Barbara C. Crosby, and Laura Bloomberg, editors.
    pages cm — (Public management and change series)
  Includes bibliographical references and index.
  ISBN 978-1-62616-261-7 (hc : alk. paper)—ISBN 978-1-62616-262-4 (pb : alk. paper)—
ISBN 978-1-62616-263-1 (eb)
  1. Public administration.   2. Common good.   3. Public interest.   I. Bryson, John M. (John Moore), 1947– editor.   II. Crosby, Barbara C., 1946– editor.   III. Bloomberg, Laura, editor
IV. Series: Public management and change.
 JF1351.P858 2015
 351—dc23

                                                                                          2015007440

16 15   9 8 7 6 5 4 3 2
First printing

Printed in the United States of America

Cover by Naylor Design, Inc.

CONTENTS

ILLUSTRATIONS

Figures

TABLES

PREFACE

An emerging approach to public administration is eclipsing both the traditional approach and what has come to be known as new public management. This new approach is part of the continuing evolution of thinking and practice in public administration. Just as the traditional approach (with its emphasis on efficiency) was overshadowed in the 1980s and 1990s by new public management (with its emphasis on efficiency and effectiveness) as the dominant view, we believe that this newer movement is likely to succeed new public management. The new approach highlights increased reliance on networked and collaborative *governance* in which governments, businesses, nonprofit organizations, and civil society all play roles in addressing public challenges, creating public value, and honoring values beyond efficiency and effectiveness—especially democratic values. The term "governance" in this case can go well beyond government and refers to collective direction setting and decision making about important issues related to some aspect of public life.

Clearly, values-related questions are central to the emerging approach. These concerns are not new to public administration, but much about the contemporary context is. Key features of the context include the urgency, scope, and scale of public problems facing the world; the recognition that governments alone cannot effectively address many of these problems; and a concern that public values have been and will be lost as a consequence of a powerful antigovernment rhetoric and a host of market- and performance-based reforms (Bryson, Crosby, and Bloomberg 2014).

The emerging approach does not have a name that is agreed upon, though there are several contenders. We prefer to call it *public value governance* given the need for effective cross-sector, cross-level, multistakeholder governance in a shared-power world that can effectively address important public problems while simultaneously attending to the creation of significant public value and protecting and furthering desired public values.

Exploring questions of value can help public and nonprofit managers, government officials, and citizens participating in all sectors to think about what kind of society they seek to build and also to counter the perception that value generation occurs almost exclusively in business enterprises and markets (Bozeman 2007). In *Public Value and Public Administration*, scholars from Australia, Europe, and the United States present an overview of major issues and debates focused on the frameworks, skills, methods, measurements, and processes related to creating public value. This book does not settle the debates; instead it provides needed intellectual order, helps clarify the issues, and demonstrates how the meaning of public value and public values is intimately related to how they are theorized and addressed by managers, elected officials, and other stakeholders.

The book has grown out of the editors' and authors' belief that time is right for a new approach to public administration and management that can align the values of efficiency and effectiveness with other important values—especially broadly democratic values. We believe that the new approach will be most robust and influential if it is infused appropriately with the language, concepts, and methodologies of public value. The public value conversation is growing rapidly, with contributions from across the globe, but especially Australia, New Zealand, the United Kingdom and Continental Europe, and the United States. Up to this point, however, scholars developing the concepts have often been working in different camps and applications have been fairly limited, which has resulted in different streams of understanding, very uneven application across policy fields, and occasionally inappropriate use of the concepts.

In order to make connections among these different streams, foster deeper understanding of public value in practice, and advance the emerging new approach to public administration and management, the Center for Integrative Leadership at the University of Minnesota organized a conference, "Creating Public Value," in fall 2012 that brought together some of the leading public value scholars along with researchers who focus on how public value can be discerned and measured in practice. For three days conference participants engaged in lively cross-disciplinary exchanges of views about the nature of public value, its potential for revitalizing democracy, and the possible pitfalls of public value rhetoric.

Three main scholarly products have resulted from the conference. The first was the symposium "Exploring the Value of Public Value," published in *Public Administration Review*, volume 74, number 4 (2014), featuring a lengthy introductory literature review and foundation papers developed for the conference. The second is a book we edited titled *Creating Public Value in Practice: Advancing the Common Good in a Multi-Sector, Shared-Power, No-One-Wholly-in-Charge World* (Bryson, Crosby, and Bloomberg 2015) that contains sections on democracy and citizenship, institutional design, cross-sector collaboration, and cases in public value creation from the local to the global levels.

The third is the present volume, *Public Value and Public Administration*, which represents an intellectual advance on the earlier two publications. This book introduces scholars, practitioners, and students of public affairs to the main streams of public value scholarship and debates about public value's relation to democracy. This book highlights six key practices by which public managers, public officials, and citizens can foster a wide range of public values and cope with some of the tensions and trade-offs among them: policy analysis, design, and evaluation; leadership; dialogue and deliberation; institutional design; formal and informal processes of democracy; and strategic management, including performance measurement and management. We try to capture some of this intellectual advance with the public value governance triangle (PVGT) that we present in the introduction and pursue further in the conclusions at the end of the book. The PVGT and our discussions of it show in greater depth how the various streams in the public value literature relate to one another and how the six key practices may be used to address public value and concerns about it. For scholars, practitioners, students, and citizens the book demonstrates ways in which public managers can create public value, measure and assess it, and use performance measurement and management to promote it.

Our fond hope is that this book and the other publications resulting from the conference help scholars and practitioners to develop a stronger global learning community focused on the creation of public value. Ultimately we hope that this book and its companion publications will contribute to better public value governance and strengthened democracies throughout the world.

John M. Bryson
Barbara C. Crosby
Laura Bloomberg

Acknowledgments

In September 2012, the Center for Integrative Leadership (CIL) at the University of Minnesota brought together many of the leading scholars of public value and other academics and practitioners to explore conceptions of public value from different disciplinary perspectives, develop a comprehensive view of the different streams of theorizing about public value, and consider how public value is enacted in communities, cross-sector collaborations, and public organizations.

The chapters in this book are drawn from papers first prepared for that conference, "Creating Public Value," and subsequently refined to sharpen their arguments and enhance links to the public value literature. Chapter 12, on performance information, was commissioned later. Since the time of the conference, virtually all of the chapters have gone through two sets of reviews and revisions. We wish to thank all of our authors for being such wonderful collaborators.

To gain a deeper understanding of the more philosophical underpinnings of the debates, readers may consult a special symposium on public value that came out of the conference, as published in *Public Administration Review*, volume 74, number 4 (2014). To understand more about practical applications of the public value ideas, see the first book to come out of the conference: John M. Bryson, Barbara C. Crosby, and Laura Bloomberg, eds., *Creating Public Value in Practice: Advancing the Common Good in a Multi-Sector, Shared-Power, No-One-Wholly-in-Charge World* (2015).

The conference was cosponsored by the CIL and the University of Minnesota's Hubert H. Humphrey School of Public Affairs. The CIL is a joint venture of the Humphrey School and the university's Curtis L. Carlson School of Management; we thank Dean Eric Schwartz of the Humphrey School and Dean Sri Zaheer of the Carlson School for their support. We also extend our deep appreciation to then interim dean Greg Lindsey of the Humphrey School for his strong support. The CIL steering committee also deserves our thanks for its endorsement and strengthening of the conference idea. Two CIL staff members, Angie Stehr and Girija Tulpule, provided marvelous help throughout the process of putting on the conference.

The conference was also cosponsored by the Minnesota Humanities Center, a state-sponsored nonprofit organization focused on bringing the unique resources of the humanities to the challenges and opportunities of our times. David O'Fallon, president of the center, has been a wonderful partner.

The faculty and staff of the Humphrey School's Public and Nonprofit Leadership Center were strong supporters throughout the process of putting on the conference. We would especially like to thank Mary Maronde and Jodi Sandfort for their help.

The coeditors taught a seminar on creating public value during the fall 2012 semester, and our dedicated students served as facilitators at the conference and afterward engaged in deep reviews and syntheses of the conference papers. Their intelligence, enthusiasm, and hard work were a constant joy and helped us sharpen our own thoughts about the public value literature; our thanks go to Libby Caulum, Abigail Felber-Smith, Ana Gabilondo, Will Harrison, Brad Hasskamp, Wendy Huckaby, Ashley James, Jason Johnson, Laura King, Romina Madrid Miranda, Todd Maki, Margaret McKenna, David Milavetz, Maria Moeller, Kristen Murray, Andrea Nadel, James Scheibel, Nichole Sorenson, Katharine Thomas-Tielke, David Thorpe, and Girija Tulpule.

Kassira Absar and Jeff Ochs were excellent graduate assistants throughout the process of putting this book together. We could not have pulled this project off without them!

Last, and by no means least, we want to express our deepest thanks and gratitude to the former president of the University of Minnesota, Robert Bruininks. Over the years he has been a steadfast friend of the Humphrey School, the CIL, and the coeditors. Beyond that, and more to the point, he is deeply committed to creating public value; he provided very strong moral support and significant tangible resources that helped make the conference—and therefore this book—happen.

Introduction

John M. Bryson, Barbara C. Crosby,
and Laura Bloomberg

Public administration practitioners and scholars are paying considerable attention to the creation of public value, to public values more generally, and to the health of the public sphere within which public value is created and public values are achieved (Williams and Shearer 2011; Van der Wal, Nabatchi, and De Graaf 2013). This trend is part of the continuing evolution of thinking and practice in public administration. As noted in the preface, we anticipate that the public value approach may well displace new public management, the dominant view at the end of the twentieth century.

Many authors, including ourselves (Bryson, Crosby, and Bloomberg 2014, 2015), point to the need for a new approach and to aspects of its emergence in practice and theory (e.g., Moore 1995, 2013, 2014; Boyte 2005; Stoker 2006; Bozeman 2007; Kettl 2008; Alford and Hughes 2008; Osborne 2010; Talbot 2010; Denhardt and Denhardt 2011). For example, Janet and Robert Denhardt's excellent and widely cited book *The New Public Service* (2011) captures much of the collaborative and democratic spirit, content, and governance focuses of the movement, and values and governance are central to this new public service.

Based on citations, "new public service" appears to be the leading contender for the emerging approach's name. We ourselves, however, prefer "public value governance" because of the emphasis on both *public value* and *governance* and because, to most people, "public service" typically refers to public employment or to a government-provided service, both of which are narrower conceptions than that implied by the scope of the emerging multisector approach. Regardless of the name, a new approach to public administration clearly is in the offing, and the creation of public value in democracies is a central part of it.

While efficiency was the main concern of traditional public administration, and efficiency and effectiveness are the main concerns of new public management, values beyond efficiency and effectiveness are pursued, debated, challenged, and evaluated in the emerging approach. In this regard the emerging approach reemphasizes and brings to the fore value-related concerns of previous eras that were always present but not dominant (Denhardt and Denhardt 2011; Rosenbloom and McCurdy 2006).

Exploring questions of value can help public and nonprofit managers, government officials, and citizens participating in all sectors to think about what kind of society they seek to build and also to counter the perception that value generation occurs almost exclusively in business enterprises and markets (Bozeman 2007). In this book, scholars from the Australia, Europe, and the United States present an overview of major issues and debates focused on the skills, methods, measurements, and processes related to creating public value. The book does not settle the debates; instead it helps clarify the issues and demonstrates how the meaning of public value and public values is intimately related to how they are theorized and addressed by managers, elected officials, and other stakeholders. Attention is devoted in particular to the two most dominant approaches to public value: Mark Moore's (1995, 2013) managerial action-focused ideas about how to create public value and Barry Bozeman and his colleagues' focus on public values embedded in public policy and supported by society, and to how these dominant approaches relate to each other.

This book is intended for scholars, students, reflective practitioners, and citizen activists. For scholars teaching or conducting research focused on public and non-profit management, policy analysis, leadership, performance measurement and management, cross-sector collaboration, democracy and citizenship, or institutional design, the present volume brings together theories, critiques, skills, measurement approaches, and processes that foster understanding of public value and public values. It also describes methods for assessing the worth of particular organizations, policies, programs, and projects designed to achieve public purposes. The book is also well-suited for students in public affairs, public administration, urban and regional planning, education, and public health, as well as those studying corporate social responsibility and social entrepreneurship programs in business schools. For practitioners the book suggests practical tools for discerning what particular stakeholders value and assessing whether and how much public value is created. Citizen activists can employ this book's ideas and tools to advocate for particular management or policy changes; judge whether particular laws, policies, and projects are likely to benefit their communities; and hold their elected representatives accountable for the creation of public value.

THE CONTRIBUTIONS OF THIS BOOK

A significant contribution of *Public Value and Public Administration* is to broaden previous theorizing in the public value literature. The book offers language, frameworks, and approaches for helping people talk about the worth of what elected officials, leaders, managers, and citizens can achieve together. It reveals the potential for discerning, measuring, assessing, governing, and managing public value within and across multiple sectors and not just governments and markets. Instrumental and end-state values are encompassed. Elaborating and operationalizing the concepts of public value and public values seem especially important at a time when scholars and practitioners alike recognize that many complex public challenges can only be solved through collaborations of business, nonprofit, media, and/or community organizations in addition to government (Stoker 2006; Crosby and Bryson 2005, 2010; Forrer, Kee, and Boyer 2014). These collaborations, however, pose particular challenges to those who care about democratic accountability. We believe that public value discernment, measurement, and assessment methods may be a way to help public managers and other stakeholders make informed decisions about when collaborations should be pursued, restructured, or disbanded. Several chapters in the book offer explicit or implicit examples.

Following some background in John Bryson, Barbara C. Crosby, and Laura Bloomberg's chapter 1, the book is organized by sections focusing on three interrelated themes: helping managers focus on creating public value, ways of measuring and assessing public value, and ways of measuring and managing performance. Addressing these themes puts the book on the cutting edge of an important and burgeoning new development in public administration—linking the various strands of public value theorizing to the developing array of approaches, skills, methods, and techniques for creating, measuring, and assessing public value.

HELPING MANAGERS FOCUS ON CREATING PUBLIC VALUE

Part I comprises five chapters focused on helping public managers who are involved in the process of creating public value. These chapters address political astuteness, facilitated dialogue and deliberation, system dynamics modeling, contingent decision frameworks, and the requirements for successful innovation—competencies that are very unevenly taught, if at all, in schools of public affairs and administration. The chapters focus mainly, though by no means exclusively, on capabilities and creating public value via integrative approaches (as represented in figure 1.2). The driving conception of public value is essentially Moore's rather than Bozeman's.

Chapter 2 highlights the need for political astuteness on the part of public managers if they are to help create public value in necessarily political environments. Authors John Alford, Jean Hartley, and Owen Hughes assert that public managers should be doubly adept at dealing with their political environments by engaging in politics while at the same time appearing not to be so engaged. Drawing on the results of their studies of senior public servants in Australia, New Zealand, and the United Kingdom, the authors identify a number of ways in which public managers can use political astuteness to both discern and create public value; these include reading collective aspirations, securing a mandate, enlisting external parties to get things done, and knowing where the line between politics and administration is. Political astuteness most obviously should be part of effective policy analysis, design, evaluation, and leadership, but it should also inform use of the other practical integrative approaches. Political astuteness is hard to overestimate as an important competency public managers should have if they are to help create public value.

In chapter 3, Jodi Sandfort and Kathryn Quick analyze the work of facilitators in three examples of the dialogical and deliberative process known as the Art of Hosting and Harvesting Conversations that Matter (http://www.artofhosting .org/). The Art of Hosting is an assembly of facilitated group engagement processes that is rapidly gaining adherents and users across the globe; the approach fosters dialogue and deliberation among participants and offers innovative methods of gathering and summarizing the results of those conversations. Prime features of the process are the sharing of power among participants and mutual learning about the process itself, so that everyone is prepared to become a host of "conversations that matter." The chapter's three case examples are all aimed at community problem solving. The authors find that the particular design of events using the Art of Hosting and harvested information will affect the extent to which the events generate public value and build civic deliberative capacity. The Art of Hosting and other methods of facilitated dialogue and deliberation are important approaches to exploring, revealing, and often integrating public values and creating public value;

skill at designing and facilitating such conversations is an important capability public managers and others involved in public value creation should have.

Chapter 4, by George Richardson, David Andersen, and Luis Luna-Reyes, describes a facilitated computer-assisted dialogue and deliberation process. The Art of Hosting techniques are not strong on sophisticated analysis; in contrast, the process profiled in this chapter includes system dynamics modeling and analytic capabilities that help participants identify and analyze important systemic relationships—especially those involving feedback. The process the authors describe is called system dynamics group model building (SDGMB), which involves key stakeholders, group facilitation, and formal computer simulations in order to "join minds" and help public managers and policymakers who are grappling with a complex problem achieve a policy consensus about means and ends for value creation. Like Art of Hosting, the SDGMB process includes "conversations that matter," but the key differences include formal model building using system dynamics methodology; computer support to develop the system model and test policy options based on that model; and carefully scripted conversations aimed at helping participants draw on their expertise to build the model, understand the results of computer runs, and converge on desirable policy options. The authors illustrate the process via a case in which SDGMB supported welfare reform initiatives in three county governments in New York State. These exercises generally resulted in policy prescriptions, organizational designs, and performance management regimes that were very different from those the participating experts initially thought would be best. Richardson, Andersen, and Luna-Reyes conclude with an assessment of SDGMB from the perspective of public value creation. Again, skill at designing and facilitating dialogue and deliberation processes that include sophisticated analyses is an important capability public managers and others involved in public value creation should have.

In chapter 5, John Alford identifies weaknesses in the current contingency framework used by public managers when making decisions about the "externalization" of government functions to nonprofit and for-profit organizations via contracting. Contrary to the "one best way" stance of externalization's proponents and opponents—that is, either provide services via external arrangements or provide them with internal staff—Alford argues that externalization is neither always valuable nor always problematic; its usefulness simply depends on whether benefits outweigh costs in specific circumstances. Based on the assertion that a conventional contingency framework misses strategic costs and benefits related to the positioning and capabilities of a government organization within its environment, Alford provides a set of decision rules for weighing up the new public value likely to be created or not created by a given externalization effort. The ability to think contingently about policy options in a broad public-value context is clearly an important management skill that can lead to very different policy and organizational prescriptions and performance management regimes.

Chapter 6, by Jean Hartley, argues that public managers are typically called upon to "innovate" when that term signals continuous improvement. Less frequently, but often enough, they are also called upon to help create step changes of some kind, which is how Hartley defines innovation—as disruptive rather than incremental change. She methodically contrasts government and business-sector innovation in relation to creating public value in each of the three phases of the innovation process: innovation, implementation, and diffusion.

Hartley notes that studies of organizational innovation tend to focus on business enterprises, and argues that this research may not apply to public-sector organizations because of the different assumptions and demands that characterize them. For example, while both business and public administration literatures attend to innovations in terms of products, services, processes, strategies, and positions, generally only the public administration and political science literatures pay attention to policy, governance, and rhetorical innovations. She also notes that whereas the sources of innovations in any sector can be employees and managers, networks of practice, and users of products and services, when it comes to public innovations elected politicians are often the sources and thus must be taken into account. In addition, where public innovations are concerned, users are typically also citizens. In short, the context of the public sphere "fundamentally affects aims, behaviors, and understanding." As in chapter 5, the ability to think contingently about innovation options in a broad public-value context is clearly an important public management skill that can lead to far-reaching effects in terms of policy, institutional and organizational designs, and strategic management regimes.

MEASURING AND ASSESSING PUBLIC VALUE

Part II comprises five chapters focused on the important issue of how to measure and assess public value. Each author or group of authors presents an approach to systematizing the collection and assessment of public value information and presenting it in relatively easy-to-understand form. The chapters thus address issues in the use of policy analysis, design, and evaluation—and the competencies needed for doing so—in order to help create public value. Collectively the chapters illustrate an array of approaches and techniques to measuring and assessing public value that public managers and others interested in creating public value should know about. The approaches and techniques can be helpful to leaders, inform dialogue and deliberation processes, influence institutional and organizational designs, be useful as part of the formal and informal processes of democracy, and serve as useful aids to strategic management processes.

In chapter 7, Clive Belfield describes the role of cost-benefit analysis (CBA) in creating public value. CBA is perhaps the prototypical analytic technique in liberal, market-oriented societies for determining whether or not something creates public value on balance. Since the 1960s, when policy analysis was developing as a field, CBA has held something like pride of place, though many other techniques are now widely used as well (Radin 2013). Belfield takes a standard economics view when comparing and contrasting CBA and public value and then addresses specific theoretical and practical objections to the use of CBA in ascribing value. He asserts that CBA has far more potential than is typically recognized by noneconomists to assist in the discernment, measurement, and assessment of public value. Finally, Belfield illustrates how even a basic application of CBA can improve the policymaking process by drawing on practical examples.

In chapter 8, Mark Moore discusses the challenges public-sector agencies face in articulating a clear bottom line to measure the value of governmental activities and the performance of public-sector managers. He suggests that the challenge lies not on the cost side of the equation but instead on finding an appropriate analogue to the revenues earned by a business through sales of products or services to willing customers. As an alternative, Moore proposes both a public value account that outlines categories for assessing public value propositions and a public value scorecard that incorporates the public value account as a bottom line for government. The account includes, on the cost side of the ledger, the use of collectively owned assets and associated costs, including financial costs, unintended negative consequences, and the social costs of using state authority. On the benefit side of the ledger (the analogue to business revenues) is the achievement of collectively valued social outcomes; these include mission achievement, unintended positive consequences, client satisfaction (including service recipients and obligates), and justice and fairness (at the individual level in operations and at the aggregate level in results). Cost-benefit analysis at least theoretically might produce a similar account, particularly on the cost side, but in practice it is hard to imagine that it would.

In chapter 9, Jennie Welch, Heather Rimes, and Barry Bozeman describe public value mapping (PVM), in which two dimensions are juxtaposed: market success or failure and public value success or failure. The result is a matrix that helps clarify the ways in which—and reasons why—public policies succeed or fail. The approach is case-based and includes the following steps: (1) identifying relevant public values; (2) assessing whether public value successes and failures have occurred; (3) mapping relationships among values; and (4) graphically representing the relationships between public value success and failure and market success and failure. PVM has been used to assess public policies in a variety of areas, including housing, science and technology, social policy, and others. This chapter provides a summary of the approach's rationale, the techniques used as part of PVM, the approach's strengths and weaknesses, and major findings from its application across fields. The mapping technique might be used to inform policy and managerial action to create more public value successes and fewer failures.

In chapter 10, Timo Meynhardt defines public value as fundamentally both value *from* and value *for* the public and provides a framework for understanding value creation as a deeply interactive process in which actors contribute to and share both the benefits and the risks. Against this background Meynhardt introduces a public value scorecard (PVSC) that is different from Moore's but is somewhat analogous to scorecards currently implemented in business, government, and nonprofit organizations.

Meynhardt's scorecard comprises five dimensions, each of which is assessed by individuals using a questionnaire; the individual results are then aggregated to produce a collective view of the public value created by an organization or service. The five dimensions include four outlined in an earlier Meynhardt study (2009); the fifth—a financial measure—is theoretically a subdimension of instrumental-utilitarian values but, as Meynhardt notes, "practitioners are unlikely to accept a PVSC unless it includes a financial measure." The five dimensions are:

1. "Is it useful?" (drawing on utilitarian-instrumental values)
2. "Is it decent?" (reflecting moral and ethical values)
3. "Is it politically acceptable?" (capturing political and social values)
4. "Does it allow for positive experiences?" (embodying hedonistic and aesthetic values)
5. "Is it financially beneficial?" (reflecting utilitarian-instrumental values)

In chapter 11, John Thomas, Theodore Poister, and Min Su analyze survey and other feedback data received by the Georgia Department of Transportation (GDOT) from a variety of its stakeholders, including legislators, local government administrators, and partners. The authors explore a number of questions about stakeholder perspectives: What public values do different constituent groups view as more or less important relative to GDOT? How well do these values fit standard categorizations of public values? And how do stakeholders view the relationship between and among public values? The study highlights the importance as a public value of the quality of the working relationships with stakeholders through which public agencies achieve their outcomes. Thomas, Poister, and Su argue that the quality of working relationships should be added to the values inventory compiled by Beck Jørgensen and Bozeman (2007).

MEASURING AND MANAGING PERFORMANCE

Creating public value and assessing it are clearly crucial, but both also need to be incorporated into performance measurement and management systems if public value is to be produced over time. The chapters in parts I and II for the most part do not really consider this requirement for effective managerial action (in Moore's terms), for achieving public value success (in Bozeman's terms), or for creating a beneficial experience for the public (in Benington and Meynhardt's terms). The chapters in part III are helpful for thinking about measuring and managing performance when public value is fully appreciated.

In chapter 12, Alexander Kroll and Donald Moynihan explore the role of performance information in identifying and creating public value. The chapter summarizes knowledge about factors affecting—and skills involved in—performance information use, and the authors emphasize that performance information should be relevant not just to the organization's explicit mission but should also encompass important non-mission-related and public-value-relevant information. Kroll and Moynihan identify four broad categories of performance information use: passive, political, perverse, and—ideally—purposeful use; they go on to identify a range of factors that influence whether purposeful use is made of performance information and conclude with a set of lessons on performance management for public value.

In chapter 13, Anthony Cresswell, Meghan Cook, and Natalie Helbig address the practical problems government agencies and managers face when attempting to use public value creation as a guide for decision making and investment in new initiatives, especially when they are confronted with political polarization and competing public values. The authors present a relatively new decision support instrument known as the public value assessment tool (PVAT) and discuss how various government agencies responded to the tool during a grant-funded pilot project.

The PVAT assesses public value against seven dimensions that can be tailored appropriately to fit specific circumstances. The seven dimensions, along with examples of potential content, are:

1. Financial—including impacts on current or anticipated income, asset values, liabilities, entitlements, and other aspects of wealth or risks to any of the above.
2. Political—capturing impacts of personal or corporate influence on government actions or policy, on government's role in political affairs, or influence in political parties or prospects for current or future public office.
3. Social—reflecting impacts on family or community relationships, social mobility, status, and identity.
4. Strategic—focusing on impacts on economic or political advantage or opportunities, goals, and resources for innovation or planning.
5. Ideological—indicating impacts on beliefs; moral or ethical commitments; alignment of government actions, policies, or social outcomes with beliefs; and moral or ethical positions.
6. Stewardship—reflecting impacts on the public's view of government officials as faithful stewards or guardians of the value of the government itself in terms of public trust, integrity, and legitimacy.
7. Quality of life—capturing impacts on individual and household health, security, satisfaction, and general well-being.

The dimensions are different from—yet seemingly complementary to—Moore's, Bozeman's, and Meynhardt's. Additional work would be required to clarify and reconcile the differences.

In chapter 14, Enrico Guarini explores how governments can shape policymaking, performance measurement, and reporting in order to account for the contributions of civil society, business, and government to public value. Guarini analyzes a multiyear experiment in boundary-crossing public value measurement and reporting in the Italian region of Veneto. He describes the process used for community engagement and the extent to which public value measurement and reporting are relevant for government, nonprofit, and business leaders. In terms of what many of the authors in this book assert, the designers and implementers of the Veneto process did much that was right; unfortunately, the experiment ended when the elected regional government representatives changed. Reasonably analogous experiments are underway elsewhere and are likely to become more common as the emerging approach to public administration takes a firmer hold. For example, in the United States, there are the federally sponsored Partnership for Sustainable Communities (http://www.sustainablecommunities.gov/mission/about-us); the State of Virginia's Virginia Performs (http://vaperforms.virginia.gov/); and the City of Portland, Oregon's 2035 Comprehensive Plan and the process that created it (https://www.portlandoregon.gov/bps/article/497622). Each of these efforts works at building the legitimacy and authority to pursue the effort, invest in needed capabilities, and endeavor to create public value via the various approaches to addressing public value concerns.

CONCLUSIONS

The public value literature is thriving and is now a major focus of work in the public administration field. Unfortunately, most of the work to date has occurred in disconnected streams, with *public value* scholars in one group, *public values* scholars in another, and scholars interested in the *public sphere* in yet another. While some cross-fertilization has occurred, the time has arrived to more explicitly link the conversations around creating public value, measuring and assessing it, and performance measurement and management. This book represents the first attempt in that direction and thus contributes to the field as a whole.

While the book brings many important scholars together and showcases a range of approaches, it is important to keep the important distinctions among public value, public values, and the public sphere in mind. We find it helpful to view the public value achieved in any particular case as a summary assessment of the extent to which more specific public values have been achieved or realized in practice. The summary may be achieved by drawing on many different processes, including policy analysis, design, and evaluation; leadership; dialogue and deliberation; institutional and organizational design; formal and informal processes of democracy; and strategic management, especially including performance measurement and management. Since the public values that might enter into that assessment are potentially quite numerous, contested, and not necessarily compatible, the process of reaching agreements on which values will prevail and in which ways may well be messy. Who gets to be involved in that process is yet another often-contested issue. These contests will take place in the public sphere seen as the occasions, settings, and context within which public values exist and public value might be created. That public sphere will either be maintained, strengthened, or diminished depending on how the contest is settled.

Because of this volume's focus, it does not give much attention to the barriers to creating public value. The challenges of addressing adverse politics and an array of structural and other barriers are certainly attended to in various ways, but the focus in the book is more on how public value creation, discernment, measurement, assessment, management, and governance might be approached in a way that informs politics and decision making. In that regard the chapters offer a variety of approaches to improving government agency, nonprofit, and cross-sector collaboration performance within the public sphere more generally. The book is thus part of, and helps point the way toward, the public value literature's promising future and practical consequences.

NOTE

This introduction draws on Bryson, Crosby, and Bloomberg (2014, 2015).

1

DISCERNING AND ASSESSING PUBLIC VALUE

MAJOR ISSUES AND NEW DIRECTIONS

JOHN M. BRYSON, BARBARA C. CROSBY,
AND LAURA BLOOMBERG

This chapter explores the meaning of value, compares Moore's and Bozeman's views of public value, connects public value to concepts like the public interest, and suggests how different public value approaches might be integrated. Because a workable public sphere is vital to conceptions of public value, we also consider the meaning of the public sphere.[1]

THE MEANING OF VALUE

For most readers, the term "value" is straightforward, meaning "relative worth, utility, or importance" ("Value" n.d.).[2] This commonsense definition, however, begs a number of questions apparent in the current debate over public values, public value, and the public sphere (Beck Jørgensen and Bozeman 2007; Rutgers 2008). These questions concern at least the following: (1) whether the objects of value are subjective psychological states or objective states of the world; (2) whether value is intrinsic, extrinsic, or relational; (3) whether something is valuable for its own sake or as a means to something else; (4) whether there are hierarchies of values; (5) who does the valuing; (6) how the valuing is done; and (7) against what criteria the object of value is measured. The chapters in this book demonstrate the variety of ways in which these questions can be addressed productively.

TWO CONTRASTING VIEWS OF PUBLIC VALUE

What we will call the *public value literature* includes the related themes of public value, public values, and the public sphere, in which the adjective "public" before value, values, and sphere extends well beyond government purview. This body of work has grown dramatically in recent years.

Based on an extensive review of the literature, Williams and Shearer (2011) find an increasing popularity of the concept of public value (singular) within both academic and practice settings. Indeed, Stoker (2006) argues that a new paradigm he calls "public value management" is emerging to replace "traditional" public administration and what has been called the new public management. Similarly, Van der Wal, Nabatchi, and de Graaf (2013) assert that "the study of public values [plural] is not only gaining in importance in our field [but] might be one of the most important themes." Finally, scholars and practitioners have paid substantial attention to the public sphere, whether in terms of government's proper role (e.g., Kettl 2002, 2008; Osborne and Hutchinson 2004; Goldsmith and Eggers 2004), public engagement (Cooper, Bryer, and Meek 2006; Bryson et al. 2013; Nabatchi and Leighninger 2015), active citizenship (e.g., Boyte 2005, 2011), or the desire for strengthened democracy (e.g., Fung 2003; Nabatchi et al. 2012).

In this section we focus on the two main strands of the public value literature. The first, developed by Mark Moore and his colleagues, is a managerial action-focused concept of creating public value, while the second is Barry Bozeman's and his colleagues' policy and societally focused conception of public values. In the next section we attend to the public sphere, the third main theme in the literature. In the section after that we present a conceptual framework that incorporates all three perspectives and discuss ways of integrating them in practice.

Mark Moore on Creating Public Value

Mark Moore's 1995 landmark book *Creating Public Value: Strategic Management in Government* helped popularize the language of public value and suggested how it might be realized in practice. Moore explicitly offered the language of "creating public value" as a counter to the more dominant language of creating shareholder value and to the assumption that government is suspect and businesses are more legitimate. The book concentrated specifically on what US public managers—meaning in this case government managers—could do that would benefit the public and that the public would value as well. The action focus was managerial, while the desired outcome was organizations that meet (or can appropriately and legitimately change) their mandates; generate political support in such a way that they can deliver public value and what the public values; and do so efficiently, effectively, accountably, justly, and fairly in the context of democratic governance. Public value is thus a summary term assessed and measured against the extent to which it achieves or realizes in practice more specific public values at reasonable cost.

Moore's approach is a normative, doctrinal argument about what public managers should do and how they should develop appropriate strategies. For this latter task he directs attention to what he calls the strategic triangle (see figure 1.1), which involves finding appropriate ways of taking into account the "authorizing environment" of mandates and political support, doing what is necessary to create operational capability to produce results, and actually delivering public value to the citizenry at reasonable cost. The strategic triangle thus incorporates input, process, output, and possible outcome measures, although the public value "point" to the triangle is essentially about outputs and outcomes. Moore's work has had a significant impact on public management thinking in the United States and has been particularly well received in the United Kingdom and Commonwealth countries. In more recent work Moore has related his public value theory more thoroughly to democratic values, institutions, and processes (Moore 2013, 2014). He also has applied the strategic triangle to nonprofit organizations (Moore 2000).

Figure 1.1   The strategic triangle

Source: Reprinted by permission of the publisher from Mark H. Moore, *Recognizing Public Value* (Cambridge, MA: Harvard University Press, 2013), 103. Copyright © 2013 by the President and Fellows of Harvard College.

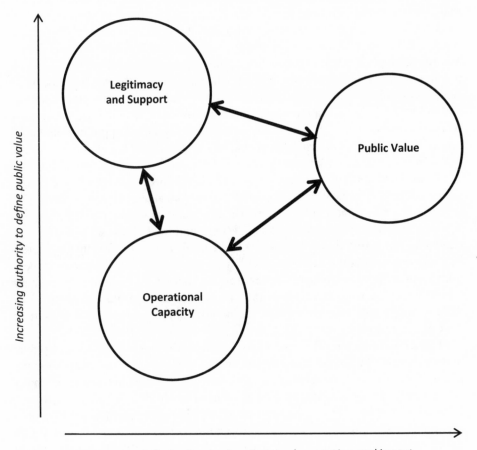

Direction of policy development, implementation, and impact

In this book Moore makes a significant contribution to answering the question of how to discern, measure, and assess public value in his chapter on public value accounting.

In terms of the questions about the meaning of value, for Moore public value generally refers to objective states of the world that can be measured. Moore also sees public value in a democracy as extrinsic, intrinsic, and relational. Something being evaluated may be deemed to hold inherent value or may be seen as a means to something else, as reflected in the criteria used to assess it. Moore does assume a hierarchy of values in which effectiveness, efficiency, accountability, justness, and fairness are prime. For Moore, elected officials and the citizenry are the ultimate arbiters of value, but public managers also play an important role in valuing. He presents the public value account and public value scorecard as aids for assessing value.

Moore's approach has received sharp criticism, particularly from R.A.W. Rhodes and John Wanna (2007). They note that at varying times its proponents view it as "a paradigm, a concept, a model, a heuristic device, or even a story. . . . [As a result,] it is all things to all people" (408). Rhodes and Wanna also charge that Moore's approach downplays the importance of politics and elected officials, over-emphasizes the role of public managers, and trusts too much in public organizations, private-sector experience, and the virtues of public servants (409–12).

John Alford (2008; see also Alford and O'Flynn 2009) mounts a spirited defense of Moore and refutes each of Rhodes and Wanna's points. He emphasizes Moore's strategic triangle that gives the authorizing environment a crucial role to play in placing "a legitimate limit on the public manager's autonomy to shape what is meant by public value" (177). Alford believes Rhodes and Wanna operate out of an "old" public administration paradigm that draws a sharp distinction between politics and administration and do not recognize that political appointees and civil servants often have considerable justifiable leeway to influence policy and decisions in the face of unavoidable ambiguity and uncertainty.

Adam Dahl and Joe Soss (2014) also criticize Moore's conception of creating public value. In their view, by posing public value as an analog to shareholder value, seeing democratic engagement in primarily instrumental terms, and viewing public value as something that is produced, Moore and his followers mimic the very neoliberal rationality they seek to resist and run the risk of furthering neoliberalism's de-democratizing and market-enhancing consequences. Public managers might unwittingly be agents of "downsizing democracy" (Crenson and Ginsberg 2002). The cautions Dahl and Soss raise are serious and should be addressed by those seeking to advance the public value literature; Moore himself addresses these concerns in chapter 8.

In addition, Lawrence Jacobs (2014) questions Moore's hopeful view of public management in the United States, given sharply divided public opinion on many issues, intensely partisan politics, the power of organized interests, and the many veto points built into governance arrangements. Clearly, public managers are constrained in a democratic society—and rightly so—but many examples of enterprising, public value-producing activities also demonstrate public managers can be active agents in creating public value. The public value literature thus should explore much further the conceptual, political, organizational, managerial, and other opportunities and limits on public managers' seeking to create public value in particular circumstances. The chapters in this book contribute to this exploration.

Barry Bozeman on Public Values

In contrast to Moore's managerial action focus, Barry Bozeman's 2007 book, *Public Values and Public Interest: Counterbalancing Economic Individualism*, significantly expanded the conversation to the policy or societal level and highlighted the intersection of market successes and failures with what he calls public value successes and failures. The action focus is thus broader than management, and the view of public value is even more emphatically normative as well as more specific than Moore's. The book explicitly takes issue with the dominance, especially in the United States, of economic individualism and the neoliberal agenda embodied in the new public management (Hood 1991; Pollitt and Bouckaert 2011). Bozeman's work has had a significant impact on public management thinking in the United States and abroad.

Bozeman (2007, 17) begins by defining public values as "those providing normative consensus about the *rights, benefits, and prerogatives* to which citizens should (and should not) be entitled; the *obligations* of citizens to society, the state, and one another; and the *principles* on which governments and policies should be based." Bozeman's definition implies that public values in a democracy are typically contested, meaning the consensus on them is hardly ever complete. Nonetheless, in operational terms one can discern relative consensus on public values from constitutions, legislative mandates, policies, literature reviews, opinion polls, and other sources (Beck Jørgensen and Bozeman 2007).

What Bozeman terms public values "failure" occurs when neither the market nor the public sector provides goods, services, or enabling institutions required to achieve public values. As a way of helping understand whether public value successes or failures have occurred, Bozeman and Japera Johnson (2014) propose a set of ten public values criteria, which are presented in table 1.1 (Bozeman 2002, 2007; Bozeman and Johnson 2014). The criteria in part mirror market failure criteria and combine input, process, output, and outcome measures. Public value creation can be conceived as the extent to which public values criteria are met. Public values for Bozeman thus are measureable, although clearly there can be disagreements about how the values are to be conceptualized and measured.

Bozeman has developed a "public value mapping process" that juxtaposes public value and market successes and failures in order to create a matrix onto which particular policies may be "mapped." The process produces a picture of the nature and extent of public value created by a policy. In this book Bozeman and his coauthors Jennie Welch and Heather Rimes contribute a chapter detailing the public value mapping (PVM) process.

One implication of Bozeman's approach is that analysts, citizens, and policymakers should focus on what public values are, and on ways in which institutions and processes are necessary to forge agreement on and achieve public values in practice (Davis and West 2009; Jacobs 2014; Kalambokidis 2014).

Note that Bozeman's approach is both positive, when he asks what the normative consensus on values is, and normative, when he argues that public values failures should be corrected. Bozeman (2007) is relatively silent on the role of the nonprofit sector; on the rights, responsibilities, or weights to be given to noncitizens; and on the role and importance of power in contests about public values. Regarding the effects of political power, Jacobs (2014) believes that in the US context Bozeman in his 2007 book severely underestimates the extent of dissensus, the disproportionate influence of affluent citizens and organized interests, and the extent to which governing structures favor inaction and drift. More recently, Bozeman has rectified some of these concerns; he and Johnson have added as public value criteria the creation, maintenance, and enhancement of the public sphere and progressive opportunity, defined as addressing structural inequalities and historical differences in opportunity structures. The changes are reflected in table 1.1 (Bozeman and Johnson 2014).

In terms of the questions about value noted above, for Bozeman, like Moore, public values are objective states of the world that can be measured. Also like Moore, public value in a democracy is extrinsic, intrinsic, and relational. Again like Moore, a policy or other object being evaluated may hold inherent value or

Table 1.1. Public values criteria

Criterion	Definition	Illustration of Public Value Failure and Success
Creation, maintenance, and enhancement of the public sphere	*As a public value:* open public communication and deliberation about public values and about collective action pertaining to public values. *As a public value enabling institution:* the space, physical or virtual, in which the realization of the public sphere value occurs.	Failure: An authoritarian regime seizes control of the Internet or other social media in an effort to exert control of protestors and thereby thwarts open public communication. Success: A deliberative democracy group is established to bring together diverse stakeholders in a local environmental dispute and these stakeholders engage in free and open public values–related communication.
Progressive opportunity	An "equal playing field" is less desirable than collective actions and public policies addressing structural inequalities and historical differences in opportunity structures.	Failure: "Merit-based" policies that fail to distinguish the effects of opportunity structures on achievement. Success: Compensatory education programs.
Mechanisms for values articulation and aggregation	Political processes and social cohesion should be sufficient to ensure effective communication and processing of public values.	Failure: Combination of US Congress' seniority system and noncompetitive districts leading, in the 1950s, to legislative bottlenecks imposed by just a few committee chairs who held extreme values on civil rights, national security, and other issues. Success: The US Congress seniority system reforms taking into account such factors related to relevant subject matter experience and expertise.
Legitimate monopolies	When goods and services are deemed suitable for government monopoly, private provision of goods and service is a violation of legitimate monopoly.	Failure: Private corporations negotiating under-the-table agreements with foreign sovereigns. Success: Uses of patent policy in allocating intellectual property rights.

text continues on page 8

Table 1.1. (continued)

Criterion	Definition	Illustration of Public Value Failure and Success
Imperfect public information	Similar to the market failure criteria, public values may be thwarted when transparency is insufficient to permit citizens to make informed judgments.	Failure: Public officials developing national energy policies in secret with corporate leaders of energy companies. Success: City councils' widely advertised and open hearings about proposed changes in zoning.
Distribution of benefits	Public commodities and services should, ceteris paribus, be freely and equitably distributed. When "equity goods" have been captured by individuals or groups, "benefit hoarding" occurs in violation of public value.	Failure: Restricting public access to designated public use land. Success: Historical policies for the governance of national parks.
Provider availability	When there is a legitimated recognition about the necessity of providing scarce goods and services, providers need to be available. When a vital good or service is not provided because of the unavailability of providers or because providers prefer to ignore public value goods, there is a public values failure due to unavailable providers.	Failure: Welfare checks are not provided due to a lack of public personnel or failures of technology for electronic checking transactions. Success: Multiple avenues for rapid and secure delivery of income tax refunds.
Time horizon	Public values are long-term values and require an appropriate time horizon. When actions are calculated on the basis of an inappropriate short-term time horizon there may be a failure of public values.	Failure: Policy for waterways that consider important issues related to recreation and economic development but fail to consider long-term implications for changing habitat for wildlife. Success: Measures taken to ensure long-term viability of pensions.

(continued)

Table 1.1. (continued)

Criterion	Definition	Illustration of Public Value Failure and Success
Substitutability vs. conservation of resources	Actions pertaining to a distinctive, highly valued common resource should recognize the distinctive nature of the resource rather than treat the resource as substitutable or submit it to risk based on unsuitable indemnification.	Failure: In privatization of public services, contractors have to post bond-ensuring indemnification but provide inadequate warrants for public safety.

Success: Fishing quotas or temporary bans allowing long-term sustainable populations of food fish. |
| *Ensure subsistence and human dignity* | In accord with the widely legitimated Belmont Code, human beings, especially the vulnerable, should be treated with dignity and, in particular, their subsistence should not be threatened. | Failure: Manmade famine, slave labor, and political imprisonment.

Success: Institutional review boards' protections of "vulnerable populations," including children, prisoners, and the mentally ill. |

Source: Barry Bozeman and Japera Johnson (2014), "The Political Economy of Public Values: A Case for the Public Sphere and Progressive Opportunity," *American Review of Public Administration* 45 (1): 7–8. Copyright 2014 by the authors. Reprinted with permission of the authors.

may be seen as a means to something else; this will be reflected in the specific criteria used to judge it. Unlike Moore, Bozeman posits no preordained hierarchies of values. Citizens, managers, public officials, and other groups can and do apply the market and public value success and failure criteria. Makers of a PVM identify important values by assessing a variety of documents and other sources.

Bozeman joined with Torben Beck Jørgensen (Beck Jørgensen and Bozeman 2007) in developing an inventory of public values found in the public administration literature (see table 1.2). They identified seven "constellations" of public values: (1) the public sector's contribution to society, (2) transforming interests to decisions, (3) the relationship between public administrators and politicians, (4) the relationships between public administrators and their environment, (5) interorganizational aspects of public administration, (6) the behavior of public employees, and (7) the relationships between public administration and the citizens. A more complete list would also articulate the relationship between public officials and society and between citizens and society. (Thomas, Poister, and Su in chapter 11 add the quality of agency working relationships with legislators and others.) The constellations of values touch on all three points of Moore's strategic triangle.

Beck Jørgensen and Bozeman also made an important distinction between "instrumental" and "prime" public values, meaning values that help achieve other values and values that are ends in themselves. Other scholars have taken different approaches to cataloging public values; for example, Stephanie Moulton (2009)

Table 1.2. Elicited public values, by category

Value Category	Value Set	Closely Related Values
Public sector's contribution to society	Common Good	Public interest
		Social cohesion
	Altruism	Human dignity
	Sustainability	Voice of the future
	Regime dignity	Regime stability
Transformation of interests to decision	Majority rule	Democracy
		Will of the people
		Collective choice
	User democracy	Local governance
		Citizen involvement
	Protection of minorities	Protection of individual rights
Relationship between public administrators and politicians	Political loyalty	Accountability
		Responsiveness
Relationship between public administrators and their environments	Openness/secrecy	Responsiveness
		Listening to public opinion
	Advocacy/ neutrality	Compromise
		Balance of interests
	Competitiveness/ cooperativeness	Stakeholder or shareholder value
Intraorganizational aspects of public administration	Robustness	Adaptability
		Stability
		Reliability
		Timeliness
	Innovation	Enthusiasm
		Risk readiness
	Productivity	Effectiveness
		Parsimony
		Businesslike approach
	Self-development of employees	Good working environment
	Accountability	Professionalism
		Honesty
		Moral standards
		Ethical consciousness
		Integrity
Relationship between public administration and the citizens	Legality	Protection of rights of the individual
		Equal treatment
		Rule of law
		Justice

(continued)

Table 1.2. (continued)

Value Category	Value Set	Closely Related Values
	Equity	Reasonableness
		Fairness
		Professionalism
	Dialogue	Responsiveness
		User democracy
		Citizen involvement
		Citizen self-development
	User orientation	Timeliness
		Friendliness

Source: Torben Beck Jørgensen and Barry Bozeman (2007), "Public Values: An Inventory," *Administration and Society* 39 (3): 360–61. Copyright Sage Publications. Reprinted with permission of the authors.

ties sets of values to institutions and Lotte Andersen and colleagues (2012) assign different values to archetypal forms of government organizations.

A Note on the Psychological Sources of Public Value

Timo Meynhardt (2009), in an important though less widely cited approach, takes a very different tack from the previous authors. He is particularly interested in the philosophical and psychological roots of valuing. He concludes that valuing is ultimately both psychological and relational and that public value is constructed out of "values characterizing the relationship between an individual and 'society,' defining the quality of the relationship" (206). The relationship's quality is assessed subjectively by individuals, but when there is intersubjective weight attached to these assessments, they become more objective and quantified and might ultimately reach Bozeman's requirement of a reasonable normative consensus. Meynhardt believes that public value is for the public when it concerns "evaluations about how basic needs of the individuals, groups, and the society as a whole are influenced in relationships involving the public" (212). Public value is also about value from the public when it is "drawn from the experience of the public." Public value for Meynhardt, too, can refer to what might be called input, process, output, and outcome measures linked to different stages in the creation of public value.

Meynhardt posits four basic dimensions (or content categories) of public value closely connected to a widely cited psychological theory of basic needs (Epstein 1989, 1993, 2003) and related to categories in traditional welfare economics. The categories are moral-ethical, political-social, utilitarian-instrumental, and hedonistic-aesthetical. (He adds a fifth, financial, in chapter 10, which is related to the utilitarian-instrumental category.) The "value" an individual attaches to an experience is based on how well the experience satisfies his or her basic needs as assessed against these dimensions. Note that the assessment is a subjective, emotional-motivational, and valenced reaction to an experience involving the "public," such as an encounter with a government program, an election, or visit to a public space. Intersubjectively equivalent assessments are a broad, reasonably objective measure of the extent to which public value has been created or diminished.

In contrast to Bozeman's and Moore's approaches, Meynhardt's is nonnormative, in the sense of being nonprescriptive; is far more psychologically based; and emphasizes more the interpenetration of public and private spheres. He also highlights far more the interrelatedness of the subjective and objective. Finally, unlike the other two authors, he pays little attention to the institutions and supraindividual processes involved in public value creation. However, like Bozeman and Moore, Meynhardt also sees public value as measurable, in his case against the dimensions he outlines.

HOW PUBLIC VALUE RELATES TO SIMILAR CONCEPTS

Public value is related to, but is not the same as, a number of other concepts. Part of public value's importance is that it encompasses a number of related concepts. John Alford and Janine O'Flynn (2009, 175–76) point out that public value includes but is not limited to public goods, by which are meant nonexcludable and indivisible goods. Public value differs in three ways: First, it includes remedies to market failures beyond inadequate provision of public goods, such as addressing negative externalities, natural monopolies, and imperfect information, along with the institutional arrangements that make the remedies possible. This fits clearly with Bozeman's (2007; Bozeman and Johnson 2014) view. Second, these authors assert that public goods are outputs and that public value includes the outcomes made possible by public goods. This fits well with Moore's (1995, 2013) view. Finally, public value has value for the valuer, which accords well with Meynhardt's (2009) psychological approach.

Public value is also not the same as the public interest, although there are again commonalities in that the public interest also includes a wide range of desired outcomes, outputs, processes, and even inputs (e.g., when early childhood education is described as in the public interest because it would produce better educated, law-abiding, and economically productive citizens). As Alford and O'Flynn (2009, 176) note, however, "rather than being about value itself, interest is one of the reasons or reference points for which people value things." Beyond that, the term "public interest" originally was associated with the state, not with the public sphere more generally (Gunn 1969). The public interest thus typically refers to the reasons for, or consequences of, government action. Ernest Alexander (2002, 226–27) expands on this point in relation to urban and regional planning, a field in which "the public interest has always remained relevant as a legitimating principle and a norm for practice, even while philosophers and political theorists debated its existence." Specifically in relation to spatial or land-use planning, Alexander asserts that the public interest helps legitimate planning as a state activity, serves as a guiding norm for planning practice and practitioners, and is useful as a criterion for evaluating planning and its products (227). However, Alexander goes on to note that "the critics' assertion that the public interest concept lacks any substantive content is irrefutable. Worse, their related contention—that the value-loaded nature of decisions and their intrinsic complexity make the *a priori* identification of any substantive public interest criterion impossible—is undeniable" (238). The public interest is clearly "an essentially contested concept" (Gallie 1956; Sorauf 1957) and attempts to operationalize it have proved difficult (Mitnick 1976), although not necessarily in the case of applying relatively clear public laws and regulations to specific decisions (Steiner 1970; Alexander 2002).

Public value is also not the same as dimensional publicness, an approach to organizational analysis championed by Bozeman (1987) and a number of colleagues (Walker and Bozeman 2011). The approach posits that publicness is best defined according to "the degree of political authority constraints *and* endowments affecting organizations" (Bozeman and Moulton 2011, 365). Privateness, in contrast, is the extent to which market authority constraints and endowments affect the organization. Juxtaposing the two dimensions indicates which organizations are more public and which are more private. Via the PVM model, dimensional publicness can be used as part of a strategy to see which public values are realized in practice and the extent to which publicness and privateness affect those outcomes (see chapter 9).

"Public value" is clearly not the same as "social value" as the term is used in the business world. Michael Porter and Mark Kramer (2011), writing in the *Harvard Business Review*, are among the strongest advocates for having businesses create shared value, "which involves creating economic value in a way that *also* creates value for society by addressing its needs and challenges" (italics in original). They go on to assert, "Businesses must reconnect company success with social progress" (64). In this view, "shared value is not social responsibility, philanthropy, or even sustainability, but a new way to achieve economic success. It is not on the margin of what companies do, but at the center" (64). Social value is thus narrower than public value, because it requires the creation of economic value, but it also helps open the way toward more cross-sector collaboration. As Porter and Kramer note, "The principle of shared value cuts across the traditional divide between the responsibilities of business and those of the government or civil society. From society's perspective, it does not matter what types of organizations created the value. What matters is that the benefits are delivered by those organizations—or combinations of organizations—that are best positioned to achieve the most impact for the least cost" (72). Social value thus provides a conceptual bridge from those interested in public value to potential allies in the business world. Note, however, that Dahl and Soss (2014) would be deeply troubled by the neoliberal and antidemocratic potentials of Porter and Kramer's view and would take strong exception to their assertion that it does not matter to society what types of organizations are involved in creating the value, given that businesses, for example, cannot be expected to embrace some of society's most important democratic values.

The English noun "commonwealth" may come closest to capturing the meaning of public value in its broadest sense, although its meaning is also contested. ("Res publica" is a synonym; "public weal" and "common good" are the more frequently used terms today.) As Harry Boyte (1989) points out, in what is now the United States, from the colonial era through the World War II era, commonwealth meant two things. First, it meant a republican or democratic government of equals concerned with the general welfare and an active citizenry throughout the year. Second, the term "brought to mind the touchstone, or common foundations, of public life—the basic resources and public goods of a community over which citizens assumed responsibility and authority" (4–5). The term had particular resonance for colonials with regard to property. Commonwealth implied a view of private property and public goods that "highlighted their social nature" (17). These meanings date from the fifteenth century and draw directly on joining the Old English words "common" and "weal," meaning "public welfare" or "the general good" (oxforddictionaries.com). Note as well that "weal" embodies an old meaning of wealth, which is well-being; "commonwealth" thus meant "common well-being." In the seventeenth century the definition of commonwealth expanded from its original sense of common well-being to include a republican or democratic government in which ultimate power rests with the people (Boyte 1989, 16–17). The Commonwealths of Massachusetts, Pennsylvania, Virginia, and Kentucky are based on this idea. Thus, while similar to public value in meaning, commonwealth is also not the same; the identification with democratic or republican government narrows the definition.

We believe that the idea of public value offers a way forward theoretically, philosophically, and practically beyond these other concepts (Bryson, Crosby, and Bloomberg 2014, 2015). The public interest and the common good, in particular, have a deep resonance in Western democracies—and especially in the United States—but both have become essentially scholarly dead ends, both because of their abstraction and vagueness and the related difficulties in creating operational measures for each (Mitnick 1976; Alexander 2002). The public values conversation, by contrast, has strong philosophical foundations but also has spawned, explicitly or implicitly, operationalization efforts in a variety of fields internationally, including public economics, political science, public administration, nonprofit management, evaluation, education, urban and regional planning, journalism, and law. The discourse in these fields typically does not specifically reference the terms "public value," "public values," or "public sphere," but nonetheless the ideas are clearly present. A major purpose of this book is to bring together contributors to the emerging public value literature that otherwise might not encounter one another's work, thereby stimulating cross-fertilization and advancing the conversation.

INTEGRATING THE APPROACHES

The two main contrasting views of public value have not been formally integrated to date, but we believe they can be. Indeed, many of the chapters in this book do so, at least implicitly.

In terms of theory, the key challenge is articulating the connections between Moore's managerial action-focused approach and Bozeman's policy or societally oriented public values. Moore goes some way toward doing so when he argues that creating public value should involve such public values as effectiveness (especially in achieving collectively defined desired outcomes), efficiency, justice, and fairness in the context of democratic governance at reasonable cost. Public value for Moore is thus, as noted previously, a summary term indexed against what is achieved or realized in practice in terms of more specific public values. Any assessment of net value created will take account of both costs and benefits broadly conceived and aligned with public values. A fuller integration simply requires that Moore's approach incorporate a broader range of public values, such as those suggested by Beck Jørgensen and Bozeman (2007), Van Wart (1998), Rosenbloom (2007), Meynhardt (2009), Box (2014), and others. The relevant values in any particular case will vary, but a broad range of public values should at least be considered, including those related to inputs, processes, outputs, and outcomes. Bozeman also goes some way toward integration by explaining how to determine public values and by developing his public values criteria and public value mapping tool, which can be used by public managers to determine what, how, where, when, and why public value should be created, and often by whom, or at least by which organizations or institutions. Beck Jørgensen and Bozeman (2007) also make a conceptual contribution by outlining "constellations" of values that bridge from managers to the public and do include values related to inputs, processes, outputs, and outcomes.

In terms of practice, the challenge of integrating managerial action with societal or policy values is more difficult, because public values are numerous, often contested, and indeed may be in conflict or even contradictory. Again, however, there is little mystery about ways to proceed, since managers, their overseers, and other stakeholders are engaged in the process of deciding what to do all the time. We argue that at least six practices are available for addressing public value questions, besides avoiding or suppressing them. These include policy analysis, design, and evaluation; leadership; dialogue and deliberation; institutional and organizational design, including cross-sector collaboration; the formal and informal processes of democracy; and strategic management, including especially performance management regimes and models. Each of these is standard fare in public life. We believe that as public managers and others engage in these key practices they should take more explicit account of a broader range of other public values beyond efficiency and effectiveness, and especially those related to the effective functioning of a democracy.

As an initial step in showing how the strands of the public value literature relate, we offer figure 1.2, the public value governance triangle (PVGT), which is obviously adapted from Mark Moore's strategic triangle. The PVGT expands Moore's strategic triangle to the multisector, multilevel realm; incorporates a broad range of definitions of public value; highlights the role of public values in the creation of public value, as articulated, revealed, or realized through the six key practices for addressing public value questions listed above; and shows how each of these elements is embedded in the public sphere.

We rely on the strategic triangle as a base for several reasons. First, Moore developed it through intensive interactions with practitioners as a way of clarifying how they approached their work. Second, though sparse, subsequent research has supported Moore's conceptualization. For example, Laurence O'Toole, Kenneth Meir, and Sean Nicholson-Crotty (2005) found in a large-N study of Texas school superintendents that the superintendents did see the points of Moore's triangle as constitutive of their roles. And Meynhardt and Jörg Metelmann (2009) in a study of the German Federal Labor Agency also found evidence that middle managers think in much the same way as Moore's public value entrepreneurs would. Based in part on this research support, and also other evidence of broad support that Moore's approach finds among public managers (Rhodes and Wanna 2007; Alford and O'Flynn 2009; Williams and Shearer 2011), we have offered the PVGT as a way of conceptualizing the move from Moore's more narrow focus on managers of government agencies to the broader idea of managing for the creation of public value in a cross-sector, multilevel world in which the challenges of governance have moved beyond government. In other words, we believe the PVGT is

Figure 1.2   The public value governance triangle

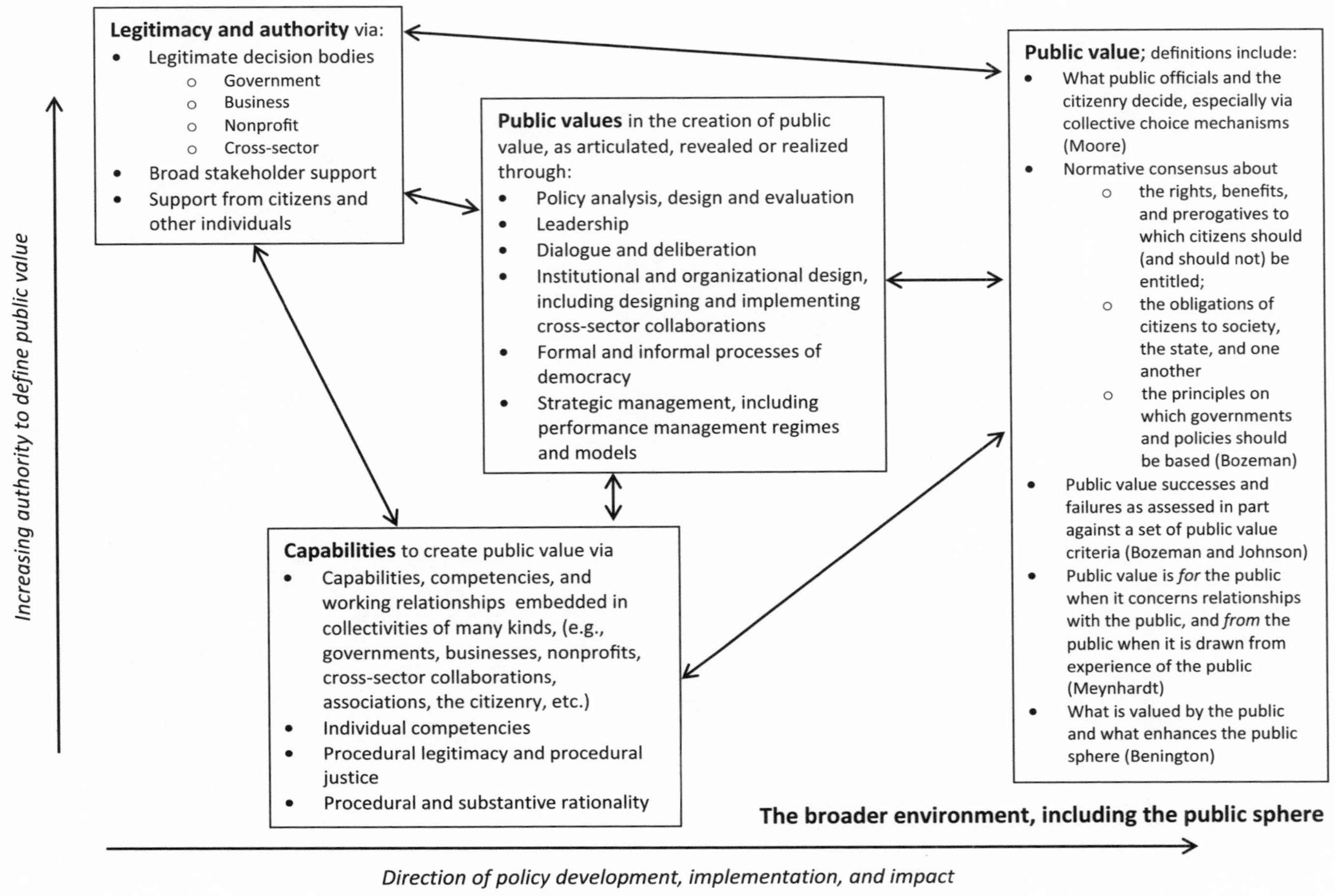

Public value; definitions include:

- What public officials and the citizenry decide, especially via collective choice mechanisms (Moore)
- Normative consensus about
  o the rights, benefits, and prerogatives to which citizens should (and should not) be entitled;
  o the obligations of citizens to society, the state, and one another
  o the principles on which governments and policies should be based (Bozeman)
- Public value successes and failures as assessed in part against a set of public value criteria (Bozeman and Johnson)
- Public value is *for* the public when it concerns relationships with the public, and *from* the public when it is drawn from experience of the public (Meynhardt)
- What is valued by the public and what enhances the public sphere (Benington)

Public values in the creation of public value, as articulated, revealed or realized through:

- Policy analysis, design and evaluation
- Leadership
- Dialogue and deliberation
- Institutional and organizational design, including designing and implementing cross-sector collaborations
- Formal and informal processes of democracy
- Strategic management, including performance management regimes and models

Legitimacy and authority via:

- Legitimate decision bodies
  o Government
  o Business
  o Nonprofit
  o Cross-sector
- Broad stakeholder support
- Support from citizens and other individuals

Capabilities to create public value via

- Capabilities, competencies, and working relationships embedded in collectivities of many kinds, (e.g., governments, businesses, nonprofits, cross-sector collaborations, associations, the citizenry, etc.)
- Individual competencies
- Procedural legitimacy and procedural justice
- Procedural and substantive rationality

The broader environment, including the public sphere

Direction of policy development, implementation, and impact

Increasing authority to define public value

better suited for the emerging approach to public administration in which government is one vitally important player among many.

The legitimacy and authority box includes legitimate decision bodies from all sectors (including cross-sector bodies), broad stakeholder support, and support from citizens and other individuals. For our purposes, we accept Mark Suchman's (1995, 574) widely cited definition: "Legitimacy is a generalized perception or assumption that the actions of an entity are desirable, proper, or appropriate within some socially constructed system of norms, values, beliefs, and definitions." We also accept the standard definition of authority as legitimate power.

The public value box includes the range of definitions of public value discussed so far, that is, those of Moore, Bozeman, Bozeman and Johnson, and Meynhardt. It also includes John Benington's definition to be discussed later and might include others as well. The capabilities box includes capacities to create public value embedded in collectivities of many kinds, including those beyond government; individuals' competencies; procedural legitimacy and procedural justice; and procedural and substantive rationality.

The latter two components are included because they clearly are relevant to the success of government initiatives in general (e.g., Van Ryzin 2011) and also to the success of cross-boundary, cross-sector, and cross-level situations that are typical of the emerging context of public administration (e.g., Bryson, Crosby, and Stone 2006). The procedural legitimacy of any undertaking rests on processes that are fair, transparent, rational, and intentional (Blader and Tyler 2003; Majone 1998). Procedural legitimacy helps generate public value by ensuring those involved in an initiative of some kind, their authorizers, and the public accept the results that it produces (Leach and Sabatier 2005), and it increases the likelihood the effort will be managed and implemented responsibly and effectively. Procedural justice refers to the extent to which a decision is seen as fair and transparent (Nabatchi 2012). Those affected by decisions will often accept decisions they dislike as long as they feel the decision procedures are fair (Susskind and Field 1996; Leach and Sabatier 2005). Procedural justice thus reflects stakeholders' perceptions of the fairness and openness of the processes by which those involved in an initiative reach decisions.

Procedural rationality is "the extent to which [a] decision process involves the collection of information relevant to the decision and the reliance upon analysis of this information in making the choice" (Dean and Sharfman 1993, 1071). A procedurally rational process thus embodies a reasonable and sound course of action that those involved can justify on technical, administrative, legal, and ethical grounds (Simon 1996, 26–27). A procedurally rational process can be expected to help produce decisions and, ideally, outputs and outcomes that are substantively rational, though there can be no guarantees that it will (Wildavsky 1979).

The central box in the PVGT refers to the public values involved as instrumental or ends in themselves in the creation of public value. These are where the work of integrating Moore's and Bozeman's (and others') conceptions of public value takes place via the six practical approaches to addressing public value questions. Beyond that, however, we also noted earlier that public value questions may be "addressed" by avoiding or suppressing them. Each of the six practices (or more precisely, sets of practices) may well do both. Whether public value is created or destroyed in the process would depend on the situation and who is doing the judging. We now discuss the six key practices in more depth, but before doing so we need to reemphasize that the boxes rest within the public sphere.

Policy Analysis, Design, and Evaluation

Obviously policy analysis, design, and evaluation can help address public value concerns, although decision makers and the public may ignore them. Indeed, Radin (2013, viii) argues that because of today's highly partisan and fragmented decision environments, we live in "a period when reliance on any form of analytic approach has become an act of hope." Analysis, design, and evaluation thus are hardly panaceas, but they can be used to clarify values; sharpen understanding of the values served—or not—by organizations and institutions; and identify what values do and do not underlie, and will or will not be served by, existing or proposed policies, programs, and projects. They can identify value complementarities, conflicts, contradictions, trade-offs, and so on (Weimer and Vining 2010; Bardach 2011; Wholey, Hatry, and Newcomer 2010). The broad field of policy analysis, design, and evaluation has expanded and matured to the point that it can be an important input into the world of political, and often very politicized, networked, and collaborative governance in which, as noted, governments, businesses, nonprofit organizations, and civil society all have roles to play in addressing public challenges and creating public value. The field now provides a variety of analytic approaches and methods that enable "speaking truths to multiple powers" (Radin 2013, 225). Most chapters in this book may be viewed as contributions to the field of policy analysis, design, and evaluation.

Leadership

Addressing public value questions is intimately related to leadership (Burns 1978; Crosby and Bryson 2005). Because of their roles or personal commitments, citizens, managers, elected officials, and journalists (among others) may step forward to draw attention to public values or ensure that stakeholders in a public issue have opportunities to air competing public values and consider areas of agreement and divergence. Elected officials and government managers have particular responsibility for defending the public sphere and inspiring and mobilizing fellow citizens to value public life and engage in democratic problem solving. Leaders and leadership of many kinds are featured in the chapters of this book.

Dialogue and Deliberation

Thoughtful, often lengthy conversational engagement with others is also an important way that managers, officials, and citizens can address values concerns and what to do about them when the answers are not purely technical (Heifetz 1994; Heifetz and Linsky 2002). Through dialogue and deliberation, participants can clarify values and their relationships and agree on which values to prefer, which to trade off, and which to avoid or downplay. Dialogue around value-laden public issues is actually surprisingly extensive in the United States, despite a sense that the citizenry is not engaged much in talking about those issues (Jacobs, Cook, and Delli Carpini 2009). Many authors in the public value literature make a case for the importance of dialogue and deliberation in discerning and assessing public value and public values and how they might be achieved (e.g., Moore 1995; Bryson et al. 2013; Fisher 2014; Kalambokidis 2014).

When engaging in dialogue and deliberation, participants must take into account the "deliberative pathways" that are possible and available for use as part of mutual efforts at persuasion.[3] The term was coined by Bryan Garsten (2006, 131) to describe Aristotle's sense of "the landscape of thoughts and patterns" that might exist in an audience and thus "the pathways" that might exist from one belief to another. These pathways are the starting point for understanding how mutual understanding, learning, and judgment might proceed. The pathways will influence a listener's beliefs via the structure and logic of an argument (logos), trust in the judgment and good will of the speaker (ethos), and/or the emotion evoked (pathos). Analysis can help illuminate these pathways. If attention to public value and public values is to occur more broadly, it will be through use of these pathways. This book may be viewed as an attempt to highlight and reinforce the paths along which the public value conversation may gain a broader hearing.

Institutional and Organizational Design, Including Designing and Implementing Cross-Sector Collaborations

Institutions—such as the family, markets, democratic arenas, and primary, secondary, and higher education—embody public values and also channel public values. In more formal terms, Douglass North (1990, 3) defines institutions as "the rules of the game in society . . . the humanly devised constraints that shape human interaction . . . complexes of norms and technologies that persist over time by serving collectively valued purposes . . . some have an organizational form, others exist as pervasive influences on behavior."

Richard Scott and Søren Christensen (1995, xiii) define institutions similarly broadly as "the cognitive, normative, and regulative structures and activities that provide stability and meaning to social behavior. Institutions are transported by various carriers—culture, structures, and routines—and they operate at different levels of jurisdiction."

Institutional and organizational design are processes of intentionally shaping institutions so that they embody particular public values and make it more likely that other particular values are realized in practice (Alexander 2015). For example, developing and amending constitutions, developing and changing city charters, and changing voting rules are all exercises in institutional design. The design of organizations and collaborations is more focused on shaping the way they are configured structurally and process-wise to do their work and achieve their goals (Bolman and Deal 2008; Bryson, Crosby, and Stone 2006). Several of this book's chapters focus directly on designing (or choosing) structures and processes so that varying public values are emphasized and public value is more likely to be created.

Formal and Informal Processes of Democracy

The formal and informal processes of democracy are also important vehicles for making reasonable and acceptable, if not necessarily wise or good, decisions involving public values (Moore 1995, 2014; Bozeman 2007). Policy analysis, design, and evaluation; leadership; dialogue and deliberation; and institutional and organizational design can help as part of these processes. More formal processes include at various times and for various purposes the following: constitution writing; campaigns and elections; direct and representative democracy; majority and supermajority voting; initiative, referendum, and recall; administrative procedures; public hearings; formal participation processes; protection of minority rights; and administrative and other court action. More informal processes include political activism of many kinds, lobbying, consensus-building efforts, and social movements. These formal and informal processes are ways for people with diverse values, interests, beliefs, and opinions to accommodate their differences and to make decisions about how to prioritize, compromise, trade off, settle, manage, or otherwise deal with value-related questions. The formal and informal processes of democracy show up directly or indirectly in virtually every chapter in the book.

Strategic Management, Including Performance Management Regimes and Models

The final key practice for integrating managerial public value and policy or societal public values is the use of strategic management, including performance management regimes and specific approaches to, or models for, performance management. A number of important recent books have appeared on this theme, including Radin (2006, 2012), Moynihan (2008), and Van Dooren, Bouckaert, and Halligan (2010).

Colin Talbot (2010, 205–15) for example, in an important synthesis of the performance literature, argues that a good theory of organizational and service performance in the public domain should attend to three elements. They are public values, performance regimes, and specific performance models. The chapters in this book collectively contribute to knowledge about all three elements.

For Talbot, public values are the frame within which the other two elements sit. Talbot highlights four sets of broad categories of public values: solidarity (co-production, redistribution, and social cohesion), equality and equity (standards, entitlements, and consultation), authority (regulation, reliability, and efficiency), and autonomy (choice, competition, and personal benefit).

Talbot defines the second element, performance management regimes, as "a combination of the institutional context within which public agencies work, and the institutional actors that can seek to steer or shape their performance together with the actual ways in which these actors exercise their powers (or do not)" (92). For governments, institutional stakeholders include the chief executive and line departments, along with their partners; the legislature, judiciary, and auditors and inspectors; and citizens, users, and the professions. Cross-sector collaborations would involve an expanded list. The third element is performance management models, or multidimensional approaches to performance management that are more specific to organizations and programs. These would include the many specific models available to manage inputs, processes, outputs, and outcomes. As examples, Talbot cites Total Quality Management, the European Union Common Assessment Framework, the second Bush administration's Program Assessment and Rating Tool, and indeed John Bryson's (2011) Strategy Change Cycle (169–84). Bryson (2011) explicitly argues that a major purpose of good public strategic management is to create public value.

Note that all six ways of integrating Moore's and Bozeman's approaches to public value presume the importance of a workable public sphere. The public sphere is the space within which public values exist and public value might be created. The public sphere is the third key term in the public value literature and is the topic to which we now turn.

THE PUBLIC SPHERE

John Benington (2011, 32) sees the public sphere as "a democratic space" that includes the "web of values, places, organizations, rules, knowledge, and other cultural resources held in common by people through their everyday commitments and behaviors, and held in trust by government and public institutions." The space is thus psychological, social, political, institutional, and physical. It is "what provides a society with some sense of belonging, meaning, purpose and continuity, and which enables people to thrive and strive amid uncertainty" (43). He believes that the public is not given, but made—it has to be continuously created and constructed. He also agrees that public value is necessarily contested and is often established through a continuous process of dialogue.

Benington draws on deep philosophical roots, including the Greek notion of the polis, and modern philosophers such as Jürgen Habermas, to argue for the importance of maintaining and enhancing the public sphere and of recognizing public value creation as producing what the public values and what enhances the public sphere. Of course, those interested in fostering a more democratic public sphere certainly have their work cut out for them in the United States. In the United States sharply divergent public beliefs and opinions are easily exploited for partisan ends by organized interests and siloed information channels, wherein affluent individuals and business and professional interests exercise disproportionate influence and the governing structures favor inaction and drift (Jacobs 2014). In such circumstances, pushes by public managers to create public value may well stall, fail, or even worse, reinforce rather than ameliorate the highly flawed or even antidemocratic forces in the system (Dahl and Soss 2014).

Note that Bozeman and Johnson (2014) have recently incorporated the creation, maintenance, and enhancement of the public sphere into their public values criteria (see table 1.1), but they argue that Benington's conception actually includes two components. The first is the public value of "open public communication and deliberation about public values and about collective action pertaining to public values." The second is the importance of "public value enabling institutions" or "the space, physical or virtual, in which the realization of the public sphere value occurs."

CONCLUSIONS

This book focuses, first of all, on the worth, utility, and importance of the idea of public value, along with the public values that might compose it in specific situations. Second, it attends to the frameworks, skills, methods, measurements, and processes needed to create public value and to assess values. This chapter has explored key questions about public value and described some of the most important public value scholarship. We have contrasted two main strands of the public value literature—Mark Moore and colleagues' focus on public managers' creation of public value and Barry Bozeman and colleagues' exploration of public values held, at least implicitly, by citizens and their representatives. We offered a framework, the PVGT, which incorporates both of these views and can apply to cross-sector as well as government initiatives at multiple levels, from local to global. The PVGT also includes six key practices for addressing public value questions. We believe the framework is a helpful way of viewing the chapters to come; it also suggests future directions in public value research and practice.

NOTES

1. Chapter 1 draws on Bryson, Crosby, and Bloomberg (2014, 2015).
2. In philosophy, "value theory" is an umbrella term for the broad subfields that emphasize making evaluations (e.g., moral philosophy, social and political philosophy) and in particular are concerned with the study of value or, more generally, goodness. The narrower field of axiology "can be thought of as primarily concerned with classifying what things are good, and how good they are" (Schroeder 2012).
3. This paragraph and the following two are drawn from Bryson (2011, 7–10).

PART I

HELPING MANAGERS FOCUS ON CREATING PUBLIC VALUE

2

POLITICAL ASTUTENESS AS AN AID TO DISCERNING AND CREATING PUBLIC VALUE

JEAN HARTLEY, JOHN ALFORD, AND OWEN HUGHES

Most public managers subscribe simultaneously to two quite contradictory beliefs. On the one hand, they affirm the political neutrality of appointed managers like themselves, placing their professional competence at the disposal of the elected government of the day without fear or favor. This means that they should stay out of their elected masters' domain of politics. On the other hand, they know full well that it is very difficult to secure mandates from their elected masters, and to get things done in government, without dealing with politics. Indeed, former Australian cabinet minister Sir Paul Hasluck has observed that "the public service cannot avoid politics any more than fish can avoid the water in which they swim" (Keating 1999, 444). Many public managers lament this state of affairs, but processes of "reading" situations, framing issues, presenting arguments, negotiating, maneuvering, and exercising influence are a necessary part of life as a public manager (Bryson 2004b); this is political activity even if it is not party politics (Crick 1993). Public managers need to be doubly adept in dealing with their political environments: engaging in politics, but simultaneously not appearing to cross the line into overtly partisan behavior.

There is a substantial public administration literature about the political dimension of public managers' jobs. But surprisingly little of it has explored what that dimension requires on the part of those managers—how they see politics, what their political skills are, what uses they put those skills to, where and how they acquire them, and how important they are to their work. One purpose of this chapter is to help fill this gap in the literature, setting out the ways in which managers' political astuteness can contribute to the practical enterprise of discerning and creating public value.

That practical enterprise is burdened with normative challenges, however. Much of the public value literature has centered on debate about the legitimacy or otherwise of public managers engaging in politics, or at least about how far they should do so (Rhodes and Wanna 2007; Alford 2008; Williams and Shearer 2011). This debate harks back to a presumed dichotomy between politics and administration: the principle advanced by Woodrow Wilson (1887) and Max Weber (1922) that there should be a separation between the realm of politics (the domain of elected politicians) and administration (the domain of appointed bureaucrats). Empirically, the weight of the evidence indicates that the pure dichotomy rarely holds in practice, and the line between the two domains is at the least rather blurred and often crossed by politicians and/or bureaucrats in the course of their work (Waldo [1948] 1984; Svara 2001; Hughes 2012). In particular, the research shows that public managers vary in the extent to which they venture into the political realm, but that those who do so are more prevalent (Aberbach, Putnam, and Rockman 1981; Peters 1987); that while politicians tended to dominate the setting of the policy agenda, career public servants exercise predominant influence in generating alternative options and in modifying policies in light of operational feedback (Kingdon 2011); and that ministers prefer their senior bureaucrats to exercise political sensitivity in their policy advice and implementation ('t Hart and Wille 2006).

Peters offers a likely reason for the persistence of the debate: the dichotomy serves as a "useful fiction" (2001, 82). For public managers, the alleged separation of politics and administration allows them to engage in organizational if not partisan politics "without the bother of being held accountable politically for the outcomes of their actions" (2001, 82). Thus the dichotomy is a poor description of actual circumstances but a valuable normative ideal to which politicians and bureaucrats find it convenient to point when there are questions about problematic issues. However, it means that public managers must juggle the contending imperatives of stretching their roles politically to create value, and recognizing how far it is acceptable for them to do so.

This relates to the second purpose of this chapter: to explore the limits of political astuteness, and in particular to enhance awareness of the "line" beyond which it is inappropriate to engage in politics. It turns out that, paradoxically, these limits are best understood and negotiated through the exercise of political astuteness.

In this chapter we set forward the case that political astuteness may enable public managers to do their jobs better in a variety of ways while still loyally serving the government. Precisely because we focus on the work of public managers, our conceptual framework primarily derives from Moore's (1995) concept of the public value triangle (see chapter 1 of the present volume) rather than Bozeman's conception of "public values" (2007). Moore offers a way of theorizing and operationalizing the key concepts in terms useful both to academics and to public managers in practice. To the extent that Bozeman understands the objects of value as objective states of the world, his analysis is partly germane to Moore's approach. But his use of the plural term tends to oscillate between understanding "values" as objective phenomena (different kinds of worth or utility) and seeing them as subjectively held norms. By contrast, we consider how political astuteness may assist managers to perform their key strategic tasks: to better discern what is valuable to the public, especially through public deliberative processes; to obtain consent for particular value propositions from the key players in their authorizing environment, especially elected politicians; and/or to elicit contributions of time, effort, and resources from internal or external actors. At the same time, political astuteness can help managers delineate the boundaries beyond which their wielding of political influence is inappropriate.

It should be acknowledged that criticism of Moore's work has not yet taken account of his most recent writings—notably, *Recognizing Public Value* (2013) and related papers about the philosophical underpinnings of his framework (Moore and Fung 2012). These publications challenge claims that Moore is merely about "management improvement" (Bozeman and Johnson 2014); that his approach lacks a coherent underpinning theory (Rhodes and Wanna 2007); or that he is in effect prosecuting a neoliberal agenda aimed at embedding market logic into the machinery of the state, as well as "downsizing democracy" (Dahl and Soss 2014). For instance, Moore writes that

> public management cannot be a purely utilitarian enterprise. Managers occupy a particular fiduciary role in a democratic system that requires them to behave in certain ways regardless of the consequences for themselves and others. They are entrusted with both public authority and with money raised through public authority. This obliges them to use the assets entrusted to them fairly and equitably, as well as efficiently and effectively. Consequently, utilitarian values alone cannot guide the value they seek to produce and reflect in the operations of their organisations. They also need to rely on deontological ideas about their own proper role, right relationships between government and citizens, and what makes a society not only good but just. (2013, 57)

PUBLIC VALUE AND THE AUTHORIZING ENVIRONMENT

Moore (1995) argues that a strategy for effectively creating public value must address three key challenges, each of them difficult. First, the strategy must be directed toward achieving publicly valuable purposes. Second, it must attract sufficient legitimacy and support from the organization's authorizing environment. This authorization comes from formal political stakeholders and institutions as well as other stakeholders, with due recognition of their differential legitimacy and power. It is likely that elected politicians will have the dominant say in this environment. Third, it must be operationally feasible—that is, achievable with available organizational and external capabilities. A valuable strategy is one where there is an alignment among these three sets of factors (Benington and Moore 2011a; Alford and O'Flynn 2009). Moore argues that the manager's job is to bring them into some degree of congruence.

That task is beset by the challenges inherent in each corner of the triangle as well as the tensions between them. First, discerning a purpose that is valuable to the public sphere can be difficult because citizens have varied and sometimes conflicting interests. Moreover, their differing interests register in political decision making in complex ways.

Then there is the authorizing environment, from which the manager needs legitimacy and support in order to pursue a particular "value proposition" (Moore 1995). Some of the key people in that environment have formal authority over the manager—that is, they are empowered by legislation or an organizational chart to direct the manager. Most significant here are politicians, who have the most direct say about what policies and actions the manager should undertake, as do legislatures and courts.

Other stakeholders amplified by the media, such as lobby groups, businesses, other public organizations, and communities, have no formal authority over the manager. In strict legal terms, a manager can ignore their demands or criticisms. But this would be risky because these stakeholders can influence those who have formal authority and because, in a shared power world, those with informal authority can provide or withdraw their consent (and their resources) to particular proposals, making implementation more or less difficult (Crosby and Bryson 2005). The manager needs to consider the variety of actors in the whole authorizing environment.

A significant implication of the strategic triangle is that sometimes what the manager judges as the most valuable thing to do is also politically unpalatable. In other words, there is misalignment between the value proposition and the more dominant influences within the authorizing environment. In this situation the manager has to determine how far to advocate for the value proposition in the face of adverse reactions from ministers and various other stakeholders. If she pushes too far, the value proposition might be overturned, or she could lose her credibility or even her job. If she doesn't push far enough, some potential value to the public could be left uncreated.

The third corner of the triangle is operational capacity, which is prone to the problem that the public manager may have little or no formal managerial authority over the people or organizations who provide that capacity—either because they sit outside the organization in question or because other agencies (such as personnel commissions or finance departments) have formal authority over resourcing issues such as staff employment or the reallocation of monies. In these circumstances the public manager is less able to command and must rely on persuasion or other techniques to bring about cooperation.

For our purposes, which concern managerial action, Moore's framework is more strategic than Bozeman's in both theoretical and practical terms. It takes into consideration both the big picture and the long term, and the interconnections among those factors, in a way that is conceptually grounded but makes sense to public managers in their work.

Moreover, Moore offers a rigorous way to operationalize the distinction between "what is" and "what ought to be": the strategic triangle can be used both positively, to diagnose where an organization or program currently sits (i.e., what value it is producing, how much support it has for that value, and whether it has adequate capabilities to deliver), and normatively, to consider where it *should* sit (i.e., what value it should produce, what level of authorization is necessary to support that, and the capabilities it requires). Thus, value is a norm or aspiration tempered by the realities of the environment and by capabilities. By contrast, Bozeman frames public values as those providing either normative consensus or content-specific preferences about citizens' rights and obligations and principles for government (2007, 13–14). While Bozeman considers value primarily in normative terms, Moore's framework encompasses both positive and normative value and establishes a coherent relationship between them.

This is not to say that normative values lack standing in this analysis but instead that their meanings register indirectly. Where they do have significance, they can act as powerful shapers of government policies and actions. In other words, subjective norms can be as real in their impact as features of objective reality. For instance, there is a very powerful subjective norm in most societies that it is wrong to harm children. That norm has significant impact on the range of policy options open to those dealing with children's services.

THE CONCEPT OF POLITICAL ASTUTENESS

Political astuteness is increasingly recognized as a valuable element in managerial work across all sectors due to the presence of diverse interests inside and outside an organization (Hartley and Fletcher 2008). This is particularly salient for those in senior or leadership positions where their role is to influence others, and even more so for middle and senior managers working in or with government and public services (Hartley, Fletcher, and Ungemach 2011; Gandz and Murray 1980).

Political astuteness as defined here, following an extensive literature review (Hartley et al. 2011), can be used to pursue personal or sectional interests as well as organizational or societal ones. The literature covers both types of interests. Political astuteness is conceptualized as a set of skills and judgments exercised in context for a range of legitimate or illegitimate purposes where there are divergent or potentially divergent interests.

This definition of political astuteness can cover a range of circumstances where there is contention over purposes, priorities, and resources. Thus, "political" is not solely about formal institutions and actors. It encompasses "small p" as well as "big P" politics—the informal as well as the formal—that can take place among the larger group of citizens, employees, and other stakeholders who may also form part of the authorizing environment. Finally, it includes the machinations of cliques and factions operating within, across, and outside organizations.

Attempts to identify and assess the political skills of managers have been sparse (see Buchanan 2008; Silvester 2008). The extensive work of Ferris and his colleagues (e.g., Ferris et al. 2005; Ferris and Treadway 2012; and many others) focuses on the skills of any employee regardless of level or sector, and thus tends to be focused on career-based, small group, or dyadic influence.

From empirical research with UK managers across all sectors, Hartley and Fletcher (2008) identified the key skills of political astuteness as given by the managers themselves across a range of contexts. A conceptual framework of the skills of political astuteness was then created and tested (see table 2.1), then subjected to statistical analysis for the robustness of its domains and of the overall framework (Hartley et al. 2011).

LINKING POLITICAL ASTUTENESS WITH PUBLIC VALUE

We can now link the concepts of public value and political astuteness. We propose that effective public managers need to be politically astute on several fronts, for the simple reason that they operate in both formal and informal political environments, where there are complex, varied, and sometimes competing interests. It is difficult for them to do their job (helping to define what is valuable, engendering acceptance of that definition, and making it happen) unless they have the skills of understanding people's interests, reading situations, fashioning workable solutions,

Table 2.1. The framework of political astuteness skills

Dimension	Elements	
Strategic direction and scanning	• Strategic thinking and action in relation to organizational purpose. • Thinking in the long term and having a road map for the journey. • Not diverted by short-term pressures. • Scanning: thinking about longer-term issues in the environment that may potentially have an impact on the organization.	• Attention to what is on the horizon. • Analytical capacity to think through scenarios of possible futures. • Noticing small changes that may herald bigger shifts in society. • Analyzing and managing uncertainty. • Keeping options open rather than reaching for a decision prematurely.
Building alignment and alliances	• Detailed appreciation of context, players, and objectives of stakeholders in relation to the alignment goal. • Recognizing difference and plurality and forging them into collaborative action even where there are substantial differences in outlook or emphasis. • Working with difference and conflicts of interest, not just finding consensus and commonality.	• Actively seeking out alliances and partnerships rather than relying on those already in existence. • Ability to bring difficult issues into the open and deal with differences between stakeholders. • Knowing when to exclude particular interests. Creating useful and realistic consensus, not a common denominator.
Reading people and situations	• Analyzing or intuiting the dynamics that can or might occur when stakeholders and agendas come together. • Recognition of different interests and agendas of both people and their organizations. • Discerning the underlying (not just espoused) agendas.	• Thinking through the likely standpoints of various interest groups in advance. • Using knowledge of institutions, processes, and social systems to understand what is or what might happen. • Recognizing when you may be seen as a threat to others. Understanding power relations.
Interpersonal skills	• "Soft" skills: ability to influence the thinking and behavior of others. • Getting buy-in from those over whom one has no direct authority. • Making people feel valued.	• "Hard" skills: ability to negotiate, stand up to pressures from other people, handle conflict in order to achieve constructive outcomes. • Coaching and mentoring individuals to develop their own political skills.

Table 2.1. (continued)

Dimension	Elements	
Personal skills	• Self-awareness of one's own motives and behaviors. • Ability to exercise self-control, being open to the views of others, ability to listen to others and reflect on and be curious about their views.	• Having a proactive disposition (initiating rather than passively waiting for things to happen).

Source: Hartley et al. (2007); Hartley and Fletcher (2008).

and influencing others. Sophisticated political skills are required to foster deliberative processes in which diverse actors grapple with complex issues and arrive at understandings that allow valuable purposes to be accepted and pursued.

DISCERNING PUBLIC VALUE: READING COLLECTIVE ASPIRATIONS

If we take a traditional administrative view of the role of public managers, their task of reading the "public value proposition" is relatively simple, because the managerial purpose is set by politicians, with the managers merely executing that policy. The research literature and our own studies show that the real picture is more complex, however.

For a start, sometimes a politician does not have a clear idea of the policy or purpose—especially if, as is often the case, incumbency in a particular portfolio changes frequently (Campbell and Wilson 1995, 23–24). Various factors—technical complexity, emergent political ramifications, fear of being held to account, wishing to avoid taking sides on a hotly contested issue—can deter a minister from handing down a clear mandate to bureaucrats. Alternatively, a minister may have a clear outcome in mind but not be sure of which policy might best lead to that outcome. Either way, the politician may procrastinate or prevaricate, even at a time when the public interest dictates that a decision be made. In this context the public manager has a responsibility to try to catalyze a decision. As one manager in a study by Jean Hartley and Stella Manzie stated, "we were trying . . . not to take their decisions for them, but to understand the pressures that were on them, that might make some of the decisions they were trying to take harder for them. . . . So it's about trying to open back up the full range of judgments and decisions for politicians, rather than about saying why don't you do the thing we want you to do" (2013, 21).

One relatively passive approach public managers can take in dealing with this is to try to "read" or "divine" (Page 2012) the minister's position, either by having developed a sense of his or her broad policy approach or by talking with the politician's personal staff. Where a slightly more active approach is necessary, the public servant may seek in good faith to assist, enable, encourage, or even gently push the minister into articulating what he or she wants.

Occasionally, public managers find themselves in disagreement with politicians—for example, when a minister's preference skates close to the edge of propriety or good policy. If the issue is important enough, one technique Page has observed is "mobilizing force majeure: using a third party within the structure of the state to persuade politicians to change their minds" (2012, 166). But this is very rare.

Interaction with formal political systems and processes is not the only way in which politics affects public managers' roles; because politicians seek support from (and therefore listen to) citizens, public managers must also understand what citizens need and desire.

The most authoritative indications of citizens' desires are, of course, democratic elections. Election results are often hard to read in aggregate, however, because citizens have different and often conflicting preferences about different issues. Elections are therefore "too rare and too crude" to provide the level of detailed guidance needed for most government activities (Moore and Fung 2012, 182); or societal and/or environmental conditions may change so that commitments made before elections seem less convincing over time. Moreover, citizens' preferences can change in time. Therefore, understanding what is valuable to the collective citizenry is a challenge for public managers.

It follows that managers can deepen the democratic process and increase the value of their advice by "reading" (sensing, discerning, analyzing) society's various and collective aspirations, especially as they change with the passing of time. Managers need to have a sense about what a sustainable plurality of citizens wants regarding a given issue, and must be able to shape it into a value proposition—not to supplant politicians' views and policies but to supplement and enhance them or to provide an alternative perspective that politicians may find helpful.

On a practical level, managers can (and do) use various techniques for reading collective aspirations, including public comment or consultation periods, public meetings, citizens' advisory committees, citizen juries, and deliberative polling (Thomas 2012; Williamson and Fung 2004). A key component of more recent civic innovations in public deliberation is improvement in the representativeness of participants, reducing the participation bias (wealthier and better-educated citizens self-selecting for participation) made likely in more traditional forms of engagement such as town hall meetings (Williamson and Fung 2004). Tools required for successfully negotiating public engagement include "people" skills (a tolerance for ambiguity, the ability to get along with a variety of people from different backgrounds, and the flexibility to move smoothly between them) and enablement skills (facilitation, knowing which actors to bring to the table, knowing how to mobilize them to solve problems, and knowing how to convert the suggested solutions into political realities; Thomas 2012).

Reading collective aspirations is about discerning rather than creating public value, and it entails observation, analysis, and intuition. The requisite capabilities (see table 2.1) go beyond implementation skills because they include the political astuteness skills of strategic direction and scanning (sensing what the key priorities are and how they may be influenced by context and future developments) and reading people and situations to understand the nuances of their positions. They are reinforced by certain personal skills (particularly curiosity and openness about the views of others), and also by the interpersonal skill of making others feel valued so that they will share their priorities and concerns.

SECURING LEGITIMACY FROM THE AUTHORIZING ENVIRONMENT

To the extent that public managers seek to articulate conceptions of what is publicly valuable and press for action, they must obtain permission from their authorizing environment to have the public value proposition(s) adopted and enacted. In short, they must secure consent from those in a position to provide legitimacy, support, and resources.

A public value proposition is not simply tested against the authorizing environment; it is negotiated, adapted, and sometimes bartered in attempts to get a sufficient degree of alignment among different stakeholders to get things done. This involves reading how well aligned the value proposition is with the balance of forces in the authorizing environment—that is, whether it is acceptable to key actors. Where it appears that there is misalignment the manager has to work to reframe the value proposition, persuade key players to come on board, or both. Securing consent requires skills about discerning differences among those in the authorizing environment, negotiating trade-offs, crafting propositions that appeal across stakeholders, getting permission and support, and outmaneuvering opposition. Traditionally this has been seen as the domain of the elected politician, and of course this continues to be so, but public managers of all levels also engage in these activities, though not necessarily as the final arbiters (Campbell and Wilson 1995; Page 2012; Kingdon 2011; Peters 2001; Aberbach, Putnam, and Rockman 1981). For example, Moore and Fung (2012, chap. 9) describe the efforts of a captain in the US Coast Guard to bolster security of US ports. Lacking formal authority over matters of port security, she designed a consultation process to determine the best way to both enhance security and build stakeholder commitment to the goal.

An important determinant of public managers' influence on policy is their perceived expertise and effectiveness (Nicholson-Crotty and Miller 2012; 't Hart and Wille 2006). The more important their capabilities are to key tasks such as crafting policy advice and implementation, the more the political sphere is likely to take notice of what they have to say.

On occasion the situation calls for the public manager to exercise political skill to persuade politicians *not* to pursue a particular path. As Campbell and Wilson note, "Ministers need to be talked out of impracticable plans with which they have become infatuated during weekends in their constituencies. Yet fulfilling this task requires skill. Too little determination in emphasizing the difficulties of ministers' favourite but unworkable projects may mean those ministers will stumble into disaster; too much determination shades into obstructionism, which ministers may believe reflects a political hostility to their policies" (1995, 24).

In the United States, evidence shows that by innovating and then mobilizing interests in support of innovations, agencies can influence other political actors to change their positions in response to this support (Krause 1996). Some agencies use recruitment and mobilization of clientele to influence policy; by building and maintaining effective constituency relationships, agencies can remain important players in the "policy subsystem" and ultimately produce outcomes close to their preferences (Clarke and McCool 1996). Even street-level managers are regularly concerned with how to build legitimacy and support from the public for efforts consistent with their democratic mandate (Mashaw 1983; Lipsky 1980).

Securing permission is a dynamic, interactive process not fully captured by the static figure of Moore's (1995) strategic triangle. Many managers believe that they can best support their political masters—who, after all, have the formal mandate—by being alert to the kaleidoscope of interests, crosscurrents, and goals of the various stakeholders, many of whom are trying to influence outcomes. These skills are the daily bread and butter of public management. But they see them as an addition to, rather than a substitute for, their technical and professional skills.

In order to do these things managers draw on a range of skills outlined in the political astuteness framework (see table 2.1). Understanding the overall strategic context is important, as is being alert to changes and weak signals in the strategic environment: this is the domain of strategic direction and scanning. Particularly important is the domain of building alignment and alliances—it is a real skill to create alignment out of different interests, timescales, priorities, and aspirations. A skill for reading people and situations is also crucial; it is a dynamic activity given the fluid nature of the authorizing environment. Interpersonal skills are central, both the "soft" relational skills of making other people feel valued, and the "hard" skills of handling negotiation and conflict.

ENLISTING OTHER PARTIES TO GET THINGS DONE

Implementing government policies is, of course, a legitimate and significant role of public managers and squarely on the administrative side of the dichotomy. In certain senses, however, managers have to cross to the political side simply to get their jobs done. They not only need to garner permission; just as important is the need to induce contributions of resources, time, and effort from people inside and outside their own organizations, without which they find at best that they lack the means to carry out their roles, or at worst that powerful others block them from their task. A telling example was Diana Gale, head of the Seattle Solid Waste Utility, who turned herself into a "garbage goddess" for the media in order to boost the use of recycling services, making Seattle the recycling capital of the United States (Moore 2013, chap. 5).

The reality of modern governance is that many of the more pressing (or "wicked") problems that governments seek to solve now span organizational boundaries: "the existing structures do not fit," and the resources required to act on a problem are not contained within a coherent operational structure (Moore and Fung 2012, 194). It is often argued that solutions to these problems (e.g., poverty, crime, and climate change) can only come via collaborative discussion and action through networks of government and community actors (Crosby and Bryson 2005; Weber and Khademian 2008; Head and Alford 2013). In fact, network collaboration models now operate in nearly every area of government, from workplace safety insurance to crisis management to welfare-to-work programs (Eggers 2008).

There has also been a shift in public management theories, away from those that positioned citizens as individualized consumers at the end of a long supply chain and toward a more empowering conceptualization of citizen participation and coproduction, where they contribute time and effort to the delivery of services (Ryan 2012; Alford and O'Flynn 2009). Managers' political astuteness can help them to not only navigate the potentially fraught cultural space of convincing stakeholders to collaborate on the development of governance arrangements but also to know when and how much to "let go" of the process—to observe and assist when necessary but allow the stakeholders enough autonomy to "own" the outcomes within an overall governance framework. For instance, as a UK manager talking about ownership argues,

> You can corral [people] through the party political process, but at the end of the day the better they understand it, the more they own it. I remember a politician saying "I don't want ownership, I just want people to get on and do it". And me trying to say, "well people won't get on and do it unless they believe in it". We depend on the knowledge and abilities of the people out there, and our job is to catalyze it and to harness it and to focus it, not to actually just tell people what to do, because it won't happen. (Hartley et al. 2013)

If mobilizing capabilities and resources means eliciting contributions from other parties such as staff, other government agencies, private contractors, nongovernmental organizations, volunteers, or client coproducers, managers need to be able to understand what makes them tick and how to influence them. All strategies—both coercive and cooperative ones–aimed at enlisting external actors to help get things done require more than official authorization from ministers, bureaucratic superiors, or legislation. Thus political astuteness in reading and influencing informal stakeholders to assist in implementing policies also necessitates political astuteness in understanding and securing formal authority and in managing what may sometimes be divergent interests.

RECOGNIZING THE LINE BETWEEN POLITICS AND ADMINISTRATION

The discussion thus far indicates that political astuteness is a very useful skill for public managers. But there is also a question of whether using political skills is *legitimate* in a democratic political system. This brings us back to the dichotomy of politics versus administration.

To the extent that the dichotomy has normative weight, it is seen as inappropriate for the line between the two domains to be breached (Rhodes and Wanna 2007). Yet at the same time we have seen that public servants do engage in political interactions of one kind or another in order to do their jobs. So a key issue for managers is how far they can deploy their political astuteness skills without compromising the legitimacy of their decisions and actions.

We do not argue that public servants should engage in partisan politics or usurp the decision-making role of politicians. If a policy or strategy is not acceptable to political overseers, the manager ought to abandon or modify it to take account of that opposition. Where managers can play an important role is in finding integrative solutions to these kinds of problems by shaping policies or strategies that maximize public value while remaining acceptable to the political decision makers (Alford and Hughes 2008). In short, managers need to be particularly cognizant of where the line between politics and administration is.

Mainly this is a matter of judgment, about governmental structures and processes in a broader sense and about the politicians in question. It involves building up a detailed understanding of their values, thinking styles, attitudes toward risk, and particular pet policy loves and hates. Effective public managers also seek to build trusting relationships with politicians, and this calls for demonstrated loyalty, perceived effectiveness, and political sensitivity ('t Hart and Wille 2006). The greater the accumulated trustworthiness of the manager, the more license to engage in political activities he or she is likely to have. Of course, encroaching into the political sphere also runs the risk of diminishing trust, so the manager needs to make subtle judgments about when to "spend" accumulated trust and when to invest in building it up.

Campbell (2012) found that lower- and midlevel public managers often have a strong sense of the underlying policy intent or fundamental values behind directives from higher up, but that some of these directives impede local implementation and goal attainment. In such cases their sense of the value potentially created by the broad policy goals can lead them to use evasive tactics or work-arounds to help them comply with the spirit—if not the letter—of the policy. For example, Kathleen Ahearn and her colleagues report that child welfare teams in a US state agency share practical advice for "finessing" the bureaucracies of other states, or information about the quirks of powerful people in their authorizing environment (Ahearn et al. 2004, 317). Strong personal skills, such as self-awareness of one's own motives and behaviors, can assist managers to use such tactics in pursuit of public value goals.

From a normative point of view it is potentially risky to assign to the public manager the task of determining where the line is: the manager may abuse that authority, either from insufficient competence or dishonorable intent. One response to this is to rely on the "public service motivations" of civil servants (Perry 2000)— the hope that their ingrained values will incline them to do the right thing and respect the authority of the elected politician. Although there is considerable empirical evidence demonstrating the salience of such motivations in many public services (Perry, Hondeghem, and Wise 2010), it would be naive to rely on them and, in any case, this relies on value rather than competence. More telling is their perceived self-identity—especially their desire to be regarded as capable in the social context, which forays into politically risky areas are likely to undermine. As Page puts it, "Where the written rules do not tell bureaucrats what to do, a range of generalized rules, norms, and expectations not only prevents them from doing as they please, but makes the whole notion of 'doing as they please' problematic. . . . [A] bureaucrat might feel it is desirable . . . to abolish a particular regulatory scheme and is perfectly free to suggest it, but if it has no chance of gaining political approval, all the civil servant stands to achieve is the prospect of being regarded as someone without any political sensitivity" (2012, 167).

The calculus to be followed by a public manager in deciding whether or not to intervene in a political matter is complex, but it is unrealistic to assume that it does not take place.

CONCLUSION

The "moving part" of the political job of the public manager is to deploy political astuteness in identifying what is valuable, in eliciting consent from political masters and the public, and in persuading actors to contribute time, effort, and re-

Table 2.2. Managerial activities potentially harnessing political astuteness

Activities	Discerning Public Value	Creating Public Value
1. "Reading" collective aspirations: having a sense of what a sustainable majority of people want as regards a given issue/situation and shaping it into a value proposition (i.e., discerning what is *valuable* to citizens).	✓	
2. Securing a mandate (obtaining permission). a. "Reading" degree of (mis)alignment between authorizing environment (AE) and value-proposition (i.e., discerning whether value proposition is politically *acceptable* to key actors).	✓	
b. Eliciting permission (1): discerning a value proposition that will attract enough support to be sustainable (i.e., shifting the value circle).	✓	✓
c. Eliciting permission (2): seeking to influence key players in the authorizing environment to support or at least not oppose the value proposition (i.e., shifting the AE circle).		✓
d. Orchestrating countervailing power to outmaneuver/overwhelm key players opposed to the value proposition (also shifting the AE circle).		✓
3. Enlisting capabilities to get things done (e.g., externalizing, coproducing, collaborating, etc.). a. Eliciting work (1): representing a purpose that attracts support from potential contributors of time and effort (i.e., shifting the value circle).		✓
b. Eliciting work (2): persuading, enabling, incentivizing, putting on peer pressure, obliging, or collaborating with key players to get them to contribute time and effort in implementing/delivering the value proposition (shifting the productive capabilities circle).		✓
4. Knowing the limits of political astuteness: "reading" AE for sense of how far a public servant can "be political."	✓	

sources to creating what is deemed valuable. The seemingly stationary constraint is the line between politics and administration, which must be treated with political insight and circumspection. For both aspects, public management entails exercising sophisticated political insight in the public interest. More dauntingly, it entails judging the appropriate balance between the two. Table 2.2 summarizes the managerial activities described here, and shows how the theory of public value relies on a theory about political astuteness.

What table 2.2 indicates is that the existence of a dichotomy is questionable. In reality, politics exists on both sides—for managers and for politicians. This is likely to increasingly become the case over time as the complexity and interdependency of public-sector functions deepen even further. Public managers' contexts will become even more fluid and dynamic, putting a premium on their political astuteness—their skill, judgment, and wisdom in interpreting the views of players whose interests sometimes converge with their own and at other times are in opposition. The political astuteness of public managers needs to be seen as an asset in creating public value and as a substantive skill in its own right.

This chapter has aimed to fulfill three goals. First, it used a conceptual framework derived from earlier research (Hartley and Fletcher 2008) to identify the political astuteness skills public managers might use. Second, it has mapped these skills onto the key aspects of public-sector strategy making articulated by Moore (1995): defining value, securing consent, and mobilizing capabilities. In the process, it has elucidated some of the differences and similarities between Moore's (1995) and Bozeman's (2007) models of public value. Third, it has explored both empirical and theoretical research to address the difficult question that inevitably arises when we start talking about public managers engaging in political processes— namely, that they risk breaching the dichotomy between politics and administration. The answer emerging from this chapter is that political astuteness enables managers to not only push the boundary between the two realms but also to better appreciate how far they can do so to create public value.

3

Building Deliberative Capacity to Create Public Value

The Practices and Artifacts of the Art of Hosting

Jodi Sandfort and Kathryn S. Quick

In the second decade of the twenty-first century, polarization in American politics is undermining civility in the public sphere (Jacobs 2014). Amid the acrimonious debates surrounding much policymaking, it is hard to sustain the core practices of our democracy: the ideal of engaging citizens and their representatives in articulating goals for government policies and programs. Public management practice has taken a turn toward market-based principles of performance measurement and competition (Pollitt and Bouckaert 2004; Moynihan 2008; Soss, Fording, and Schram 2011), thereby reinforcing a framework attending to customers who demand to be served rather than citizens working with their representatives to cocreate public policy (Dahl and Soss 2014).

Yet, as public affairs scholars, we take a different tack of studying public engagement initiatives as potential mechanisms for exercising and creating public value rather than customer service. Our notion is consistent with others (Alford 2008; Benington and Moore 2011b) in that we believe public value can be created by the actions of public affairs professionals, by what they do and how they do it. In this view, a central principle of modern democracy is citizens' abilities to deliberate with each other about social values and public policy, a process described by Reich (1990) as the "civic discovery" of public interests. Capacity for and enactment of democracy through deliberation have inherent public value as expressions of a democratic state (Benhabib 1996; Young 2000; Cooke 2000; Dryzek 2002; Gutmann and Thompson 2004) and forms of public work (Boyte 2012). When public affairs professionals build deliberative capacity, they create public value in two ways: deliberative capacity both advances democratic participation in governance and provides a means to produce effective and efficient policy solutions.

Our arguments about the contribution of deliberative capacity to public value are grounded in the emerging construct of public value governance (Bryson, Crosby, and Bloomberg 2014). This idea emphasizes that deliberation and other forms of democratic participation are themselves public values, defined as inherently desirable features of good governance. Thus deliberative capacity can advance some of the particular public values identified by Bozeman (2007) relating to the rights and obligations of citizens to be accounted to and responsible for good governance. It also suggests that deliberative capacity supports the production of other kinds of public value in that these decision-making processes help to generate policy outcomes that more strongly reflect what it is that the public values. In this respect, deliberative capacity can advance what Moore (1995) means by creating public value—namely, that good governance produces policies and social outcomes that reflect values about justice, efficiency, or equity. Deliberative processes move citizens beyond a role as either consumers or recipients of policy decisions to being active partners in both defining public issues and developing strategies to solve shared problems.

Yet, to assure public engagement efforts contribute to creating public value by building deliberative capacity—and not merely add fuel to cynicism about public institutions—we must learn more about what occurs when deliberative democratic projects are implemented. Moore (1995) asserts that public managers, through their practices, influence whether and how public value is created. And, often, deliberation is advocated as a practice for engaging diverse perspectives in policymaking and bringing a variety of ways of knowing into policy decisions (Young 2000; Nabatchi et al. 2012). This chapter provides guidance on how public managers, other policymakers, and citizen activists might organize and use deliberative processes to create public value. We look at a wider domain of actors because there are many potential leaders and sites beyond the formal boundaries of government institutions (Bryson et al. 2014). Indeed, national groups have developed many formats for exercising and building deliberative capacity, such as citizen panels, national issue forums, polling, and twenty-first-century town meetings. However, there is wide variety among the consequences of these models and, as we point out in this chapter, significant differences among particular uses of any one model in actual implementation.

In this chapter we provide ethnographic analysis of facilitators applying an international body of engagement practice, the Art of Hosting and Harvesting Conversations that Matter (hereafter, "Art of Hosting"; Block 2009; Holman 2010; Wheatley and Frieze 2011), which highlights the actual process of building deliberative capacity as a public value. Compared to common democratic participation measures, such as Arnstein's (1969) ladder of citizen participation, Roberts's (2004) typology of types of participation, or the spectrum of public participation developed by the International Association for Public Participation, the Art of Hosting approach is highly deliberative. Our examination of what facilitators actually say and do can shine new light on the ways in which deliberative processes both contribute to and/or deplete the creation of public value. The analysis highlights the dynamic and fluid process of public value creation, showcasing how the practicalities of public deliberation can enhance or reduce it in particular applications and settings. It is not an intervention guaranteed to deliver public value creation.

RESOURCING PUBLIC VALUE THROUGH DELIBERATIVE PROCESSES

Deliberative theorists and pragmatists argue that communication is the fabric of democratic life (Forester 1998; Innes and Booher 2010). By talking together, citizens learn about opposing views and develop shared understanding of issues, building what Jacobs, Cook, and Delli Carpini (2009) term "discursive capital." Such capital can be invested in the development and deployment of civil society organizations that increase citizens' motivations to engage in electoral politics. Yet deliberation is a distinct form of political participation. Through conversations that examine a range of problems and solutions, people learn how to participate in a polis (Dewey 1927). This conception sees democracy—and by extension, public value creation—as a never-ending project accomplished through the process of engaging with others (Young 2000; Dryzek 2002).

Deliberative theory scholars also articulate certain ideal conditions that must be met to realize deliberation's potential to invigorate authentic democracy. Processes must be inclusive and involve people being affected by decisions, assuring that all voices can be heard (Young 2000). Additionally, they must support the engagement of reason and the consideration of various forms of evidence in coming to conclusions (Mendelberg 2002; Gastil and Dillard 2006; Rosenberg 2007). Finally, the overall process should ultimately yield shared understandings and enable broader political engagement (Fischer and Forester 1993). Carried out in these ways, deliberative processes influence both how citizens understand substantive issues and how they understand their agency in developing or acting on solutions (Sirianni and Friedland 2001; Gutmann and Thompson 2004; Fung 2004, 2006).

Amid a general recognition that these ideals are desirable, many scholars challenge the prevalence and potential of their implementation in practice. Pragmatists suggest the emphasis on reason is artificial, stressing the social construction of problems and solutions (Briggs 2008). Others worry about ideological capture and stress the importance of content-neutral process experts to facilitate deliberation (Schwarz 2002; Nabatchi et al. 2012). At the same time, there is concern that public and nonprofit managers frequently do not possess the skills necessary to foster authentic engagement in practice (Escobar 2011). However, this literature has a tendency to valorize facilitators, expecting them to wade into knotty and complex community settings and render miracles through the exercise of process expertise. Ironically, this frame centralizes responsibility for deliberation not in the participants but in the facilitator of dialogue, thereby decreasing the experience of practicing deliberation among equal citizens in a polis.

All democratic processes do not inherently produce public value; it is a resource that must be generated and activated.[1] There are many choices available for designing and implementing deliberation (Bryson et al. 2014). Depending on how and how well they are organized, ostensibly democratic processes may enhance or reduce public value. Public participation processes *may* endogenously create results, such as improved understanding of problems, discovery of innovative solutions, or improved connections and commitments for implementation (Feldman and Quick 2009). They may also create the opposite dynamic—diminishing capacity and willingness to deliberate—if the public feels the invitation to participate is inauthentic or the outcomes have been predetermined (Arnstein 1969; Flyvberg 1998). The extant literature suggests choices are highly consequential for public value, as they generate or diminish the individual and collective capacity of the participants to deliberate and articulate public interests and goals (Reich 1990;

Mansbridge 1999; Quick and Feldman 2011; Nabatchi et al. 2012). Yet, few studies enable controlled comparison across cases.

RESEARCH CONTEXT AND METHOD

To systematically explore the ways in which deliberative processes are designed and implemented, we exploit facilitators' common training in a particular facilitation method and natural variation in project implementation in a statewide, foundation-supported initiative, InCommons (Sandfort and Bloomberg 2012). The InCommons project focused on building opportunities for community engagement that addresses complex problems across diverse geographic areas, socioeconomic groups, and topical issues in the state of Minnesota. While the initiative deployed a range of strategies, early on its managers identified a need to enhance citizens' capacity to effectively facilitate challenging community conversations. As its name suggests, InCommons was explicitly focused on public value creation across diverse communities.

The Art of Hosting was identified as a potent tool for building capacity to facilitate uncommon conversations. The Art of Hosting is an international community of practitioners working in diverse contexts, focusing on youth employment, economic development, indigenous people's rights, and governance in the European Commission.[2] For example, Columbus, Ohio, is using Art of Hosting practices to reenvision health care, higher education, business networks, and social services in that community (Wheatley and Frieze 2011). The Art of Hosting training workshop functions as an immersive practicum in the hosting approach, concentrating on a number of engagement techniques, theories, and practical design frameworks. All enable facilitators to coproduce participatory engagement processes within complex social systems (Holman 2010; Wheatley 2006; Success Works 2011). While the Art of Hosting resembles other approaches to whole systems change (Holman, Devane, and Cady 2007; Wheatley and Frieze 2011) and deliberative democracy (Creighton 2005; Kaner 2007; Escobar 2011), there are several distinctive features that are relevant to our discussion of its potential for generating public value.

First, the Art of Hosting brings together a range of engagement techniques that were developed and are used by others outside the Art of Hosting into an overall collection. Peer circle process (Baldwin and Linnea 2010; Baldwin 1998), Open Space Technology (Owen 1997), the World Café (Brown and Isaacs 2005), and appreciative inquiry (Cooperrider and Srivastva 1987) are taught as techniques for enabling deep dialogue and high-quality conversations, spurring collective analysis of external trends, and motivating action planning. As the Art of Hosting website (www.artofhosting.org) explains, "The Art of Hosting training is an experience for deepening competency and confidence in hosting group processes— Circle, World Café, Open Space, and other forms. Each of these processes generates connection and releases wisdom within groups of people." The training workshop also focuses on a set of practical frameworks to support implementation of these techniques in community engagement processes. Some frameworks—such as one for understanding divergence and convergence in group processes—assist with design, helping facilitators systematically explore how various techniques can be applied to particular issues. Additionally, the workshop showcases "harvesting," a word that transforms conventional note-taking into creating artifacts that allow meeting participants to make meaning and share it with others. In the workshop, trainers stress that harvesting can take many forms: personal journal writing, visual artifacts (such as photographs and drawings), video, song, or more conventional formal proceedings. As we will see, attention to creating and using artifacts is significant, as in the cases we examine they seem to fuel or deplete public value creation.

Second, the engagement techniques and practical frameworks embody a frequently asserted normative public value (Bozeman 2007)—namely that they are *public*: they are freely available and accessible to anyone who would like to use them. What is presented in the training workshop is not owned by an institution or copyrighted but, like code shared by open-source computer programmers, seen as a public resource by the international Art of Hosting community. Through application, members in the community of practitioners make additional refinements to both techniques and frameworks that they subsequently share online, in training workshops, or in reference workbooks. For example, in the course of this research, two new engagement techniques—Pro Action Café (which combines other techniques and enables more refined action planning) and Storytelling Harvest (which uses the age-old power of storytelling and focused listening to impart insight)—were developed, refined, and incorporated into the Art of Hosting suite of techniques.

Third, the workshop itself produces public value as an experience in deliberation and opportunity to build the trainees' deliberative capacities. It is an experiential practicum in which trainers and participants just being introduced to the Art of Hosting are encouraged to "practice" the techniques and to "colearn." One dimension of this is deepening relationships among the diverse participants. Satisfaction surveys of those who have participated in the training in Minnesota, found 99 percent ($n=89$) agreed they had formed deeper relationships during the training. Yet, more fundamentally, learning to host—acquiring the skill to convene meaningful conversations that situate knowledge in context-appropriate ways—involves devolving authority from a centralized, heroic facilitator role to coproducing the means and ends of deliberative processes with the people being hosted (Quick and Sandfort 2014). Coproduction, in which authority for content and process is shared (Bovaird 2007; Quick and Feldman 2011), happens in the workshop. The experience teaches people to facilitate by practicing—namely, by facilitating their own workshop (Sandfort, Stuber, and Quick 2012). Thus the workshop is not a simulation of deliberation or merely a way to build participants' capacities to support public value creation in other venues. Rather, it is itself an emergent democratic space and a project of building community (Quick and Sandfort 2014). The training reflects the deep commitment of the hosting model's ongoing collective learning through practice, making it a potentially powerful means and ends of generating public value.

In sum, the Art of Hosting model is ambitious about generating public value. There are now enough people trained in it to begin to analyze whether or how it accomplishes the outcomes it claims, a project we take on through studying the population of individuals trained in Minnesota. Previously analyzed data is promising, but speaks primarily to the quality of the training and what participants learned.[3] Herein we analyze whether or how the workshops and Art of Hosting model have produced public value as the model is carried out in community settings. InCommons created and supported the expectation that Art of Hosting training participants would use this approach to facilitate deliberative processes in various contexts. After participating in the free workshop, participants were asked to devote an equivalent of three days, pro bono, to designing and implementing projects focused on enhancing public value. The data is drawn from these projects.

We particularly focus on three cases to delve into the means and results of purposeful attempts to engage in public value creation. Each of these cases highlights instances in which professionals and citizens from diverse regions and points of view were invited into a deliberative process about significant public services redesign. Each involved a team of hosts trained in the Art of Hosting to design and implement the engagement efforts. Each drew upon public or philanthropic resources to support the project costs. Each had sponsors willing to enter into a deliberative process that did not have predetermined outcomes but instead focused on improving both substantive content issues and relationships among participants. As described in table 3.1, however, the cases varied in terms of their intensity and size; hosting team configuration; intent of involving participants in defining the problem, process, and outcomes; and primary sources of participant diversity.

We utilized multi-sited ethnographic methods (Marcus 1995; Gupta and Ferguson 1997) for data collection and analysis. Extended participant observation has

Table 3.1. Variation in cases

	Local Government Innovation	HIV/AIDS Field Realignment	Resilient Region
Engagement intensity	Three-hour dinner forum, 6 distinct audiences	Three full days over 2 weeks	Five 4-hour meetings of large consortium, 4 additional sessions for working groups, all over 18 months
Total participants	400+	26	484
Hosting team configuration	One core host, plus 22 trained Art of Hosting volunteers, who assisted single sessions	Three core hosts	Four core hosts, working together and in distinct work groups
Intent	Generating commitment to local government innovation	Coproducing topics, deliberative process, and field change	Coproducing insights and shared plan through deliberation
Dimension of participant diversity	Geography, jurisdiction, political party	Geography, demographic	Jurisdiction, profession, political party

allowed us to learn the practices and become members of the community of practice (Dewalt and Dewalt 2002). We were participant observers in the InCommons-sponsored training and in two of the subsequent engagement cases we analyze here. In the third case, we reviewed videotapes taken of community gatherings. In addition, we conducted and analyzed semistructured interviews with sixty-nine people, comprising 100 percent of the participants in January and April 2011 Art of Hosting training cohorts and members of the training team in the InCommons project. We interviewed them six to eight months after the workshops. To analyze the three engagement cases, we conducted thirty additional interviews with their core hosts, sponsors of community sessions, and participants. In these interviews we probed the nature of the engagement design and implementation. For each interview we consulted materials developed before, during, and after the engagement processes. We analyzed all of these data inductively with qualitative analysis software, Nvivo, using iterative rounds of data collection, data analysis, and thematic coding in a grounded theory development process (Glaser and Strauss 1967).

HOSTING AS A METHOD OF BUILDING DELIBERATIVE CAPACITY FOR CREATING PUBLIC VALUE

In our interviews we explicitly asked training participants, as well as the sponsors and participants involved in the cases, to consider how the use of the Art of Hosting approach creates results, particularly when compared to traditional meetings and conferences. Facilitators believe the approach has impact. The training workshop acquaints people with techniques and conceptual frameworks side by side in a complete package that enables them to understand the strengths and limitations of each particular tool and provide theories and language that describe otherwise ambiguous group dynamics. The workshop also describes the development of the Art of Hosting approach and its use around the world. Invoking the reach and impact of the approach increases its legitimacy with workshop participants and sponsors. Overall, interviewees believed these dimensions improved the efficiency and effectiveness of planning and implementing deliberative events.

When interviewed, facilitators and participants also stated that—compared to traditional formats for meeting—people experiencing these deliberative processes are more satisfied. They describe this partly in terms of cocreation. As one facilitator said about her use of these techniques, "People always say, 'That is the best meeting I've ever had.' When I ask them to say more, they tell me, 'The [way you organize it] provides a space for everyone in the room to be heard. There are people who have gone to fifteen meetings and have not been able to say anything. To be heard and seen, through the Post-it notes and graphics around the room, is to be honored.'" Another seasoned facilitator explained, "By participating in the process, they own what comes out of the process. It is cocreation. What comes out is a result of what they brought . . . and what they are willing to do together." In other words, the people we interviewed saw participation as the first step to enthusiasm, buy-in, and ownership for decisions. The hosting approach ideally provides a way for participants to "own" what develops, even if it is not necessarily what they—as individuals—would have created or planned.

Art of Hosting gatherings also create opportunities for people to develop relationships based on unpredictable connections. Because these connections arise from sharing and listening to stories, many participants saw this learning, and potential new relationships, as a unique result of the Art of Hosting approach. Our interviewees also believe deliberative techniques lead to higher-quality decision outcomes. Some stressed that engaging people more deeply and removing any excuses for detachment generate a pool of ideas that are both of higher quality and more comprehensive. Art of Hosting techniques can help a group confronting a "big thorny issue" to explore significant questions that get to the heart of the matter. Through delving more deeply, participants better understand the challenge and see a range of potential solutions better than mere content experts' presentations.

These interviews suggest potential in the Art of Hosting model for creating efficiency and effectiveness in project implementation, and a number of potential mechanisms through which public value might be created. As we will see through our in-depth analysis of cases, however, there is variation in how this possibility is realized in practice.

REALIZING DELIBERATIVE CAPACITY: AN ANALYSIS OF IMPLEMENTATION

We now turn our analytical eye to three cases of community engagement undertaken by teams of hosts trained in this approach. Before delving into what we can learn across these cases, we first describe the origins and ambitions of each. At the beginning of this chapter we asserted that process design and implementation create the capacity for public value creation. We now focus our account and analysis on certain hosting frameworks and artifacts to showcase how this capacity is or is not realized in these particular projects.

The Local Government Innovation Process

Our first case engaged local elected officials from counties, cities, and school districts to consider government services redesign. Undertaken during significant state-level budget shortfalls, facilitators trained in the Art of Hosting designed and implemented meetings to spark dialogue and engagement around promising solutions to operational problems. State legislators had come together to create the bipartisan Redesign Caucus, a volunteer body charged to solicit, review, and support implementation of innovative changes in public service redesign. One of the strategies they identified was to bring together local government officials in "listening sessions" for legislators traveling around the state to hear from local constituents. The Redesign Caucus cochair secured funding from a local foundation interested in using deliberative forums to inspire public-sector redesign and engaged three membership associations: the state's League of Cities, the school boards association, and the counties association. Together the groups identified several goals for the proposed meetings: enabling the exchange of ideas among grassroots managers; generating political momentum for local government funding from the state; and strengthening relationships and trust among elected officials from all kinds of local government.

The planning group began to hear about a growing number of local facilitators being trained in the Art of Hosting approach. They engaged one, who led a design that incorporated extensive outreach to invite participants, a shared meal, a brief informational presentation, and what was initially described as an "adapted World Café." In the end, six meetings were held throughout the state in November 2011, bringing out more than four hundred agency staff and elected officials. Participants attended a single meeting that lasted about three hours. Each meeting followed the same agenda. After a welcome and brief presentation about economic and demographic changes, people were encouraged to introduce themselves by describing their own pathway to public service to highlight the urgency and significance of the evening's work. The groups then began dialogues in small groups. A facilitator supported each table. Because of time and logistic constraints, several typical features of the World Café engagement technique were modified for these small group discussions. Participants were preassigned to tables and stayed in one group for the whole session. They first brainstormed services or programs that could be redesigned and then explored opportunities for implementing change. Each table assigned a note taker to document the conversation using written templates provided by the hosting team, although participants were also encouraged to informally jot down or draw on large paper with markers. A representative from each table reported a short overview of what was discussed.

The major output of the forums was the final, glossy summary report, which provided an overview of the process, summarized the need for significant changes in local government, and shared key principles offered at the forums for effective redesign and high-level lessons learned about barriers to change and innovation ideas. The report's recommendations were aimed at local and state leaders, with a particular emphasis on changes coming from legislative and statewide action. It was presented publicly at a press conference by the head of the Redesign Caucus, and copies were shared with the twenty-two Art of Hosting trained facilitators who had volunteered as table hosts.

In our follow-up interviews, participants and facilitators hungered for next steps or more opportunities to engage in similar conversations. The process was new to them, and most reported really enjoying having smaller groups walk through a structured conversation. Yet many participants were not completely clear about the desired outcome of the gatherings. Some expressed pessimism about the report, believing it would not be used by the legislature in spite of the press conference fanfare. In addition, while an expressed purpose was to build relationships and trust across jurisdictional boundaries, many noted that building more durable relationships takes time beyond merely a shared meal and conversation. One participant reflected a sentiment expressed by others: "I don't think they realized what the turf issue was and how strong it is. People say we should work together, but it just never happens."

HIV/AIDS Field Realignment

Our second case also involved the sustainability and redesign of public services. When HIV/AIDS erupted as a public health crisis in the United States in the early 1980s, nonprofit agencies providing food, supportive housing, and health care developed to help people die with dignity and advocate for more effective and responsive action. In recent decades, advances in prevention and treatment have significantly reduced disease transmission and enhanced survival, changing the service needs of HIV-infected people. When a statewide council of nonprofits offered resources for groups to use the Art of Hosting deliberative process to explore opportunities to improve and realign services in their field, four leaders stepped forward and invited people from their field to a three-day gathering.

To prepare for the gathering, staff members conducted background research, highlighting critical policy and fiscal issues in briefing documents. A three-person team, all trained in Art of Hosting practices, designed the gathering in an iterative process, working with the four field leaders to shape significant questions that would bring content to the more general circle practice, World Café and Open Space Technology techniques were deployed. The agenda for the three days was represented on a visual landscape learned in the Art of Hosting training workshop.

The first two days focused on building relationships among this diverse group and planting ideas for change. Participants shared stories of their motivation for this difficult work, learned more about the field through a cocreated timeline of key historical events, and worked in triads to analyze briefing documents. Facilitators also sat on the floor and taught three theories from the Art of Hosting workshop, focusing on helping participants understand the intent to diverge in views before converging around some common understandings or action steps at the end of the third day. Through an Open Space Technology process, participants also generated conversation topics about issues relevant to the future of HIV/AIDS services.

The final day, held two weeks later, began with a presentation by one of the sponsors about a realignment spectrum. This set the tone for focusing the day more explicitly on realignment and restructuring. While the facilitators used the same Open Space Technology process as in the prior session, a few features of its implementation were notable. First, the facilitators explicitly wanted to create more convergence among participants, so they entitled the work period "Considering Realignment Possibilities" rather than "Open Space" in the agenda. Second, even though participants were encouraged throughout the three days to help direct how the sessions unfolded, this part of the process revealed that they were not always willing or able to do so. When the participants were asked to consider the question "How could we realign ourselves to achieve more effective user-centered services?," nonprofit leaders hesitated. Public-sector leaders proposed the majority of the conversations convened that day, even though they comprised a minority of the attendees. Although the sessions were well attended and people engaged deeply in dialogue, nonprofit leaders were unwilling to lead conversations about strategic realignment in front of their peers.

A month after the gatherings, a five-page, colorful newsletter was sent to all participants. As facilitators related in interviews, this was intended to evoke the spirit of the gathering and inspire further action; it shared content discussed and also provided photos of activities. Participants pointed to its significance in reconnecting them to the feeling of the gathering and their intentions for field realignment. The background briefing documents, a realignment spectrum offered by the sponsor, and visual documentation of the conversations also helped orient them to the work at hand. Some results were already becoming visible as of the third meeting day—in the opening circle, one public manager reported her efforts to start implementation of the centralized intake process they desired; a statewide advocacy organization invited others to develop a shared policy agenda; and another participant opened up a training she had developed for her own agency to others. Nonetheless, there were not ultimately huge results in relation to the ambitious goal of field redesign. While those interviewed reported improved communication and plans to convene in the future, the deliberative process did not yield significant systems change.

The Resilient Region Project

The final case explores a regional planning process taking place over eighteen months that generated a plan to chart economic, environmental, and social sustainable development. A five-county region in rural Minnesota began to consider how to purposively prosper in the wake of the economic recession, elevated unemployment, eroded natural resources, and outmigration. After seeing a federal government call for proposals, the executive director of the regional development commission engaged others and successfully applied for a federal government grant that enabled them to develop a process to create a strategic and implementation plan for long-term development.

The Resilient Region Project was structured around four work groups—housing, land use, transportation, and economic development—and larger consortium meetings of all 220 participants, including the work groups. Most work groups involved thirty people who were intentionally recruited to include diverse backgrounds and areas of expertise. Information developed by these groups was brought to the larger consortium meetings' participants to garner feedback and connect the work of the different groups. Additionally, other key stakeholders in the region, such as utility companies, educational institutions, and alternative energy groups, were consulted.

Initially leaders imagined a typical planning process, but just as the grant was being finalized, four leaders attended the Art of Hosting training workshop and decided to adapt their approach. The facilitators heavily used a World Café technique in the work group and full group consortium meetings to inspire people to engage in dialogue with others who might not share their point of view. They combined the technique with others to help the participants identify key issues, develop recommendations to address them, and identify action steps. As in the HIV/AIDS case, facilitators shared theories from the Art of Hosting approach with participants—for example, noting the natural tendencies for groups to diverge and enter the "groan zone" before converging on areas of resolution. They also used techniques from outside their Art of Hosting training, such as the nominal group process, when it helped advance the purpose of a particular meeting. They used information technology to share results and be transparent, although facilitators noted that sharing electronically was not a substitute for personal connections and relationships.

When interviewed, facilitators and participants identified a number of results. Some shared stories about participants engaging in new relationships, using insights developed, and their own heightened attention to listening in other arenas of their lives. As one person suggested, "Because everyone got to go around the table and offer their opinion, there was more even chance for everyone to hear from others." A host shared a similar observation about the work group he assisted, noting, "Using Open Space Technology and World Café is helping people understand they are not as far apart as they seem to think they are [or] as you've been told; they start to understand that there is more commonality. That has been the benefit in facilitating conversations and letting *them* talk to each other, and solve their own problems, and work through some of these issues, and create recommendations together. In a typical approach, where we just did lecturing and nobody spoke to each other, they wouldn't see how close together they were." To document how people engaged across their differences, the facilitators decided to create a video testimony of six ideologically diverse participants. In our interviews, people emphasized the importance of civility and including diverse opinions, suggesting that the deliberative methods used strongly contributed to a civil and inclusive process. Facilitators and participants also expressed their long-term commitment to the region and indicated they had discovered, strengthened, or honed it through the inclusive process. The Resilient Region Plan summed up the project's work into themes, goals, recommendations, and action, and implementation began immediately. The first small but significant changes implemented so far include private employers, pooling resources to build a homeless shelter, the creation of trail projects developed at military training facilities, and technical and financial resources for wastewater treatment.

BUILDING DELIBERATIVE CAPACITY TO CREATE PUBLIC VALUE

These data indicate how engagement processes may build deliberative capacity for creating public value. They reveal that the mechanisms through which this occurs are neither static nor determined by use of a particular deliberative model. In the three cases, the Art of Hosting model provided a consistent group of techniques, theories, and practical design frameworks that enabled facilitators to more efficiently design and implement deliberative process. Hosts' experience in the immersive training workshop provided them a common palette from which to create the deliberative projects, as well as experience as participants in cocreating agendas and visual artifacts. The Local Government Innovation forums benefited from many volunteer facilitators who, having been trained in the Art of Hosting method, were eager to contribute their time to honor their commitment to the In-Commons initiatives. In the HIV/AIDS realignment and Resilient Region conversations, the facilitator teams were made up of groups trained in the model who used it more extensively—for example, by employing a wider variety of techniques and by introducing participants to the convergence-divergence Art of Hosting practical framework, which participants said helped them to orient themselves and accept the sometimes uncomfortable or meandering process of public deliberation.

Yet these cases also showcase the significance of both facilitator choices and participant engagement in generating or undermining public value in deliberative projects. They point to two kinds of public value that may potentially be built by deliberative processes. The first is to incorporate publicly held values into outcomes aimed at addressing public problems. This is accomplished through enhanced participant involvement in understanding and developing better-informed actions on substantive policy issues and public program delivery systems. The second involves enhancing underlying deliberative capacity to work on not only the issue at hand but also potential other issues as an essential public value of good governance. Building this kind of public value—deliberative capacity—involves not only design and skill, but also how the participants understand their agency in developing or acting on solutions.

Although an espoused goal in the Local Government Innovation process was to build relationships among participants, facilitators did not pursue relationship-building processes in a sustainable way. In fact, rather than enabling spontaneous connection, the process limited opportunities by preassigned seating throughout the event and offering participants no opportunity to coorganize discussion topics. While the material collected ultimately appeared in the glossy report, it did not build a collective sense of value from the deliberation because it was not "harvested" in a coproduced manner with the participants. Created by consultants to advance a state-level policy goal rather than to document shared understandings among participants, the Local Government Innovation process created cynicism among some participants who, while enjoying the conversations, knew it wasn't so easy to work together across jurisdictional boundaries because "it just never happens."

The facilitators in the HIV/AIDS project made many more explicit decisions to involve participants in cocreating the events, from shaping the design and questions to enabling people to critique the briefing documents. Yet, while this did create an expectation that field changes needed to come from participants' own leadership, the results were more modest than had been initially hoped. The deliberative process was not able to help nonprofit leaders overcome the risks they sense about fundamentally redesigning their system. In the Resilient Region case, both facilitator choices and participant engagement generated public value. In this instance the process and results were coproduced through the use of a range of Art of Hosting techniques and practical design frameworks. The process generated new relationships, appreciation of differences, and concrete plans and projects in the community related to their ambitious goal of regional resilience.

These cases also highlight time as potentially significant in how deliberative processes create public value. As is noted in table 3.1, The HIV/AIDS Field Realignment and Resilient Region Project brought participants together for several hours at a time, repeatedly, over an extended period for analysis and discussion, whereas the Local Government Innovation project brought participants together just once for a few hours. The hosting model is agnostic on whether there is a desired amount of time, duration for a process, or particular sequencing of steps. However, greater time—to permit reflection and in-depth work—does seem to support opportunities for systemic change, a finding echoed in the literature on designing engagement processes (Bryson et al. 2014; Nabatchi et al. 2012).

CONCLUSION

This study has allowed us to examine in some detail how a new approach to engagement, the Art of Hosting, may offer opportunities for creating public value through building deliberative capacity. Potentially, these opportunities contribute to creating public value in two ways: by enhancing the influence of publicly held values in framing public problems and formulating policy solutions, and in building deliberative capacity as an intrinsically valued feature of good governance. The data was drawn from three specific public service redesign projects that used some elements of the Art of Hosting approach. Like other deliberative scholars (Fung 2004, 2006; Gutmann and Thompson 2004; Sirianni and Friedland 2001), we find that the design and implementation of deliberative processes influence both how citizens understand substantive issues and how they understand their agency in developing or acting on solutions. Thus, for public managers, other policymakers, and citizen activists, this research practically stresses that *how* they enact deliberative processes has a powerful impact on *whether* they create public value. Deliberative processes do not guarantee that these important results are achieved.

As these cases highlight, no silver bullets are contained in the democratic process—even one that trains facilitators to be more deliberative than in many other engagement methods. While Art of Hosting advocates make ambitious claims in regard to creating public value, the practicalities of public engagement processes and building deliberative capacity are very significant. They suggest that the impacts of public participation design choices extend far beyond the success or failure of a particular project. Facilitators' skillfulness in coproduction is not merely important for solving a particular challenge but for what it teaches participants about their abilities, or lack thereof, to influence collective actions through engagement with others. These capacities are core to leveraging the power of engagement for creating public value through building deliberative capacity on a larger scale.

NOTES

1. This reflects an understanding that resources are not fixed but endogenously generated and brought into use in particular ways. Frameworks or schemas have a recursive relationship with resources in which they help to bring one another into use (Feldman 2004; Feldman and Pentland 2008; Feldman and Quick 2009; Sandfort 2013).
2. For an illustration of this breadth and depth, see http://artofhosting.ning.com/.
3. In repeated satisfaction surveys taken after the three-day workshop in Minnesota, the vast majority of participants rated it useful or very useful (89–100 percent). For many the workshop provided exposure to new techniques and frameworks that—though they might have heard about before—they had not had the chance to experience. For copies of reports, including photos from training events, see http://www.leadership.umn.edu /education/leadership_forum.html. When we interviewed the first two cohorts of workshop participants six to eight months later, all could recall notable techniques, frameworks, and experiences from the three-day workshop; while not all were deploying them, the Art of Hosting workshop was memorable for all who had participated (Sandfort, Stuber, and Quick 2012).

4

JOINING MINDS

SYSTEM DYNAMICS GROUP MODEL BUILDING TO CREATE PUBLIC VALUE

GEORGE P. RICHARDSON, DAVID F. ANDERSEN,
AND LUIS F. LUNA-REYES

System dynamics group model building (SDGMB) engages public managers and policymakers in strategic discussions that can help create public value for their organizations, their direct clients, and the public at large. These techniques link people, process, analysis, and policy design as an approach to helping create public value. SDGMB involves key stakeholders, group facilitation, and formal computer simulations in a transparent process designed to "join minds," by which we mean create a shared view and set of commitments. The goal is to assist public managers and policymakers grappling with a complex problem achieve a consensus on what the problem is and a consensus on how to address it. This chapter summarizes more than twenty years of experiences with SDGMB, as documented in the systems thinking and management sciences literatures, and emphasizes the potential of the approach to generate public value. It outlines the process in an extended example dealing with welfare reform, and synthesizes the results of evaluation studies to identify conditions that affect the success or failure of group modeling. SDGMB can help public managers engage stakeholders, build on their mental models to help them understand complex systems, define problems, articulate viable solutions, and link them to desired public values and outcomes. Although SDGMB serves primarily as an analytical method to help managers to create public value (Moore 1995), the same models and techniques can be used to promote conversations and dialogue about public value to a wider audience (Bozeman 2007). We view SDGMB as an approach that spans both of these views.

WHAT IS SYSTEM DYNAMICS GROUP MODEL BUILDING?

In 1987, New York State was facing a crisis in its medical malpractice system. Doctor- and hospital-paid premiums into the state-sanctioned system were skyrocketing. Physicians, especially obstetricians, were refusing to treat new patients, and some were moving out of state to practice elsewhere. The governor and the legislature were caught in crossfires across hospital associations, medical associations, trial lawyer associations, and insurance carriers. Actuarial calculations predicted that the malpractice insurers' reserve funds were statistically insolvent to the tune of $2 billion, which implied the need for dramatic hikes in doctors' premiums. A problem of this magnitude, based on complex legal and technical arguments and involving the core interests of competing powerful stakeholders, would now be characterized in the literature as a "tangled," "messy," or "wicked" problem.[1]

As a partial solution to this crisis, the commissioner of the New York State Insurance Department convened a group of expert political, financial, and actuarial stakeholders internal to his agency to design possible solutions to this connected set of issues. As previously reported in the management science literature (Reagan-Cirincione et al. 1991), with the support of the Decision Techtronics Group (DTG) at the University at Albany,[2] the group designed and implemented a series of computer-based simulation models and multicriteria decision-making models that helped to guide the state toward a resolution of the crisis that focused squarely on enhancing public value.

These meetings became the first published example of what system dynamics modelers later came to call group model building (GMB). For sake of clarity here, we shall refer to this process as system dynamics group model building (SDGMB) to distinguish it from other forms of group-oriented modeling practices. Four developments came together right around 1988 to make the first case of SDGMB possible: (1) the field of computer simulation was maturing and its practitioners were beginning to work directly with multiple competing stakeholder groups; (2) microcomputing and early computer projection technology had made it possible for the first time to bring live computer support into group meetings; (3) methods of group facilitation had formed the basis for the emerging field of group decision support systems;[3] and (4) the recent development of icon-oriented system dynamics simulation software (initially STELLA, later Vensim and Powersim Studio) enabled modelers to develop high-level simulation models in real time with client groups in the room. While many of the formulation and calibration tasks of the modeler still remained "in the back room," key system conceptualization and problem-defining tasks could now be accomplished in front of, and with the active involvement of, client groups representing diverse stakeholder interests.

Since 1987 the field of SDGMB has made considerable progress. It has diffused out from its origins in public-sector work (where it was uniquely suited to support complex and conflicting stakeholder groups of clients) to become the mainstay of a growing consulting practice used in business, government, and nonprofit organizations. In a meta-analytic survey, Rouwette, Vennix, and Van Mullekom (2002) reported on over one hundred cases appearing in the published literature. In addition, a literature documenting systematic methods of carrying out SDGMB has emerged, giving practice guidelines to consultants and practitioners new to the field. Finally, researchers are beginning to grapple with the complex issues of defining and measuring the effectiveness of this class of interventions.

This chapter presents an update on what has been happening with SDGMB since its inception in 1987 and links that ongoing work to efforts to generate public value. Table 4.1 provides thumbnail sketches of eleven illustrative interventions, tracing some of the recent developments in the art and practice of group modeling. After presenting an interpretation of public value that is embodied in these studies, we present an extended example. Then we briefly review some of the

Table 4.1. Thumbnail sketches of a number of published group model building interventions with a public-sector focus

Client Organization	Problem	Processes	Outcomes
New York State (NYS) Department of Social Services (DSS) Key reference: Wulczyn and colleagues (1991)	Understanding foster care caseload dynamics	Group model building workshops with foster care experts; a model-based master's essay with policy analyses	Continuation of research in New York City (NYC), NYS DSS, and Chicago on the dynamics of foster care caseloads
Vermont (VT) Department of Health and Human Services (DHHS) Key references: Vennix and colleagues (1994); Richardson and Andersen (1995)	Rising VT Medicaid costs	Group model building with VT Medicaid experts and stakeholders	Resistance from traditional quantitative approaches; no clear implementation of system dynamics insights
NYC Office of Management and Budget (OMB)	Caseload growth in NYC foster case	Group model building workshop with practitioners, NYC managers, and OMB	No clear policy implementations; motivation for continued research between NYC practitioners and NYS DSS researchers
NYS Office of Mental Health (OMH) Key references: Richardson and Andersen (1995); Huz and colleagues (1997)	Studying the failed efforts to integrate vocational services of OMH and Vocational and Educational Services for Individuals with Disabilities (VESID) for mental health clients	Group model building workshops in four counties; building shared understandings between OMH and VESID county workers	Group modeling increased alignment, achieved greater agreement on means, and built significant improvements in intergroup goal clarity, team cohesion, and openness
NYS Office of Real Property Services (ORPS) Key reference: Griffen and colleagues (2000)	Moving from an adversarial role for ORPS with localities to a consulting model	Several group modeling workshops involving both system dynamics and strategic mapping	Increased clarity in the nature of a consulting role for ORPS with localities; enhanced motivation and capabilities to pursue it

text continues on page 57

Table 4.1. (continued)

Client Organization	Problem	Processes	Outcomes
National Cancer Institute Key reference: Best and colleagues (2007)	Dynamics of tobacco prevalence and control, as a test of the Initiative for the Study and Implementation of Systems (ISIS) in public health	Policy-oriented systems, maps, and models of the dynamics of prevalence and control linked with the other ISIS approaches: networks, knowledge management, and organization change	Research report capturing the individual and combined contributions of the four components of the ISIS approach to studying tobacco prevalence and control efforts
Center for Technology in Government (CTG) at UAlbany and National Science Foundation Key reference: Luna-Reyes and colleagues (2006)	Building grounded theory on implementing information integration among public sector agencies	Several group model building workshops with CTG staff evolving a model representation of the structure and dynamics of their interventions	Increasingly sophisticated model-based understandings (theories) of the problems and possibilities involved in implementing information integration among public sector agencies
Consortium of offshore oil platform developers interested in developing wind farms Key reference: Howick, Ackermann, and Andersen (2006)	Financial feasibility of offshore wind farms depended on unknown mix of risk and government policy factors	Consortium used group model building to understand the structure and dynamics of the offshore wind farm market	Simulations identified and quantified risk factors; report was sent to national legislative bodies
British National Health Services Key references: Ackermann and colleagues (2010); Eden and colleagues (2009)	Provision of long term dementia services in the Scottish Borders was straining service capacity	Local coalition of service providers met in group mapping sessions to plot new directions	Sessions did not result in a formal running simulation, but did lead to a service integration proposal
CERT National Cyber-Security Center Key reference: Martinez-Moyano, Conrad, and Andersen (2011)	Insider Threats provided an ill-understood source of cybervulnerability for the US internet	Cybersecurity experts joined behavior scientists to craft a dynamic theory of cyberattacks by insiders	Published theory of insider attacks supports national policies on cybersecurity aimed at insider threats

Table 4.1. (continued)

Client Organization	Problem	Processes	Outcomes
NYS DSS Key reference: Kim, MacDonald, and Andersen (2013)	Perceived long-term decline in Social Security Administration clients requiring layoffs in NYS DSS	Several group model building sessions followed by extensive model collaboration with agency data	Agency discovered endogenous management policies and began outsourcing client screening activities, avoiding layoffs

emerging literature on methods, present an overview of several of the key studies that are evaluating group modeling efforts, and conclude with reflections on current practice and future prospects.

CREATING PUBLIC VALUE

SDGMB aligns with Moore's strategic triangle (discussed in chapter 1), which shows the importance of aligning three interrelated processes: defining public value, building and sustaining a group of diverse stakeholders to create an authorizing environment, and mobilizing the resources from inside and outside the organization to achieve the desired outcomes (Benington and Moore 2011b). Each of the group model building interventions shown in table 4.1 was an effort to generate public value highly consistent with these three key concepts.

In a parallel development, colleagues from the Center for Technology in Government (CTG; see Harrison et al. 2011) at the University at Albany have identified what they argue are the seven generators of public value (see http://www.ctg.albany.edu/projects/opengov). These seven generators—described in detail in chapter thirteen of this volume by Cresswell, Cook, and Helbig—add efficiency, efficacy, enablement, and intrinsic enhancements in government actions to the three dimensions emphasized in the Open Government Directive of the administration of President Barack Obama—namely, transparency, participation, and collaboration (see http://www.whitehouse.gov/sites/default/files/omb/assets/memoranda_2010/m10-06.pdf). These generators are not ends in themselves but instead are "instrumental to the accomplishment of democracy," enabling "citizens to perform their roles as citizens" (Harrison et al. 2011). The work of the CTG further emphasizes the multiple and diverse stakeholders that would be involved in any in-depth analysis of an initiative designed to create public value.

The values identified in the work of the CTG are related to three of the seven constellations of values identified by Beck Jørgensen and Bozeman (2007). The values of efficiency and effectiveness belong to the constellation of intraorganizational aspects of public administration. Transparency, collaboration, enablement, and intrinsic enhancements are closely related to the constellation of relationships between public administration and its environment, and participation belongs to the constellation of relationships between public administration and the citizens.

In this sense, this framework is only incorporating explicitly values in the realm of public administration activity and its relationships with the environment and the citizens, leaving out those values in the constellations that involve politicians and the society at large.

SDGMB targets Moore's three elements in the strategic triangle, and all six of the CTG generators of public value, and does so in contexts made complex not only by the difficulty of the problems but also by the diversity of the stakeholders involved. SDGMB thus can serve as a facilitator of what Stoker (2006) calls public value management, in fact including values from those constellations representing the relationships between public administration and the society at large (Beck Jørgensen and Bozeman 2007). Moreover, as argued by public failure theory (see chapters 1 and 9 of this book), SDGMB provides a tool to build causal hypotheses related to instrumental, sometimes competing values, and uses simulation as a form of empirical testing of such hypotheses. Looking at the results of simulations over time contributes to understanding the impact of policies in the short and long terms, helping to reduce public value failure.

AN EXTENDED EXAMPLE

In order to give a better sense of what happens in one of these group model building projects and how they target public value, we describe in the next section an extended example that used SDGMB to support welfare reform initiatives in three county governments in New York State.[4] We chose to present this example because it is particularly well documented, with aspects of the project having been reported previously in the literatures on public affairs (Rohrbaugh and Johnson 1998; Rohrbaugh 2000; Zagonel et al. 2004) and simulation (Rogers et al. 1997; Lee et al. 1998; Lee 2001; Andersen et al. 2000; Zagonel 2003).

Background on the Case

In 1996, President Bill Clinton signed into law the Personal Responsibility and Work Opportunity Reconciliation Act. While many of the implications of this law have been made clear with the passage of time (Ewalt and Jennings 2004), at its inception policymakers and researchers had no steady intuition or theoretical knowledge to guide them in considering plausible outcomes: What if there were a recession while clients are facing time-limited benefits on federal funding that were part of the act? How could counties cope with increased demands for scarce resources as clients lost Federal welfare eligibility? What if neighboring states were forced to cut back benefits? In New York these questions have a special edge because Article 17 of the state constitution mandates local governments to provide for the indigent and needy. While the federal government can end entitlements after five years, New York State and its local governments cannot suspend all benefits. A coalition of state agencies and county governments agreed to use simulation technologies supported by SDGMB techniques to address these questions (Richardson and Andersen 1995; Andersen and Richardson 1997; Vennix 1996).

A Thumbnail Sketch of the New York State Welfare Simulation Project

The project emerged in four overlapping phases. The first phase involved building a simulation model of the basic federally mandated Temporary Assistance to Needy Families (TANF) system for Cortland County, a rural county located in central New York State (Rogers et al. 1997; Rohrbaugh 2000; Zagonel 2003). In this phase a preliminary simulation model was constructed with the commissioner and her management team using SDGMB.

The second phase of the project concentrated on formulating the "safety net" sectors of the model, which would serve clients after they lost federal eligibility. This portion of the modeling effort imported the TANF model developed in Cortland County, but had it calibrated and joined with the safety net model developed for Dutchess County, a midsize suburban county located in the Hudson River Valley (Zagonel 2003). The simulation model was thus extended and elaborated.

The third phase of the project was conducted in conjunction with a network of service providers located in Nassau County, a large and demographically complex county directly adjacent to New York City. After calibrating the model for this area, the group explored how approaches developed in smaller regions applied in the more complex environment in the metropolitan area, adding yet more refined detail to the simulation model.

The final phase of the project was aimed at implementing policy insights from the model. Follow-up workshops were held in these counties with broadly based groups of stakeholders, including new participants who were not involved in model development. To facilitate this process, the joined TANF–Safety Net model was wrapped in a graphical user interface that allowed it to be used by managers, policymakers, and laypersons who had not been previously involved in the model construction process (Rohrbaugh and Johnson 1998).

Policy Insights from the Simulation Model Contributing to Public Value

An important policy insight produced by experiments through the modeling process involved the comparison of two investment policies labeled Edges and Middle. The Base run (or "reference" run) shows the model's projection of what would happen to the county's welfare system if no policy changes were made and if there were no external scenario changes.[5] The Middle policy simulated a high investment in assessment, monitoring, and job finding and promotion functions traditionally associated with a social services unit. The Edges policy contained a mixture of resource investments that concentrated on the "front" and "back" ends of the system (i.e., prevention, child support enforcement, and self-sufficiency promotion).

Figure 4.1 compares the Base run to the Middle and Edges policy packages for one key performance indicator—*total clients finding jobs* from TANF. The X-axis is time, measured in years, and the Y-axis is the total flow of people out of TANF, measured in people per year.[6] As shown in figure 4.1, significant new investment in the Middle policy package greatly accelerates this presumably beneficial trend.

Figure 4.1   Total job-finding flows from TANF (base vs. middle vs. edges policy packages)

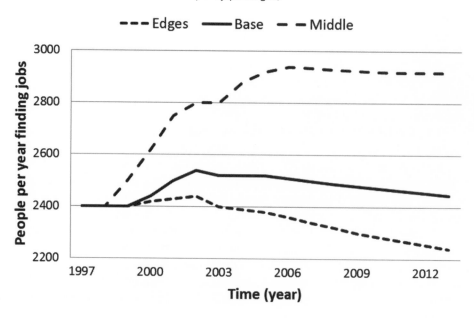

Investing in the Edges of the system appears in the simulation actually to retard job finding relative to the Base run.

The conclusion from figure 4.1 is misleading, however. By focusing on a less commonly articulated performance measure—total recidivism, defined as the number of people losing their jobs and returning to welfare—figure 4.2 reveals an important structural insight lurking behind these graphs. The Edges policy has the effect of significantly reducing recidivism in the model. Since the total number of persons coming on to TANF at any point in time is the sum of first-time recipients plus recidivists, this reduction in recidivism can dramatically decrease the overall TANF caseload. By contrast, the Middle policy actually has the simulated effect of increasing recidivism. Richardson, Andersen, and Wu (2002) have demonstrated that in the simulation model the high influx of families on TANF into the post-TANF employment support system had the effect of "swamping" these downstream resources, leading to long-term increases in recidivism. Since federal legislation does not require that recidivism be tracked and it is hard to document, the increased TANF caseload could easily be misinterpreted as the result of some external influence such as rising unemployment rather than as a natural, endogenous consequence of the Middle policy intended to reduce caseloads.

To summarize the mechanism at work here, the Middle policy is great at getting people into jobs, but then they lose those jobs and cycle back into the system because there aren't enough resources devoted to help them stay employed. The Edges policy lets them trickle more slowly into jobs but then does a better job of keeping them employed.

Whatever the final policy choice, the simulation model provides a level playing field for evaluating the implications of multiple policy and scenario changes, al-

Figure 4.2   Total recidivism flows back to TANF (base vs. middle vs. edges policy packages)

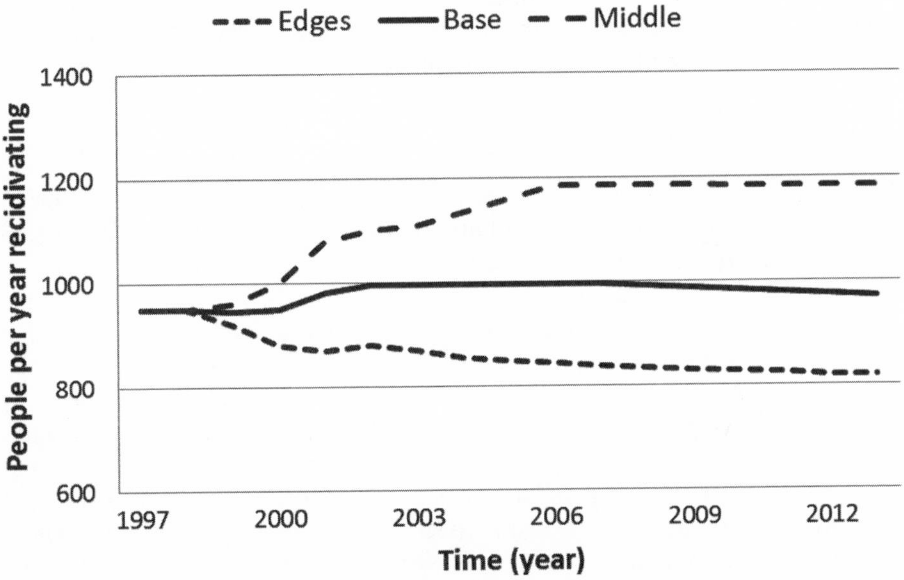

ways using precisely the same agreed-upon set of assumptions and numbers. Of course, these inferences are only as good as the model upon which they are based. In this case, SDGMB has the great strength that the model and its parameters emerged from facilitated conversations among experts in the problem. In addition, the overall project paid careful attention to qualitative and quantitative model testing, sensitivity analyses, and calibration (Lee et al. 1998; Zagonel et al. 2004).

This intervention illustrates the potential contributions of the approach to public value. From simulations and analyses the idea of recidivism emerged as a robust measure of policy performance and public value. The analyses were transparent: model building and model evaluation took place in public. The work was participatory and collaborative: the model was not the work of one group but instead a highly participative process, with most stakeholders present and active. Additionally, the diverse group was actively involved in stressing the model to test it and to help build confidence in its structure and dynamic implications.

What Happened in the Three Counties?

The patterns of pursuing implemented results from the modeling process varied considerably in the three counties. The commissioner of social services in Cortland County used the model and its results to plan her investment priorities to implement welfare reform for the mid- to long term (Rogers et al. 1997). In Dutchess County, the commissioner created a public-private task force to design and implement concrete initiatives aimed at the Edges policies (Rohrbaugh and Johnson 1998; Rohrbaugh 2000). Implementations in Nassau County were the least extensive of the three sites. The commissioner convened her direct staff to work with the model but did not involve a wider group of community stakeholders to implement model-based implications. In a sense, the commissioners from Courtland and Dutchess Counties were more effective in using the model to increase their operational capacity (as described in Moore 1995) when compared with the commissioner from Nassau County. Moreover, the commissioner in Dutchess County was the most effective in creating an authorizing environment to create public value.

HOW THE SDGMB METHOD WORKS

There is much to say about approaches to group conversations about messy problems. There are many approaches, all presumably designed to enhance discussion about and creation of public value. SDGMB is better suited for multistakeholder complex "messy," "tangled," or "wicked" problems involving feedback and dynamic changes over time that require collaboration and shared understanding to design policies to create public value. These problems are sometimes recognized by the fact that several policies have not been effective in solving the problem or they only alleviate some symptoms temporarily. The method helps to better understand public value failure, particularly doing a good job at helping managers to understand trade-offs between the short- and long-run effects of policy choices. The inclusion of multiple stakeholders considered in SDGMB also supports the creation, maintenance, and enhancements of the public sphere. Below we describe the defining characteristics of the SDGMB approach and touch upon some practical considerations associated with helping groups of managers develop policy and strategy.

Team Facilitation

Experts in group decision support point to skilled facilitation as a key success factor for any group method. Because of the nature of the tasks involved in facilitating SDGMB sessions and model development, a single person has difficulty accomplishing all of them. SDGMB works best with team facilitation; each member of the facilitation team plays a different role in a coordinated manner. Through experience over the years, our group has identified five different roles: facilitator, modeler/reflector, process coach, recorder and gatekeeper; Richardson and Andersen (1995) have described these five roles in detail. A key feature of creating and sustaining multiple roles is the ability to separate the facilitation work into two specialized tasks, facilitation and analysis (Rohrbaugh 1992; Zagonel 2002; Vennix et al. 1994; Richardson and Andersen 1995).

Scripts for Group Model Building

SDGMB sessions are the result of a very careful planning process (Andersen and Richardson 1997). Tasks are usually broken up into discrete periods of fifteen to twenty minutes' duration throughout the day, promoting continuous change of activity and group dynamics to improve group engagement. A variety of convergent, divergent, and evaluative group tasks are cast as "scripts," all of which cumulate to create pieces of model structure that can be assembled into the final formal simulation model. Usually, the client group sits in comfortable chairs arranged in a *U* shape, with the facilitator in the front with a computer or an overhead projector. The ideal room has lots of wall or board space on which to write down diagrams and ideas. The modeler/reflector and the recorder sit at the back of the room.

Detailed descriptions of the process and scripts used in SDGMB have been reported in the simulation literature (Andersen and Richardson 1997; Luna-Reyes et al. 2006). Although the planning stage is very important, the facilitation process requires flexible improvisation after compulsively detailed advance planning (Andersen and Richardson 1997).

The In-Meeting and Between-Meeting Work of Team and Clients

A typical SDGMB project involves effort from the facilitation team and the client team both during the sessions and between them. The main activities of the facilitation team include facilitating the sessions, working in model development, coordinating the effort, writing reports, and gatekeeping (Luna-Reyes et al. 2006). Besides participating in the SDGMB sessions, the client group participates in defining the scope of the project and in providing soft and hard data for model calibration. With the present state of the art, much of the technical model formulation, testing, and validation are completed by the SDGMB team outside the group sessions.

Recent Developments in SDGMB: From Artful Practice to Structured Craft

One of the limitations to the use of SDGMB to support the generation of public value has been the perception, if not the reality, that completing a group model building project was an art form that blended multiple talents that are hard to assemble in a single team. Typically an SDGMB team would involve a skilled system dynamics modeler as well as at least one more person with facilitation skills. Often a recorder joined the modeling team. In addition, a team needed to have training in how to organize a full day or more of activities with a client group. While the benefits of these sessions in terms of generating public value are high, the barriers to doing successful work were also high and the risks of a less-than-successful session with high client involvement could prove to be a barrier to successful implementation.

Recently Hovmand and colleagues (2012) have been working to make SDGMB less of an art form and more of a structured craft; They have published a series of scripts that describe precisely small bits of behavior that a skilled facilitator or modeler should engage in when working with a group. The intention of this "scriptapedia" is to produce an easy-to-use handbook that would allow teams with little background in SDGMB to get started. Increasingly, teams with no experience in using SDGMB in a public value creation project have been able to pick up the manual and begin to make progress working with a group.

Ackermann et al. (2011) have contributed to this conversation by creating what they call a "Scriptsmap," a structured system for "snapping together" various smaller scripts into a larger all-day workshop for the purpose of working with client groups in a public value–creating exercise. These two recent developments promise to move the art of SDGMB into a more easily replicable form of craft.

Finally, and with the purpose of adding more science to the craft, Black (2013) describes visual representations in SDGMB using theories of distributed cognition and the sociological concept of boundary objects. In other words, visual representations of problems, in the form of causal maps and graphs of behavior over time, serve as tools to dialogue and reach agreements on problems, means to solve them, and values. Moreover, Black describes simulation forums as a way to take the dialogue about public values beyond the modeling team and public managers to a broader audience in the public at large.

EVALUATING SDGMB

SDGMB is a promising technology for creating public value, and many case-based stories of its use can be found in the literature. However compelling such case stories may be, they also involve serious limitations as evaluation tools. We summarize in this section some key group modeling evaluation studies.

Several evaluation efforts have attempted to identify keys to success in group sessions with managers working in the field. One of these studies found that the introduction of group decision support technologies substantially changes the way that groups function and how decisions are arrived at (McCartt and Rohrbaugh 1995). They also found that organizations open and receptive to change, or those who value adaptation, flexibility, and creativity in the decision process are more likely to succeed. Moreover, good managerial decision making in this group context is enhanced when the experience combines an effective empirical process and information that is not in the form of spreadsheets or databases (Schuman 1995).

A second study compared managerial teams using SDGMB with teams that did not use the approach in nine domains across three separate levels of analysis: reflections of the modeling team, participants' self-reports of the intervention, and measurable system change (Huz et al. 1997). Results of the experiment show statistically significant differences in six of the nine domains measured. Overall, participants were satisfied with SDGMB. Additionally, while the study found significant differences in goal alignment among participants, it found they were aligned around strategies to implement.

In their meta-analysis of 107 case studies of SDGMB, Rouwette and colleagues (2002) coded case studies with respect to eleven classes of outcomes, sorted into individual, group, and organizational levels. While recognizing limitations of the research design, they found high percentages of positive outcomes along all eleven dimensions of analysis. Rouwette (2003) followed this meta-analysis with statistical analysis of a series of SDGMB interventions held mostly in governmental settings in the Netherlands. He was able to demonstrate how SDGMB sessions moved both individuals and groups from beliefs to intentions to act and ultimately on to behavioral change.

In sum, what is emerging from this body of study is a mixed "good news and bad news" picture: all studies that take into account a reasonable sample of field studies show some successes and some failures. About one-fourth to one-half of the SDGMB studies investigated showed low impact on decision making (Rouwette 2003). On the other hand, roughly half of the studies have led to system-level implemented change, with approximately half of the implemented studies being associated with positive measures of success (Rouwette 2003). Nonetheless, from about three-fourths to all of the cases report some positive outcome at the individual, group, and organizational levels.

"Success" is a multidimensional concept in the evaluation studies, having important components on the individual, group, and organization or system levels.

A promising result is that explanations of differences between successful interventions and less successful ones have not been associated with the complexity of
the task environment. Rather, success appears to be conditioned by the user team's
openness to new problem-solving approaches and by an appreciation for and orientation toward empirical problem-solving methods.

DISCUSSION

While recognizing and respecting the difficulties of scientific evaluation of
SDGMB, we remain quite optimistic about the method's utility as a policy design
and problem solving tool capable of generating public value. A method that can
deliver—in a compressed time frame—implemented changes up to half of the time
and implemented results in up to half of the cases examined (Rouwette 2003) is
an improvement over alternative approaches that can struggle for months or even
years without coming to closure on important policy directions.

SDGMB can be effective because it joins the minds of public managers and
policymakers in an emergent dialogue that relies on formal modeling to integrate
data, other empirical insights, and mental models into the policy process, contributing through the process to the creation of an authorizing environment as well
as consensus on how to improve operational capacity to create public value (Moore
1995). Policymaking begins with the preexisting mental models, values, and policy stories that managers bring into the room. Policy consensus and direction
emerge from a process that combines social facilitation with technical modeling
and analysis. The method blends dialogue with data. It begins with an emergent
discussion and ends with an analytic framework that moves from "what is" base-
line knowledge to informed "what if" insights about future policy directions. In
his dichotomy of model as boundary object (Carlile 2002; Black and Andersen
2012) able to bridge differences versus model as microworld, analytic device, Zagonel (2002) has captured this distinction between SDGMB as a storytelling tool
and an analysis tool. In other words, SDGMB is both.

Nearly two decades ago, when we began this work, we primarily saw ourselves
as technical analysts who were building microworlds in an accelerated way in real
time with client groups. Early on we strove to incorporate insights relating to
facilitation and group process from our colleagues working in the Decision Techtronics Group (Milter and Rohrbaugh 1985; Quinn, Rohrbaugh, and McGrath
1985; Reagan-Cirincione et al. 1991; Rohrbaugh 1992; Rohrbaugh 2000). More
recently this work has showed increased sensitivity to stakeholder issues (Bryson
2004b; Bryson, Cunningham, and Lokkesmoe 2002), to visible maps of individual and group thought processes (Bryson et al. 2004), and elements of strategic
planning (Bryson 2011; Eden and Ackermann 1998).

These group process insights help make formal models easier to develop and
more powerful, but we are convinced that the models themselves are a key element
in the future success of such work. The key to the success of SDGMB interventions is a formal computer simulation model that reflects a negotiated, collaborative, consensual view of the "shared mental models" (Kim 2009) of the managers
in the room (the problem structure). This formal simulation model must be tested
and tried against existing administrative and time series data (the problem behavior)

whenever possible. The final simulation models that emerge from this process are crossbreeds, sharing much in common with data-based social scientific research while at the same time being comparable to the rough-and-ready intuitive analyses emerging from backroom conversations. Furthermore, system diagramming tools both useful for group process and embedded in modern simulation software provide support for dialogues among managers, their mental models, and both structural and behavioral data. In this work teams join minds, linking people, process, and analysis in the policy design process.

In sum, we believe that a number of the process features related to building these models contribute to their appeal for public managers:

- **Engagement.** Key managers are in the room as the model is evolving, and their own expertise and insights drive all aspect of the analysis.
- **Mental models.** The model building process uses the language and concepts that managers bring to the room with them, making explicit the assumptions and causal mental models managers use to make their decisions.
- **Complexity.** The resulting nonlinear simulation models lead to insights about how system structure influences system behavior, revealing understandable but initially counterintuitive tendencies like policy resistance or "worse before better" behavior.
- **Alignment.** The modeling process benefits from diverse, sometimes competing points of view as stakeholders have a chance to wrestle with causal assumptions in a group context. Often these discussions realign thinking and are among the most valuable portions of the overall group modeling effort.
- **Refutability.** The resulting formal model yields testable propositions, enabling managers to see how well their implicit theories match available data about overall system performance.
- **Empowerment.** Using the model managers can see how actions under their control can change the future of the system.

These process features of SDGMB provide effective tools to create public value as described by Moore in the strategic triangle (Moore 1995; Benington and Moore 2011b). Group modeling merges managers' causal and structural thinking with the available data, drawing upon expert judgment to fill in the gaps concerning possible futures. In this process, managers define collectively and iteratively public value by defining the key variables to be included in public discussion and debate. Publicly defined public values are also present in the conversation through the inclusion of legal mandates and regulations as well as the ways in which they constrain or enable policy options. Moreover, the resulting simulation models provide powerful tools to ground what-if thinking and to identify and align the key operational capacities needed to deliver such value. Using the model as a boundary object to communicate results to a variety of stakeholders has the potential of creating the necessary authorizing environment to act, as well as continuing with the dialogue about rights, obligations, and principles that constitute public values (Bozeman 2007).

Finally, the same process features are very well aligned to the public value management paradigm (Stoker 2006). Bringing together different stakeholders and public managers in a problem-solving process, SDGMB supports networked governance by providing a space for dialogue about goals, alternatives, and necessary capabilities to deliver public value. The extended example presented in this chapter also shows ways in which the SDGMB process serves several categories of values (Beck Jørgensen and Bozeman 2007). By helping to develop more effective programs, SDGMB promotes values belonging to the intraorganizational aspects of public administration. By providing tools for collaboration and participation, it contributes to the creation of public values connected to the relationship of the public administration with its environment and the society at large.

NOTES

1. The terms "wicked" (Rittel and Webber 1973) and "messy" (Eden, Jones, and Sims 1983) refer to problems lacking a clear definition, goals to pursue, or feasible solutions. Problems are "messy" partially because of a diversity of stakeholders with different—sometimes conflicting—points of view about a given situation. Dawes, Cresswell, and Pardo (2009) had in fact coined the term "tangled" for those problems whose main source of complexity is such diversity of interests.
2. The Decision Techtronics Group has a long tradition developing computer-based models with groups of managers to analyze policy and strategy (Rohrbaugh 1992). The group's approach has been used to understand and tackle problems in a diversity of areas using many kinds of models (Milter and Rohrbaugh 1985; Schuman and Rohrbaugh 1991), and particularly using system dynamics models (Reagan-Cirincione et al. 1991; Richardson and Andersen 1995; Andersen and Richardson 1997; Rohrbaugh 2000).
3. Group decision support systems are computer-based systems and techniques developed for group decision support (Quinn, Rohrbaugh, and McGrath 1985; Desanctis and Gallupe 1987).
4. This section is based on a note published in the *Journal of Policy Analysis and Management* (Zagonel et al. 2004).
5. Base policy assumed that all welfare programs were funded at their 1996 levels. The Base assumption about unemployment was that the economy was at the exact unemployment rate that would cause no growth but also no decline over the time frame 1984–98 (the modeling team "backward-computed" this figure as part of the model-testing and confidence-building phases. This calculation was intended to "hold constant" the very large effects of unemployment on TANF caseloads so that the runs could show "pure" effects of policy changes.
6. Note that in order to show the pattern of the dynamics, the scales on figures 4.1 and 4.2 are not zero-based scales and are different. Thus, the visual intervals between graphs in figures 4.1 and 4.2 are not comparable.

5

WEIGHING THE PUBLIC VALUE OF ALTERNATIVE METHODS OF PROVIDING PUBLIC SERVICES

TOWARD A CONTINGENCY FRAMEWORK

JOHN ALFORD

S ince the 1970s, externalization of public services—that is, government agencies transferring all or part of their work to external providers—has been popular for reasons that have changed over time. Initially the rationale was mainly an ideological one: the assumption that the private sector is inherently more efficient and therefore the role of government should be minimized (e.g., Bennett and Johnson 1981; Savas 1987), just as public-sector advocates argue that government should keep doing everything it currently does. More recently some have advocated a more contingent approach in which the question of whether to privatize services depends on the context, wherein privatization makes sense in some situations but not in others (see especially Donahue 1989). Given that there are different kinds of services and contexts, they argue, externalization will be optimal in only some situations. While it is useful as far as it goes, even this critique takes insufficient account of key contextual factors.

This chapter draws on a public value framework and research on types of externalization both to challenge "one best way" thinking and to call for a broader contingency approach. It offers an elaborated framework for making decisions about whether and in what form to externalize services and sheds light on the public value model in the process. After first reviewing the literature and setting out what is meant here by public value, the chapter examines the case of a large urban fire brigade, arguing that assessing the public value of any given externalization is a matter of weighing three different types of benefits and costs, only some aspects of which have been acknowledged hitherto.

EVOLVING RATIONALES FOR EXTERNALIZATION

The view that the private sector is inherently more efficient and therefore the role of government should be minimized gained louder voice from the 1970s on as a public reaction against "big government" was fostered by a growing advocacy of market-like mechanisms for the public sector (Savas 1987; Wolf 1988; Friedman

1962; Niskanen 1971). In 1995 former US secretary of defense Donald Rumsfeld delineated the parts of government that should be privatized:

> The first task is to decide what the core business is. . . . For the federal government, the four basic departments—State, Defense, Justice, and Treasury—have a solid basis for existence. The other departments were either more narrowly based, an afterthought, or both. Some had utility when they were established, but no longer do. Others, in my view, probably should not have been established in the first place. . . . Once one has determined the core functions to be performed by the federal government, all other activities should be scrutinized for elimination, downsizing, reorganization, movement to state and local governments, or privatization. I begin with the conviction that activities should first be undertaken by individual citizens and private organizations. (1995, 3)

This philosophy was applied to the Pentagon after Rumsfeld once again became defense secretary in 2001. Between then and February 2011, at least $177 billion was spent on contractors to provide protection for Coalition missions in the Iraq and Afghanistan wars, their numbers at times exceeding the number of military personnel there—with mixed results, according to a bipartisan congressional commission (2011).

In fact, the assumption that "private is best" had already become solidly embedded as an orthodoxy among politicians, business leaders, and senior public servants, transmitted by consultants, think tanks, and institutions like the World Bank (Henig, Hamnett, and Feigenbaum 1988; Hefetz and Warner 2004). But the ways of acting on this assumption were varied. Privatization meant not only transferring ownership of productive assets from the public to the private sector but also other long-standing methods such as competitive tendering on the basis of price.

From the late 1970s on, the focus on cost gave way to broader attention to service quality, effectiveness, or responsiveness—the operative term being "value for money." Pragmatism about the relative merits of public- and private-sector production had led to greater openness to market testing of both, although government delivery still tended to be regarded as guilty until proven innocent (Savas 1987; Wolf 1988).

Further delineation came from a growing recognition that external providers to a public agency could include not only private firms but also other types of organizations. From the 1980s onward, the contribution of nonprofit agencies to public services generally increased around the world (Salamon and Sokolowski 2001; Smith and Lipsky 1993). Similarly, various forms of interorganizational collaboration within government, such as whole-of-government coordination (Christensen and Lægreid 2007), joined-up government (Hood 2005), or between levels of government in federal systems demonstrated that, for any given public-sector agency, other government organizations can be external providers—hence the label "externalization" rather than "privatization."

Meanwhile, some scholars began to point out that value for money did not account for all the benefits and costs of engaging external providers. They demonstrated that in addition to the benefits and costs of the service itself, the transaction costs of ensuring that the provider delivers also had to be considered. Donahue (1989; see also Williamson 1975) showed how government organizations contracting out services incurred transaction costs of various types (see also Prager 1994; Brown, Potoski, and Van Slyke 2006). These factors inhibited the capacity of government to act as a "smart buyer" (Kettl 1993), with the risk that not only would government fail to reap the benefits of privatization, but it might also suffer *diminished* value as a result of the reduction in accountability.

This thinking gave rise to a contingency approach to the externalization of services in which it is neither inherently good nor inherently bad; rather, it depends on the circumstances, including not only whether an external party can do it better or cheaper but also the transaction costs of controlling that party's performance. The contingent perspective is an intellectual counterweight to "one best way" positions, lending coherence to the pragmatic decisions of many public managers. It is now well established, but although it is a considerable advance on earlier thinking, it still misses four important factors.

First, in a world of proliferating management innovations, the range of alternative types of contributors to service outcomes has grown to include, for instance, volunteers, clients, and regulatees (Parks et al. 1981; Alford 2009). Relatedly, the mechanisms for coordinating the actions of the government organization and the other party have also proliferated, encompassing not only classical contracting but also other forms such as collaboration, persuasion, regulation, or negotiation.

Third, the established categories of benefits and costs—that is, those to do with the service and those to do with transactions—are each too narrow, especially in accounting for public value. There is more to service benefits and costs than value for money. And the notion of transactions costs doesn't quite cover some aspects of the coordination mechanisms, such as collaborative partnerships. They also include what we might call collaboration costs (White 2005)—which together with the transaction costs will be labeled generally as relationship costs.

Finally, the established contingency approach misses another category of benefits and costs that cannot be conceived in terms of the service itself or the relationship with providers. This category, drawn from the public value framework, concerns institutional benefits and costs—those relating to an agency's positioning both within its environmental context and over time, and to the distinctive set of competences it brings to that environment.

This chapter offers an elaboration of the contingent view, by broadening the array of potential contributors to value creation, coordination mechanisms, and benefits and costs to consider when deciding whether to externalize.

PUBLIC VALUE

Public managers do not spend their working hours cogitating about public value. Their time is mostly taken up solving problems emanating from their task environment, which throws up situations in the social or natural world that need remediation. This task environment is inexorably changing. For instance, factors like global shifts in economic power, new technology, and new patterns of demand have led to population shifts, urban blight, fiscal crisis, and crime. How a manager understands and reacts to these problems has value implications. Any particular arrangement for delivering a service or implementing a policy creates a specific bundle of types of value.

This perspective on public management is drawn unambiguously from Moore's framework (1995) rather than Bozeman's (2007). Like Bozeman, Moore sees economic individualism as an inadequate basis for recognizing what is valuable—for instance, pointing out that public value goes beyond satisfying individual preferences through collective means such as public goods or other remedies to market failure. Not only does Moore acknowledge abundantly that we have more than economic needs, such as normative or symbolic aspirations, but we also have more than individual goals, such as for the whole society (Moore 2013, 57; see also chapter 8 in the present volume).

But Moore's framework differs from Bozeman's in that it enables articulation of key distinctions in a way that is both coherent and useful for public management practice, which Bozeman acknowledges obliquely (and perhaps a little dismissively) by referring to Moore's model as being about "management improvement." The first of these is that between private value, which is received and "consumed" by individual clients, such as welfare recipients or pupils in government schools; and public value, which is received and consumed collectively by the citizenry. This has two managerial implications. One is that it enables both a recognition that there is a multiplicity of types of recipients or consumers of value (e.g., citizens and taxpayers for public value, and clients, customers, beneficiaries, and obligatees for private value) and clarity about their respective entitlements from, claims on, or exchanges with the organization. The other is that it allows for the consideration and enlisting of a wide range of ways to do things. It registers that value is not public by virtue of being produced by the public sector but instead because it is enjoyed by the public. It can be created not only by government organizations but also by a variety of external parties such as those considered here.

To say that public value is collectively consumed is to imply an expansive conception of the notion (Moore 1995; Bozeman 2007). At a minimum, as even libertarian writers would affirm, it involves provision of the preconditions for the operation of the market, which does not just fall fully formed from the sky. The market needs nonmarket mechanisms—such as ways of safeguarding people's personal security, observing property rights, and enforcing contracts—to function. These preconditions are usually provided by a central authority such as a state applying the rule of law.

Also in the modest version of public value are various types of remedies to market failure, such as externalities, natural monopolies, and imperfect information (Stokey and Zeckhauser 1974; Hughes 2012). But as both Moore (1995) and Bozeman (2007) point out, these forms of value are predicated on a preference for markets, to be used only if markets fail. Yet people also have goals or aspirations for the society as a whole beyond their individual self-interest, founded in social or normative commitments or purposes. They seek what can be seen as collective benefits in the way society is ordered: citizens' rights and prerogatives, as well as their obligations, and the principles underpinning government (Bozeman 2007; Moore 2013). Notably, these include both views about substantive policies and views about the mechanisms of government deliberation. In the former case, key considerations will include not only efficiency but also social equity—which can be framed in various, sometimes contending ways. In the latter case there may be public value in facilitating the conditions for deliberation about these purposes, such as constitutional arrangements, consultative mechanisms, educational processes, and cultural norms.

From all of this, and from the fact that managers create public value in response to problems arising from their task environments, it should be no surprise that public value is not an orderly, unified concept. There is no absolute standard of public value but instead differing types that can sometimes be in harmony with each other, sometimes in conflict, and sometimes just different from each other.

So far we have been considering public value in terms of what is *desirable*, but for the benefits of a particular arrangement for service delivery or policy implementation to be realized, it also has to be *feasible*. If circumstances are such that a valuable policy is stymied by, for example, powerful opposition from key players in the political environment or the organization's lack of appropriate skills to undertake it, then its value will simply not be realized. This is the focus of Moore's strategic triangle (see figure 1.1 in chapter 1), which posits that a strategy for a government organization must be aimed at creating something substantively valuable; be legitimate and politically sustainable (attracting sufficient ongoing support and resources from the authorizing environment); and be operationally and administratively feasible with the available organizational and external capabilities (Moore 1995, 71).

These three factors are rarely in alignment, so public managers must work constantly to bring them into at least some degree of congruence. If the most valuable course of action does not square with what the authorizing environment prefers, the manager can either alter the value proposition to bring it into line or try to persuade key players to shift their position. If a valuable goal is not achievable with available operational capabilities, then the purpose has to be amended accordingly (or the capabilities improved).

Thus, the potential value can be constrained by the other two factors, which do not in themselves constitute categories of public value. Rather, they are factors that affect how far a particular value proposition can be taken. More important for the present discussion, the causality can run in the other direction as well. Different options for externalization can, quite apart from their *value* in service and relationship terms, have varying effects on the government organization itself as an institution—for example, its positioning and capabilities beyond the externalized service in question. This in turn will affect the broader or longer-term value it might create now or in the future.

There are three kinds of public value (or loss of value) that might emanate from a particular service delivery arrangement relative to any given alternative. Two of them relate to the value circle in Moore's triangle. The first is *service* benefits and costs—that is, the net value gains of the service, such as effectiveness, efficiency, quality, or equity—set against the money paid for it. The second type is *relationship* benefits and costs—those incurred by the government organization in managing the relationship with the provider, including benefits in clarifying the relationship and social connection, as well as the costs of defining the service, determining who is to produce it, ascertaining whether it has been provided satisfactorily, and inducing good performance on the part of the provider. Difficulty in any of these matters is not a reason to avoid externalization, but they do need to be weighed against each other and against the net service benefits and costs.

The third kind of value is *institutional* (or *strategic*) benefits and costs. It has two aspects, each of which can be affected by choices made in respect to the service and the relationship. One relates to the potential impact of the value proposition on the organization's positioning in its environment. The adoption of a particular arrangement can be either beneficial or detrimental in this respect. For instance, any government organization that hired the security firm Blackwater would probably suffer reputational damage because of that company's track record of misuse of deadly force in Iraq and elsewhere, and consequently be less able to pursue other value-creating initiatives (Barton 2012).

The other aspect is that some externalization initiatives might add to or subtract from an organization's core competences and therefore its ability to produce other values besides the service in question or the same value in future situations. Key among these is the organization's capacity to act as the principal in its dealings with providers (Kettl 1993). For example, the US Federal Protective Service has been criticized several times in Government Accountability Office reports for divesting itself of the capability to oversee the large contract guard force protecting nine thousand federal buildings (Davidson 2010). Also potentially important is the preservation of unique knowledge, experience, capabilities, and systems.

Another distinctive competence in the public sector is the use of public power: the state's legitimate monopoly on the use of force to compel people to do things for the sake of the citizenry. This power is indivisible; there cannot be competing public powers in the same jurisdiction. Even where government delegates coercive power, such as vehicle inspections or occupational licensing, it is subject to state authority and monitoring. Where it is externalized, the issues in debate are to do with potential misuse of coercive power. These are just some of the distinctive competences residing in government organizations, which may be enhanced but more often are lost through externalization. A particular externalization may offer service and relationship benefits but entail a larger cost in institutional terms.

What follows is an explanation of these concepts with reference to the case of a large urban fire brigade—that of the city of Melbourne, in the state of Victoria, Australia. The case was chosen because the service is recognizable, of middling complexity, and is open to multiple service arrangements. The purpose of this analysis is not to demonstrate how to measure public value quantitatively; discerning public value is often a matter of judgment rather than calculation. The framework is put forward for use as an *aid* to decision making, not as a substitute for it.

MELBOURNE'S FIRE SERVICE

In Australia, fire services are the responsibility of state governments. Victoria, like the other states, has one fire service for its capital Melbourne, a metropolis of 4.2 million people, and another for the rural area, the Country Fire Authority. The Metropolitan Fire and Emergency Services Board (MFB) covers more than one thousand square kilometers and employs over 2,100 people: 1,850 firefighters and 300 corporate staff. It provides prevention, preparedness, and response and recovery services, the shape and relative weight of which reflect an evolving service philosophy with implications for the role of external parties. First I will analyze the public value of fire brigades, and then the benefits and costs of using them.

Fire services are partly private goods, in that extinguishing a fire at a house is of clear private benefit to the householder, and partly public goods, in that they combat the negative externalities of fires. In urban settings fires can spread to adjoining properties, as occurred in the Great Fire of London in 1666 (Carlson 2005), and in rural contexts they can spread literally like wildfire, as Victoria itself experienced in the Black Saturday Fires of 2010 (Padula 2011). The overwhelming majority of fire services around the world were established to remedy the failings of private fire brigades established by insurance companies.[1] There is also an element of natural monopoly in a fire service, whose stations constitute a network.

Fire services therefore create value for the public, which can be expressed in terms of *outputs*, such as fires suppressed, measured in terms like average time to arrive at the fire, percentage of fires contained to the room of origin, and so on. We can identify and compare three options for producing these outputs that have been adopted in different places. One, of course, is the fire brigade itself, which will be treated as the base case against which externalization options will be weighed. A second option is to externalize the whole service to a private contractor—as has been tried in Denmark and in a small number of US counties or municipalities. A third option is to create a mostly volunteer service, an arrangement found in most rural fire services around the world (Carlson 2005).

If we think of the work of the fire brigade in terms of *outcomes*, such as minimizing fire harm to life, property, and the environment, there is another potentially important type of contributor to at least part of the task: building owners or occupants. They are effectively the brigade's customers and undertake fire prevention, ensure that properties are built to be less flammable, and have well-rehearsed response plans ready. Part of the MFB's work is devoted to engaging with the community to prompt these harm-reducing behaviors—not only via specialist education and technical support units but also via frontline firefighters who spend about 10 percent of each shift checking hydrants or building safety, signing off on sprinkler or smoke alarm installations, or engaging with the community (e.g., school talks). We will therefore consider owners/occupants as a fourth option.

BENEFITS AND COSTS

The remainder of this chapter analyzes the benefits and costs of these options. It shows that consideration of only those benefits and costs of externalization relating to the service itself—that is, its value for money—leaves two other types of benefits and costs unexamined: those to do with managing the relationship with the external provider and those to do with the organization as an institution. Table 5.1 summarizes and draws together the costs and benefits, as defined in this chapter, of the four options.

CONTRACTING THE SERVICE OUT TO A PRIVATE PROVIDER

Considering the service itself, the value of contracting with private providers (column 2 in table 5.1) varies according to whether the service is specified as an output or an outcome. A private provider of sufficient substance could well deliver better on the standard outputs of a fire service: suppressed fires. If it had

Table 5.1. Types of benefits and costs of externalization options for fire services compared to in-house production

Type of benefit/cost	1. In-House Production	Externalization Options		
		2. Full-Service Contract	3. Volunteers	4. Community Engagement
Service benefits	Established systems, knowledge, and staffing	Potential for better fire suppression • economies of scale/scope • specialization • flexibility • innovation Likely lower cost than in-house	No wage costs Specialized skills Support paid staff "Volunteer intangible"	Interdependency → better achievement of purposes • fast fire-suppression → reduced damage Lower cost likely
Service costs	Budget amount fairly high (esp. unionized labor costs)	Contract price	Indirect service costs Resistance by staff "Amateurs"	Minimal
Relationship benefits	Possibilities for high-engagement human resources management, but labor relations tend toward the adversarial	Clarify relationship by specifying deliverables	Commitment of volunteers Goodwill to organization	Likely increase in civic-mindedness
Relationship costs	Costs of supervision, performance management, incentive schemes, and disciplinary processes	Specification costs (uncertainty) Low competition, asset-specificity Monitoring: feasible Incentives/penalties can be applied	Recruiting/selection Induction/training Managing volunteers: supervisor	Costs of mobilizing community • engagement staff • advertising campaigns • events, etc.

(continued)

Table 5.1. (continued)

Type of benefit/cost	1. In-House Production	2. Full-Service Contract	Externalization Options	
			3. Volunteers	4. Community Engagement
Strategic benefits	Retains core competences within organization	Transfer technical and economic risk	Reputational standing from committed volunteers	Reputational standing in community
Strategic costs	Risk borne in-house Potential lack of interest in innovation	Possible loss of core competence • accumulated experience • commitment to public good (cf 9/11 firemen) • natural monopoly complicates partial externalization	Mission rigidity No pay = lack of leverage → dependence on volunteers	Element of mission rigidity

contracts for adjacent jurisdictions, it could reap economies of scale. It might have greater flexibility to call in extra staff from other parts of its operations in a major emergency (although public fire brigades generally do this on a cooperative basis). It could also be less constrained than a public fire service in finding innovative methods or technology. On the other hand, a private contractor is less likely to perform tasks outside its official remit that the MFB currently does as extracontractual favors, such as rescuing pets.

The degree of difficulty of managing the relationship with the provider, and hence its relative costs, would be mixed. The MFB is already able to specify and monitor performance clearly, most notably in its requirement that fire crews should be able to reach a fire within a particular number of minutes.[2] On that basis a plausible system of incentives and penalties to induce performance could be developed, but it would have some complexities. First, the specified measure does not allow for uncertainty—for instance, the possibility of traffic jams or malfunctioning traffic lights. Second, even before performance management, the task of choosing a private provider may be complicated by the absence of a robust market of fire suppression companies—not least because it has previously been a solely governmental role.

To the extent that other factors—in particular, the behavior of building owners/ occupants—affect the incidence, severity, and harm arising from fires, the private provider is likely to be less successful in achieving the outcome of minimizing the damage to life, property, and the environment. This is primarily because dealing with those factors calls for institutional standing that it may not have. Specifically, it may attract less cooperation from the public than a government-run service because its basic rationale of earning a profit does not engender the same level of trust or credibility as a body seen as working for the public (see Brudney 1990; Toppe, Kirsch, and Michel 2002).

In any case, whether the fire brigade is oriented to outputs or outcomes, the institutional benefits and costs—those concerning the positioning and core competences of the government organization—add to the negative side of the ledger.

One possible institutional benefit of externalization is that risk is transferred from the government to the private provider. Yet while this might be true for technical or financial risk, it may be less likely for political risk: citizens often continue to see the government as responsible for the shortcomings of a service long after it has been outsourced to a private entity.[3]

Much more important is the institutional cost of handing over core competences to external parties, detracting from public value. First, the government may diminish its capacity to exercise control over the provider in either of two ways. One is divesting itself of the requisite knowledge of the service and thus becoming less able to act as the principal. Fire service expertise is specialized and held within a close compass. Externalization can also reduce government control by altering the relative power of the two parties. In Williamson's terms, the provider gains "specific assets" by virtue of having gained the contract, such as inside knowledge and connections, technology and systems, and particular staff (1975). When it comes time to renew a contract, the incumbent fire service provider will have an advantage in a retendering process. This may translate into opportunistic behavior.[4]

Finally, externalization may entail discounting a government organization's role as repository of values important to the public interest. The now substantial literature on public service motivation (e.g., Rainey 1982; Perry and Wise 1990) raises the idea that public employees have some degree of commitment to serving public purposes beyond what is of personal benefit to them. The evidence on this factor is inconclusive, but it is arguable that these *motivations* of public servants may be accompanied by particular *capabilities*, including an awareness of how a particular measure might affect the broader public interest; a willingness to "go the extra mile" for a worthwhile purpose; and an understanding of proper behavior in functions like public expenditure, recruitment, and procurement. These values and beliefs are infused over time, forming part of organizational memory and culture.

The events of September 11, 2001, provided poignant indications of this phenomenon in the publicly employed firefighters of New York City, who along with other emergency workers repeatedly endangered themselves, and in many cases lost their lives, in order to rescue trapped civilians. Subsequently, a number of firefighters made it clear that they did the job because they wanted to safeguard the welfare of others. The question this raises is whether firefighters working for a privately contracted fire service would have made the same sacrifices.

In summary, weighing these benefits and costs shows that contracting the full service out to a private provider is of mixed value.

CREATING A VOLUNTEER SERVICE

This option (column 3 in table 5.1) entails emulating numerous rural fire brigades the world over: engaging volunteer firefighters to work with a core group of paid fire service employees. In Victoria, the Country Fire Authority (CFA) has 1,400 paid employees, including 500 firefighters, and 58,000 volunteers, of whom 35,000 are trained as firefighters.

The reason the CFA uses mostly volunteers while the MFB uses entirely paid staff is largely due to network economics. In rural Victoria, the thin population means both that fires are less frequent (albeit very serious when they do occur) and the availability of personnel is limited, making it less economic to have paid fire crews providing ready response. It is also true that MFB staff have developed expertise in urban fires, which call for some different skills and knowledge than rural ones.

Engaging volunteers incurs a particular mix of costs and benefits. On the benefits side there is the simple fact that volunteers don't have to be paid—although the service may have to pay indirect costs, such as providing protective clothing, insurance, facilities and equipment, and out-of-pocket expenses.

Perhaps just as important as the unpaid contribution (indeed, closely related) is what Brudney (1990) calls the "volunteer intangible." This is quite similar to public service motivation; people volunteer because of a normative commitment to the purposes of the organization and are more likely to go the extra mile as a result. They are also more likely to show interest in the service and acquire knowledge about it.

There are also relationship and institutional costs and benefits. The relationship benefits of engaging volunteers arise from the sense of communal interaction that typically accompanies their use, fostered by social events such as barbecues, with a consequent sense of ownership by staff.

Relationship costs, on the other hand, are partly different from those for private contractors. Recruiting and selecting volunteers in the CFA entails a relatively low-key process including a local interview, followed by three to six months of part-time training and a six-month probation period. The recruit is then managed alongside other volunteers by senior local officers, who have themselves been trained to play management roles. Thus, training constitutes the most significant relationship cost, substituting for the carrots and sticks of contracting.

The most significant institutional benefit from using volunteers, if done well, is the likelihood that it will lead to enhancement of the government organization's standing in the community, as its members disseminate positive stories about it to their families and friends. Against this are two potentially important institutional costs, each constituting the downside of one of the beneficial aspects of using volunteers. One is that volunteers receive no pay for their effort, which is obviously valuable, but this also renders the organization vulnerable in a particular way: it lacks leverage over volunteers and is consequently dependent on their continued willingness to serve. The related problem is their high commitment to the established purposes of the organization, which again is valuable, but becomes problematic when the organization seeks to alter its purposes—for example, by becoming a first-responder organization offering ambulance services as well as fire suppression. In this situation commitment to the mission becomes mission rigidity, in which volunteers resist the proposed change.

ENGAGING THE PUBLIC

The third possibility is to place greater emphasis on engaging members of the public, especially building occupants or owners and their neighbors, in undertaking fire prevention and mitigation activities to minimize fire-related damage to life, property, and the environment (column 4 in table 5.1).[5] In a sense this is not so much an option as an imperative: it is virtually impossible for the fire brigade to achieve this outcome without these contributions from the public. The question, therefore, is not so much *whether* to engage the public as *how* to do so.

The service benefit is that there are more prepared, vigilant, and responsive behaviors from the brigade's clients, without having to pay them. Engaging volunteers also entails certain relationship costs—namely, those of mobilizing the community. In the MFB's case, this includes influencing the media to promote fire safety; running paid advertisements; education work by fire officers in schools, community organizations, and workplaces; and, in recent times, harnessing social media to spread the word. While these are all specific costs, they are likely to prompt a more diffuse benefit in that they foster civic-mindedness.

At the same time, these public manifestations are of institutional benefit to the organization in that they promote commitment to the organization's purposes and perhaps even its standing in the community. On the other hand, relying on community engagement can be prone to a degree of mission rigidity. This is because strong popular commitment to the organization's purposes can mean that, if there were an attempt to amend the mission in some way that is unpopular, community cooperation might be diminished.

This analysis shows how the choices managers might make between alternative service-delivery arrangements entail consideration of more than the value-for-money criteria conventionally applied. They need also to be informed by an understanding of the value of different types of relationships, and of the likely effect of externalizing services on the organization's strategic positioning and capabilities (see table 5.1).

In this particular case, each broad alternative is shown to be better in some respects but not in others. One way of making sense of this is to deconstruct the value creation process, which can enable more finely grained contingency judgments—selectively for parts of the service rather than in broad-brush fashion for the whole organization. Thus it might make sense to subject the supply of vehicles, equipment, information technology, and payroll to a contracting process, probably involving competitive tendering. At the same it would probably be useful to call on volunteers in aspects such as ancillary services or community education. And we have already seen that community engagement is very necessary in some parts of the MFB's work but not relevant to others. This would enable each contingency within the service to be recognized in a tailored way. Notably, with only a few exceptions, these suggested arrangements are similar to what the MFB is already doing.

CONCLUSION: A CONTINGENCY FRAMEWORK

These understandings can be encapsulated in a series of decision rules that can assist judgments about whether and in what form to externalize. These rules are iterative. They are not replacements for the practical means of implementing externalization, such as competitive tendering, but instead are for use a priori, at the stage of contemplating whether to engage external providers. The fact that they are for the contemplative stage means that not all requisite information will be available and that the manager will need to exercise judgment as part of the analysis.

1. The first question is critical, and usually takes a lot of thought: *What is the purpose of this organization, program, or policy?* It is only in the context of the answer to this question that the subsequent questions make sense. The answer might include not only the required outcome(s) but also an acknowledgment of certain process or input values that need to be accommodated (e.g., increase police conviction rates, but don't transgress the rule of law).

2. Next is a threshold question: given a specific purpose, *is there a compelling institutional reason why this activity should be kept in-house?* Answering this question will call for analysis of the organization's authorizing environment as well as its productive capabilities. If externalization is likely to undermine the organization's positioning in its environment or deplete its core competences, then it probably makes sense to retain it within the organization. If not, the next question is . . .

3. *Are there any external parties who might contribute to this purpose?* If not, then it will either be impossible to arrange external providers or doing so will incur costs in developing a market that need to be weighed in the overall decision. If so, then the next question needs to be addressed.

4. *Does the external provider offer, or seem likely to offer, net service benefits (i.e., benefits exceeding the price)?* This is a matter not only of the relative value but also of the probability of it being delivered. It calls for sage judgment about the capacity and motivation of the provider. When the type of provider is not likely to deliver what is required, other types should be considered and, failing that, consideration given to producing the service in-house.

5. *Do the likely relationship costs outweigh other net benefits?* Where these costs are considerable, then alternative service-providers should again be considered. More generally, these costs should be weighed against the other costs and benefits to ground an overall decision about whether to externalize, and to whom.

None of these decisions can or should be simply "read off" from the available information at the contemplative stage. They require judgment not only about the service, relationship, and institutional issues but also about the surrounding political and organizational dynamics—in a similar vein to Vickers's "appreciation" (1995).

Thus, Moore's public value framework offers some tools for public managers to imagine and seek out value-creating solutions to the problems emanating from their task environments. It does not supplant the need to exercise judgment nor the need to take account of political realities, but it does provide aids to public managers seeking to determine courses of action.

In providing at the least a guide to decision making and action for public officials and those with whom they deal, Moore's approach differs in focus from Bozeman's account, which is aimed at analysis and appreciation of values at a societal level. But this very difference is the basis of an important affinity between the two—namely, that like the objects to which they are applied, both are fit for their purposes.

NOTES

1. For instance, the government of Victoria replaced multiple competing fire brigades with the Melbourne Fire Brigade in 1891, imposing levies on insurance companies but also giving them positions on the MFB board (Wilde 1991).
2. See the MFB's *Annual Report* for 2010–11.
3. The public transportation system of Melbourne was franchised to private operators in 1999, but the citizenry has blamed its continued late running and canceled trains on the state government, with unambiguous election results.
4. In the case of the fire brigade, its quasi-network nature means that to some degree it has the characteristics of a natural monopoly and therefore the asset-specificity problem could not be overcome by running parallel competing services.
5. The Report of the Royal Commission into the Victorian Bushfires underscored this when it noted that "responsibility for community safety during bushfires is shared by the State, municipal councils, individuals, household members and the broader community" (Bushfire Royal Commission, 2:9).

6

THE CREATION OF PUBLIC VALUE THROUGH STEP-CHANGE INNOVATION IN PUBLIC ORGANIZATIONS

JEAN HARTLEY

This chapter examines the literature on innovation in order to ask questions about whether, which, and how innovations in governance and public services may lead to the creation of public value. Public value can be created by any sector, whether private, public or voluntary (Benington and Moore 2011b; Porter and Kramer 2011), but there is a particular onus on public organizations to create public value through innovation. Until recently, however, the innovation literature was dominated by analysis of private-sector institutions and innovation processes, with insufficient attention to the distinctive features of public organizations and democratic contexts that create public value.

Furthermore, as hybrid organizations become more prevalent, as public services are externalized to a greater degree to the private sector, and as there is a shift toward greater partnership working and collaborative innovation (Hartley, Sørensen, and Torfing 2013), there is a need to analyze whether and how public value is created in a variety of institutional arrangements. Unless citizens, public officials, and public managers understand the contribution that publicness makes to the creation of public value, there is a danger that the key opportunities for valuable and effective innovation will be lost in the rush to make the public sector more "businesslike."

This chapter is more concerned with public value (Moore 1995; Benington and Moore 2011b) than public values (Beck Jørgensen and Bozeman 2007) for two reasons. First, in examining whether innovations are beneficial or detrimental (or both) to society, the focus is on the value added when compared with not having the innovation. This points to public value theory, which is output- and outcome-focused. Second, while subjectively held values or norms as analyzed by Bozeman may shape whether and how innovations develop, his framework has less to say analytically about what is added by the creation of innovation.

After briefly defining both innovation and public value, the chapter examines the dominant models of private-sector innovation in the literature and the misleading assumptions about organizational design, outputs, and outcomes that these models can create when applied to public organizations. The binary division between public and private is of course overly simple, as there are many interrelationships and interdependencies between the two sectors (Crouch 2011). Yet the distinction between public and private is worth pursuing in order to draw out some key issues about public organizations and public value. Public and private organizations are compared through the analytical device of three innovation phases: invention, implementation, and diffusion. This chapter shows the insistent presence for public organizations of the formal political environment, the role of citizens (not just as customers) in the innovation process, and the influence of public accountability. Innovation is not purely a managerial matter but has to take account of processes, outputs, and outcomes for a range of stakeholders. This is because innovation creates or destroys not only private value but also public value.

DEFINING INNOVATION AND PUBLIC VALUE

Varied meanings are given to innovation in public policy (Osborne and Brown 2011; Lynn 2013) and in academic writing (Lynn 1997; Hartley 2005; Borins 2012). Altshuler and Zegans (1997) define it as "novelty in action," and Bessant (2005) emphasizes that innovation is not just having a bright idea (which can be termed "invention") but is about implementation. In addition, many writers argue that innovation is disruptive, involving *step change*, not just incremental improvements; otherwise innovation is indistinguishable from general change (e.g., Osborne and Brown 2005; Lynn 1997). This chapter, as the title suggests, adopts the view of innovation as step change. It is therefore very different from continuous improvement (Hartley 2011; Osborne and Brown 2011). Inevitably, the degree of innovation is socially constructed (Greenhalgh et al. 2004). Innovation may or may not be successful (Moore 2005; Hartley 2011), and indeed, some innovations may fail (Tidd and Bessant 2009); in addition, the assessment of value created may change over time as new uses are found for an innovation or as negative effects of an early success are discovered (Hartley 2011). The separation of innovation and outcome is important analytically, avoiding the assumption prevalent in parts of the policy literature that any innovation is an improvement and enabling a clear-headed analysis of the varied relationships between innovation and public value.

As with innovation, the concept of public value has acquired a multiplicity of meanings and connotations (Williams and Shearer 2011; Alford and O'Flynn 2009). The term gained currency through the writings of Moore (Moore 1995, 2013; Benington and Moore 2011b). Public value, according to Benington (2011) has two major dimensions: what the public values (which may be different from what it wants or needs), and also what adds value to the public sphere. It is an output rather than an input concept (it is different therefore from public values; see also Rainey 2009; Davis and West 2009; Bozeman 2007) and it includes not only goods, services, and obligations that are valued by the public collectively and that contribute to the public sphere but also the rules and governance arrangements that shape how society conducts itself—including fairness, justice, and efficiency (Marquand 2004). According to Benington (2011), at its most basic, public value can be thought of as the "dividends" added to the public realm by activities, services, or relationships, or investments of human, financial, and technical resources. Analysis of innovation through the lens of public value reveals some substantial differences in approach between the public and private sectors. O'Flynn

(2007, 359) notes that the kinds of relationship that exist and the fact that public managers undertake their work in a democratic political context means that there is "something fundamentally unique about the public sector." Public organizations, in certain circumstances and within certain legal limits, are also able to use state authority to oblige or force citizens to engage in certain actions (e.g., policing, military conscription, and taxation payments) and thus often act on behalf of the state, not simply as organizations providing a service.

Public value can be conceptualized within an open systems perspective (Scott 2007; Benington 2011) that analyzes interdependencies between the organization (as the open system) and its external environment (the political, economic, social, and physical environment). Open systems theory predicts that the complexity of those interactions means that outputs and outcomes are bound to be emergent as well as planned. This suggests that public value theory has to be able to address unstable as well as stable contexts with risky and uncertain outcomes. Innovation is generally more relevant to unstable contexts than stable ones (Hartley 2011) because in the latter, continuous improvement may suffice to achieve valuable outcomes.

PUBLIC AND PRIVATE INNOVATION

The view is sometimes expressed—or implied—in both policy and academic writing that the private sector is "better" at innovation than the public sector and that therefore public organizations should emulate private ones in their organizational forms and managerial processes (Hartley, Sørensen, and Torfing 2013). A great deal of the innovation literature is derived from the private sector, particularly from manufacturing, as noted by several scholars (Altshuler and Behn 1997; Hartley 2005; Albury 2005; Moore 2005; Osborne and Brown 2011; Koch and Hauknes 2005). A literature about innovation in service industries is emerging (Gallouj 2002; Miles 2000; Osborne, Radnor, and Nasi 2013) but still has to develop in terms of theorizing innovation as being about creating value for citizens as well as customers and clients. Important technological developments are occurring in public services—for example, e-government technologies or new health equipment—but applying concepts derived from *product* innovation to *service* and *organizational* innovation can be difficult (Alänge, Jacobsson, and Jarnehammar 1998). Service innovations typically have high levels of ambiguity and uncertainty since they are affected by the variability of the human characteristics of both service provider and service receiver (who is sometimes also a coproducer). The innovation is often not a physical artifact but a change in service, which implies a change in the relationships between service providers and their users. Many features are intangible and include high levels of tacit knowledge (Nonaka 1994). For example, a service innovation occurred in some UK policing organizations a few years ago when there was a strategic shift from a primary focus on crime to a primary focus on harm in society. It was a step change that reoriented the strategy; the deployment of staff, resources, and equipment; and the nature of interactions with the public.

Finally, not only is the academic literature on innovation largely based on the private sector, but often few people realize that it is. Given this "sector-blindness," there is a need to sift through the literature on innovation carefully to ensure that the insights are relevant and applicable to public organizations and that innovation is designed and implemented in ways that create public value. Understanding the limits and possibilities of learning across and between sectors is critical if public services organizations are to avoid the fads and fashions of the private management field (Abrahamson 1991), avoiding overadoption and hyperinnovation (Rogers 2003; Moran 2003).

Allison (1983) famously argued that the public and private sectors were "alike in all unimportant respects"—there are similarities but also fundamental differences. The boundaries between public and private sectors are "neither clear nor permanent" (Flynn 2007, 1), there is increasing hybridity in organizational form, and academic disciplines vary in their emphases of similarity or difference (Rainey and Chun 2005). Here I focus on the issues relevant to innovation and public value.

Any simple division between public and private is neither theoretically or empirically feasible. First, there are a number of interrelationships and interdependencies between sectors (Bozeman 1987; Bozeman and Moulton 2011), including, for example, firms operating under regulatory frameworks devised by the state; privatized and contracted-out public services; commissioned services; the increasing prevalence of hybrid organizations; and collaborative governance.

Second, there are substantial variations within sectors. Organizational and industry characteristics such as size, task, or function vary (Rainey 2009), and each of these may affect innovation processes and outcomes. This highlights the need to examine innovation not solely in terms of public and private sectors but also at the institutional level.

Third, Bozeman (1987) argues that all organizations have some degree of publicness (e.g., all private firms work under state legislation and regulation to some extent). To clarify differences across sectors and across organizations he outlines two key dimensions, economic authority and political authority, which together create a number of combinations. Economic authority concerns the degree to which the organization has control over its revenues and assets. Political authority is derived from the legitimacy conferred by citizens, legislative bodies, and governmental bodies and enables the organization to act on behalf of those institutions and to make binding decisions for them. Both of these dimensions are valuable to consider in relation to innovation in public service organizations. I will argue that the second (political authority) is particularly salient in considering public innovation and any public value created. Hartley and Skelcher (2008) argue that one of the distinctive elements of public management is that it operates within a democratic and political context, with governance by elected politicians and accountability to the electorate. Summing up, Rainey and Chun (2005) note that differences between sectors are most salient where the organization interacts with its external environment.

INNOVATION PHASES AND PUBLIC VALUE

It is common in the management literature to find innovation being considered in terms of stages or phases in the process, though the number of phases and their description may vary (e.g., Tidd and Bessant 2009; Rogers 2003). Although these management stages can appear linear and rational, in practice innovation can be chaotic, emergent, unpredictable, and interconnected (Rickards 1996; Van de Ven 1986; Bason 2010). In public services, innovation may sometimes reverse the sequences of the phases (Hartley 2005). For example, a politician may announce the implementation of an innovation and public managers may then have to work out how to invent the processes that will enable that implementation. Nevertheless, closely examining phases or stages can be analytically valuable even though empirically and managerially more complex. Here I use three main phases derived from viewing innovation as a process: invention, implementation, and diffusion.

The first phase, invention, is the creativity and ideas phase. It covers the processes of inventing, finding or harvesting ideas, or recognizing needs and opportunities that have potential as the starting point of innovation. The second phase, implementation, is about turning those ideas into practices and products for the organization or service, including working out whether and how it needs adjustment in the shift from idea to action, and how it will fit with other organizational processes (Denis et al. 2002). The third phase is the diffusion of innovation, which, it will be argued, is a particularly crucial element of innovation for achieving public value.

Bearing in mind my earlier caveats about oversimplification and overgeneralization from the private-sector literature on innovation, this chapter uses those three phases as an analytical device to examine some key features of innovation actors, processes, and outcomes in terms of public value. Of course, there are exceptions—where a private firm acts in the same way as a public organization, or vice versa. The aim is to show differences in emphasis in order to highlight some aspects of the innovation process that may have been neglected by the context-blind literature and that provide insights into public value creation.

INVENTION AND PUBLIC VALUE

Private- and public-sector approaches to innovation in this initial stage display a number of similarities and differences.

Dimensions of Innovation

Various typologies of innovations exist, but I argue that it is more helpful to conceptualize innovation in dimensions rather than types, because any innovation may involve more than one feature (Hartley 2005). For example, a new piece of medical equipment (a product innovation) may also entail new ways of providing the service (service and process innovation) and may also enable the hospital to cater for new types of patient (position innovation).

For both the public and private sectors, many dimensions of innovation can be similar—product, service, process, strategic, and position (Hartley 2005) as well as business model (Birkinshaw, Hamel, and Mol 2008). However, three aspects of innovation are absent or rare in the private-sector literature though critical in the public innovation literature. Political scientists point to the existence of policy innovations—the adoption and implementation of new policies by governments (e.g., Berry 1994). Scholars also discuss innovations in governance (Hartley 2005; Moore and Hartley 2008; Voss 2007) that concern new procedures and institutions to make decisions about policies and resources for the public sphere. Finally, Hartley (2005) identifies rhetorical innovation—new language and new concepts that are used to mobilize support from the public or other significant stakeholders. (For example, the terms "climate change," "food miles," and "congestion charging" have been used to galvanize changes in behavior among citizens.) Innovations in policy, governance, and rhetoric each signal the salience of the political context for public service organizations. It means that public value can be created by a range of features, not just service delivery. How things are done, using state authority, may be important as well as what is achieved, and this affects the public value that may be created.

The Unit of Analysis

In the generic management literature, the firm is the primary unit of analysis (though there is some interest in strategic alliances and collaborative networks of organizations; see, for example, Belussi and Arcangeli 1998). Innovation is seen to be important in order to help a firm survive or develop, or for a sector to maintain competitive edge in global marketplaces.

A focus on the single organization can be helpful in understanding public innovation, and a number of studies have used this unit of analysis (e.g., Newman, Raine, and Skelcher 2001; Walker, Damanpour, and Devece 2011). However, innovation to create public value may require consideration of whole sectors or sector clusters, such as schools, hospitals, or health care provision (Greenhalgh et al. 2004) because value is created not only by a single organization creating an innovation but by wide or wholesale adoption of the innovation such that services as a whole are improved in quality, reach, efficiency, or other criteria. There are thus differences in emphasis in the literature about the unit of analysis for the public and private sectors, though theoretically each of these levels of analysis is appropriate across both sectors. The public value of innovations can be analyzed at organizational and service-system levels.

The Environmental Drivers of Innovation

For private firms, and for the market economy, market competition is an important driver of innovation, and innovation is a key driver of economic change and development. Schumpeter (1950) is a key writer in this regard. It has sometimes been assumed that the corollary of this is that since public services do not (usually) operate in competitive markets, innovation is low in the public sector.

A number of writers challenge the assumption that market competition is the primary driver of innovation in public service, however, arguing that different mechanisms operate in the public sector (Hartley et al. 2013; Lynn 2013). There is substantial empirical evidence of considerable innovation in the public sector (Hartley 2005; Albury 2005), and many of the key innovations of the last few decades originated in the public sector—not least the internet. These writers argue that innovation is a crucial element of public policy and management in a dynamic society, where needs and aspirations are shifting (Lynn 2013). Innovation is also a critical method for improving the performance of government and enhancing government's legitimacy with citizens (Moore and Hartley 2008). The pressures for innovation derive from the wider society, and the public value impacts may be particularly relevant at that level.

The Catalysts of Innovation

People in a number of different roles may contribute to the initiation, design, development, and diffusion of an innovation. Until recently, the literature focused primarily on the creativity of managers and employees within the organization and how to enhance their capacity to come up with creative ideas, to recognize needs in the market or society, and to use "recombinant" innovation (taking an innovation that works in one area and using it in a quite different application through knowledge brokering; see Hargadon 2002). This is a drive for innovation that is not sector-specific.

Networks can also be an important source of invention (and also of diffusion) in both sectors, whether these are supply chains, communities of practice, business associations, or professional networks (e.g., Hartley and Downe 2007; Birkinshaw, Bessant, and Delbridge 2007). Again, one can find similarities across sectors, though learning and knowledge transfer is easier in collaborative compared with competitive networks (Inkpen and Crossan 1995).

A third catalyst of innovation is the users of products and services. Von Hippel (1988) has noted that many innovations are developed or improved by "lead users" who are familiar with the product or service through regular use and who communicate and collaborate with the producing organization to develop the innovation. Chesbrough (2003) and Von Hippel (2005) have analyzed the burgeoning phenomenon called open innovation, which occurs when individuals or groups in society coproduce innovations. Increasingly, firms invite the participation of users to help them design new products and services. They may also employ staff to actively search for and co-opt ideas from the public.

In the public sector there is less use, as yet, of open innovation (which is very different from public consultation on existing proposals), though some examples exist—for example, the expert patient initiative in UK health care, or engaging with citizens to create and implement new ideas in Denmark (Bason 2010). Notably, while the processes of open innovation could be similar across sectors, public services have to maintain awareness of who is involved. Open innovation for public organizations is not solely concerned with customers or users because of the wider public nature of the organizational goals and values and the need to create public, and not only private, value. Some users may have ideas for innovation that cut across the needs of other groups. Some stakeholders may be more articulate, or hold access to power and influence compared with others, and thus open innovation in the public services has to take account of different motivations, needs, and consequences compared to private-sector innovation. Such open innovation brings both opportunities and difficulties, which suggests a more contingent approach to public innovation (Hartley et al. 2013).

The fourth key catalyst of public innovations is elected politicians. Both national and local politicians, along with their advisers, can have a central role in innovation. They can be engaged in developing new policy frameworks (Albury 2005); announcing innovation intentions (Hartley 2005); mobilizing support among the public for the innovation (Moore and Hartley 2008); helping to create an organizational climate receptive to innovation; and fostering support inside the organization (Newman et al. 2001; Rashman, Downe, and Hartley 2005; Borins 2012). Even when innovations are initiated by managers and staff, political support will in some cases contribute to the nurturing and continuation of the innovation (Hartley and Rashman 2010). Sometimes policy initiatives can lead to large-scale, universal, and radical innovations across a whole nation (Albury 2005), such as has happened in setting up the NHS in the 1940s and now its commercialization in the first decades of the new millennium. Top-down innovation through policy announcements by politicians creates a different challenge and climate for managers and staff compared with innovations originating inside the organization. Thus, public managers who seek to foster innovation must work with politicians and their policies and show a sensitivity to the dynamics of the wider political and societal environment than is the case for many private-sector managers who are pursuing innovation.

This consideration of the roles that catalyze innovations shows a sharp difference between the public and private sectors. While both sectors use managers, staff, networks, and users to create and/or harvest innovations, there are two major differences in the public sector—the need to think about citizens, not just users, and to think about elected politicians as well as paid managers in initiating and pushing forward innovation. These again relate to the wider democratic and policy context and how public value is created.

IMPLEMENTATION AND PUBLIC VALUE

Turning ideas into practical application happens in the implementation phase, and there are a number of similarities but also some differences between the public and private sectors. I won't repeat some issues from the invention section (e.g., politicians as catalysts), though these remain relevant.

Organizational Design

Much of the implementation of innovation takes place within organizational settings, as managers and staff work out the practicalities of the new initiative and try to ensure that it is embedded with other practices and processes—in both sectors. Yet some implementation occurs in interorganizational collaboration (e.g., Moore and Hartley 2008; Tidd and Bessant 2009; Hartley et al. 2013) and in processes of coproduction (Von Hippel 2005) in both sectors. Collaborative innovation also involves paying attention to organizational structures, cultures, and processes as well as partnership working. It is not possible in the space of this discussion to address all organizational features that foster or hinder innovation.

Some characteristics of organizations appear to foster or dampen innovation in general, and others may help or hinder different phases of innovation. For example, small organizational size tends to be conducive in the invention phase, but large organizational size makes it easier to allocate funds to implementation and to embed the innovation in organizational processes (Hage and Aiken 1967). Large organizations, contrary to common opinion, tend to be better overall at exploiting innovation and taking it through all stages to completion (Damanpour 1992).

Potentially also relevant is the role of bureaucratic structures (taken here to mean a particular form of organization with hierarchy, division of labor, rules, and prescribed roles) compared with more organic structures. The literature suggests that innovation is harder to foster in bureaucratic forms of organizing (Burns and Stalker 1961; Thompson 1965), and there is some evidence that public managers face greater degrees of formalization and centralization (Rainey 2009). Rainey and Chun (2005) conclude, however, that there is mixed evidence as to whether public or private organizations are more bureaucratic, and that where differences are found they are not that large.

Having a strong innovation culture—one that values new ideas—supports innovation (Rickards 1996), while some cultures suppress it (Kanter 1984). "Culture" refers to the shared norms, values, and assumptions that are typical of the organization or work group. At the level of employees, surveys have found that private and public managers express similar levels of receptivity to innovation, reform, and organizational change (e.g., Rainey 1983; Elliot and Tevavichulada 1999). Employees across sectors also perceive similar levels of risk-taking by their own organizations (Bozeman and Kingsley 1998). It is sometimes assumed that public service organizations have a poor climate for innovation, but the evidence—to the extent that it exists—suggests no clear differences between sectors.

The Criteria of Success

In some of the academic and policy literature, innovation is treated as though it has inherent value—as though any innovation is, by definition, good for a firm, an organization, or for society and essential as a means for firms to be competitive and successful (e.g., Chesbrough 2003; Tidd and Bessant 2009). Within this perspective, if profits are increased, or if market share is enhanced or competitive position maintained, then an innovation may be considered successful because for a private firm success is largely judged by market criteria. Use value or value for the public sphere is here seen as less central than private appropriation of value.

This is rarely the case for the public service sector. Innovation is mainly justifiable to the extent that it increases the quality, efficiency, or fitness for purpose of services; improves the ways in which decisions about services and priorities are made; or addresses a performance gap (Walker et al. 2011). Furthermore, successful public innovation is not only about organizational performance metrics but also about added value to the public sphere (Hartley 2011), and this may include creating a fairer, more tolerant, or more resilient society.

Public value has to be created without the benefit of hindsight (given that innovation by virtue of being new is inherently risky and uncertain), and it often requires political and managerial judgment as to whether a particular policy or strategy will achieve the sought-after outcomes. Because innovation is novel for the organization, it is discontinuous with previous products, processes, and/or services, so there is a risk that it will fail. The estimate for the private sector is that 30 to 45 percent of innovation projects fail and that half overrun their budgets or timelines (Tidd and Bessant 2009). So there are risks as well as benefits with innovation. Therefore, the question of how public value outcomes can be measured can never be fully and finally answered; there may be different assessments according to context and organizational capacity, according to short-term and longer-term perspectives, and amplified by the different judgments, values and priorities that varied stakeholders may place on the innovation (Hartley 2011). Thus, right at the heart of any public innovation is the existence of a tension not only about what the public values compared with adding value to the public sphere but also about who judges public value, on what basis, and whether this will change over time. For example, it is hotly contested as to whether large coastal wind farms in shallow UK waters are beneficial in safeguarding future generations through the use of renewable energies or whether they are a blot on the landscape. Such views and evaluations may shift over time and in debate due to a range of factors.

Accountability and Transparency

Accountabilities differ between the sectors and may affect the ways in which innovation is driven, decisions evaluated, and public value created or sustained. In the private sector, accountability for the innovation resides in the firm or strategic alliance, with shareholders as the justification for this. Transparency (or lack thereof) is a strategic choice; it can be restricted to those directly involved in design and development, and a new product or service kept secret until fully ready—both to capture market interest and fend off competitor replication. A different strategic choice is to create novelty in products and services through open innovation (Von Hippel and Von Krogh 2003), engaging customers in the design and even the build. The decision to be secretive or open lies with the organization itself, however.

By contrast, most public services tend to design and implement innovations in ways that enable greater access to both the ideas and the decision making of the public and sometimes in the full glare of media publicity. (There are some exceptions, such as national security or custodial services, but the degree of secrecy can itself be subject to legal recourses in some situations.) Some innovations may be scrutinized at the national government level or in local governments. The political opposition may attack the proposed innovation; the public may be consulted about the ideas or comment vociferously; the media may comment on the innovation and its implied costs and consequences; and evaluation data may be published. Accountability is not just within the organization but also to elected political representatives and the public. Furthermore, politicians, interest groups, and citizens may engage in considerable public debate as to whether a particular innovative effort in public services should be prioritized or not and with what amount of resources. All are likely to be aware that an innovation that improves the service for a certain type of user or citizen may make it worse for another. Here not only the innovation but its potential public value (or public loss) is under scrutiny before the innovation is complete—and sometimes well after. This brief analysis suggests that developing innovation in a democratic context may carry different pressures from the private sector in the efforts to add value.

DIFFUSION AND PUBLIC VALUE

Diffusion (sometimes also called dissemination), describes the spread of innovative practices over time among members of a social system (e.g., Greenhalgh et al. 2004; Rogers 2003). Here the focus is on diffusion among organizations, not diffusion through individuals or of particular types of innovation. There is a large though fragmented literature on diffusion and it is not feasible here to cover all the aspects.

The Motivation of the Innovator to Diffuse

The motivation to engage in the sharing of promising practices has a different set of social norms in the public sector compared with the private sector. In the latter, given the competitive pressures to exploit innovation in the marketplace, there are often intense pressures to keep the innovation confidential within the organization or within a tight circle of collaborators. This may involve the use of patents, copyrights, design rights, and so on, to keep intellectual property or to at least delay replication by competitors. The public sector also commercializes certain innovations once developed (e.g., medical equipment), but mainly there is a public value imperative for the innovator to share ideas and practices across the sector for societal benefit. An innovation in treating cancer, or helping the unemployed back into regular work, is useful to the extent that it is widely adopted or adapted across similar organizations. An innovation that originates in one public service may also have value when it is adopted in other services. Some innovation award schemes have been set up at least in part to support the spread of promising practices across public services (Borins 2008; Hartley and Downe 2007). Notably, diffusion also serves a particular function for public service organizations in managing risk in that the uncertainties—including political risk—of innovation implementation are ameliorated by adapting what another organization has done rather than inventing something from scratch (Hartley and Benington 2006).

The Motivation of the Adopter to Take Up the Innovation

Organizations do vary within and across both sectors in their preparedness and their ability to engage with promising practice, to search for promising ideas, to notice and take concepts on board, and to learn from and adapt ideas into a particular organizational setting (Zahra and George 2002). It is possible to find organizations in both sectors that are relatively resistant to diffusion. Yet, in general, many private-sector organizations likely face pressures to obtain knowledge of the innovation that is providing a competitor with a market lead and to try to "reverse-engineer" the innovation in order to understand it, replicate it, or improve it (e.g., the replication or improvement of smartphone technologies between competing firms).

Enthusiasm and drive to adopt promising practices is evident in parts of the public services (Rashman et al. 2005), but there are also parts where the barriers are high, making diffusion difficult to achieve (e.g., Buchanan, Fitzgerald, and Ketley 2006). The public service sector sometimes lacks the incentives associated with competition, and is rarely rewarded for adoption of innovation by, for example, keeping savings. Furthermore, given the public nature of many innovations, an organization may face criticism from a number of quarters when an innovation is introduced (as noted earlier). Notably, both political and managerial leadership are particularly important in creating a climate for public service organizations to enable diffusion to take place (Greenhalgh, et al. 2004; Hartley and Rashman 2007).

In diffusion overall there is wide variation within and across sectors, but again the obligation on public service organizations to create wider public value means that diffusion is more central to the innovation endeavor than it often is for the private sector. This relates again to the earlier point about the unit of analysis being the firm or the organizational field. Again, this underscores the importance of understanding the political and environmental context in which innovations take place.

CONCLUSIONS

This chapter set out to analyze whether, which, and how innovation (defined as step-change innovation, not continuous improvement) leads to the creation rather than the reduction of public value. This was undertaken by examining the innovation literature to explore where the public and private sectors converge or diverge in their approach to innovation, and what this tells us about public innovation and about the creation of public value.

The chapter has viewed innovation as a process that is partly led and managed. Phases are used as analytical devices to explore different aspects of innovation; this has enabled key questions to be asked about who is involved in innovation, in what ways, with what intentions, and with what outcomes for the public sphere.

The comparison between the private and public sectors provides interesting insights into how innovation arises, is developed, and is diffused in public organizations, particularly in areas and processes that have been understudied due to the dominance of private-sector perspectives on innovation. The caveats are manifold: there is no hard and fast distinction between public and private, and organizations vary in the degree to which they are influenced by the wider political and policy context and the extent to which they add public value through their activities and innovations. There is thus considerable variation within as well as across sectors, and this chapter highlights emphases within sectors rather than rigid distinctions (so there are inevitably exceptions). The chapter's broad generalizations are intended to elucidate when, where, and why the public features of innovation have an impact on innovation processes and on the creation—or not—of public value.

Whether the focus is on the dimensions of innovations, the environmental drivers of innovation, the unit of analysis of innovation, or the roles played by different catalysts, one finds an insistent presence of the formal political environment and of the role of users not just as customers but as citizens—and of the need to consider public value creation. Implementation shows the greatest degree of similarity across sectors, but even here public managers have to operate within a wider field of actors, including citizens (not just customers) and politicians. The outcomes being sought are often different, since public service organizations are expected to achieve not organizational gain alone but to add public value. (Of course, private firms can create public value, but that is not their primary task, whereas it is for public organizations.) Diffusion appears to show particularly large differences because there are social norms and expectations that innovative public organizations share their ideas and practices with others in their sector to extend the quality, efficiency, and effectiveness of the service across the society. Thus publicness (Bozeman 1987) and public value (Moore 1995) in the innovation field seem to matter—and matter very substantially.

This context of the public sphere is not just the "wraparound" in which to set management theory and research about innovation; it fundamentally affects aims, behaviors, and understanding. Unless innovation research takes sufficient account of the wider political and policy context in which innovation takes place, it will miss key ways in which to theorize, explain, and understand innovation. Public value is increasingly a matter of concern to private-sector organizations as some firms try to address corporate social responsibility, so firms may also obtain crucial learning about public value from public innovation. Additionally, unless some of the broad differences in purpose, actors, and processes between public and private sectors are understood, then collaboration between the sectors will be more difficult or will be inadequately theorized in terms of the opportunities for public value creation.

PART II

MEASURING AND ASSESSING PUBLIC VALUE

7

How Can Cost-Benefit Analysis Help Create Public Value?

CLIVE BELFIELD

In theory, there is no difference between theory and practice. But in practice, there is.

YOGI BERRA

Cost-benefit analysis (CBA) is the method used by economists to evaluate public policies. It rests on a theory of public goods and externalities almost universally accepted by economists that in principle can be applied across almost all domains of public policy. Yet CBA is rarely undertaken, in part because there is considerable resistance on theoretical grounds. But the theory of CBA is not the problem. When CBA is undertaken, the gap between theory and practice is enormous. The real concern is with the practice of CBA. Thus, CBA might be fruitfully related to public value theory, which incorporates a political as well as a methodological framework. Our exposition links directly to the "bottom-line management" described by Moore (2014) and accords with his conclusion that such management, while merit worthy, is neither "simple" nor "within close reach." Kalambokidis (2014), adopting a macroeconomic perspective, reaches similar conclusions to ours about both the rigor of theory and the muddle of practice. However, Welch, Rimes, and Bozeman (chapter 9, this volume) describe a public value map that is intended to serve as a counterweight to cost-benefit analysis.

The structure of this chapter is as follows. First, I review the theory of CBA and relate this to the theory of public value; the two theories are compatible with each other, although the latter is more comprehensive in that it addresses the political nature of government in a way that CBA does not. I emphasize the importance of CBA—and by implication the importance of public value theory—for policymakers as a way to help create public value (i.e., to implement policies that yield net benefits to the public). I then describe the use of CBA across government agencies, finding this to be far less than might be justified. Next, I address the reasons for this lack of attention to CBA. Typically, CBA is rejected on theoretical grounds; I argue this rejection is not always correct and is used too frequently. Rather, CBA might be rejected for practical reasons; I argue instead that these grounds are much less appreciated. To illustrate the practical role of

CBA, I describe a series of case studies in which the practice of CBA falls far short of what is needed. I conclude with predictions as to the application of CBA in the future.

COST-BENEFIT ANALYSIS AND PUBLIC VALUE: THEORY

Despite its attention in public administration, the concept of public value is not a familiar one to economists. Yet the concept is quite complementary to how economists understand what government should do. The economic theory behind this role for government is the theory of public goods and externalities.

Every economist accepts the basic theory of public goods and externalities. Public goods are goods that provide benefits that society values but that are underprovided by private markets. Externalities are indirect effects of production and consumption behaviors that are not captured in market transactions. Disagreement arises over when and where public goods and externalities exist, whether there is any remedy and, if so, whether that remedy should be a regulatory one or involve public provision. But there is little disagreement over the general principles for providing public goods or remedying externalities once this need has been established. To determine the optimal amount of a public good, government—or any agency charged with creating public value—must take into account the full social (private and public) consequences. This accounting is done with a cost-benefit analysis—indeed, this is often the strict definition of what cost-benefit analysis is. Similarly, the remedy for externalities is that private producers or consumers must be forced to make decisions based on their marginal social (private and public) costs and benefits. The enforcement mechanism is the imposition of a tax (or subsidy). The optimal size of this tax is determined using "shadow pricing" methods developed within CBA (see Boardman et al. 2006). Hence, CBA is the fundamental economic approach to understanding and creating public value when markets fail.

The literature on CBA and public value has not coevolved, but there is broad overlap. The textbook definition of CBA is "a policy assessment method that quantifies the value to a given agency of public policy impacts and consequences in monetary terms" with the goal being "to help effective social decision making through efficient allocation of society's resources when markets fail" (Boardman et al. 2006, 23). This corresponds to the idea of creating public value, as described by Alford and O'Flynn (2009, 173), with the explicit difference being that CBA does not address whether an action is "legitimate and politically sustainable." At least at this general level, the two constructs conform. CBA should help policymakers adopt policies that create public value.

Bozeman (2002), however, argues that this economic approach and public value theory are not compatible. First, he objects to the equation of the two approaches on the premise that an economic approach is "less a reflection of public value than of the private value of public things" (2002, 146). But this objection is overstated; economic approaches can and do use public valuations for public goods. Contingent valuation methods explicitly ask individuals to value the full value of public goods, including non-use and existence value (i.e., including how important goods are to society as a whole). Second Bozeman (2002, 150), in developing a public failure model, writes that "the key policy question becomes, if the market is efficient, is there nonetheless a failure to provide an essential public value?" To most economists this question would suggest a semantic confusion: if something of public value is not being created, then the market is, ipso facto, allocatively inefficient. Again there may be disagreement about what specific public value should be created, but if the market does not provide it, then that market is not efficient.

Overall, unless one interprets economic approaches narrowly and defines CBA dogmatically, there is no glaring conflict with the theory of public value. Bryson, Crosby, and Bloomberg (2014) describe how thinking about public value has moved on from an emphasis on efficiency and effectiveness toward dialogue and responsiveness to active citizenship. But the need to take account of efficiency remains. Perhaps more sympathetically, Moore (2014) sees "bottom-line" management as helping clarify what is at stake in creating public value. Welch and colleagues (chapter 9, this volume) are more emphatic in rejecting CBA, but this rejection is founded on a very strict interpretation of the process. More importantly, any terminological distinctions pale in comparison to the much larger problem of the use and practice of CBA.

THE USE OF COST-BENEFIT ANALYSIS

The US federal role for CBA is identified under the Regulatory Right to Know Act, which requires the Office of Information and Regulatory Affairs (OIRA) within the Office of Management and Budget (OMB) to submit annually to the US Congress an "accounting statement and associated report" that includes estimates of the benefits and costs of federal rules. In 1993, Executive Order 12866 included as its objective 6, "Each agency shall assess both the costs and the benefits of the intended regulation, and recognizing that some costs and benefits are difficult to quantify, propose or adopt a regulation only upon a reasoned determination that the benefits of the intended regulation justify its costs."[1] This assessment is applied to rules designated as major and those meeting a threshold under the Unfunded Mandates Reform Act of 1996. This threshold—labeled "economic significance"—is in practice any rule with an effect of over $100 million. Thus, those who object to CBA should be comforted by the knowledge that unless the policy involves $100 million of resources, CBA is not required.

But the scope of CBA is far narrower because there are several ways in which this executive order is circumscribed. First, government agencies are not bound to respond to a CBA if it conflicts with their legislative mandate. The two most significant exemptions here are for regulations regarding National Ambient Air Quality Standards (where public health concerns are the mandate) and the Endangered Species Act (where species preservation is the mandate).

Second, independent agencies are not subject to the executive order. This exempts at least thirty-three agencies, including many with substantial influence over how the economy is structured (such as the Department of the Treasury, the Federal Reserve, and the Securities and Exchange Commission), and those agencies with potentially enormous consequences for public value (such as the Defense Nuclear Facilities Safety Board, the Nuclear Waste Technical Review Board, and the Council on Environmental Quality). In addition, it exempts agencies with significant societal influence, such as the National Science Foundation, the National Endowment for the Arts, the Social Security Administration, the Equal Employment Opportunity Commission, and the Farm Credit Association.

Finally, regulations may be devised strategically to avoid CBA. Rules may be implemented before a CBA has been completed; rules may be devised to avoid the designation "economically significant." An egregious example was the Environmental Protection Agency's new rules on new source review for power plants in 2003. These rules were declared to fall below the "economically significant" threshold based on anecdotal evidence from industry executives—the beneficiaries of the new rules (see Chettiar, Livermore, and Schwartz 2009). This evasive technique was regularly employed during the administration of President George W. Bush from 2000 to 2008, with several acts being exempt from review under the National Environmental Policy Act.

Consequently, the proportion of rules that actually undergo CBA is very small. Of the 3,773 rules published in the Federal Registrar in 2007–8, 277 were reviewed by OMB. Of these, 42 were identified as major rules for the OMB but 21 were federal budget transfer programs (and thus exempt). Of the remaining 21, 13 had a statement of costs and benefits. Overall, less than one-half of 1 percent of rules was subject to CBA. Since 1990, only 7 percent of the 41,724 reviews performed by the OIRA were deemed "economically significant"—that is, above the $100 million threshold. But even these figures overstate the implementation of CBA because most analyses that are conducted fall far short of a full CBA. In their review of seventy-four regulatory impact analyses, Hahn and Tetlock (2008, table 1) found that not every analysis estimated costs and not every analysis estimated benefits. In fact, only 12 percent of these analyses actually reported costs and benefits together to allow for the calculation of a benefit-to-cost ratio. Rule review times are also very short. For those not deemed economically significant, the average review time was thirty-two days; for reviews of rules that were deemed economically significant, the average review time was forty-four days.

Of course, federal governments are not the only agencies providing public goods and regulating public "bads." State and local government spending is approximately one-half the size of federal spending, and nonprofit charitable agencies play an important role. Unfortunately, economic evaluation by these other agencies is not remotely as advanced as that of the federal government. In a comprehensive summary of regulatory review by state agencies across the United States, Schwartz paints a very dismal picture: "almost no states have balanced or meaningful processes to check the ongoing efficiency of existing regulations" and "most states struggle to assess the basic costs of regulations—and completely forgo any rigorous analysis of benefits or alternative policy choices" (2010, 8). Few nonprofit agencies, including large international concerns, have sufficient capacity to perform economic evaluations. Finally, the situation appears no better in Europe. Reviewing impact assessments there, Hahn and Tetlock concluded starkly that they "seldom estimated costs, almost never quantified costs to business, did not specify benefits, and virtually never compared the costs to the benefits." Emphatically, CBA is a "custom more honored in the breach than the observance" (2008, 72). Policymakers with concerns about the use of CBA may thus rest easy.

CRITIQUES AND REASONS FOR NEGLECT OF CBA

This lack of use of CBA makes debate about the value of it somewhat moot. Perhaps the absence of CBA reflects its weakness as a method for evaluating public policy, however. I will divide these weaknesses into theoretical and practical ones, emphasizing that the latter is the real concern.

Theoretical Critiques

Fundamentally, the biggest reason for neglect of CBA is that it is viewed as illegitimate (Sandel 2009). As noted above, this argument is substantially overstated.[2] First, no economist is arguing for a CBA of every individual decision. As argued by Posner (2000), the criterion for using CBA is whether it improves decision making. Economists might argue that the scope of decisions under which CBA would improve decision making is large, but I suspect that many non-economists would agree that a $99 million federal policy—or any large-scale state government policy or any World Bank intervention—would merit some form of economic evaluation.

Second, categorical imperatives assume away any policy issues. It is not enough to say that slavery is wrong or education is a human right. Policymakers have to implement policies that ensure and maintain the abolition of slavery and provide students with schooling. Both imperatives require resources and those resources, once allocated, cannot be used for an alternative purpose. If an entire society is agreed that the Asian tiger should not be allowed to become extinct, there is no reason for a CBA unless one realizes that the cost of preservation is such that it is not possible to save the Asian tiger from extinction instead or until one asks how many Asian tigers should exist.

Third, many of the supposed illegitimacies can be incorporated into policy-making independently from CBA. The overarching critique is that one cannot measure values using prices. This critique comes in many forms. CBA reflects the existing pattern of wealth such that prices of goods do not reflect their value and CBA calculations will be unfair. For example, a vaccine research program should not be funded but a seat belt subsidy for Rolls-Royce owners should be because the latter have a higher willingness to pay for lifesaving policies. No weight is placed on the morality of values used in CBA; that is, it does not matter whether the beneficiaries are saints or sinners, and it does not matter if due process has not been followed. Some things cannot be priced—for example, due process. And there is a saliency mismatch because CBA counts only what it can see. Finally, preferences cannot be aggregated using money because it does not correspond to utility or satisfaction.

The method of CBA, however, is not prescriptive on these issues. If the analyst believes that public valuations better capture willingness to pay or opportunity cost, then these assessments of public value should be used. The literature on contingent valuation and passive use—individuals valuing things that they will never use—is substantial and growing. Similarly, the analyst can choose to exclude benefits that accrue to sinners and disproportionately weight those that accrue to saints. In addition, there is a sizable literature on differential valuation of voluntary risks (driving at high speed) versus involuntary risks (breathing contaminated air). There may be some debate about the precise weights to use, but this debate is helpful in illustrating the trade-offs policymakers face. When there are benefits that cannot be measured, such as due process, CBA is still helpful because it clarifies what due process is really "worth" to society when a policy is found to have costs that exceed its benefits. In other cases, CBA may be useful in persuading those with no strong moral opinions. People who are not bothered about a particular policy may be persuaded simply by an argument that the policy will not increase their taxes or will generate net benefits for some group.

The final—ultimate—version of this critique is that one should not use aggregations of private values but instead use those of the community or collective. (This criticism seems to be separate from the one above regarding skepticism that money can proxy for satisfaction.) Unfortunately, how these community or collective valuations are to be determined is left unspecified. If they are the whims of a politician or bureaucrat, one might argue in favor of aggregations of private values. If they reflect the enlightened views of a legitimately elected official in a representative democracy, one might inquire as to what information and rules this official used to make his or her benevolent decisions. It is incumbent on opponents of CBA to specify in detail how elected officials might—in the absence of CBA—determine which policies create the most public value. Alternatively, these opponents need to specify in detail how citizens might—in the absence of CBA—understand why a particular policy has been selected.

Critically, CBA does not compel a decision. Policymakers must still make decisions. If these policymakers choose to override the findings from a CBA and that choice can be justified or rationalized, then the policy process has been improved; not only is policymaking more transparent, but the legitimacy of the policymaker has been affirmed. If a community knows that to save the Siberian tiger from extinction will cost $200 million, but goes ahead anyway, this is not a critique of CBA. Moreover, if policymakers choose to override the findings from a CBA on the grounds of political expedience or because of special interest lobbying or for legitimate reasons, then the policymaking process has also been improved: the CBA provides the electorate with information as to the policymakers' integrity or judgment. Indeed, Levin (2001) has argued that this is one of the main reasons policymakers do not value CBA: it makes clear when policies have been subverted to satisfy the policymakers' self-interest or, relatedly, the interests of powerful stakeholders.

Additionally, the criticisms of CBA are almost never accompanied by a credible alternative. Simply finding policies that are effective is not sufficient. For example, CBAs of interventions to reduce crime illustrate why looking just for effective programs is misleading. Marsh, Chalfin, and Roman (2008) reviewed 106 interventions intended to reduce crime where there was information on costs and benefits. In 74 of these, crime fell and the benefits exceeded the costs, and in 3 studies crime rose and the costs exceeded the benefits. In 7 studies crime rose, but because the intervention significantly reduced costs, the benefits exceeded the costs; and in 22 studies crime fell, but the intervention was so costly that it was deemed not worth it. So, in approximately one-fourth of studies, a determination based on CBA would differ from one based on the change in crime.

The standard alternative to CBA is to identify particular public values such as personal freedoms, desires, and rights and then work to meet those goals (see the work by Nussbaum and the instruments developed by World Health Organization Quality of Life program at www.who.int/mental_health/publications/whoqol /en/). But this alternative is too vague, too narrow, and incomplete. The vacuity arises because this approach does not specify to what extent these rights should be satisfied; in other words, when is the elimination of hunger satisfied? The approach is too narrow because it does not cover many policy decisions; for example, what personal desires and rights are satisfied by the decision to build a road instead of a bridge? And specifying rights is incomplete because it requires resources (eliminating hunger requires food, and eliminating abortion requires prosecution of noncompliers) and all resources are scarce. Thus, unless all freedoms, desires, and rights are satisfied—in which case the policymaking process is redundant—a choice has to be made as to which one can be satisfied first. This critique also applies to the public value map of Welch and colleagues (chapter 9), although in this case the authors recognize their map serves as a "loose set of heuristics," arguing that this allows for necessary flexibility in policy.

Practical Challenges to CBA

Ironically, denigrators of CBA might have more "success" if they focused on the practice of CBA rather than on the theory. Certainly there is scope for considerable error in using inaccurate prices (e.g., valuing a lifesaving device at $10,000 per life saved) or in failing to count an important benefit from a policy (or double-counting it), and there are going to be forecast errors in ex ante CBAs. There are, however, other—more fundamental, practical—questions that CBA researchers face.

First, there is a practical concern over which method to use to calculate the benefits of a policy. The two general classes of method are contingent valuation and revealed preference. The former is typically sensitive to several important biases, such as hypothetical bias (survey respondents do not know how to value something they have never experienced) or embedding bias (survey respondents give general answers to specific questions) and to whether the benefits are expressed as willingness to pay or willingness to accept a loss. There is no easy way to evaluate differences in results across the two classes of method.

Second, there are distributional issues for any policy. In theory it does not matter who the winners and losers are as long as the former gain more than the latter lose. In politics, it does matter. Some groups are considered more deserving than others, but there is no clear guidance on how to weight the more deserving groups. Kalambokidis (2014) describes how distributional concerns—captured in economics by the idea of a social welfare function—can be distorted by policy choices.

Third, the choice of the discount rate matters. Discounting is the method by which benefits that occur in the future are made comparable to costs that occur in the present. Choosing a high discount rate will mean that future benefits are worth less. Moore and colleagues (2004) provided an important clarification on how to choose the discount rate, but the actual number can vary for several plausible reasons. For example, they propose a discount rate of 3.5 percent for the first fifty years of a policy. But this choice is based on a set of quite restrictive assumptions. In fact, no US government agency uses this specific rate. The OMB, for example, uses a much higher 7 percent discount rate.

Fourth, there is the challenge of how to measure the change in risk associated with a project. If a community is risk-averse, then a policy such as a hydroelectric dam that reduces risk (e.g., from flooding) may well have a value beyond the benefits of electricity generation. At issue is how to measure this reduction in uncertainty. It requires information about how the community values reductions in risk, and this information is very hard to collect (and hence is almost never collected).

Thus one might be much less concerned about the theoretical legitimacy of a CBA, because if it does not improve decision making it can be neglected or ignored. Rather, policymakers should be much more concerned about how to interpret a CBA in light of the practical decisions made by the analyst with respect to the method used to calculate benefits; distributional weights; the choice of the discount rate; and the value of risk reduction. Of course, only someone trained in CBA and willing to take the method seriously can understand the implications of these choices. The case studies below illustrate this dilemma.

POLICYMAKING IN PRACTICE AND THE ROLE OF CBA

Case studies of policymaking illustrate the many challenges of CBA and how difficult economic analysis is in practice. Notably, our examples do not deal with the practical challenges listed above. Instead, their deficiencies are far more basic and show how policymaking is distorted by incomplete, weak, or manipulated economic analysis. Nevertheless, the case studies also show that CBA uniquely sheds light on some important aspects of the policymaking process, albeit not a good light.[3]

The Importance of Getting the Costs Right: The Iraq War

Most military decisions are presumably to be determined based on military strategy. However, the Bush administration made a number of ex ante bold assertions that the Iraq War (2003—2011) would not be a costly campaign, amounting perhaps to less than $2 billion (see Stiglitz and Bilmes 2008, 10–15). Yet a conservative estimate of the ex post costs of the Iraq War was $3 trillion, of which $1.7 trillion was budgetary (materiel, care for veterans, and debt interest); and this was not counting any costs imposed on the Iraqi people or US allies (Stiglitz and Bilmes 2008). Almost certainly there would have been more opposition to the war from fiscal conservatives had this information been made available ex ante.

We can use a simple thought experiment to consider the value of CBA even in the context where decisions are supposedly non-economic. The Iraq War was declared on March 19, 2003. Although that date was not arbitrary, it could have probably been postponed by one week. This postponement would have reduced "interest payments" on the $3 trillion amount by one week. Assuming perfect capital markets and a 5 percent interest rate, this postponement would have been worth at least $120 million in present value terms on March 19, 2003. In theory, society should have been willing to pay at least this amount for a Department of

Defense economist who could have successfully argued for a delay of the invasion by one week.

The Importance of Getting the Costs and Benefits Right: Mega-Events

The economic rationale for mega-events such as the Olympics or the World Cup and the associated policy decisions regarding stadium siting has been widely acknowledged to be weak, yet the persistence of cities in vying for these events is partly a consequence of the poor quality of the CBAs performed. Each bidding city can find an economic evaluation (or "economist") that makes the case look attractive.

Many of these evaluations are flawed. Mega-event CBAs have large errors on both the cost and benefit sides. Cost estimates are systematically understated, often enormously. The estimate at the time of the bid for the London 2012 Olympics was for a gross public cost of $6.3 billion; four years later in 2007, this estimate was revised upward to $14.5 billion (National Audit Office 2007, 6, table 2). These understatements are not prediction error; instead they reflect a failure to perform a full costing exercise with sensitivity testing. Such an exercise would recognize that contracts of such large scale cannot be costed out using prevailing wage rates for construction workers, for example, and that amortization of capital assets such as stadia is critical. A common error is to overestimate private-sector contributions. (For the 2012 London Olympics, this overestimate was by a factor of five; see National Audit Office 2007, 6, table 2.) Another common source of error is that the proposal is changed after the cost estimate is conducted—and not to reduce the scale of the event. These sensitivities are well documented, not least because of the errors in prior mega-event costing exercises—for example, Montreal in 1976 (see Harrington, Morgenstern, & Nelson 2000).

On the benefit side there are also errors, and again these are not forecast errors. Some errors are gratuitous and no longer common in the literature, such as counting the wages paid to construction workers as a benefit of the games. Others include failure to model switched expenditure by residents (e.g., fewer trips to museums), tax exemption for Olympic committees, and the crowding out of other tourists. But, of course, the most salient issue is the benefit that is not counted: the value of "public spirit" associated with such a world event, a benefit typically cited as an important justification for hosting it. Yet there are almost no studies as to what this public spirit is worth for any mega-event. It seems highly unlikely that it is worth the $8.2 billion error in the cost accounting for the London Olympics. Policymakers clearly felt no obligation to provide an estimate of the value of this public spirit. Indeed, it is not obvious that public spirit will be enhanced. Events at both the Munich and Atlanta Olympics probably adversely affected those cities' reputations.

The Importance of Measuring Benefits (Not Just Impacts) and Costs

Much has been written about the low quality of CBA in education (Levin and McEwan 2002; Levin 2001). In a review of over thirteen hundred relevant academic papers in education on cost-effectiveness, Clune (2002) divided them on a quality scale as follows: 56 percent, "rhetorical"; 27 percent, "minimal"; 15 percent, "substantial"; and 2 percent, "plausible." As an indicator of the low quality of the research, Clune's (2002) definition of "substantial" was an "attempt to mount data on cost and effectiveness but with serious flaws." "Rhetorical" was defined as "cost-effectiveness claims with no data on either costs or effects."

Education research has not improved considerably since Clune's (2002) review. There is no strong research on the economic value of achievement or test scores, for example, despite substantial policy attention to raising scores and reducing achievement gaps (e.g., No Child Left Behind). There is a growing literature on the economic benefits of high school graduation (Belfield and Levin 2007; Rumberger 2011), but the costs of effective interventions are rarely reported. Economic evaluations of small-scale reforms also fall far short of CBA. For example, the US Department of Education's Institute for Education Sciences summarizes research findings through its What Works Clearinghouse (http://ies.ed.gov/ncee/wwc/). The WWC performs a lengthy and complete review of research using a detailed protocol for evaluating and interpreting the evidence. For comparability, the research findings are reported using a standardized outcome such as effect size gains in achievement. However, the WWC pays little attention to the costs of the interventions. For example, in 2007 it reviewed all available research on reforms to math curricula. The review identified four curricula that satisfied the WWC's methodological standards and reported the effect size gains for each, but these curriculum reforms required very different cost amounts. They lasted between one year and three years; they required either no teacher training or up to one week of teacher training; they required from zero additional hours of instruction to forty-nine additional hours.

The Importance of Specifying the External Costs: The Social Cost of Carbon

The social cost of carbon (SCC) is perhaps the most important price on the planet. The SCC is the estimate of the global economic damages of an incremental increase in carbon emissions each year. Failure to accurately calculate this price will impose potentially enormous social burdens on current and future generations. Yet the SCC is extremely difficult to estimate; it requires modeling of an enormous proportion of global economic activity in relation to global environmental change, and is often predicted across centuries. In February 2010, in a collaborative effort across twelve departments, the US government published a "technical support document" to calculate the SCC. Using a 3 percent discount rate, the SCC was estimated at $21 per ton in 2010, rising to $26 by 2020 (in 2007 dollars). This document might therefore provide a consensus as to the SCC to be used in cost-benefit analyses of policies that involve significant changes in carbon emissions.

Three cases illustrate why such a consensus is desperately needed. One is the opposition of the Bush Administration to the Kyoto Protocol. In a letter opposing the protocol in March 2001, President Bush asserted that it "would cause serious harm to the U.S. economy." As Nordhaus (2007, 686) concludes, "This policy . . . was undertaken with no discernible economic analysis." A second case, documented by Chettiar and colleagues (2009), involves the setting of Corporate Average Fuel Economy standards by the National Highway Traffic Safety Administration (NHTSA). Under the Bush administration, NHTSA argued that because the SCC could only be measured imprecisely it was better to assume that its actual value was zero. After a US Court of Appeals ruling, the NHTSA was forced to estimate the SCC. Its estimate excluded global effects of climate change; any economic activity not in the United States (e.g., mining in Canada to meet US demand for energy); and any noncarbon emissions. Finally, in their CBA of offshore drilling in the Arctic National Wildlife Reserve, Hahn and Passell (2010) use a social cost of carbon of $0.91 per ton, far below any reasonable estimate. The authors' justification is that US citizens should only care about climate change damage felt by US citizens. As the United States makes up only 5 percent of the earth's population, any estimate of the SCC should be reduced to 5 percent of its actual value. This assumption makes a mockery of efforts to identify and apply a social cost of carbon as part of a cost-benefit analysis.

The Importance of Specifying the External Costs: The Senior Death Discount

Another social cost that has attracted considerable controversy is the value of life (more strictly now referred to as the value of a micro-risk reduction in mortality). In deciding on health care coverage, it is necessary to weigh the value of drugs that save some lives against the value of operations that save other lives. In environmental policy, clean up of polluted sites requires assessing the impacts on mortality rates across different groups in society. One balancing act that has attracted the most attention (albeit far disproportionate to its practical application) is whether to value the mortality of seniors at less than that for children. This is the so-called senior death discount.

One can think of plenty of reasons why policies to help preserve a senior's life might be less valuable than those for a child's, the three most obvious being that risks children face are often involuntary, that senior citizens have already had "fair innings," and that children themselves have not had children. Indeed, the consensus from most studies is that the value of a statistical life is higher for children (Viscusi 2010). Thus, many countries do have senior death discounts, but the Environmental Protection Agency (EPA), which performs the most significant CBAs in the United States, does not. The EPA's decision was made after significant political pressure when it attempted to apply lower weights for health benefits for persons over the age of seventy. Critically, policies that affect the lives of children are therefore now weighed the same as policies that affect the lives of seniors. Of course, seniors might disagree with a reweighting (just as children might disagree with the status quo), but this does not mean that the problem of valuing life has been avoided.

The Importance of Understanding the Fiscal Implications

Typically, CBA is performed from the social perspective—that is, the costs and benefits are totaled across all entities with standing regardless of whether these are government agencies or private individuals. Yet it may be that a policy that passes a CBA test from the social perspective does not do so from a fiscal (government/taxpayer) perspective. This has led some economists to call for multiple-account CBA where it is explicit who the winners and losers are (Shaffer 2010).

Policy on smoking is a particularly interesting case. Imagine a policymaker faced with an antismoking lobby group; what economic information would be useful to him or her? A full treatment of this question is given in the excellent book by Sloan and colleagues (2004). First, the marginal net external cost of smoking to society is currently not very high. Over the lifetime of a twenty-four-year-old regular smoker, the present value net external cost is only $6,200, or about $150 per year (Sloan et al. 2004, table 11.3). Smokers now bear almost all the costs of smoking themselves. The benefits they get in public health care are offset by the Social Security and private pension payments they are entitled to but never claim because they die before they can collect them. Second, the fiscal implications of smoking are slightly positive, meaning the taxes on smoking cover any additional claim on public resources made by smokers. In other words, reducing the rate of smoking would likely cost the US Treasury money. Finally, the two groups that are biggest losers from having a large population of smokers are perhaps surprising. The first group is the spouses of smokers who incur higher mortality costs (Sloan et al. 2004, table 11.2); the second group is participants in life insurance markets who lose out because historically premiums paid by nonsmokers have subsidized those of smokers. This is useful information that can only be gleaned from performing a CBA.

CONCLUSION

Our case studies highlight the gap between theory and practice. The focus on the presumed theoretical shortcomings of CBA, rather than the failure to recognize its general absence or its practical manipulability and misapplication, has undermined the creation of public value. In environmental policy, an area where CBA has the greatest applicability, under the Bush administration CBA became a tool used by those who did not want regulation rather than a tool to decide the optimal amount of regulation (Revesz and Livermore 2008). A similar dynamic occurs in education policy: by failing to calculate the full benefits of education, proeducation groups are not able to make as forceful a case for investments in public schooling or subsidies to other schooling alternatives. In addition, state governments have limited capacity to make an economic argument for investments in state infrastructure. Our other cases suggest a more general cynicism in favor of not using rigorous CBA; for example, when policymakers wish to implement policies that serve their expediencies, they simply focus on the elements of CBA that lend their case the most credence. Indeed, these many shortcomings may justify a movement away from simply creating public value through efficiency and effectiveness and toward a more democratic understanding of public value (Bryson et al., 2014).

Yet the case studies also illustrate the value of CBA in making clear what is known, what is not known, and what needs to be known. For example, if the civic spirit of hosting a mega-event is very large, then these events are justifiable. But the extent of civic spirit cannot be presumed, it must be established. As another example, if smokers are already fully compensating society for smoking, then the policy questions change. Society is not losing out; the losers are the smokers themselves and their families, against which policymakers should weigh the value of freedom of choice to smoke.

In attempting to create public value in any form, all those involved in government—be they public managers, politicians, active citizens, or what Moore (2014) calls arbiters of public value—face a dilemma. Difficult decisions have to be made, but often there can be no acknowledgment that these decisions are difficult. The choice typically needs to look easy so that the favored decision will gain sufficient political support. Recognizing that there are arguments in favor and arguments against a policy, but that the pros outweigh the cons, can be seen as too complicated and too risky. The more mixed assessment can give political ammunition to obstructionists who will only mention the cons and argue that the policymaker must acknowledge those while never mentioning the pros. The policymaker may think it better to proceed as if there are no trade-offs. CBA, which has the trade-off in its name, then becomes (unsurprisingly) not welcome. We have reached potentially even more of a stalemate, however. As discussed in the context of work by the Government Accountability Office in the first decade of the twenty-first century, Shipman (2012) basically concludes that all evaluation decisions are regarded as partisan. If so, the need for a rigorous, formalized method of evaluation—which does not preclude and indeed illuminates policymaker discretion—becomes even more necessary, and this method must be able to reconcile both sides of a policy argument. CBA could, if practiced more often and to a higher standard, meet this need.

Indeed, it is likely that CBA will play a greater role in policymaking. First, it can yield much valuable information even before it provides guidance on the net benefits of public investments. Second, there is growing consensus on shadow prices such that CBAs are becoming more standardized and policies can be more easily compared. Demographic changes, in combination with the health care crisis, will force tough decisions on policymakers; specifically, allocating resources to prolong life will become more fraught. Finally, and by far most important, climate change has raised the stakes on how we should value the planet's public resources. In helping to articulate and derive shadow prices for carbon and other greenhouse gases, CBA can play a vital role in creating or sustaining public value. Ultimately, carbon emissions cannot be regulated using heuristics; there is overwhelming evidence that the shadow price is too low and—critically— policymakers should use this "bottom line" evidence regardless of how distorted the political process is. Preservation of the planet's sustainable resources for future generations might be regarded as the ultimate way to create public value.

NOTES

1. This order was reaffirmed on January 18, 2011, under Executive Order 13563; http:// www.whitehouse.gov/the-press-office/2011/01/18/improving-regulation-and-regu latory-review-executive-order.
2. Sandel writes that, strictly, "our hesitation points to something of moral importance— the idea that it is not possible to measure and compare all values and goods on a single scale" (2009, 46). This leaves open the possibility that *some* values and goods might be measured on a single scale. Therefore, the question becomes, Are too many public decisions being valued this way or too few?
3. These case studies are chosen to be "big picture" illustrations. Thus I do not dwell on, for example, the CBA of New York City's Second Avenue subway line, which was performed over a decade before the final plans for the subway were completed and included no estimate of dislocation costs to residents living on the path of the subway during the five to ten years of construction.

8

CREATING A PUBLIC VALUE ACCOUNT AND SCORECARD

MARK H. MOORE

Creating Public Value (Moore 1995) left a large, important question unanswered: How would public managers, the elected representatives of the people who monitored their work, the citizens in whose name public enterprises were carried out, the taxpayers who provided much of the funding for government, and the individuals who had interactions with governments as clients properly determine whether public value was, in fact, being created in a particular government enterprise? Presumably the answer to that question lay in the development and use of some kind of accounting scheme that could recognize when costs to the society were incurred and value to the society produced.

In this chapter I sketch the outlines of an accounting scheme that might be useful to the various stakeholders described above—citizens, taxpayers, elected representatives, political executives, public managers, and clients of public agencies—as they seek to define, create, and measure governmental efforts to create public value. Other chapters in this volume offer excellent alternatives to my proposed approach, but I will concentrate here on the particular concepts I have been trying to develop and test (Moore 2013).

The concepts are, admittedly, inspired by the private sector. In this respect, I expose myself to three criticisms, namely that my work is: (1) a thinly disguised effort to smuggle inappropriate "neoliberal" concepts into the world of political economy and public administration; (2) an approach that neglects the effort to develop a coherent, clear conception of the public values that should be advanced by a good and just government in favor of helping managers cope with the world they find around them; or (3) a view of democratic politics that makes politics instrumental to the achievement of valued ends and ignores democratic politics as a valued end to be achieved in itself and as the proper author of the public values to be produced in government activity (Dahl and Soss 2014).

In my defense, I entered the fray at a time when neoliberal ideas about the "proper" role of the state and private-sector concepts of managing government organizations were becoming dominant in public discourse. Two of these influential ideas focused on the proper role of the state in a modern society: (1) that creating conditions that could promote economic prosperity was a key function of government that was at least as important if not more important than advancing any particular procedural or substantive conception of social justice; and (2) that unregulated markets were both the best means of achieving economic prosperity and the embodiment of a particular idea of social justice that emphasized the priority of individual property rights. A third idea focused more on improving the management of public-sector organizations by importing private-sector concepts of accountability that focused on satisfying customers' demands for services and using metrics (ideally *financial* or *monetized* metrics) to animate, guide, and evaluate agency performance.

Although it is both possible and important to separate these ideas from one another, in the practical world of politics they were packaged as a coherent whole that could restore government to its proper function in modern liberal societies. Packaged together, these three distinct (and contestable) ideas became one big (apparently uncontestable) idea that sought to shift basic ideas of political economy, the role of the state, and the idea of social and political justice—not just ideas about the efficient and effective administration of government agencies.

Somewhat surprisingly, this package of ideas made significant headway in the worlds of politics, government, and public administration. But they did so, I think, not as the result of a serious, broad public discussion of how societies as a whole ought to deal with significant public problems such as poverty, unemployment, crime, health care, child abuse, educational inequality, and aging. That discussion would have been much slower and more hotly contested.

Instead, this neatly packaged set of large political ideas moved ahead under the cover of a simpler, more general, and much less controversial idea—namely, the procedural idea that government, whatever its purposes and its size and scope, should be accountable to the people.

This, of course, is the core idea of democratic accountability. But the kind of accountability associated with *democratic* accountability is very different than the kind of accountability associated with *market* accountability. As a philosophical matter, the idea of democratic accountability makes the body politic the appropriate arbiter of social value, not individual consumers. As a practical matter, democratic accountability moves backward along the process of policy from formulation through implementation to the creation of public value to the goal of satisfying the aspirations of the individual citizens and taxpayers who authorize and pay for government activities (and those who represent them) rather than out to the clients of government agencies who might benefit from government largesse or find themselves burdened by government-imposed duties all justified in terms of a collectively made decision to use the assets of the collectively owned state to achieve particular publicly defined purposes.

On this view, the principle of democratic accountability—the idea that the state should be accountable to its citizens—exists independently of any particular substantive ideas about a good and just society and the role of the state in helping to create such a thing. Presumably a liberal who sought to ensure the goal of equality of educational opportunity by establishing uniform, high-quality public schools for all could be as committed to the principle of democratic accountability as a libertarian who believed that providing choice to parents among publicly financed schools would be the best way to achieve educational outcomes—not only for some students, but for all. Their differences would lie in their particular conceptions of the sort of education that a good and just democratic society needed and the best means for creating that particular educational system; they would not lie in differences about the core question of whether democratic governments were accountable to their citizens.

Somehow the indisputable idea that a democratic government should be accountable to its citizens was transformed into the idea that what its citizens wanted was not just a *liberal* state that protected political rights, and sought to advance equality in social and economic terms, but a *neoliberal* or *libertarian* state whose principal responsibility was to protect property rights and, in so doing, advance both economic prosperity and the liberty that goes along with making one's way in a market economy. In this way the widely accepted and universally embraced idea that democratic government should be accountable to its citizens provided cover for a much more controversial idea about what constitutes a good and just society and what role government should play in helping citizens achieve that goal.

The demand for government accountability (as opposed to any particular political idea of a good and just society) also leaked over into the narrower world of public management and added fuel to the enthusiasm for libertarian principles. The reason is that when the public sought a conception of tough accountability that forced organizations to pay attention to their efficiency and effectiveness in meeting the needs of individuals as an idea that was consistent with the broad principle of democratic accountability, they naturally turned to the structures and processes that seemed effective in creating private-sector concepts of accountability.

In the private sector, the accountability of powerful organizations making decisions about how to deploy valuable assets is constructed from three distinct structures and processes: (1) the fact that individual customers can choose whether to buy the products and services offered, creating incentives for producing firms to produce what individuals (with discretionary money to spend) want to buy; (2) the existence of shareholders represented by a vigilant board unified in their desire to maximize their long-term shareholder wealth by controlling costs and increasing profits even as they try to serve customers; and (3) the widespread availability and use of financial metrics that reliably show the degree to which the enterprise has created value for both shareholders and customers.

To many, the private system of accountability seemed more powerful in driving efficient and effective organizational performance than the public system. The market had self-interested customers and individual choice that could call producing organizations to account. Democratic accountability had to rely on citizens and democratic politics to create the required discipline. The private sector had powerful, objective financial metrics to show investors whether the enterprises in which they have invested were or were not profitable. Compared with these simple, straightforward processes, the idea that citizens and their representatives could effectively call government agencies to account for their performance by articulating a clear purpose for government, and then developing and using measures to show whether the collectively defined purposes had actually been achieved, seemed very weak indeed. Consequently, if one wanted accountable government (which every democratic citizen does), one had to have government agencies that sought to satisfy customers and had financial metrics for performance. Thus the concepts of market accountability, substituted for democratic accountability, were used not only as a guide to improved government management but also as a compelling reason to justify a wholesale shift in discourse about the proper role of government. The only way for government to be accountable to citizens was to embrace neoliberal or libertarian principles.

One can reasonably be in favor of or opposed to the large political ideology advanced by neoliberal or libertarian thought. But one should recognize the difference between a simple argument for the importance of government accountability and an argument that the only government that can be accountable is one that operates in accord with private-sector concepts and methods of accountability.

There are three key ideas associated with market-based, or neoliberal approaches to government that I have consistently opposed: (1) that government's main purpose should be promoting economic growth rather than the pursuit of economic, social, and political justice as an existing democratic polity defines these conditions; (2) that the sole arbiters of value in society are individual customers who seek to advance their own material welfare rather than the collective aspirations of citizens, taxpayers, and their elected representatives to achieve a vision of a good and just society; and (3) that the process of developing a public that can become articulate about the purposes for which a government enterprise is launched is important only instrumentally and not intrinsically as an expression of democratic life. In fact, in each case, I believe the opposite: (1) the arbiter of value is a collective public rather than individual customers; (2) the interests of that public include limiting the use of authority and ensuring the justice and fairness with which government operates as well as its efficiency and effectiveness; and (3) a democratic government cannot act legitimately, responsively, efficiently, or effectively without a process that can call a public into existence that can understand and act on its own interests.

Where I have found common cause with neoliberalism is in emphasizing the critical importance of improving the processes of democratic accountability on both the supply side and the demand side. It is not easy to call a public into existence that can become clear and articulate about the public values it wants to see achieved by and expressed in government operations. It is not easy to sustain the public commitment to remain vigilant and insistent that the results be produced. And it is not easy to develop the measures that can reliably tell us the degree to which the desired results have been achieved.

But I have described the work that has to be done to help citizens, taxpayers, and their elected representatives "recognize public value" precisely to help meet these current deficiencies in democratic accountability (Moore 2014). Consistent with my previous work, I have focused much attention on public managers and what they have at stake in developing and using effective performance measures. But, following Bozeman (2007), I have also tried to construct a more general philosophical framework of the values that democratic governments must seek to advance as a matter of democratic principle. Responding to those who think I have given insufficient attention to the intrinsic as well as instrumental importance of democratic policymaking, I have discussed the useful role that public deliberation about developing performance measurement systems might play in allowing publics to become more articulate about the values they would like to see advanced

(Moore and Fung 2012). Whether I have succeeded, or at least moved the ball down the field, others will have to decide.

The core concepts of my suggested approach are presented in two graphics: a *public value account* that is the functional equivalent of the private sector's famed bottom line and a *public value scorecard* inspired by Kaplan and Norton's (1996) balanced scorecard that helps public managers understand how they might best create value in the particular context of the public sector. To review whether, how, and to what degree concepts from the private sector can help public managers meet the challenges of determining whether value is being created for the society, meeting demands for accountability from the citizens, taxpayers, and elected representatives who authorize and finance their operations, and guide their enterprises toward improved performance, it is useful to start with a clear understanding of the private sector's financial bottom line.

THE PRIVATE SECTOR'S BOTTOM LINE

In the private sector, the bottom line is essentially a measure of the financial performance of a commercial enterprise. It consists of a simple comparison between the revenues earned by the sale of products and services to willing customers and the costs the organization incurred in the production and distribution of those goods and services. Sometimes financial bottom lines are calculated for the performance of the organization as a whole, sometimes for a strategic business unit within the organization, and sometimes for a particular product line or service. The only information system the organization needs to support this financial assessment is a financial system that keeps track of costs and revenues. Since all companies have such systems in place, it is not hard for them to use bottom-line performance evaluations to assess performance at many different levels of aggregation in the organization, nor is it difficult for them to use these bottom-line assessments to increase pressure to improve performance and to make better resource allocation decisions.[1]

In principle, public-sector accounting systems can be as good as private-sector systems in capturing the most obvious material costs of producing desired social results.[2] Government organizations rely on inputs of labor and materials—often purchased in open markets at market prices—to produce results. The costs can be assigned to particular organizational units and activities. So there is very little difference between private- and public-sector cost accounting.

What is crucially missing in the public-sector accounting system is the functional equivalent of the revenue measure that the private sector relies on to recognize value. It is not that the public sector doesn't have financial revenues to account for; money flows to the government in the form of taxes, and those funds are used to sustain government activities. What is different is not just the *sources* of the revenues but, more important, the *philosophical meaning* of the revenues used in private and public accounting.[3]

In the private sector, when an individual puts hard-earned money toward a particular good or service we have evidence that the individual valued the good or service; even a precise estimate of how *much* he or she valued it. We can also directly compare the value that individuals attach to particular goods and services and the cost of producing them simply by comparing the revenues earned to the costs of production. If that comparison shows a profit, and society believes that individuals are the important arbiters of value, then those who manage the company can assume that some kind of individual (and therefore, social) value has been created.[4]

This reasoning that connects financial revenues to judgments about individual and public value is much less tight in the public sector. There productive enterprises are financed not by individuals purchasing goods and services for themselves at a point of sale but instead through taxes that are imposed on them as their fair share of financing an enterprise that a collective has judged valuable. Revenues are less directly attached to the satisfaction of individual citizens, taxpayers, and clients, and less directly attached to the performance of government organizations. They are instead attached to the aspirations of citizens as they are expressed in the decisions of their elected representatives in the form of public policies.[5]

These are all well-known facts, but their full consequences have not yet been fully appreciated. First, when tax dollars finance public agencies, the appropriate arbiter of value shifts from individuals making consumer choices to a public that comes into existence and becomes articulate about what it would like to do with the collectively owned assets of government. Second, the purposes that a public might embrace—the values they would like to see produced by and reflected in government operations—will not necessarily be easily monetized. The collective says it wants a safer, greener, more educated, or less discriminatory society; it pays for such purposes by taxing and regulating itself. But the value of achieving the particular results registers not in the till but in the changes made in the world that register in the hearts and minds of the citizens (Moore 2013, 2014).

Consequently, it is very difficult for public managers to provide simple, convincing, objective evidence of the value they create. The link between what individuals value and the particular values they are supposed to produce and reflect in their operations is attenuated. The collective articulation of the values to be realized and affirmed is muddy and incoherent. The capacity to measure the degree to which the values are being produced is limited. And it is very hard to monetize or create some common metric that can be used to compare the value of different particular results.

MANAGEMENT ACCOUNTING IN GOVERNMENT

Of course, government agencies could not escape the demand for accountability. They needed some kind of system to report to their "investors" and "shareholders" about their performance and to manage their operations for efficiency and effectiveness no matter how challenging the task.

Government's response was thus to create accounting and measurement systems that focused on activities observed at different points along the production process that converted the assets of government into collectively valued results. These systems began with efforts to monitor government control over assets, check compliance with established policies and procedures, and measure the quantity and quality of organizational outputs that occurred at the boundary of the organization.

Internal audits sought to ensure that government money was not stolen or diverted to unauthorized purposes (Allen 2002; Moore and Gates 1986). Compliance audits sought to ensure that government assets were being used according to established policies and procedures (Hood et. al. 1999, 61–68). Outputs of organizations were counted to measure productivity and workload (Poister and Streib 1999, 325–35).

This was all fine as far as it went; it was important to assure citizens and taxpayers that tax dollars were not being diverted through official fraud, waste, and abuse. Indeed, insofar as many government programs involved little more than the distribution of financial resources from the treasury to individual client beneficiaries of government programs, ensuring that government dollars went to individuals who were the intended beneficiaries and not to others went a fair distance toward ensuring that the program was creating the value legislators and policymakers intended (Moore 1986).

Moreover, insisting on compliance with existing policies and procedures was potentially valuable for two slightly different reasons. On one hand, since treating like cases alike was considered an intrinsically valuable characteristic of government activity, and since compliance with policies guaranteed such consistency, one could say that compliance audits produced a much-desired fairness in government operations (Mashaw 1983; Moore 1994). On the other hand, if existing policies and procedures embodied the best possible methods for using government assets to achieve desired results, then compliance with those policies would ensure efficiency and effectiveness as well as fairness.[6]

The problem was that these accounting systems did not reach far enough along the "value chain" that links government-controlled assets to internal public agency activities, agency outputs, and ultimately to clients who encounter the government and to socially desired outcomes experienced by society as a whole (Wholey, Hatry, and Newcomer 2010). Figure 8.1 presents a picture of this value chain with different points of monitoring and accountability indicated.

The historical lack of measurement and accounting beyond organizational boundaries left government unable to account for the experience of the clients or the ultimate socially valued results. Nor could the government note and seek to mobilize contributions of those beyond the boundaries of the organization that could contribute to the achievement of social objectives (Alford 2009). That left citizens, taxpayers, and their representatives uncertain about what value had actually been accomplished and who had actually produced it.

More recent efforts to fill this gap with cost-benefit analyses and program evaluation have not, for a variety of reasons, been entirely satisfactory in providing guidance to public managers and accountability to citizens.[7] First, the expense and difficulty of organizing these analyses meant that relatively few government activities could be evaluated. Second, the results of these analyses tended to come late in organizational decision-making cycles. While these results might be useful in making big policy decisions, they were hard to use for managing operations and adapting them in medias res when they did not seem to be working. Third, these methods often focused on the evaluation of policies and programs, not organizational units. If a policy cut across several different organizations or a program was only part of what one organizational unit did, then these systems were less useful

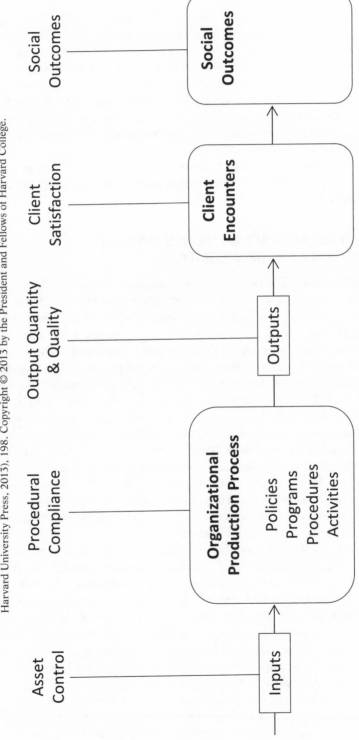

Figure 8.1 Measuring along the public value chain

Source: Reprinted by permission of the publisher from Mark H. Moore, *Recognizing Public Value* (Cambridge, MA: Harvard University Press, 2013), 198. Copyright © 2013 by the President and Fellows of Harvard College.

than private-sector financial measures in managing organizational resource allocation, motivation, or learning.

Finally, all of these efforts to measure the social or public value of government operations lay within a utilitarian philosophical framework (Moore 2014). This is problematic because government cannot insulate itself from continuing public concerns about the protection of individual rights, the fair treatment of those it regulates and to whom it provides benefits, and its success in producing a civil and just society. These concerns for fairness, justice, and right relationships are associated with a deontological rather than a utilitarian philosophical framework, and they arise over and over again when government acts in a democratic society (Frankena 1973). To the degree that citizens want a government that acts fairly and justly and helps to encourage fairness and justice in the society as a whole, there must be some method for incorporating these concerns into the measurement of public-sector operations.

KAPLAN AND NORTON'S BALANCED SCORECARD AS CHALLENGE AND OPPORTUNITY

The publication of *The Balanced Scorecard* and its follow-up, *The Strategy-Focused Organization*, shook up the world of performance measurement—in both the private and public sectors (Kaplan and Norton 1996, 2001). These books, intended principally for private-sector managers, argued persuasively that managers had long overestimated the value of their financial systems to guide their organizations. The authors did not argue that maximizing long-term profitability should not be the goal of private-sector organizations; nor did they raise any doubts about the adequacy of financial measures to capture the value of what had been produced. They were not recommending the use of double, triple, or quadruple bottom lines to capture the full range of effects that commercial enterprises could have on individual and social life (Savitz 2006). They were simply saying that financial measures were always about the past. They reliably captured what the organization had done in previous years, but revealed very little about what the organization needed to do now to sustain profitability in the future. And from their point of view the issue of how past profitability could be sustained in the future should be the important issue facing private-sector managers.

To answer that question, business executives had to shift their attention from backward-looking financial performance measures to developing a plan for future profitability, described as the business strategy of the organization. To do that these executives needed good information about their market position—particularly their standing with customers. They also needed to understand whether current operations could be sustained and how investments could be made to change what the organization was producing or how it was producing it.

This led the authors to propose a performance measurement system that embraced four perspectives. They began with the financial perspective, which still occupied pride of place as an accurate description of the value the organization produced, then added three more: the customer perspective (the current and future state of the organization's relationship with customers), the operations perspective (the efficiency and sustainability of operations), and the learning perspective (the ability to adapt products and services and the methods used to produce them for future profitability).

This did not come as big news to business executives who had long deployed many measures other than financial ones to monitor operations and guide investments for future-oriented strategy execution. But it did serve to emphasize the importance of nonfinancial measures, including measures of the environment beyond the organization and at its boundaries and process measures focused on both internal operations and investments being made to transform current product lines or operations. Insofar as the ideas began to undermine the dominance of the financial bottom line as the best way to capture an organization's value and manage future performance, *The Balanced Scorecard* deeply challenged and reordered private-sector measurement practices.

To government managers *The Balanced Scorecard* seemed as much an opportunity as a challenge.[8] The idea that high-performing organizations needed nonfinancial measures as well as financial measures—measures that focused on internal organizational processes and investments as well as ultimate outcomes and aligned with an explicit theory of value creation, not just a demonstration of past accomplishment—reflected exactly what they had long been saying about the inadequacy of financial measures for organizations whose revenues came from taxpayers rather than paying customers. Finally, they had someone—indeed, two business experts—who could champion their cause! A cottage industry grew up that applied the ideas of *The Balanced Scorecard* to government organizations.

What public managers who tried to apply these measures found, however, was that *The Balanced Scorecard* left unanswered two critical questions about performance measurement in government. The first was the old bugaboo: Who exactly should be viewed as the proper arbiter of the value produced by such organizations, and what exactly was it that they either did—or should—value? Kaplan and Norton's book directed organizations to identify their customers. But confusion reigned about who the customers of government organizations were. Were they the citizens and taxpayers who provided the money and authorization that government organizations used to create public value? Or were they the folks who met government in individual transactions and received benefits (and/or obligations) as individuals? There was no guarantee that taxpayers wanted the same things as individuals receiving government benefits. In fact, it seemed likely in many cases that their interests were opposed. Similarly, it was not obvious that citizens wanted the same things from government that the tax cheats, criminals, or polluters that government encountered in regulatory and enforcement organizations wanted. If there was a difference, which of these different possible customers would be properly viewed as the morally compelling or practically important arbiter of value?

The second problem was that, like cost-benefit analysis and program evaluation, applications of the balanced scorecard remained in a utilitarian framework (Frankena 1973); they were not particularly attuned to questions about justice and fairness in government operations or the kinds of social relationships public agencies were structuring. This was problematic when so much government activity was justified by individually or collectively held views of what was good for others, what one's duties were to others, and an ideal of a good and just society.

RECOGNIZING PUBLIC VALUE: A STRATEGIC APPROACH TO PERFORMANCE MEASUREMENT

In *Recognizing Public Value* (2013), I have tried to find a different path for the future development of measures that could more or less reliably capture the public value being produced by a government enterprise, meet public demands for accountability in government, and help managers use performance measurement systems to guide their organizations toward improved performance. Three key assumptions about the nature of the work to be done guide this path.

Taking a Developmental Approach

The first assumption is to recognize that, while the development of suitable performance measures for government might eventually simplify oversight and management in the public sector, in the short run it is likely to create some increased complexity. To many this will come as unwelcome news. After all, part of the appeal of "bottom-line management" for government is precisely that it might make things relatively simple and objective, and many enthusiasts of measurement and accountability assume that it can't really be that hard.

I am all in favor of being tough and determined in the pursuit of accountability through quantitative, objective, performance measures. But I am painfully aware of how much can be lost both in organizational performance and in the cause of performance management when government makes a large commitment to the wrong set of measures. One can walk into virtually any public organization and find the rusty hulks of previous efforts to measure performance. Of course, one could say that the reason these systems have been abandoned is that the bureaucrats finally wore down political and managerial efforts to impose a reasonable kind of accountability. But more often the fact is that the measurement systems were not very good. In a surge of enthusiasm for performance measurement, the overseers and managers of organizations reached for a convenient set of measures without worrying much about whether the measures could reliably capture the value that the organization was producing, whether the measures were aligned with the values citizens and their representatives wanted produced, or whether the measures could attract the loyalty and commitment of the organization's employees.

A better approach would recognize that the development and use of a performance measurement system is like the construction of a cathedral. Initial construction could inspire hope, command commitment, and create a space for worship. But it is never quite finished. However much work it takes to build the foundation, anchor the buttresses, and erect the spire, more work would be necessary to create the embellishments, even more to make significant renovations as conditions change, and still more to rebuild when the cathedral is razed by barbarians! Just as a firm's balanced scorecard might change in response to environmental changes and strategies to deal with them, so should a public agency's performance measurement system change with the times. A strong performance measurement system does not come from a single moment of insight or a surge of effort; it comes from relentlessly pursuing a path of development and learning over a long period of time.

Embracing a Strategic Approach That Integrates Values, Politics, and Operations

The second assumption is that a strong performance measurement system should not only account for past performance but also lay a basis for defining and pursuing a future-oriented, public value–creating strategy. In *Creating Public Value* I argued that a good, value-creating strategy had to (1) make a plausible claim that the envisioned purposes were publicly valuable, (2) command legitimacy and support from those who authorized and financed the activity, and (3) be operationally achievable. The challenge was to integrate these pieces in the short run and to envision how to move an organization or enterprise to an improved position on each of these dimensions in the future. These three requirements were graphically represented in the strategic triangle presented in chapter 1 (see figure 1.1).

The requirement that managers attend to and manage conceptions of public value, the mobilization of legitimacy and support, and the development of the operational capacity required to produce the desired results meant that government managers needed not only measures of ultimate outcomes and value but also (like the private-sector managers using the balanced scorecard) some way of monitoring their current position and capacities and the ability to envision and execute strategies that would sustain or improve their position and performance in the future.

Different Kinds of Managerial Work

The third assumption is that public managers would have to understand that the effort to develop an effective performance measurement system would require them to do both more and different kinds of work than their private-sector counterparts. Private-sector managers usually enter their organizations with much of the work of building a performance measurement system already done. They have at least the financial measurement system and human systems that are comfortable using it for both external and internal accountability. Public managers, however, often have to create both the systems and the cultural commitments to the use of those systems.

In *Recognizing Public Value* I claim four different kinds of managerial work have to be done: technical, managerial, philosophical, and political. The first two are familiar and widely acknowledged but still difficult. The second two are less widely recognized as important in the development of performance measures, but, in my view, crucial to the development of a value-creating, sustainable measurement system (Bryson and Patton 2010). Indeed, I think part of the reason we have not done very well in developing performance measures is that we have concentrated on the technical and managerial and ignored the political and philosophical.

Technical work refers to the challenge of developing specific measurement instruments that can accurately capture the degree to which valued effects are occurring in the world. This may seem simple, but it is not always so. The police, for example, have as their mission to reduce crime and enhance security; for many years that goal was measured by observed changes in levels of crime reported to police forces. We later learned that many crimes went unreported and that citizen fears were not closely related to actual crimes. Consequently, the police added victimization surveys to their performance measurement systems to get a more accurate picture of the real level of crime, and to ask citizens about their fears and their own self-defense efforts, thus giving the police a more accurate picture of their fundamental goals (Coleman and Moynihan 1996).

Managerial work refers to the challenge of using the measures in the context of organizational operations to animate and guide the organization toward improved performance through harder or smarter work (Behn 2008). Again, to many this seems a straightforward task: all one has to do is to attach specific performance measures to particular managers or workers and use them to reward good and punish bad performance, and the performance of the organization will improve—at least in terms of the measured dimensions of performance. But as many managers can attest, creating and using a performance management system that an organization can tolerate as fair and appropriate, and that can engage managers and workers in wholehearted efforts to improve performance (rather than bad-faith efforts to cheat or game the system), is not at all straightforward and simple. Things get even more complicated if, instead of simply driving individuals to perform better against the performance measures, managers decide that they want to help the organization *learn* about what works. The information and social relations required to create an organization passionately committed to doing its job well and continuously learning how to do it better are harder to construct than simple liability systems that impose sanctions on employees on the basis of performance statistics (Kofman and Senge 1993; Moynihan 2008).

Philosophical work refers to the work that must precede the technical work described above (Moore 2014). Public value is a normative, philosophical concept; so is the idea of performance. Government organizations can and do try to make the ideas of value and performance more objective and technical by constructing empirical measures that they hope stand reasonably well for the normative ideas. But it is important to recognize that all performance measurement and management systems have at their core a normative theory of what effects of an agency's performance will be valuable.

By far the most challenging kind of work in developing a performance measurement system in government is *political work*. This work is crucial, however, because in a democratic government the system must be not only philosophically and technically sound and managerially useful but also endorsed by those in positions to authorize, legitimate, and pay for the enterprise (Bryson and Patton 2010). This is *morally* important because the only appropriate arbiters of public value in democratic political systems are citizens, taxpayers, and their elected representatives. It is *practically* important because it is the political demands for accountability that provide the drive to create, develop, and use performance measurement systems. Without political agreement and commitment to a particular performance measurement system, there is no electricity flowing to the light that should be guiding the way. *With* political support and interest, the performance measurement system not only clarifies the mandate for government operations but also focuses and sustains the energy through the difficult implementation phase.

DEVELOPING THE PUBLIC VALUE ACCOUNT

To begin this strategic work of developing performance measurement systems for government organizations, it is useful to set out a framework that can capture the most important issues to consider and to accumulate important ideas and information. One such framework is described in *Recognizing Public Value* as a public value account. This framework is meant to do for government managers what the financial bottom line does for private-sector managers: provide a way of accounting for costs incurred and valuable results produced by a government organization.

Adapting the Financial Bottom Line to Public Assets and Public Values

The public value account helps public managers cope with three features of government operations that differ from private-sector concepts of individual or market value.

First, it accounts for the fact that the assets that government uses to produce public value include authority as well as money. Government can use its authority to create an army, regulate pollution, impose speed limits, and so on. It also uses its authority to ensure that public benefits go exclusively to the intended beneficiaries. Like money, authority is valued and in short supply. All other things being equal, if government can find a way to produce desired results using less authority, that solution would be preferred to one that made greater use of state authority (Sparrow 1994).

Second, it recognizes that individuals and their material satisfaction are not necessarily the appropriate arbiter of public value. This is particularly true when the government obliges individual citizens to do something they would prefer not to do for the benefit of the community as a whole. It is also true when the government provides benefits like job training and drug addiction treatment to individual clients. In these cases the public may have the satisfaction of the individual clients in mind, but that is usually not the only important objective. The public hopes the unemployed will find gainful employment and that addicts will get clean, get a job, stop committing crimes, and care for their dependents (Alford 2009).

Third, the public value account recognizes that when the government acts, the public will use deontological standards of fairness and justice as well as utilitarian standards of satisfying individual clients or achieving desired social outcomes to judge its actions. Individuals and their fellow citizens want to know that their rights and interests have been appropriately protected from arbitrary action and that the government is acting fairly and justly as well as expediently (Mashaw 1983). These are the normative concerns that attach to the use of state authority, and government action nearly always makes use of the authority of the state, whether it is imposing obligations on individual actors and restricting access to benefits or simply spending money to produce a good or service that is available to all, because the government's money came into its hands through the use of the state's taxing authority. If concerns about justice and fairness attach themselves to any use of state authority, then presumably they attach themselves to the use of money that was raised through the use of state authority.

The Main Categories of a Public Value Account

Working out the implications of these philosophical points for the construction of a bottom line for public agencies is a difficult but not insurmountable task. Again, government can have as good a cost accounting system as the private sector—at least with respect to financial expenditures. The problems begin, as noted above, on the revenue side. If we wanted to take a customer perspective in government we could, perhaps, substitute some measure of client satisfaction for revenues earned. But, as noted above, there are many clients of government agencies including criminals, polluters, and tax cheats who receive obligations from the government rather than services and whose satisfaction cannot be the only (and probably not even the principal) aim of the encounter. And often, even when the government is providing benefits, it is at least as interested in achieving some desired aggregate social welfare that is not necessarily captured in the satisfaction of individual clients—whether "obligatees" or service beneficiaries.

There are also many individuals in various social positions—such as voters, taxpayers, or concerned citizens—who are not necessarily clients of particular government programs. Because we are often uncertain about what values these individual stakeholders would like to see achieved by and reflected in government operations, we rely instead on a kind of collective utilitarianism in which we imagine that there is a public more or less appropriately constructed that can become articulate about what the public as a whole, or all of us acting as citizens rather than clients, want to see happen in government operations. We call this legislating or public policymaking, and it relies on there being both a collective entity that can express what the public values and the likelihood that what the public values consists not only of individual client satisfaction but also the achievement of desired social outcomes.

Given this, the public value account begins with financial costs on the left-hand side of the ledger. The right-hand side of the ledger begins with client satisfaction but adds the more important idea of the specific social outcomes that the public values as the mission or ultimate goals of government enterprises (Wilson 1989). These basic elements of the public value account give citizens and taxpayers an idea of cost-effectiveness in achieving a desired social goal, with some attention to the satisfaction of individual clients. (Taxpayers are presumably mollified by the inclusion of a focus on cost, and citizens, we hope, are satisfied with the concern given to both cost and valued social result—just as corporate shareholders would be interested in overall profit.)

The next step, however, is to recognize the use of authority as an asset and to note how much authority is engaged in any particular government enterprise. It may seem odd to think of the use of authority and force as a quantitative idea, but it is not hard to reckon the degree of force used to promote compliance with particular obligations or the magnitude of the burden that is imposed by any given regulation. We can even estimate the financial costs of enforcement and compliance. And on occasion, when the government is forced to pay compensation to those whose rights were violated, we can get a direct estimate of the financial cost of an improper use of force, which could help us monetize other abuses of authority.

Once we recognize the use of force as a cost in government operations we have to begin accounting for the fairness with which the government acts and the degree to which its policies are pushing the society toward one or more particular images of a good and just society. As noted previously, in a democratic society the use of state authority always has to be justified; it cannot be used arbitrarily or unfairly. There has to be a reason, and the reason has to be a general rule that applies to all (Tyler 2006).

Obviously it is much easier to account for fairness in government access than to account for its success in producing other important aspects of justice. But given that these matters of justice and fairness show up all the time in discussions about how government agencies are performing, it is essential to consider what facts could be gathered to show progress or problems on these dimensions of value.

Taken together, the interests in financial costs to government, the achievement of collectively desired outcomes, the satisfaction of individual clients, the degree to which state authority is being used, and the degree to which government agencies are acting fairly and helping to achieve a just as well as a prosperous society will produce a public value account like the one pictured in figure 8.2.

In addition to the categories described above, this public value account includes the idea that a public organization might want to make room in the accounting scheme for recognizing unintended and unanticipated good and bad effects of

Figure 8.2   The public value account: general form
Source: Reprinted by permission of the publisher from Mark H. Moore,
Recognizing Public Value (Cambridge, MA: Harvard University Press, 2013), 113.
Copyright © 2013 by the President and Fellows of Harvard College.

Public Value Account	
Financial Costs	*Achievement of Collectively Defined Mission/Desired Social Outcomes*

	Client Satisfaction
	  Service Recipients
	  Obligatees

Unintended Negative Consequences	*Unintended Positive Consequences*

Social Costs of Using State Authority	*Justice and Fairness*
	  At Individual Level in Operations
	  At Aggregate Level in Results

its activities. When the government acts, surprising outcomes that matter to individuals often occur, and a complete public value account needs such categories to allow a public organization to learn more about the consequences of its actions. It should also create room to change and adapt collective ideas of what values the public wants the organization to achieve.

The challenge, of course, is to begin filling in this abstract frame with more particular ideas about public value and concrete measures that could capture the degree to which these values were actually being produced in the world, agency by agency. Perhaps over time, certain classes of agencies such as police departments, schools, or social service agencies may develop concepts of value and systems of measurement specific to their particular kind of work. That would be a welcome development, since we could then begin to codify practices, improve measures, and make comparisons among different agencies in the same line of business in the interest of learning how to improve performance. Once data collection was begun in similar systems capturing different dimensions of performance, we might actually be able to see how much of what particular values could be produced using existing operational methods. This would reveal what economists describe as the production possibility frontier for each public-sector industry. It would also show us which particular agencies are defining the frontier for particular industries, and which have room to improve on all dimensions. But the start is to see if we can outline in sharper and sharper detail the target we are trying to hit: a reasonably satisfying conceptual definition of public value.

DEVELOPING A PUBLIC VALUE SCORECARD

In the effort to truly improve the performance of government organizations, however, the public value account is just the first step. Just as private-sector managers learned that their financial accounts alone were too focused on end products and past performance to provide an adequate basis for evaluating and managing their organizations' performance, so public-sector managers might learn that they need something more than the public value account to manage their enterprises. Drawing with gratitude on the example of Kaplan and Norton, I proposed in *Recognizing Public Value* the creation of a *public value scorecard* that included the public value account (analogous to the financial perspective) but added families of measures that would focus managerial attention on the current position of the organization in its environment, whether and how operations could be sustained, and how to improve current and future performance through investments that embody the organization's continuous learning.

In constructing these families of measures, I relied on the strategic categories developed in *Creating Public Value* and often presented as the strategic triangle (see chapter 1). The public value account captures the particular perspective associated with the "public value" circle of the strategic triangle. To this I added a legitimacy and support perspective (roughly analogous to the balanced scorecard's customer perspective) and an operational capacity perspective (roughly analogous to the balanced scorecard's operations perspective).

Figure 8.3 The legitimacy and support perspective: general form
Source: Reprinted by permission of the publisher from Mark H. Moore, *Recognizing Public Value*
(Cambridge, MA: Harvard University Press, 2013), 119.
Copyright © 2013 by the President and Fellows of Harvard College.

THE LEGITIMACY AND SUPPORT PERSPECTIVE: General Form

Mission Alignment with Values Articulated by Citizens
(Link to Public Value Account)

Inclusion of Neglected Values with Latent Constituencies
(Link to Public Value Account)

Standing with Formal Authorizers:
Elected Executives
Statutory Overseers in Executive Branch (Budget, Finance, Personnel)
Elected Legislators
Statutory Overseers in Legislative Branch (Audit, Inspectors-General)
Other Levels of Government
Courts

Standing with Key Interest Groups:
Economically Motivated Suppliers
Self-Interested Client Groups
Latent Interest Groups

Media Coverage
Print
Electronic
Social

Standing with Individuals in Polity:
General Citizenry
Taxpayers
Clients
- Service recipients
- Obligatees

Position of Enterprise in Democratic Political Discourse:
Standing in Political Campaigns
Standing in Political Agendas of Current Elected Regime
Standing in Relevant "Policy Community"

Status of Key Legislative and Public Policy Proposals to Support Enterprise
(Link to Operational Capacity Perspective)
Authorizations
Appropriations

Engagement of Citizens as Co-Producers (Link to Operation Capacity Perspectives)

Figure 8.4 The operational capacity perspective: general form

Source: Reprinted by permission of the publisher from Mark H. Moore, *Recognizing Public Value* (Cambridge, MA: Harvard University Press, 2013), 124. Copyright © 2013 by the President and Fellows of Harvard College.

THE OPERATIONAL CAPACITY PERSPECTIVE: General Form

Flow of Resources to Enterprise *(Link to Legitimacy and Support Perspective)*
Financial Revenues Flowing to Public Agencies
- Appropriations
- Intergovernmental grants
- Fees

Legal and Statutory Authorizations/Mandates
Public Support/Popular Opinion

Human Resource:
Current Status of Workforce
- Size
- Quality
- Morale

Recruitment and Selection Processes
Training/Professional Development of Staff
Compensation Levels
Advancement Opportunities
Performance Measurement Systems for Individual Accountability
Public Volunteer Efforts

Operational Policies, Programs and Procedures:
Quality of Operational Performance
- Documentation of current procedures
- Compliance with tested procedures
- Auditability of performance recording methods

Organizational Learning
- Evaluation and current untested policies
- Stimulation and testing of innovations
- Institutionalization of successful innovations

Internal Resource Allocation
Performance Measurement and Management Systems
- Investment in systems
- Use of systems

Organizational Outputs *(Link to Public Value Account)*
Quantity of Outputs
Quality of Outputs
- Attributes that produce desired results
- Attributes that increase client satisfaction
- Attributes that reflect justice and fairness in operations

I did not create a separate category for the learning perspective because it seemed to me that this was the dynamic quality of all the perspectives. By encouraging public managers to think strategically and developmentally, the public value scorecard took it for granted that learning would occur about what constituted the important dimensions of public value to be measured, current standing and legitimacy with authorizers and how to bolster it, and how to improve current and future performance.

Figures 8.3 and 8.4 present general outlines for the legitimacy and support and the operational capacity perspectives. Again, these abstract categories have to be given richer content by developing both more specific concepts and measures attached to those concepts. And, as we accumulate experience in constructing these sorts of measurement systems, some parts may become more easily standardized.

CONCLUSION

Citizens of democratic societies and their elected representatives have long sought something as simple as the private sector's bottom line as a basis for improving the performance of government. And they have often assumed that such a thing was easily within reach, and that it was only the resistance of self-protective bureaucrats that prevented the creation of bottom-line management systems for government.

I don't think citizens are wrong to want good measurement systems that can enable effective public oversight and accountability of public organizations. Indeed, I count myself among the most ardent enthusiasts of both political and governmental accountability to citizens in democratic societies. Where I part company with the most enthusiastic advocates of bottom-line management for government is not in the desire to achieve that goal but in the assumption that such a feat is simple and within close reach. Oliver Wendell Holmes once said, "I wouldn't give a fig for the simplicity on this side of complexity. But I would give my right arm for the simplicity on the other side of complexity." I think, like Holmes, that we ought to hold out for the simplicity that lies on the other side of complexity in seeking accurate and useful measures of public value creation. To get there we have to fight through not only the technical issues of how to construct reliable empirical measures of value concepts and the managerial issues about how to use such measures to motivate performance in organizations and help them learn how to improve but also the tough political and philosophical questions that lie behind any judgment of value in a democratic regime. We have to think about how a collective entity that we call the public can be called into existence and become articulate about what it would like to achieve through governmental action. And we have to keep talking about the important issues of justice—about the kinds of relationships we would like to have exist in our society, and what as a consequence we might owe to one another as something that government might help us achieve.

The challenge, it seems to me, is to use frameworks such as the public value account and the public value scorecard to enable the rich, swirling discussion of public value that is characteristic of a healthy democracy to connect with a concrete reality that must be managed. I hope the frameworks developed here can weather the storm and light a path toward sustained value creation.

NOTES

1. In thinking about the future development of efforts to measure the performance of government, it is enlightening to consider the history of financial measures. It took several centuries for these relatively simple measures to become the powerful managerial tools they now are (Riahi-Belkaoui 2005).
2. There is still some way to go in improving public-sector cost accounting systems even though this does not pose the same philosophical or practical problems as accounting for the public value being produced with those funds.
3. For a more extended discussion of the philosophical issues, see Moore (2013, 2014).
4. One can mount many challenges to this idea of consumer sovereignty. Individuals can be easily fooled and often make choices that are not in their long-term interests, making consumer choice a flawed arbiter of individual private value—to say nothing of collective, public value; this is the focus of much behavioral economics research. But despite the evidence that individuals are often far from rational in making choices for themselves, the core liberal idea that the only proper arbiter of value is individuals, and that social institutions should be constructed to let those individual value choices shape social outcomes, has remained vital.
5. There are as many difficulties with the story that good, just, and wise collective choices emerge from the processes of democratic governance as there are with the story that markets work well to produce the greatest good for the greatest number in a just and fair way. For a discussion of how individuals might be successfully aggregated into a public of citizens that can become articulate about the values that should be produced by and reflected in government operations, see Moore and Fung (2012).
6. If, however, procedures are costly and ineffective, enforcing compliance can reduce overall performance. This is a particularly grave danger in the public sector, where organizations have to be concerned about legitimacy as much as performance, and tests of performance are weak. Since copying the behavior of other organizations is the easiest path to legitimacy, there is a real risk that a focus on compliance with policy and procedures rather than testing and innovating can lock an entire organizational field into low performance (DiMaggio and Powell 1983).
7. For a more complete discussion, see Moore (2013).
8. *The Balanced Scorecard* also had a significant impact on the nonprofit sector, which faced performance measurement problems analogous to those of government agencies (e.g., third-party payers, social results that were difficult to measure and monetize, and concerns about justice and fairness in operations and results). Unlike government, however, nonprofit organizations could not directly deploy the authority of the state (though they could contract with government to use it!). For a discussion of the limitations of *The Balanced Scorecard* for nonprofit organizations, see Moore (2003).

9

PUBLIC VALUE MAPPING

JENNIE WELCH, HEATHER RIMES, AND BARRY BOZEMAN

At both the individual and societal levels, values can be likened to Silly Putty: moldable, changeable, and sometimes breakable if given a sharp blow. Because our values are complex personal judgments based on knowledge as well as emotional reaction, they are not static but instead continuously changing as our knowledge and emotional responses evolve (Bozeman 2007). These qualities can sometimes make value identification and measurement difficult and, as a result, easily quantified values such as economic efficiency tend to dominate public policy evaluation and debate. Yet because the vast majority of public endeavors are motivated and guided by entire constellations of values (Beck Jørgensen and Bozeman 2007), there is a need for mechanisms that systematically incorporate a broad range of value considerations in policy decision-making processes.

Public value mapping (PVM) is a tool designed to address this need. PVM is not an analytical technique or even a set of analytical techniques but instead an approach to identify public values; assess whether public value failures have occurred; map relationships among values; and graphically represent relationships between public value and market value successes and failures.

PVM should *not* be considered a replacement for market-based approaches to policy analysis such as cost-benefit analysis (CBA) and expected value models. Rather, it serves as a counterweight to these commonly applied economic approaches, allowing for a more explicit consideration of collective values. The need for this opposing force has long been noted by scholars who have pointed out the limitations of a strict reliance on neoclassical models in policy evaluation, with particular attention paid to the inability of certain evaluation tools to fully account for public values. Criticisms of market approaches include:

- The Pareto efficiency criterion is not useful for addressing distributional issues that are often at the heart of public value questions (e.g., intergenerational resource rights; see Howarth and Norgaard 1990).
- The theoretical assumptions are based in utilitarianism, a theory that many contend is insufficient for valuing equity concerns (Brown 1992; Sen 1970; Sen and Williams 1982).
- The philosophical foundation is one of economic individualism, which privileges the interests of the individual over the interests of society; treats social and government institutions as a means of satisfying individual needs; and gives the individual supreme value over society or the polity. As a result,

collective action, usually in the form of government intervention, is often treated as a possible (although not necessary) alternative to pursue only after private solutions have failed (Bozeman 2007).

- Policy tools derived from neoclassical economic theory (e.g., cost-benefit analysis) may fail to fully account for the long-term consequences of policies (Mishan 1980). Furthermore, CBA requires the monetization of all items under review—even those that some contend should not be treated as commodities (e.g., the practice of assigning a dollar value to a human life).
- Efficient markets often have very little to do with development or human happiness, and thus market frameworks are inadequate for social allocation of goods and services (Lane 1991).

Despite these limitations, economic approaches to policy evaluation and decision making in the public sector continue to dominate the analytical process. There are good reasons for the power of these tools: analyzing the marginal benefit, economic productivity, or the economic development impact of a policy or program is usually a critical component to determining the value of a policy. Market-based tools also have the appeal of being based on a concrete set of procedures and grounded in familiar economic principles. Unfortunately, tools that allow us to engage in a dialogue or analysis of additional values beyond those considered in economic models lag behind. Though still in its infancy, PVM is a tool designed to offset the strict reliance on economic considerations in policy evaluation to give more equal weight to the assessment of public values beyond those of a strictly economic nature.

The purpose of this chapter is to provide clarity around the theory that has influenced PVM, to discuss how PVM can serve to counterbalance traditional economic approaches, and to review several examples of PVM in use. We begin this chapter with a discussion of PVM's theoretical building blocks. We then describe the core assumptions of PVM and the key steps and procedures that are required for its application. Next, we examine examples of PVM applications. Finally, we conclude with a discussion of the strengths and limitations of PVM and discuss possibilities for future application. We argue that although PVM has predominately been applied to address questions related to science and technology policy and research innovation, it has potential to be useful in a number of other policy domains and has promise as a pathway to more systematic consideration of some of the most pressing questions in the field of public administration.

THEORETICAL BUILDING BLOCKS OF PVM

The cornerstone of PVM is the public value concept. Despite being heralded as "the next 'Big Thing' in public management" (Talbot 2009) and as an emerging paradigm in the field of public administration (Stoker 2006), the conceptual meaning of the term "public value" remains ambiguous. Indeed, one of the largest criticisms of the systematic consideration of public values is the marked lack of consensus in the academic community about what constitutes public value. Key questions still linger such as what the "public" in "public value" means; whether there is a hierarchy of public values; what the possibilities for assessing public values are; and how public values fit together (Beck Jørgensen and Bozeman 2007).

In order to provide more clarity around the valuation of public values, any discussion should begin by providing a clear conceptual definition. For our purposes, we define a society's public values as those providing normative consensus about the rights, benefits, and prerogatives to which citizens should (and should not) be entitled; the obligations of citizens to society, the state, and one another; and the principles on which governments and policies should be based (Bozeman 2007, 132). Note that this definition does not require government or public managers to be the sole proprietor or creator of public value. This conceptualization is aligned with others developed in the literature (see Alford and Hughes 2008) in that the "public" in public values is less about the sector in which value is created or delivered and instead a reflection of who benefits from it. However, it differs from Moore's conceptualization (1995), which suggests public value creation is a strategic problem that public managers can solve provided they have clarification on what it is they should be trying to produce; legitimacy and support from their authorizing environment; and a recognition of the operational capabilities of their organization or network.

A critical distinction between Moore's conceptualization (1995) and the approach advanced by Bozeman (2002) and applied here is the theoretical focus as it relates to public value (managerial action focus versus policy focus). Nevertheless, these two approaches are not so distinct from one another as to be irreconcilable. As Bryson, Crosby, and Bloomberg (2014) explain, both Moore's approach and Bozeman's approach contend that public value and public values are observable and measurable; emphasize the importance of healthy democracies for the achievement of public values; recognize the negative implications of privileging efficiency and effectiveness at the expense of other public values; and recognize the relationship between policy environments and the public managers that operate within them. Indeed, the public managers who are the focus of Moore's conceptualization may find the definition of public values applied here useful—and certainly may find utility in the public value mapping tool reviewed in this chapter for evaluating and analyzing policy contexts or as a tool to analyze their own decision-making processes. However, it is Bozeman's conceptualization of public value that is the foundation for public value failure theory (hereafter "public failure theory")—and it is public failure theory that informs PVM. Therefore, it is Bozeman's conceptualization that is most heavily emphasized in this chapter.[1]

Public Failure Theory

Public failure theory emerged in response to the reliance on market-based assumptions for rationalizing the provision of goods and services by the public sector (Bozeman 2002). Although market-based approaches provide a clear, concise, and easily applied approach to public policy decision making, public failure theorists argue that market explanations alone do not allow for an expansive public dialogue about policy issues (Bozeman 2002). For example, economic models may effectively deal with the efficiency criterion in environmental policy debates, but they fall short of considering conservation issues (Bozeman 2003).

Rather than relying on vague notions of the public interest, public failure theory is aligned with the work of public administration scholars who have given explicit consideration to specific aspects of public values (Beck Jørgensen 1996;

Kirlin 1996; Van Deth and Scarbrough 1995; Van Wart 1998). A key assumption of the theory is that all instrumental values (public, economic, and private) can be viewed as casual hypotheses that are, in principle, subject to empirical tests (Bozeman and Sarewitz 2011). For example, the University System of Georgia states that one of its core characteristics is "a commitment to excellence in public service, economic development, and technical assistance activities designed to address the strategic needs of the State."[2] If we treat this commitment as an organizational value, we could empirically test the organization's progress toward this desirable state.

Public failure theory does not adopt a particular normative perspective as its starting point, nor does it suggest what public values are or should be. Instead, public failure theorists argue that core values can be identified by reviewing a variety of sources, including formal scholarly literature; cultural artifacts and traditions; government documents; agency and program mission statements; strategic plans; and opinion polls (Bozeman 2007; Bozeman and Sarewitz 2011). Of course, systematic efforts to identify public values may uncover a lack of consensus surrounding certain policy domains, a number of public values that conflict with one another (e.g., security and transparency), or sets of values that may or may not be interdependent (Bozeman and Sarewitz 2011). These issues are particularly germane in pluralistic societies, where values often compete and collide (Bozeman 2007). For example, the ongoing debate surrounding same-sex marriage legislation in the United States has revealed fundamental cleavages in values among different groups of citizens.

This invites the question, How do we know when we have achieved our public values, particularly if they are fluid and changing? Proponents of public failure theory argue that if society expresses consensus on a certain value and that value is not achieved, then a public value failure has occurred (Bozeman 2002; Bozeman and Sarewitz 2005; Feeney and Bozeman 2007). Just as approaches to policymaking grounded in economic theory indicate that it is appropriate for the government to intervene when a market failure occurs, public failure theory suggests analogues in terms of public values.

The connection between public failure theory and public value mapping is that PVM provides criteria to identify public values in order to determine when public value failures have occurred (Bozeman 2007). The PVM criteria have obvious analogues to the market failures identified by Bator (1958) and Samuelson (1954; see table 1.1 in chapter 1 of this volume). For example, just as monopolies are said to be market failures that often require government intervention, one of PVM's value criteria is "legitimate monopoly"—that is, when goods and services are deemed suitable for government monopoly, private provision is actually a *violation* of this public value (Bozeman 2007). Note that just as public values are moldable and changeable, the criteria presented in table 1.1 have also evolved. "Creation, maintenance, and enhancement of the public sphere" as well as "progressive opportunity" are the latest criteria to be advanced (Bozeman and Johnson 2014).

In addition to this normative theory, at least one explanatory theory is worth noting with particular relevance to PVM applications. "Churn theory" (Rogers and Bozeman 2001) was developed to offer explanatory power for analyses specifically concerned with knowledge value successes and failures, measured by the extent to which knowledge is translated into social impact (Bozeman et al. 2003). In applications of churn theory, knowledge is conceptualized as information put into use (Bozeman and Rogers 2002), and therefore knowledge *value* derives from the breadth and use of that knowledge. The unit of analysis in this subset of PVM applications is the knowledge value collective (KVC), defined as a "set of individuals who interact in the demand, production, technical evaluation, and application of scientific and technical knowledge" (Bozeman and Rogers 2002, 769). It follows then that KVCs can have varying degrees of social impact depending upon the effects of the knowledge KVCs demand, produce, evaluate, and apply.

These two theoretical cornerstones have allowed for three types of PVM application: (1) evaluations of the extent to which public values are met within agencies, programs, and communities (Bozeman 2007); (2) examinations of the social impact that KVCs engender or could engender (Bozeman et al. 2003); and (3) attempts to detail the relationships and linkages among public values and their implications (Maricle 2011; Meyer 2011). These application types are reviewed in further detail in a later section of this chapter.

PUBLIC VALUE MAPPING

It is useful to note at the outset that PVM is not the public value equivalent of economic evaluative tools such as benefit-cost analysis. Instead it is a loose set of heuristics that allow for the development of analyses of public values (Bozeman and Sarewitz 2011). PVM is designed to address questions such as:

- Given a set of social goals and missions, are the strategies for linking and mobilizing institutions, network actors, and individuals viable for achieving the goals and missions?
- Is the underlying causal logic of a program or mission sound?
- Are the human, organizational, and financial resources in place to move from the agency, program, innovation, or policy in question to desired social outcomes?

Implicit in the design of PVM are a set of core assumptions, presented in table 9.1. In order to apply PVM to questions like those identified above, it is necessary to treat these assumptions seriously. For example, applying PVM as a rigid, technical tool ignores the flexibility inherent in its design. Of equal importance are several key steps of PVM application, which are reviewed below.

Step 1: Identifying Public Values

First, PVM requires the identification of a core set of public values. Because PVM is grounded in public failure theory, which does not offer any prescriptions for what values *should* be, it is the job of the researcher to identify values using data sources that are relevant to the analysis. For example, PVM was recently applied to a review of the state of US climate science—specifically the interagency research initiative that began under President George H. W. Bush as the Global Change Research Act of 1990 (Meyer 2011). Meyer identifies public values related to climate science research by analyzing public laws, program documents, National Research

Table 9.1. Core assumptions of PVM

Assumptions	Description
PVM is assessment-neutral	Applications of PVM can be prospective, formative, or summative
PVM maintains a social focus	PVM takes into account the highest order of impacts and therefore maintains a focus on social indices and indicators; any recommendations that evolve from PVM should be focused on possible changes that seem likely to improve social outcomes
PVM includes measurement of social context	The social context in which a program, policy, or innovation is implemented is a part of the PVM analysis
PVM is multilevel	PVM seeks to show linkages and networked relationships
Environment matters	PVM takes into account the social, economic, and political factors that influences the constraints, opportunities, and resources for the program, policy, or innovation being considered
Public values should guide	Public value theory should guide application rather than market-based approaches or theories
Public values can be derived from diverse sources	Outcome values can be identified by consulting a variety of sources including government legislation, opinion polls, organization mission statements, etc.
Values can be related to activities, programs, and outcomes	PVM assumes that values can be mapped using causal logic models to measured or hypothesized activities, programs, and outcomes. Public values can be included at the beginning of the map (i.e., from the time policies and actions are initiated)
PVM is not a technical approach	PVM should be thought of as a set of heuristics rather than a technical approach to analysis
Specific analytical techniques are not required	The analytical techniques used to test hypotheses and measure impacts and outcomes should be selected based on their appropriateness to the research aims; results should be based on the interrelationships among causal logic, environmental context, and measured impacts and outcomes
PVM should link impact and outcome measures back to social indicators	PVM concludes with a linkage of impact and outcome measures back to aggregate social indicators or other appropriately broad-based, trans-institutional, trans-research program measures of social well-being

Note: This table is informed by the core assumptions outlined in Bozeman and Sarewitz (2011).

Council reports, and interviews with agency officials. As this example illustrates, key decisions of the researcher (e.g., who is considered "in" the policy circle; what data sources are "relevant"; and the time frame of analysis) have the potential to significantly affect PVM results. Thus, it is critical to carefully frame the analysis from the outset.

Step 2: Assessing Public Value Failures and Successes

Next, PVM analysis requires an assessment of whether public value failures have occurred. The criteria presented in table 1.1 can serve as useful diagnostics to engage in this process (a more thorough review of each criterion is provided below). It is important to note that the criteria outlined in table 1.1 are designed to serve as a useful starting point for those seeking to diagnose public value failures but should not be treated as an exhaustive list. Therefore, researchers should consider additional public value failure criteria that may be applicable to their work as well as the appropriateness of applying each criterion to their policy context of interest. Moreover, the criteria are framed as public value failures in order to offer analogues to the more familiar market failure criteria for government intervention. Thus, in cases in which there is debate about the appropriateness of government action or policy development, the criteria can help to indicate whether or not such action is justified. It is also appropriate to utilize the criteria to retrospectively evaluate a specific policy or set of policies. In these instances investigators will find that for each of the criteria, outcomes actually fall along a spectrum ranging from total failure to total success, with most outcomes falling somewhere between either extreme. It is at this point that use of the PVM grid (discussed in step 4 below) plays a particularly important role.

Creation, maintenance, and enhancement of the public sphere. As a public value, this criterion is defined as "open and public communication and deliberation about public values and about collective action pertaining to public values" (Bozeman and Johnson 2014, 7). The criterion is applicable when one is seeking to evaluate policies or regimes pertaining to open dialogue, communication, and transparency. Bozeman and Johnson (2014) cite authoritarian regimes that seize control of social media platforms as an example of a public value failure when evaluated on this criterion, but one can point to public failures within democratic institutions when they are evaluated using this criterion as well. For example, there is a growing body of literature in the field of education about the space (or lack thereof) for public school students to have dialogue about a variety of public values in the classroom, and the role that public schools and public school teachers should or should not play in enabling open and public dialogue about issues of social justice and equity in America for traditionally marginalized populations (Apple 2006; Clark 2006; Cochran-Smith 2004). As Au, Bigelow, and Karp (2007) argue, public school curriculum should equip students to "talk back to the world" and pose questions such as "who makes decisions and who is left out; who benefits and who suffers; why is a given practice fair or unfair; what alternatives can we imagine; and what is required to create change?" They suggest that schools should be forums for students to examine cartoons, literature, legislative decisions, and the like in order to question social realities. This suggestion aligns with what Bozeman and Johnson (2014) consider to be a public value success along this criterion: intentionally and deliberatively making space for free and open public values-related communication (see table 1.1).

Progressive opportunity. In this criterion, "An 'equal playing field' is considered less desirable than collective actions and public policies addressing structural inequalities and historic differences in opportunity structures" (Bozeman and Johnson 2014, 7). Thus, this criterion is aligned with notions of equitable distribution advanced by Sen (1992, 1997), and concerns over the role that the market and private interests play in perpetuating inequalities in market-based economies (Matsuyama 2000; Mookherjee and Ray 2002; Stiglitz 2013). Bozeman and Johnson (2014) cite merit-based policies that fail to distinguish the effects of opportunity structures on achievement as a public failure evaluated against this criterion, whereas compensatory education programs could be considered public value successes. There are a number of additional public policies that could be assessed against the progressive opportunity criterion as well, such as corrective or restorative justice policies designed to compensate American Indians for the extreme hardship and abuses suffered as a result of policies and practices of the US government. One could argue that this criterion provides an answer to the question, "equality of what?"—focusing on the need for relative equality in the resources available to individuals (e.g., income equality). As Bozeman and Johnson argue, "There is no equal opportunity when members of society have remarkably different levels of resources available for the exploitation of opportunity" (2014, 14).

Mechanisms for values articulation and aggregation. This criterion is applicable when political processes and social cohesion are insufficient to ensure effective communication and processing of public values. An illustration of a public value failure that meets this criterion is the political gridlock that has surrounded the passage of the federal budget, with Congress resorting to the use of "continuing resolutions" in all but three of the past thirty years (US Government Accountability Office 2013). If the federal budget is considered a reflection of the nation's values, the "broken" budgeting process (Rivlin 2012) can be thought of as contributing to a multitude of public value failures. In his study of US climate science, Meyer (2011) examines this public value criterion and finds multiple points at which this type of public value failure could potentially occur. For example, he finds that the US Climate Change Science Program only offers ambiguous and broad guidance, making it difficult for agencies to make clear and agree upon connections between program priorities and public values. On the other hand, Bozeman and Johnson (2014) cite the US Congress and seniority system reforms as public value successes when evaluated against this criterion, because the reforms privilege relevant subject matter experience and expertise.

Imperfect monopolies. A clear analogue to the market failure of imperfect competition, imperfect monopolies occur when private provision of goods and services is permitted even though government monopoly is deemed in the public interest. An example of a public failure evaluated against this criterion is private corporations negotiating under-the-table agreements with foreign sovereigns (Bozeman 2003; Bozeman and Johnson 2014). Feeney and Bozeman (2007) also identify imperfect monopolies in their analysis of the 2004–5 flu vaccine shortage in the United States. They contend that because of the "public good" characteristics of vaccines it would be more appropriate for the government to provide the good rather than for private companies to sell it. Thus, they argue a public failure occurred when private companies failed to provide enough vaccine doses and the government did not have enough supply to cover the shortage. Of course, on the flip side are public value successes: one could argue that the use of patent policies creates legitimate monopolies that are in the public interest because of their protection of intellectual property rights.

Benefit hoarding. Benefit hoarding occurs when public commodities or services are captured by an individual or group, thereby limiting distribution to the rest of the population. This can be considered a public failure because, ceteris paribus, public commodities, services, and benefits should be freely and equally distributed (Bozeman and Johnson 2014). Bozeman and Johnson cite restricting public access to designated public use land as an example of benefit hoarding/public value failure and cite historic policies for the protection and governance of national parks as a public value success. Examples of benefit hoarding can also be observed when examining public education systems around the world, including the segregated education system that disproportionately benefited whites in the United States prior to *Brown v. Board of Education of Topeka* (Bozeman 2007). More recently, new schools in South Korea have been opened to specifically serve children from "multicultural" backgrounds. While the Seoul Office of Education argues that special schools are a progressive and necessary approach to educating this subset of the student population, others argue that isolating mixed-descent children from children who are the progeny of two ethnic Korean parents is disabling, inappropriate, and undesirable for the future of South Korea (Fiedler 2012). Additional failures have been cited by Slade (2011), who finds evidence of benefit hoarding in the emerging field of nanomedicine due to the lack of diversity in clinical trial participants. In this case Slade suggests that minority groups may be excluded due to limited access to participating physicians and medical centers as well as study designs that exclude participants with other chronic conditions, some of which are disproportionately found in minority groups. In this instance, the distribution of clinical trials resources and their often lifesaving benefits is disproportionately skewed toward non-minorities.

Security of providers. Failure along this criterion occurs when there is recognition of the public value in the public provision of a particular good or service but that good or service is not provided because of the unavailability of providers. Bozeman and Johnson (2014) cite welfare checks not being distributed due to the lack of public personnel as an example of a failure, but see the multiple avenues for rapid and secure delivery of income tax refunds as a success. Another example of a policy failure when evaluated against this criterion is the controversy that has plagued the Veterans Affairs Administration (VA), which has faced a demand for benefits from wounded and disabled veterans that has continually exceeded the number of claims the agency has been able to process. Recent estimates suggest there are just under 600,000 claims that have been pending for over 125 days (Dao 2013). This massive backlog has been attributed to low-performing or inadequately trained employees, inefficient claims review processes, and outdated technologies (Veterans Benefits Administration 2013). Despite having an agency in place to provide a benefit that is highly valued by the majority of Americans, the demand for veteran benefits has continually surpassed the availability of the VA to provide them.

Short time horizon. This criterion indicates that a short-term time horizon is employed when a longer-term view shows that a set of actions is counter to public values. For example, a county may adopt a new policy for its waterways based on consideration of recreation and economic development factors, but fail to consider long-run implications for the changing habitat for wildlife (Bozeman 2003; Bozeman and Johnson 2014). Logar (2011) also identifies short time horizons as a public value failure in his analysis of traditional chemistry as opposed to green chemistry. He argues that traditional chemistry, by "failing to consider the long-term sustainability consequences for new chemicals and processes, chemists and those who fund chemistry, including companies and federal institutions," creates a situation that engenders short time horizon public value failures (Logar 2011, 128). Yet a number of successes can be observed across public policies as well; for example, policies designed to ensure the long-term viability of pensions (Bozeman and Johnson 2014), or redesigned education evaluation systems that evaluate school performance with metrics that extend beyond high school graduation rates to consider career or postsecondary outcomes of students from preschool through the twelfth grade.

Substitutability versus conservation of resources. Public value failures can occur when policies focus on substitutability (or indemnification) even in cases where there is no satisfactory substitute. For example, although government contracts with private-sector companies require contractors to post bond-ensuring indemnification, these contracts may not require similar warrants for public safety (Bozeman and Johnson 2014). This is also often applicable in policies that apply to natural resources for which there is no close substitute. The federal government's no-net-loss policy regarding wetlands attempted to prevent this type of public value failure by requiring any wetland acreage diminished by development to be counterbalanced by reclamation or restoration efforts elsewhere (US Department of Agriculture 2013). A policy that could be considered a public value success when assessed against this criterion is a temporary fishing ban that allows long-term sustainable populations of food fish to replenish.

Threats to subsistence and human dignity. As Bozeman and Johnson note, "Human beings, especially the vulnerable, should be treated with dignity, and, in particular, their subsistence should not be threatened" (2014, 7). Thus, policies that produce threats to subsistence and human dignity are policies that produce public value failures. Examples of policies that could be deemed failures when assessed against this criterion abound, including policies that promote or allow for political imprisonment. Of course, there are a number of examples of success as well. In the United States alone there are numerous federal, state, and local policies designed to protect or serve children, the mentally ill, the economically disadvantaged, or individuals with limited English proficiency.

It is important to note that not all of the criteria described above are relevant in all cases: some may be more or less useful in evaluating or predicting outcomes depending on the context of the policy, program, innovation, or agency. Furthermore, this set of criteria should not be thought of as exhaustive; additional public failure criteria can be added, provided they are appropriate and justified.

Step 3: Mapping Values

One of the difficulties in value analysis is that analysts fail to consider interrelationships among values (Gaus 1990). PVM offers a way to overcome this challenge, in that step 3 requires relationships between values to be mapped (see table 9.1). Factor analysis, a multivariate statistical technique, is a useful methodology at this stage because it allows value statements to be grouped based on their factor loading scores and for the explanatory power of each factor to be considered based on its eigenvalue.

Step 4: Considering Relationships between Public Value and Market Failures and Successes

The final stage of PVM is to consider the relationship between public value failure or success and market failure or success. While scholars have long recognized the tension that exists between market-based criteria such as efficiency and public value criteria such as resource conservation (Norton and Tomen 1997; Page 1977), the PVM grid allows for a graphic representation and explicit consideration of these tensions (see figure 9.1). The idea is that any policy, program, innovation, or agency under analysis can be charted based on its public value and market value successes and failures. To take an extreme example, slave labor may be the most cost-effective way of producing a good or service, but it also presents a heinous threat to human dignity and is in direct opposition to the US Constitution, so it would be placed in

Figure 9.1   The PVM grid
Source: Adapted from Bozeman 2002. Used by permission of John Wiley & Sons, Inc.

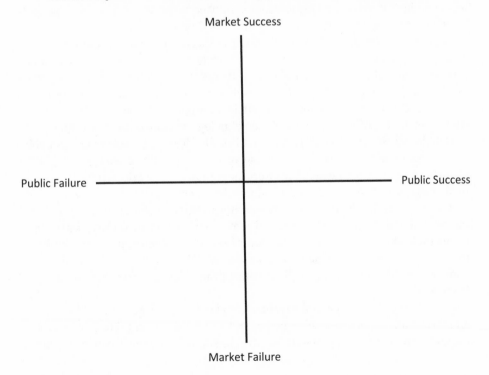

Market Success

Public Failure

Public Success

Market Failure

the upper left quadrant of the PVM grid. Placement on the grid need not be precise, but should be made with consideration for both the public value assessment and market-based indicators. Economic assessments can be conducted using a variety of evaluative tools such as cost-benefit analysis.

In sum, PVM is a conceptual tool that is applicable to the analysis of public mission fulfillment (Bozeman 2003). When used in conjunction with market-based tools, PVM allows for a deeper and richer discussion around policy implications and serves as a vehicle to drive the consideration of public values forward. The next section provides evidence for how PVM can be utilized to enhance our understanding of social impacts.

APPLICATIONS OF PVM

To date, the majority of explicit PVM applications have been in the realm of science policy (Bozeman 2003; Bozeman and Sarewitz 2005, 2011; Fisher et al. 2010; Gaughan 2003; Gupta 2003; Hays and Guston [n.d.]; Logar 2011; Maricle 2011; Meyer 2011; Slade 2011; Valdivia 2011). This work aims to use PVM to help shape science policy decisions by providing a fuller picture of what is being accomplished through publically supported scientific endeavors. As mentioned previously, these uses of PVM fall into three key categories: (1) examining the social impact that KVCs engender or could engender (Bozeman et al. 2003); (2) evaluating the extent to which public values are met within agencies, programs, and communities (Bozeman 2007); and (3) detailing the relationships and linkages among public values and their implications. Notably, the last two categories are suggestive of ways in which PVM can be expanded and applied in areas outside of science policy. Examples of each of these uses are discussed below.

The first category of PVM application is specific to science policy in that it focuses on the knowledge value collective. As mentioned previously, these applications often make use of churn theory, a theory with specific explanatory power for these applications. Slade (2011) takes this approach in her evaluation of nanomedicine. She identifies prominent stakeholder groups in the nanomedicine KVC—such as members of the National Nanotechnology Initiative, the US Department of Health and Human Services Office of Minority Health, and other various public and private research and health related agencies—and then uses content analysis to identify public value statements in over one hundred public documents produced by these groups. She focuses specifically on statements related to equity and finds that documents that address basic research very rarely include equity value statements, while those that address applied research often include these types of statements even when the same entity produces both sets of documents. Slade indicates that PVM can function to help members of the KVC identify these types of disconnects in their value pursuits and work toward a more integrated public value framework.

Another, and perhaps more typical, application of PVM is the identification and discussion of public value successes and failures. Gaughan (2003) provides an example; she evaluated public initiatives in support of breast cancer research.

Gaughan has conducted two separate case studies: one focuses on federal government efforts at cancer research, and the second examines efforts in the state of Georgia. In both cases she first identifies the relevant public values related to cancer research by examining policy documents, mission statements, and other pertinent public statements. She then discusses social outcome indicators that can be used to measure progresses toward these broader public value goals. Next she describes relevant institutional actors and their roles in cancer research efforts. She then reviews the current state of research programs at both the state and federal levels and discusses points of weakness where public value failures either have occurred or could potentially occur in the future. In this way public value mapping functions as both a prospective and retrospective evaluation tool. In particular, Gaughan states that the cancer research initiatives in the state of Georgia are too new to gauge their success in terms of social outcomes. However, applying PVM reveals lessons that agency managers and other policymakers can employ in future decision making. Conversely, PVM applied to federal breast cancer research efforts reveal several areas where public value goals are not being met and public failures are occurring. Gaughan argues that there are four particular areas of weakness. First, she notes a lack of integration and accountability in research efforts, finding that the National Cancer Institute is not fully integrated into the publicly sanctioned hierarchies for articulating and meeting social goals (Gaughan 2003, 63). Next she finds a concentration on microlevel cancer research—or a focus on cellular (and smaller) solutions to cancer—that she argues has led to biases and norms that privilege micro-perspectives over meso- and macrolevel perspectives that "may have greater potential for population impact" (Gaughan 2003, 63). She also finds that lagged effects and unclear prioritization from the National Cancer Institute's peer review process, as well as a lack of diversity in the knowledge value collective—meaning other relevant disciplinary perspectives, social institutions, and actors that could contribute in meaningful ways to cancer research—have failed to be incorporated (Gaughan 2003, 63). In this case she suggests that policymakers should use PVM evaluations to recalibrate efforts and address these areas of weakness.

A third category of the PVM approach focuses on the relationships among public values in an agency or a program's constellation of public values with an emphasis on the impact that these relationships have to public value outcomes. Maricle (2011) illustrates this approach in her assessment of the current state of US earthquake and hurricane research. She reviews legislation and academic literature and identifies increased resilience as the key public value goal of these types of research programs. Although both areas of scientific inquiry are aimed at producing the same public value (resilience), Maricle argues that each field has its own "public value logic" that results in the pursuit of divergent pathways to attain resilience (2011, 103). She illustrates the differing logics with two alternative conceptual models that are based on the idea that two secondary or instrumental values are necessary to achieve the core value of resilience; these two values are high-quality science and useful knowledge. Maricle argues that in hurricane research it is more common for the relationship between high-quality science and useful knowledge to be hierarchical, with high-quality science as the chief value.

On the other hand, she asserts that the two values are weighted equally in earthquake research. The result is that transparency, responsiveness, and collaboration are promoted in earthquake research, whereas there is a lack of these three values in hurricane research. She then plots public and market value successes and failures on the PVM grid for both research fields. The majority of earthquake research outcomes fall into the public value success quadrants, whereas most hurricane research outcomes are plotted as public value failures (see figure 9.1).

In this way Maricle demonstrates that with PVM it is not only possible to evaluate a single research program for public value failures but also to offer a means of broad-gauge comparison for two research programs that are in pursuit of the same constellations of public values. This type of approach can also have a single program focus and can be used to evaluate whether the logic of public value relationships are coherent (Meyer 2011). Incoherent public value logic within a program or agency contributes to explanations of public value failures as well as failures to achieve agency goals and missions.

While PVM has most commonly been used to evaluate science policies, it is not necessary that it be restricted solely to such applications; it also shows promise as a tool in other areas of policy research and evaluation. In particular, scholars in the fields of public administration and management have incorporated public value failure theory in their work, although they have not necessarily engaged in all four stages of PVM analysis outlined herein (Chen 2009; Feeney and Bozeman 2007; Beck Jørgensen and Bozeman 2002; Moulton 2009). For example, Feeney and Bozeman (2007) use the public value criteria outlined in table 1.1 as a tool for analyzing the public failures associated with the 2004–5 flu vaccine shortage.[3] Using a case study approach, they review the vaccine shortage across each of the criterion and find evidence of public value failures in all but one area (conservation of resources). Their analysis is similar to the approach taken by Gaughan (2003) in her evaluation of breast cancer research, but the authors stop short of identifying a conceptual model of the linkages among public values and mapping public value successes and failures on the PVM grid. Work in this vein could be extended in health policy analysis or other public policy domains, however. Taken together, the stages of PVM can serve as a tool kit for a wide range of policy areas and can offer more robust explanations of both policy problems and solutions.

CONCLUSIONS

Despite its considerable limitations, PVM has one overriding advantage: it at least seeks to identify and track the course of public value attainment (and failure) where "public value" is not coterminous with marginal economic benefit, economic productivity, or economic development. It recognizes that there are factors, ones important to citizens in democratic systems, that are not captured in any extant economic approach to impact assessment. To date, the factors that have largely been considered in PVM applications are those related to technology, innovation, and research outcomes, but there is nothing inherent in the design of PVM that limits its scope to the science and technology policy realm. For example, components of PVM could be applied to address a number of questions within the field of public administration:

- Are managers' knowledge of and commitment to public values related to their public service motivation?
- Do linkages among public values (hierarchical ordering, for example) affect managerial and stakeholder power relationships?
- How do broad public values inform managerial ethics?
- What social outcome measures should be included in agency, policy, and program evaluations?
- Are agencies that underperform based on market criteria also underperforming in their achievement of public values?
- What does a public values approach suggest for accountability measures?
- Are agencies in pursuit of similar constellations of public values more likely to have similar organizational structures?
- How is organizational capacity tied to public value failure?
- How do public value chains develop in and among networked actors?

As mentioned previously, many PVM applications are derived from public failure theory, but this does not mean that PVM applications cannot also be informed by Moore's approach to creating public values. In fact, part of Moore's strategic triangle suggests that managers should ensure that their actions are *delivering public value to the citizenry*. To aid in this process, managers might employ the PVM tool as a means of strategically planning or analyzing their own decision making processes or policies.

Still, PVM remains in an early stage of development. The fact that applications vary from one to another to such a high degree is symptomatic of this early stage development but at the same time show that the approach is robust and flexible. PVM may seem to be going in several directions at once, but another view is that it is rapidly evolving and it seems likely that those interested in public values in science and technology, as well as those simply interested in identifying approaches that do not rely entirely on traditional neoclassical economic thinking, will play a role in shaping PVM evolution, retaining promising adaptations, and discarding maladaptations.

In PVM's focus on public values it is easy to overlook the "M": mapping. The mapping aspect of PVM is an important attribute, however, because it implies that analyses must necessarily be dynamic and longitudinal, not just short case studies or cross-sectional data analyses. From the standpoint of technical progress, most has been in the nature of the mapping, ranging from carefully concatenated case studies to large-scale analyses of legislative maps and their correspondence to outcomes. But much more technical work is required, especially mapping approaches that can easily be described and straightforwardly replicated.

Another major concern for PVM is to provide a stronger theory basis. To some extent the churn theory of innovation has served as scaffolding for PVM research and, indeed, the churn theory does seem to be consonant with the methodological assumptions and evaluation approach of PVM. However, the connection between public failure theory, churn theory, and PVM could be further developed. Additional explanatory theories are also warranted to move PVM application beyond the science, technology, and research innovation realm. Future work needs to provide more concrete linkages between PVM and its theoretical base and, indeed, other theories of social innovation; otherwise, PVM is likely to remain a novelty rather than a widely accepted, useful tool for improving our valuation of public values in the policy process.

NOTES

1. A more expansive discussion of these two approaches can be found in Bryson, Crosby, and Bloomberg's chapter 1 and "Conclusions" in this volume, and elsewhere (Bryson, Crosby, and Bloomberg 2014; Davis and West 2009; Meynhardt and Bartholomes 2011).
2. The full set of core characteristics of the University System of Georgia can be accessed at http://gradschool.uga.edu/about/mission.html.
3. Feeney and Bozeman (2007) apply all criteria except for the two recent additions advanced by Bozeman and Johnson (2014).

10

PUBLIC VALUE

TURNING A CONCEPTUAL FRAMEWORK INTO A SCORECARD

TIMO MEYNHARDT

Public value "may, just possibly and as a result of the current tumultuous events, turn out to be the next 'Big Thing'" (Talbot 2009, 167). Or, in other words, "Creating public value is a hot topic" (Bryson, Crosby, and Bloomberg 2014, 445). Given the recent financial crisis, the massive loss of trust in managers, and the issues of corporate actions' unintended consequences or side effects, this topic is specifically of interest to businesses, public administrations, and nongovernmental organizations (NGOs) alike. Organizations in all sectors not only face legitimacy issues but also need to further develop their risk management with regard to social impacts. Last but not least, public value offers a new perspective to achieve innovation and growth. Public value's promise is not to supersede economic perspectives but to combine objective *and* subjective performance factors into a coherent framework. It may be seen as a way to contextualize financial and nonfinancial performance within a larger picture of human values established in the public sphere and in society at large.

Across sectors, the common denominator of shared interest in public value may be the quest for a deeper understanding of any organizational entity's contributions to the broader public—that is, to the making of community and society (Tönnies 2001). Against the larger context of "modernity" (Habermas 1988) with its changing nature of "moral commonwealth" (Selznick 1994), one may even argue that organizations cannot escape the constant challenge to create and renew normative narratives and to reflect about identity and value issues.

Thus, public value creation does not only concern democratic values, nor is it simply a means to overcome individualistic tendencies. A focus on public value avoids general deontological notions but seeks to take into account existing local deontologies and value systems. It is basically a contingent idea and draws our attention to the mechanism of how people draw value from the collective (public value as a resource for the individual), and how the experience of a collective emerges out of individual and social interactions with organizations in some way (the individual as a source of public value). On a fundamental level, relationships involving the public help people to grow, develop, and become socialized.

From a management perspective, this view shifts the focus of value creation from a narrow financial-economic performance perspective to a broader concept of value creation that maintains and influences individual well-being as well as societal progress. In this sense, public value redefines the whole notion of value creation.

Organizations contribute to the many relationships between the individual and the collective (society, community, etc.). A public value lens reveals how an organization links to its wider community and where the gaps or potentials for improvement are. Consider not only a public administration or a company, but also a soccer club or a public swimming pool: all institutions provide opportunities to engage with the public and draw value from it. Ultimately, public value shows managers where they might over- or underestimate the value they wish to create. For instance, it may be contested whether certain products or services serve a legitimate cause in society, or whether people are really prepared to pay more for more ethically sound products. Or consider a public good (e.g., internal security) that only becomes a public value if people value it. This also holds true for highly normative concepts—such as sustainability initiatives or corporate social responsibility approaches—that cannot simply claim to be taken for granted. Organizations both moderate and mediate how an individual is attracted to, or repelled by, collectively shared values that characterize a certain community and society.

Public value is value from and for the public. In my view, the public value construct is a way of looking at organizational impacts on people's experience of the public as well as of taking into account the reflexive, value-laden nature of organizational performance. Furthermore, it helps conceptualize value creation as a deeply interactive process in which different actors contribute and share both the benefits and the risks. It constitutes a way of combining and integrating one-sided approaches that favor one perspective over others—for instance, shareholder value, citizen value, and customer value but also stakeholder value, corporate social responsibility, and sustainability.

In this chapter I will describe a practical tool—the public value scorecard (PVSC). I build on my previous research and seek to help managers in business, nonprofit, and government organizations to better understand different aspects of public value creation in their daily operations. The chapter's main purpose is to present a description and illustration of the PVSC against the background of underlying theoretical conceptualization (see, e.g., Meynhardt 2009; Meynhardt and Bartholomes 2011). Following the main elements of this definition, I will describe the foundations before I turn to the method. The text is structured in a way that enables the reader to skip the theoretical section and jump to the description of the tool right away. Nonetheless, I advise reading the entire text before using the PVSC, as a proper use of the tool requires a grasp of the underlying theory.

THEORETICAL BACKGROUND

Several interdisciplinary sources (e.g., administrative science, philosophy, and psychology) fuel the public value discourse. Public value provides a platform for dialogue among different disciplines, which may be considered one of its key strengths. At a deeper level, public value is a regulative idea. It can be seen as a managerial

Table 10.1. Theoretical concepts and their consequences for a public value scorecard

Theoretical Concept	PVSC Consequence
Value exists in relationships	A measurement should focus on actions or any action-oriented characteristics that describe a relationship, not on values (as nouns) in isolation. A valuing subject and an object of valuation must be present. The aggregation of individual assessments may be viewed as an expression of a collectively existing public value. Public value as a collectively shared value is not constructed as a sum of individual values, but their common and overlapping meaning about the quality of a relationship involving the public shall be regarded as an embodiment of it.
The public is inside	There is no objective public dimension, independent of subjective meaning. Rather, "the public" (or a number of publics) as a gestalt exists in the form of psychological reality, which may take different forms and shapes. Therefore, a scorecard should consider the different publics and operationalize which part of social reality is the focus.
Public value is grounded in basic needs	A measurement can have many objects to be valued (products, services, institutions, etc.); it can credibly rely on a limited number of basic value dimensions—moral-ethical, hedonistic-aesthetic, instrumental-utilitarian and political-social, which are rooted in psychological needs theory. They can be used for combinations and more fine-grained subdimensions (e.g., as a limited number of Lego pieces for kids provide a basis for almost any imaginable construction). A PVSC cannot rely on a hierarchy of needs or values, but should treat them without a normative a priori.
Public value creation: perceived—not delivered—and relative	A measurement must focus on human perception, not on pure facts, which only give rise to emerging valuations. Assessing public value creation thus involves measuring subjective meaning and value. It should also not limit itself to certain value contexts or political systems (e.g., democracy) but should allow for perceptions that acknowledge the whole range of human experience. Such a nonnormative approach is seen as a prerequisite for public value relevance and acceptance in different sectors and political contexts.

way to consider notions such as the common good, public interest, or *bonum commune*—that is, a way that complements a legal perspective and the operationalization of philosophical ideas.

Public value *creation* suggests a more active and even entrepreneurial perspective on how organizations shape and cocreate our experience of society and social reality; it has been defined as "any impact on shared experience about the quality of the relationship between the individual and 'society'" (Meynhardt 2009, 212).

More concretely, public value creation "is situated in relationships between the individual and 'society,' founded in individuals, constituted by subjective evaluations against basic needs, activated by and realized in emotional-motivational states, and produced and reproduced in experience-intense practices" (Meynhardt 2009, 212). In this sense, public value is only created or destroyed when individual experience and behavior of individuals and groups are influenced in a way that they (de)stabilize social order evaluations, sense of community, and self-determination in a societal context. Along these lines, public value is seen as a result of valuing processes, which are collective and social in their very nature.

Such a microfoundation of public value—at the individual and social levels—might also help relate other public value approaches (e.g., Bozeman 2007; Moore 1995, 2013) to psychological realities on which people act. Ultimately they form the basis for any attempt to account, understand, or even manage public value.

As Baran notes, "In general, 'value' refers to something which—for whatever reason—is emphasized in reality and desirable and forceful for the one who evaluates, be it an individual, a societal group, or an institution representing individuals or groups" (1991, 806, my translation). "Desirability" may be seen as a synonym, or at least a reference to preference, appreciation, or object of need. Regardless of the philosophical perspective, a notion of being attracted to something is always part of the value terminology. Whether implicit or explicit, "value" manifests "in two directions, that of discourse and that of overt action" (Rescher 1982, 3).

This line of argument leads directly to (socio)psychological inquiry into antecedents and the states of subjects (individual, group, nations) to understand how public value emerges and evolves over time. It also leads us to a perspective in which value is in the eye of the beholder or, as Talbot puts it, "Public value is what the public values" (2006, 7).

I now consider in more detail several theoretical issues and what their consequences are for a public value scorecard (see table 10.1).

Value Exists in Relationships

Before discussing the idea of "the public," I shall argue that subjectivity is central to both value and public value. I will focus on the question of what value is because I assume that the answer to this has consequences for the methodology of the PVSC.

A long philosophical debate has occurred between value objectivists and value subjectivists. In short, value objectivists (e.g., Husserl, Scheler, and Windelband) saw value as a characteristic of an object (almost physically attached to it); the question remained how such value could be identified and experienced. For value subjectivists (e.g., Ehrenfels, Meinong, and Menger), value was not inherent in an object; they argued that something *has* a value—that is, that value is only agreed upon by actively valuing or evaluating subjects. The result of the debate between the two camps is very relevant for public value research, since it confronts us with the question of how public value is detected or constructed. Does it exist independent of individuals?

The ideas that value is only to be identified (objectivists) and that value is only subjective (subjectivists) are not very convincing. The value philosopher Johannes Erich Heyde (1926), who argued against both a metaphysical perspective and an overemphasis of human consciousness, presents a strong synthesis for our inquiry of value objectivist and value subjectivist positions. His solution, which I follow here, is the idea that value is a *result of a relationship* between a subject that is valuing an object and the valued object. Therefore, value exists in the relationship, not outside it; value is not a characteristic of an object, but describes the subject-object relationship. In Heyde's words, "Value is the relationship" (1926, 77, my translation). Without a subject, there is no value. In this sense, value is subjective. As a subject relates to an object, in the act of valuation or evaluation, value comes into being. Value is "value for a subject" (Heyde, 46, my translation). In this view value is always bound to relationships and is relative; it always takes subjects to call a value into existence.

Speaking of "value" as a noun is misleading, since it suggests the independent existence of a value (e.g., freedom, beauty) if it implies an ontological status independent of a relationship. A value can become objective if different subjects share a valuation. If this is a social phenomenon, one can talk about a collectively shared value. Public value can be seen as a shared or collectively held value about the quality of a relationship involving the public.

The Public Is Inside

Public value is not simply sharing values about anything; it is about sharing the individual's experience of a social environment or "the public." Thus, public value is not limited to either businesses, public administrations, or NGOs, since the individual relates to multiple institutions that contribute to his or her perception of the public.

The idea of the public is vague and serves as a regulative idea that helps us organize our experiences. Its different meanings (Frederickson 1991) are often related to a notion of a collective property—that is, something that is not to be reduced to the sum of its members. This reference to the whole (e.g., society, community, the common good, etc.) is an abstraction "generated on the basis of experiences made in daily practices, analytical insight, and all sorts of projections as to complex phenomena" (Meynhardt 2009, 204). Consequently, the public is what an individual or group regards as public, including a number of different (relevant) publics. This idea is crucial for the PVSC, since it requires a methodological idea of how to determine the public(s) under consideration. The rationale behind this view is that "individuals and groups in this view need to act 'as if' (Vaihinger 1911/2008). This constantly (re)negotiated, tested, or invented 'operational fiction' forms the 'Gestalt,' 'generalized other' (Mead 1934/1962) or 'quasi-object' (Latour 1993), as the reference point for action. The 'state,' the 'market,' or the 'society' are emerging functional generalizations, often necessary to arrange and interpret data or events in a meaningful way. Following Luhmann, meaningfulness then is 'a self-referential attitude towards complexity' (Luhmann 1984, 107, own translation)" (Meynhardt 2009, 205).

The public is, in its broadest, a reality construction and exists at the level of human experience—*the public is inside*. Similar to value, the public also comes into existence through an active process of human experience. Public value, then, is influenced when people generalize and value their experience with some social entity (e.g., organizations).

Public Value Is Grounded in Basic Needs

In earlier work I have suggested relating public value to basic needs theory (Meynhardt 2009). The main reason is that we could take advantage of such a public value microfoundation, since public value is always bound to subjects' needs (individuals, groups). Even the act of calling a public into existence—that is, to increase awareness of the public dimension—is motivated and driven by certain needs.

From a logical perspective, basic needs form a basis of evaluation in a subject-object relationship (Iwin 1975). What role do basic needs play? They serve as subjective reference points, whether or not there is a discrepancy between one's needs and the perceived reality. New information is filtered and processed not only cognitively, on the basis of fact, but also emotionally. Valuing is an emotional-motivational process, which is subjective and eludes the notions of right or wrong. Axiologically speaking, objects of evaluation are propositions, and subjects take a position toward them via a value statement. Such a position is the result of a comparison between a perceived actual state and a real, or hypothetical, speculative, or even illusionary optimum. Psychology has developed a number of constructs to study this evaluation process—for instance, emotion, attitude, motive, or fear (Graumann and Willig 1983). As the basis of evaluation, these phenomena can be regarded as initiating forces for valuing processes. It is at this level that value is linked to psychological realities.

One well-known psychological construct, which captures the affective element and the motivational one, is the notion of needs. Needs concern deficits—that is, felt discrepancies between an actual and desired psychological state—that result in a motivation to act. Needs serve as actual or hypothetical reference points for evaluation (Lewis, Haviland-Jones, and Barrett 2008). Therefore, basic needs theory is a good candidate as a tool with which to derive public value dimensions.

Epstein has developed a cognitive-experiential self-theory, in which he describes how "individuals automatically construct an implicit theory of reality" (Epstein 1993, 316; see also Epstein 2003). He distinguishes four equally important basic needs, which are closely related to this personal theory, noting that "the construction of a personal theory of reality is not an exercise undertaken for its own sake. Rather, the theory is a conceptual tool for fulfilling life's most basic psychological functions, namely, assimilating the data of reality within a relatively stable, coherent conceptual system; maintaining a favorable pleasure-pain balance over the anticipated future; maintaining relationships with significant others and maintaining a favorable self-esteem" (Epstein 1989, 8).

These four functions or needs provide a minimal and robust starting point for the development of basic value dimensions. The abstract philosophical notion of desirability is thus traced to a conception of human needs. In this view, these needs are basic or essential: They are about fundamental structures of personality and are functionally extremely relevant. Invalidating them would destabilize the "entire conceptual system" (Epstein 1993, 322).

What is important for the PVSC is that no single motive or need dominates others. As Epstein notes, "Which function, if any, is dominant varies among individuals and within individuals over time" (1989, 8). Epstein relates these functions or needs to values by arguing that people at least "implicitly value" (1989, 16) these when fulfilling their needs. An evaluation of any object against basic needs is called a value. Table 10.2 presents the basic value dimensions that result from the basic needs identified by Epstein.

First, the need for positive self-evaluation concerns a moral-ethical value. It focuses on a person's perception as an individual and human being. This basic need relates to an evaluation of the extent to which an action or decision leads more or less to equality or inequality concerning what is seen as just or unjust in a certain social context. Moral values point to standards that should apply to everyone in a given social environment. Lowering or enhancing self-worth is not moral or immoral per se, but if a person feels that it is not legitimate, then moral-ethical values are violated or invalidated. The individual bar for such an evaluation is a perceived discrepancy between what he or she feels is appropriate or fair and the actual experience. Such a psychological discomfort (Festinger 1957) is always related to one's own self-worth, self-concept, and identity. I talk about a moral-ethical dimension of public value with regard to an organization's impacts on collective moral-ethical values, which contribute to the functioning of a society or community. For example, if the value of human dignity or respect for the individual is profoundly violated, the individual may experience a destruction of

Table 10.2. The relationship between basic needs and basic value dimensions

Basic need for . . .	Translation into a motivation for . . . (examples)	Basic value dimension
positive self-evaluation	• positive self-concept and self-worth • consistent relationship between self and environment • feeling of high self-esteem (in social comparison)	moral-ethical
maximizing pleasure and avoiding pain	• positive emotions and avoidance of negative feelings • flow experience • experience of self-efficacy due to action	hedonistic-aesthetic
gaining control and coherence over one's conceptual system	• understanding and controlling one's environment • predictability of cause-and-effect relationships • ability to control expectations to cause desired outcomes	utilitarian-instrumental
positive relationships	• relatedness and belongingness • attachment, group identity • optimal balance between intimacy and distance	political-social

Source: Adapted from Meynhardt (2009, 203).

public value. A moral-ethical public value is a collectively shared value ascribed to personhood and what it means to be human.

Second, the need to maximize pleasure and avoid pain generally points to an organism's survival. Beyond this evolutionary deeply ingrained motive, it relates to positive experiences and joy. Culturally and socially mediated, new levels of experience come into play. This may range from hedonistic needs to aesthetic preferences. Beauty, happiness, and fun are examples of hedonistic-aesthetic values. Again, people evaluate their experience with organizations or other social entities accordingly—whether it be a public service or a corporation's marketing campaign. A hedonistic-aesthetic public value is a collectively shared value ascribed to pleasure and what it means to create a positive experience.

A third fundamental need pertains to control and coherence in one's conceptual system. People are motivated to maintain or increase their degree of freedom. Solving a problem, understanding the world, and orienting oneself in an environment are all considered fundamental needs; they are about the instrumental-utilitarian aspect of an action or decision, and concern means-to-ends relationships. The question whether something is efficient also belongs in this category. At the public value level, the question is whether or not any product or service provides people with some use value. This may be clear for services such as transportation, communication, and insurance, but less clear, for instance, for financial products, tax policies, and some consumer products.

Although there is no basic need for financial-economic value, money is considered part of instrumental-utilitarian needs. At a conceptual level, even shareholder value and profitability are not opponents of public value. Yet a discounted cash flow, or any public-sector equivalent such as taxes or budget savings, are not yet per se public value *creation*. Only a psychological reality, in which cash flows are appreciated in some way, can be considered value creation. An instrumental-utilitarian public value is a collectively shared value ascribed to utility and what it means to create a benefit efficiently.

A fourth need is the need for positive relationships, which addresses the motive to experience group membership, social identity, and belonging. In contrast to the moral-ethical value dimension, this basic need concerns our social nature, which places value in the group as opposed to the individual. People draw value from this asymmetry between insiders and outsiders. I call this basic value dimension political-social, because it involves diverging group interests and, thus, a power dimension. At the public value level, solidarity, cooperation, status, exclusion, and prejudice belong to this sphere. A political-social public value is a collectively shared value attached to social relationships and what it means to establish positive group relations.

The described dimensional nature of public value grounded in Epstein's basic needs has been empirically validated in the context of a German public administration (Meynhardt and Bartholomes 2011).

Public Value Creation: Perceived—Not Delivered—and Relative

To summarize my argument thus far, value is a result of valuing and "public" is a necessary fiction. The perception of public value is a process subject to human experience and is vulnerable to many distortions and biases. There is no public value without human appraisal. Thus, organizations cannot rely on their intended public value being appreciated, since it cannot simply be delivered but only comes into being at the experience and perception levels.

People perceive public value because they can positively relate their experience of the public to their basic needs. Value drawn from a public experience is considered a public value if it concerns values related to the functioning of a collective, society, or community. The experience of a (de)stabilized social order is seen as instrumental to an individual's perception of the quality of the relationship between the individual and society; if it is positive, public value is created, and if it is negative, public value is destroyed.

Public value lives in relationships and in the eyes of the beholder. This is a relativist approach, since it is not restricted to a specific public value set (e.g., humanistic values). I follow Talbot, who states, "Public Value then is the combined view of the public about what they regard as valuable" (2006, 7). Taking it a step further, such an approach implies that public value is not a synonym for democratic procedures or Western ideas of fairness or justice. Rather, it is open to human nature with all its contradictions and irrationality. Thus, public value is created in every societal or historical context; it is about everything to which people ascribe value with regard to their experience of the public. Such a nonnormative perspective prevents a conception where public value is always a force toward more humanity, or a device to safeguard democracy. It is the extent to which a perceived relationship between an individual or group and some social entity influences the fulfillment, or change, of basic needs. One could think about other resources than the public in which people can fulfill basic needs—for instance, nature, private relationships, self-reflection, or simply withdrawing from social life.

Produced and Reproduced: The Dynamics of Public Value

Public value can be viewed as a mechanism that helps people relate to their wider community and society, and it helps organizations identify the potential for (re)gaining and sustaining legitimate action. Public value is a linkage mechanism between an individual microlevel (not just a person, but also organizational entities) and a collective macrolevel. To better understand such dynamics, self-organization theory is a promising candidate; in its various forms, it provides principles to describe self-organization beyond equilibrium. Here I refer to respective propositions as developed by Haken (1977; see also Haken and Schiepek 2005), and their transfer to the value dynamics realm (Meynhardt 2004).

One of Haken's primary propositions is that of *circular causality*. The basic idea is that interaction between different elements (people, groups, etc.) leads to the emergence of collective properties (e.g., shared worldviews, norms, and values), which in turn promote consensus, coherence, and orientation in chaotic interactions at a microlevel. Once an *order parameter* is established, the individual cannot simply "escape" it. At an experiential level, a person may almost physically experience the pressure or forcefulness of group norms or a social climate. In such emotionally charged situations, public value perception is also activated and realized.

In this view, public values as order parameters only change when a system is critically destabilized (e.g., a massive loss of trust). At these *bifurcation points*, system behavior is largely unpredictable: Different order parameters compete and stabilize each other so that the system fluctuates between different states. External factors (or control parameters) can stimulate destabilization but not intentionally create a specific order parameter. Inner conditions and historically established path dependencies hinder a *linear* intervention.

The basic mechanisms of change in public value are as follows:[1] At the individual level, psychological processes constitute the elements in the system. If an evaluation of an experience emerging from a relationship involving the public is perceived as a positive contribution to one's basic needs (fulfillment), public value is created. The current "personal theory of reality" (Epstein 1993) is stabilized. If there is a negative evaluation (consciously or not), all sorts of psychological mechanisms come into play to accommodate it (e.g., distortion). If the experienced discrepancy is relevant for self-concept, considerable cognitive dissonance is triggered. Past experience is questioned, established practices and routines no longer work, and an individual feels psychological discomfort (Festinger 1957). At least parts of the system no longer work or are invalidated, and public value is destroyed for the individual.

A social system becomes destabilized (far from equilibrium) when many people feel discomfort and new alternatives emerge to deal with that. Following Haken, it is a critical state—far from equilibrium—in which the system's response is not predictable. In such situations, in which many alternatives seem possible, there is a *symmetry* between different solutions that is only broken by choosing one way or the other. If a solution works, it is highly likely that this highly emotional experience is integrated into the value system (*phase transition*) and guides further action. A value is enacted—that is, internalized at the individual level (from macrolevel to microlevel), or socialized (from microlevel to macrolevel). For example, sustainability as a public value is only enacted when people integrate associated attitudes in their mind-sets and behaviors.

FROM PUBLIC VALUE THEORY TO A PUBLIC VALUE SCORECARD (PVSC)[2]

The theoretical framework introduced above has guided and inspired method development since 2009. The different philosophical, sociological, and psychological underpinnings justify the number of methodological steps taken. In particular, they help researchers navigate the manifold empirical challenges and methodological constraints.

Moore (2003, 2013) first used the term "public value scorecard" but is, however, only concerned with public-sector organizations' challenges in democratic societies. His scorecard is conceptualized as a public-sector alternative to the "balanced scorecard," which Kaplan and Norton (1996) developed. Moore builds his approach on a strategic triangle, emphasizing that an administration must build legitimacy and support, as well as organizational capabilities, in order to produce public value. Building on cost-benefit analysis, Moore introduces an account to list different public values (see his contribution, chapter 8 in this volume).

Here I introduce a very different PVSC. It does not address capabilities or support but focuses on de facto public value creation. The PVSC epistemology allows individuals, groups, and organizations to rate the public value creation (intended or realized) of some initiative, service, product, or the like, along five dimensions. Based on needs theory (see table 10.2) there are four dimensions. I have added a fifth (financial-economic), which is theoretically incorporated within the instrumental-utilitarian dimension because practitioners are unlikely to accept a PVSC unless it includes a financial measure.

The view put forward in this chapter is the idea that public value starts and ends within the individual: it is not delivered, but perceived. Public value is therefore measured against individual evaluation, since people act on the basis of meaning they attach to their perception. This approach must not be confused with the idea of measuring individual values. Individual evaluation means that individuals assess the public value of something. Therefore, the PVSC does not ask *What's in it for me?* but forces respondents to reflect on the social impacts and the question *What makes X valuable to society?*

The PVSC takes society to the decision arena and expands the scope of value creation by linking it to a broader value set. By using the PVSC, a manager (or an institution) can now more systematically address the trade-offs between financial and nonfinancial goals and can better identify societal needs and concerns. An overview of exemplary PVSC applications is given in table 10.3.

Applications in different contexts indicate that the five interrelated yet nonsubstitutable dimensions seem to work for practitioners when a public value impact assessment is called for. The nonhierarchical framework is typically well received, since it does not suggest any normative premises. Rather, an organization would relate it to its own values and mission.

Five Different Inquiry Techniques

The PVSC was tailored to the specific strategic challenge of each of the aforementioned cases. The five dimensions of the PVSC are always constant. The method to collect data varies, and includes five different versions (see table 10.4); each version leads to either a public value score or profile, and can be used as either a standalone or a complementary method. In the following, the prioritizing version will be described in more detail than the other three, since all five share certain characteristics despite their different data collection procedures.

Version 1: Prioritizing

This PVSC builds on a trade-off logic. By means of sentence completion it prompts respondents to rank, in order of importance, the five value dimensions in different situations and in respect of opportunities and risks. The PVSC includes eighteen questions (situations) and asks the respondents to rank each value statement from 5 (highest importance) to 1 (lowest importance). There are ninety items (18 × 5). Six questions concern a general assessment, six concern the short-term perspective, and six address the medium-term and long-term perspective. This differentiation allows one to identify sustainability gaps and to operationalize a dynamic perspective of change over time.

Here the PVSC's structure is forced choice ranking. It allows one to analyze each public value dimension independently of other dimensions and their interrelationships. Given the chosen methodology of forced ranking (following the tradition of instruments such as the LIFO Method by Atkins, Katcher, and Porter

Table 10.3. Exemplary PVSC applications

PVSC	No.	Organizational Context	Strategic Challenge	Engagement specifics	Reference
Prioritizing	1	HANIEL — German family holding with multiple businesses	Do we need to disinvest due to a potential threat for the firm's public value?	Board workshop, part of CR strategy	Müller, Menz, and Meynhardt 2013; in press.
	2	TAKKT AG BUSINESS EQUIPMENT SOLUTIONS — German business equipment	What are public value consequences if we establish direct sourcing with Asia?	Expert workshop, decision-making support	Müller, Menz, and Meynhardt, in press.
	3	Die Mobiliar Versicherungen & Vorsorge — Swiss insurance company	What are implications for our public value if we would acquire a specific company?	Board workshop, sample of opinion leaders	Meynhardt, Gomez, and Schweizer 2014
Screening	4	Bundesagentur für Arbeit — Federal Employment Agency in Germany	How can we assess the social impact and innovativeness of project proposals?	Budget decisions, Leadership workshop with 120 managers	Weise and Deinzer 2013
	5	Deutsche Gesellschaft für das Badewesen e.V. — PV award for public swimming pool in Germany	How can we analyze and award public baths with the highest public value?	Since 2010 biannual process, with jury workshops	Ochsenbauer and Ziemke-Jerrentrup 2013
	6	iF PUBLIC VALUE AWARD IMPACT BY DESIGN — iF Public Value Award for innovative projects	How can we analyze and award projects addressing megatrends around the globe?	Start in 2015; online and offline jury around the globe	www.ifdesign.de

	Organization	Question	Method/Sample	Publication
Surveying				
7	German medical supply (renal dialysis)	How can we better understand the public value of dialysis clinics in the UK?	Sample of partners (e.g., doctors and politicians)	Armsen et al. 2013
8	Federal Employment Agency in Germany	How does public value relate to customer satisfaction and controlling data?	Time series of 1,000 employers across the country	Not before 2015
9	Deutsche Auslandsschulen (German Schools Abroad)	How can we better legitimize our contribution to society?	Internal view (300 managers)	WDA 2013
10	German soccer club	How can we sustain our public value in the light of our growth strategy?	Expert interviews with experts (e.g., fans, media, managers)	Beringer and Bernard 2013; Meynhardt et al., 2015
Exploring				
11	Goethe Institute, a German cultural association	What is our institution's public value? How can we improve our public value strategy?	Interviews with managers and stakeholders; board workshop	Schulze 2010; Meynhardt, Maier, and Schulze 2010
12	German Stock Exchange	Shareholder value or common good: what is our public value?	Focus on middle management	Meynhardt and Müller 2013
13	Deutsche Auslandsschulen (German Schools Abroad)	How can we better legitimize our contribution to society?	External view (25 interviews)	WDA, 2013
Sensing				
14	Swiss multinational food and beverage company	What are the most pressing public value issues as discussed in social media?	Automated semantic analysis over three weeks all over the world in multiple social media channels (ca. 4500 statements)	No publication

Table 10.4. Five different PVSC versions

	Prioritizing	Screening	Surveying	Exploring	Sensing
Main characteristic	Forced choiced ranking questionnaire	Facilitated group discussion	Likert scale–based questionnaire	Hybrid between qualitative and quantitative approaches	Automated Social Media Analysis
Typical application area	Project or product evaluation	Evaluating ideas, award juries	Survey-based stakeholder dialogue	Exploring public value in different publics	Any online channel
Scope	Workshop setting, small surveys ($n < 100$)	Workshop setting, online assessment	Survey ($n > 100$)	Expert interviews ($n < 100$)	Entire web-based communication

1967), the sum of all dimensions is always constant. The advantage of this restriction is increased validity owing to the induced permanent call for trading off different values. As a result, the profile shows the dimensions' relative importance and indicates trade-offs. Several challenges with ipsative forced ranking data concern the replication of the factor structure (Baron 1996; Meade 2004). In each adaptation of the questionnaire's items, this issue has been solved through extensive validation procedures in the field—for instance, in focus groups and expert ratings.

Table 10.5 shows all the questions and value statements for a generic version of a prioritized PVSC, which must be adapted to a specific context. For example, instead of an initiative, the inquiry might be about a tangible product or a service. The questions remain basically the same, but the value statements are tailored to the object of valuation. For example, the assessment of a local project to combat unemployment involves different political aspects, compared to the assessment of a potential takeover target in a merger and acquisition context.

In table 10.5 we can also see that the PVSC comprises not only questions on general opportunities and risks but also statements with a process view (short-term, long-term); this allows the dimension to be analyzed in more detail. Thus, a specification concerns the time frame under consideration, which varies among different organizations.

The completion of the questionnaire takes approximately fifteen to twenty minutes. The respondent ranks all five answers as regards each statement according to their relative importance or fulfillment.

For example, an *initiative* may solve a problem (instrumental-utilitarian) and may also consider different group interests (political-social) very well. The respondent is still forced to differentiate between the two public values and ranks the

Table 10.5. PVSC questions and value statements (generic)

		The aims of the initiative convince me, because they . . .	Not carrying out the initiative would above all prevent . . .	The chances of the initiative being successful in the end are great because . . .
Opportunities	General	are factually and technically coherent	a solution with innovative content being tried out	the content is well thought out
		do not regard human aspects as merely a means to an end	an important contribution to more fairness being made	the matter is not just legal but also perfectly legitimized
		incorporate different interests appropriately	the politically favorable situation being utilized	a wide range of interests is being appropriately considered
		are oriented to the satisfaction and well-being of those involved	the public image of those initiating the initiative being improved	those involved predominantly recognize the opportunities it gives them
		are financially and economically attractive	a lucrative investment being made	there is the prospect of making a profit
	Short-Term	**I believe that the initiative will be successful within a short time because . . .**	**It is immediately obvious that . . .**	**It will quickly become apparent that . . .**
		the fitness for purpose of the content will be recognized	the initiative makes sense	the objectives are achievable
		nobody suffers on a personal level	the self-worth of those involved will be increased	those in charge handle gray areas fairly
		it does not trigger any insuperable political controversies	any power conflicts that occur will not impede the initiative	conflicts that arise are dealt with constructively
		it provides fun and pleasure	those involved associate good and enjoyable experiences with it	the welfare of all is taken into consideration appropriately
		it is being handled appropriately economically	the initiative pays off financially	funding is being used sensibly

(continued)

text continues on page 164

Table 10.5. (continued)

	I am convinced that the initiative will also gain recognition in the medium- to long-term, because . . .	Over time it will be recognized that . . .	In retrospect, the initiative will be acknowledged in that . . .
Opportunities / Long-Term	the cost-benefit ratio is right	the content is worth the expenditure	the quality of the approach is right
	the matter is fair and just	the dignity of the individual is strengthened	the leap of faith is justified
	there is a balance of interests	there is a positive effect on relationships between groups	the cohesion of different groups is being influenced positively
	it helps meet important needs	the satisfaction of those involved increases	it provides fun and pleasure
	those involved will benefit materially from it	the financial resources are being used sensibly	it is worthwhile from an economic point of view

	In my view the greatest risks for the initiative are that . . .	When difficulties loom, the initiative will be reproached most for . . .	I believe that in the end the initiative is most likely to fail because . . .
Risks / General	there is too much emphasis on the current level of knowledge	not solving any really relevant problems	it is not possible to make the ideas comprehensible
	reservations on moral grounds are not dealt with honestly	having excessive moral expectations	people will have suspicions about the good intentions
	not enough attention is paid to the political effects	provoking tension between people in an irresponsible way	it does not achieve social balance
	there is no agreement among those involved	tacitly approving disproportionate individual hardship	too few people really have fun with it
	the costs are being underestimated	not working efficiently economically	financial or cost objectives are not being achieved

	With the initiative there is a risk in the short-term that . . .	The initiative is particularly vulnerable in the current situation because . . .	A failure would above all immediately . . .
Short-term	initiatives in this field that are at least as important will be dropped	the technically superior quality of the approach is not being adequately acknowledged	exacerbate material problems
	our own credibility will suffer	there are doubts whether it would also be equitable under pressure	do irreparable moral damage
	relationships among those involved will be adversely affected	existing relationship structures are being queried	put a strain on existing cooperative relationships
	too few people will be positively motivated	at the beginning it will involve losses for different parties in the first place	adversely affect the well-being of those involved
	there will be a shortage of funding elsewhere	the actual financial effects are still unclear	cause financial losses
	As things stand today it seems to me that it is very uncertain in the medium to long term whether . . .	**In the longer term it appears particularly uncertain whether . . .**	**In the medium- to long-term one might pay the price in that . . .**
Long-term	the expected long-term benefits will occur	the solution is sound and viable enough	the path for other solutions is being obstructed once and for all
	the moral and ethical claim will be realized	all will keep to their word	new injustices arise
	it will ever be accepted in the public power and relationship structure	those involved will deal with each other in a professional and cooperative way	prejudice between groups increase
	it will gain positive feedback from third parties	the results will be perceived as rewarding	too many people are dissatisfied
	the potential financial yield will be exploited	the necessary funding can be found	the economic results are not being properly appreciated

Risks

other three accordingly. Each answer is attached to one of the five PVSC dimensions. This specific data-gathering technique calls for value judgments as a means to also foster rather implicit valuation processes. It is important to clearly define the evaluation object (project, policy, product, etc.) and what is meant by the public in a concrete measurement (e.g., a local or national perspective). Another important step is the careful consideration of the respondents—that is, which public(s) is/are being called into existence. In a number of projects the organizations wanted to give their managers and employees a voice and to contrast self-perceptions with third-party evaluation (e.g., customers, lobby groups, media, citizens, or business partners).

In its most general form, this data gathering leads to a pentagonal profile indicating perceived public value creation opportunities and risks. The scores of each of the five dimensions are computed from the forced ranking results and translated into a managerial perspective. The labeling may vary according to the cultural context (business, nonprofit, or public administration). One often used version is:

- Utilitarian-instrumental values (1): Is it useful?
- Utilitarian-instrumental values (2): Is it profitable?
- Moral-ethical values: Is it decent?
- Political-social values: Is it politically acceptable?
- Hedonistic-aesthetic values: Is it a positive experience?

Figure 10.1 shows the profile of an assessment of a business divestment decision at Haniel, a German family holding (see no. 1 in table 10.3). After an accounting procedure and cost-benefit analysis had been done, Haniel wanted to assess the public value consequences. Clearly there was no simple cut-off point ("make or break") or significant threshold between the opportunities and the risks. From a business perspective (usefulness and profitability), the opportunities (the solid line) clearly outweighed the risks (the dotted line). A conflict emerged between the moral-ethical dimension and the political-social one, however. Whereas the project was seen as bearing a moral risk, the political dimension appeared less risky.[3] This assessment was carried out by the board, which subsequently decided to validate its view by extending the assessment to the investors and external stakeholders. In effect, the board welcomed the broader perspective as instrumental to the decision-making process. In particular, the managers expanded their views on what is legitimate beyond a purely legal or economic perspective. In a manager's words, "It helps us to not only see the pain, but also the gain." As a result, Haniel decided to continue the operations. Further, the management decided to better manage the obvious tensions by establishing a better monitoring system and engaging in dialogue with the stakeholders.

It should be noted that the methodology also provides a differentiated view of how sustainable any public value creation may be. The data used for the general profile is also analyzed from a time perspective. For example, the PVSC shows whether the moral opportunities are or are not sustainable over time. Figure 10.2 illustrates how the PVSC reveals potential sustainability gaps and how it indicates an anticipated change over time.

Figure 10.1   The public value scorecard (illustrative)

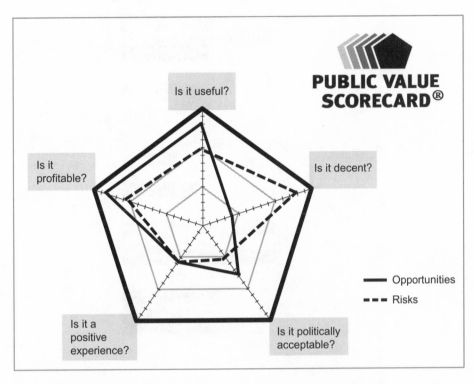

This example from the aforementioned divestment decision (see no. 1 in table 10.3) shows that the opportunities in the moral dimension are decreasing and the risks are increasing over time. However, the opportunities and risks for the business' financial return are decreasing over time.

This type of inquiry was also used in the managerial quest to reconfigure a part of the value chain of TAKKT, a business equipment firm—that is, to also extend the supply chain to Asian countries, with their different values and regulations (see no. 2 in table 10.3). This prioritizing version was likewise chosen for Mobiliar, a Swiss insurance company, which was interested in assessing the public value consequences of a potential takeover (see no. 3 in table 10.3).

Version 2: Screening
This PVSC version builds on consensus building in a dialogue format. The Federal Employment Agency in Germany used this version in a leadership workshop to assess projects that had potential both for public value creation and destruction (see no. 4 in table 10.3). Each situation involved a risky strategy, and reputations were at stake. Besides the large budgets or costs, the societal implications were of paramount importance in the management decision. Ten projects creating new services were introduced to a jury, which discussed and scored each dimension in respect of each project individually. Beforehand, each public value dimension was characterized by only three indicators so that it could be dealt with in a facilitated group discussion. In Germany, a jury deciding on a public value award for public

Figure 10.2   Assessment of changes in opportunities and risks over time (illustrative)

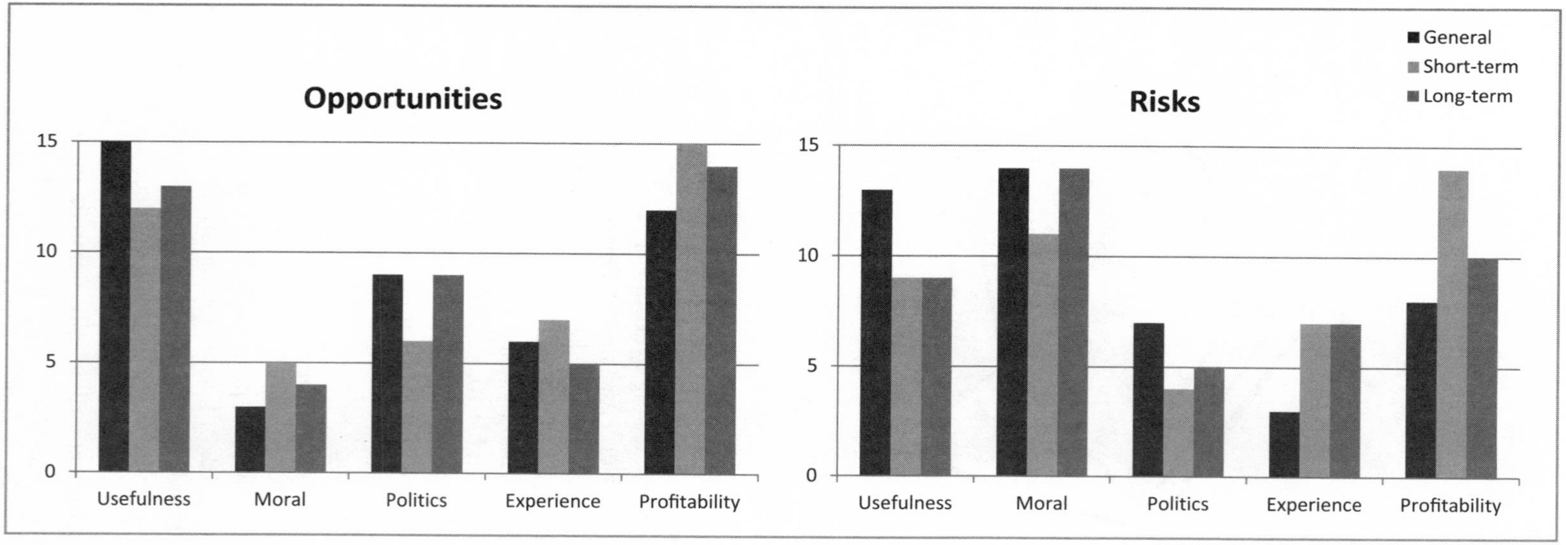

swimming pools has applied the same procedure every two years since 2010 (see no. 5 in table 10.3). This group typically receives about thirty applications from different public pool operators, who report on each of the five PVSC dimensions. Starting in 2015, there will be a global public value award, building on a similar logic to assess projects addressing megatrends such as megacities and demographic change (see no. 6 in table 10.3).

Version 3: Surveying

For large-scale surveys, the PVSC needs to be simplified. Intense forced ranking is hardly possible with a thousand customers and via telephone. Therefore, three organizations translated the indicators and adapted them to a question battery, using a Likert scale from 1 to 6. The first organization, Fresenius Medical Care (see no. 7 in table 10.3) asked major stakeholder groups (doctors, politicians, and patient groups) in different places to assess the public value of its dialysis clinics and services; the surveys assessed absolute (not relative) public value creation. At the Federal Employment Agency (see no. 8 in table 10.3), this version has been applied to analyze the relationship between public value and other measures, like customer satisfaction and controlling data. Deutschen Auslandsschulen (German Schools Abroad) used the large-scale survey version to obtain an internal view of the public value creation by German schools all over the world (see no. 9 in table 10.3). In all three cases the analyses followed descriptive and inference statistics (e.g., regression analysis).

Version 4: Exploring

The most demanding PVSC version for the respondent is the exploratory one. It builds on the value knowledge guide (*WertwissensGuide*), which allows a hybrid between qualitative exploration and quantitative analysis (a version of the repertory grid; Meynhardt 2004). Such an approach is suitable when an organization is interested in the manner and particular language in which the public recognizes and frames its public value.

Contrary to a quantitative design with prefabricated items, the semantic space and worldview were considered here. The guiding question is, *What makes our organization valuable to society?* This method requires at least forty-five minutes for completion and allows for relative (not absolute) assessment.

Beside the soccer club FC Bayern Munich, the Goethe Institute in Germany, Deutschen Auslandsschulen, and the German Stock Exchange have also relied on this inquiry technique (see nos. 10, 11, 12, and 13 in table 10.3).

Version 5: Sensing

Given the new technological possibilities of analyzing big data, an inquiry technique for social media data was developed.[4] This version of a public value scorecard directly draws on conversations and public opinion as manifested in multiple social media channels, such as Twitter, Facebook, Google+, or blogs. Similar to human beings, a software tool "reads and understands" sentences and extracts meanings (questions, intentions, ambiguity, direction, amplification, etc.). It detects not only single words or phrases but analyzes grammar and context. In contrast to sentiment analysis, this new way of semantic analysis provides much more valid results. Against this background of advanced linguistics, a huge number of indicators were attached to each public value dimension in order to determine a theory-driven interpretation of statements. Although in an early stage, it is now possible to automatically interpret a specific statement to what extent it is attached to single or multiple public value dimensions. Furthermore, each phrase is evaluated as to whether it is positive, negative, or neutral. This methodology, for example, was used to analyze the conversation in microblogs and blogposts (Twitter, Facebook, Omgili, Google+, and others) about Nestlé, a Swiss multinational food and beverage company (see no. 14 in table 10.3). Almost 4,500 statement were analyzed and mapped against each scorecard dimension. As a result, a typical PVSC (see figure 10.1) was created. Interestingly, the study revealed very much the same results previous surveys about Nestlé's public value did.

It is to be expected that this real-time sensing of public value in social media will become of greater importance in the near future. Such an inquiry technique allows for a closer monitoring of public values dynamics, even avoiding reactivity inherent in many others methods. Also, it reduces costs of collecting data.

CONCLUSIONS: FUTURE DIRECTIONS OF THE PVSC

The public value scorecard does not tell us *how* public value is created. In its current versions, it focuses on the creation of public value along five dimensions; it also tells us where the trade-offs and gaps are. Consequently, blind spots are discovered that are not otherwise noticed in strategic planning, political deliberation, and innovation process.

As the projects show, the current PVSC can be integrated into management systems (e.g., incorporated into a balanced scorecard or as an extension of customer satisfaction surveys). It may be used to evaluate projects and initiatives on an ongoing formative or summative basis. The next step for improving the PVSC will be a methodological link to dynamic perspectives. Applying ideas from self-organization theory and based on network methodology thinking (Gomez and Probst 1999), PVSC designers can deploy it to better understand interdependencies, feedback loops, and potential intervention entry points. This dynamic perspective aligns the PVSC more closely with the daily experience of constraints, sudden developments, and time lags.

The PVSC discerns, measures, and assesses public value creation in different situations across sectors. It can be seen as a theory-based effort to incorporate society's voice and will help organizations better understand their role in a given social context: What is the public value created? Where are the tensions, paradoxes, and trade-offs of which we were not aware? How do we better manage risks and opportunities in a highly contested environment? As a dialogue tool about mutual interdependencies in pluralist societies, the PVSC confronts managers with the challenge to justify their mandates or business models from a societal perspective. Although the PVSC is nonnormative, it urges managers to engage in a dialogue about where our societies are heading.

NOTES

1. For a detailed description of emotional self-organization and different views in psychology—for example, on unconscious and conscious evaluations—see Meynhardt (2004).
2. Those interested in more technical information about the PVSC (e.g., an interpretation manual with cases, validation procedure, and reliability challenges) should contact the author for further material: timo.meynhardt@unisg.ch.
3. The data analysis and interpretation is supported by guidelines and case-based material; see Meynhardt and Gomez (2013).
4. This version was co-developed together with Ernst & Young Ltd.

11

IN THE EYE OF THE BEHOLDER

LEARNING FROM STAKEHOLDER ASSESSMENTS OF PUBLIC VALUE

JOHN C. THOMAS, THEODORE H. POISTER, AND MIN SU

O ver the better part of the past decade, we have worked with the Georgia Department of Transportation (GDOT) to solicit systematic feedback from a variety of its stakeholders, including partners and oversight entities as well as customers and employees. This feedback provides a unique body of data for examining stakeholder perspectives on the public values relevant to a specific governmental agency.

This data will be analyzed in this paper to explore a number of questions about stakeholder perspectives: What public values do different constituent groups view as more and less important relative to the GDOT? How well do these values fit standard categorizations of public values? We refer, in particular, to the Beck Jørgensen and Bozeman (2007) schema, which we prefer to Moore's (1995) for its greater precision on specific values. How do different stakeholder groups see various public values relating to each other? Finally, what do the answers to these questions tell us about public values more generally?

To set the stage for this exploration, this chapter will first survey prior research on stakeholder perspectives on agency performance in general and public values in particular. A second section will briefly summarize the GDOT Stakeholder Assessment Project that produced the data for this research. We will then explore what the data tell us about stakeholder perspectives on public values relative to the GDOT before concluding by considering the implications of the findings.

COLLABORATIVE PARTNERSHIPS AND STAKEHOLDER ASSESSMENTS

Public agencies appear increasingly to perform their functions in partnership with other public, nonprofit, and private-sector entities, with many or most public services now the joint products of collaboration between governmental and nongovernmental actors (see, for example, Alford 2009). The rise in partnering is documented in a proliferation of research on collaborations and on participants in those collaborations. Researchers focusing on collaborations and networks have examined when collaborations arise, how they function, how well they perform, and the extent to which they have come to characterize the work of government (e.g., Edelenbos and Klijn 2006; Hill and Lynn 2005; Considine and Lewis 2003; Agranoff and McGuire 2003). Another line of research has focused on defining the nature and role of various stakeholders in collaborative efforts. Bryson (2004b), for example, proposed a range of techniques for identifying and engaging stakeholders at various steps in agency decision making (for an illustration, see Bryson, Cunningham, and Lokkesmoe 2002).

To date, though, few scholars have examined how collaborative partners and/or stakeholders perceive each other's performance. As the principal exception, an extensive literature and practice focuses on the use of citizen satisfaction surveys to gain perspectives on governmental effectiveness (e.g., Miller, Kobayashi, and Hayden 2008; Hatry et al. 1998; Lyons, Lowery, and DeHoog 1992). Only a few scholars have extended this research to additional stakeholders beyond citizens (e.g., Thomas, Poister, and Ertas 2010; Daley 2009; Van Ryzin and Freeman 1997).

As best we can tell, no one to date has asked the even larger question of how an agency's performance may be perceived by partners *collectively*—by, for example, citizens, customers, contractors, and public-sector partners (other governments or public agencies)—including what the various partners value about that performance and how they agree or differ in those judgments. Those perceptions and opinions could prove valuable to agencies by suggesting which aspects of their performance their service partners value most.

As that discussion implies, no one appears either to have asked how stakeholders view the public values that agencies do pursue or should pursue (as one limited exception, see Nabatchi 2012). Based on an extensive review of how public administration scholars have defined these values, Beck Jørgensen and Bozeman (2007, 360–61) propose that public values for public administration fall into seven categories: (1) the public sector's contribution to society; (2) the transformation of interests to decisions; (3) the relationship between public administrators and politicians; (4) the relationship between public administrators and their environment; (5) the intraorganizational aspects of public administration; (6) the behavior of public-sector employees, and (7) the relationship between public administration and the citizens.

The current research is designed as a first effort toward filling this void in the literature. It will explore what can be learned from examining how different stakeholders perceive the performance of a specific public agency: the Georgia Department of Transportation.

THE GDOT STAKEHOLDER ASSESSMENT PROJECT

The Georgia Department of Transportation is the principal transportation agency in state government in Georgia. Its core business consists of planning, building, maintaining, and operating nearly eighteen thousand miles of highways in the state. When this research began in 2005, approximately six thousand employees worked for the department, down from a high of more than ten thousand in the late 1960s due to a series of budget retrenchments. Among other impacts, this shrinkage of in-house staff resulted in much greater reliance on external consultants to perform the department's engineering and design work (Gen and Kingsley 2007).

Like many other public agencies, the GDOT has become more customer oriented in recent years—for example, by tracking citizen satisfaction through annual public opinion polls. Departmental leaders had also begun to recognize that succeeding in the mission of providing a safe, seamless, and sustainable transportation system for Georgia required the cooperation of numerous external stakeholders. Reflecting that recognition, one of the fourteen objectives in the GDOT's 2004 strategic plan called for improving working relationships with suppliers, business partners, and other critical stakeholders.

The GDOT Stakeholder Audit

Based on that objective, the plan specified a strategic initiative to identify the department's stakeholders and solicit their feedback regarding the GDOT's performance. This research began when the GDOT invited the authors to assist in implementing the initiative by conducting what eventually became known as a stakeholder audit, an exhaustive identification of the full range of relevant stakeholders combined with definition of the information the department might need from specific stakeholders (Thomas and Poister 2009).

Working with the department's Office of Strategic Development, we began by conducting personal interviews with twenty-eight top managers, extending all the way from the commissioner at the top down through lower organizational layers to division directors, executive staff, office heads, and program directors. We sought to talk with anyone in the GDOT who, by virtue of programmatic responsibilities, had "outward-looking" perspectives on the department's interactions with stakeholders. For each stakeholder group identified in this process, we also asked about existing communication channels, the extent to which the GDOT received systematic feedback from the group, and information the department might need from the groups.

Based on the interviews, we grouped similar stakeholders into clusters including any relevant organizations or associations, resulting in the stakeholder map shown in figure 11.1. The stakeholders on the right side of the map include customer groups such as public transit users, property owners, motorists, and citizens at large. At the bottom are nonprofit and other advocacy groups. On the left side are partners and suppliers, such as consultants, contractors, and vendors. Across the top are five clusters for (1) entities that provide oversight and resources to the GDOT, such as the Governor's Office; (2) nontransportation agencies whose missions overlap with the GDOT's, such the Georgia Departments of Community Development and Natural Resources; (3) other state agencies whose missions also focus on strengthening Georgia's transportation system, such as the State Road and Tollway Authority; (4) other public entities that also plan and deliver transportation services, such as local governments and public transit authorities; and (5) the media.

As the next step, we analyzed the interviews to define fourteen areas where the GDOT appeared to need additional feedback from specific stakeholder groups and recommended a data collection technique for meeting each need. We prioritized the recommendations by means of a brief survey asking ninety-six high-level GDOT managers to rate their usefulness. These ratings and further discussion with the four statutory officials in the department led to recommendations that the

Figure 11.1 The stakeholder universe of the Georgia Department of Transportation
Source: Poister, Thomas, and Berryman 2013.

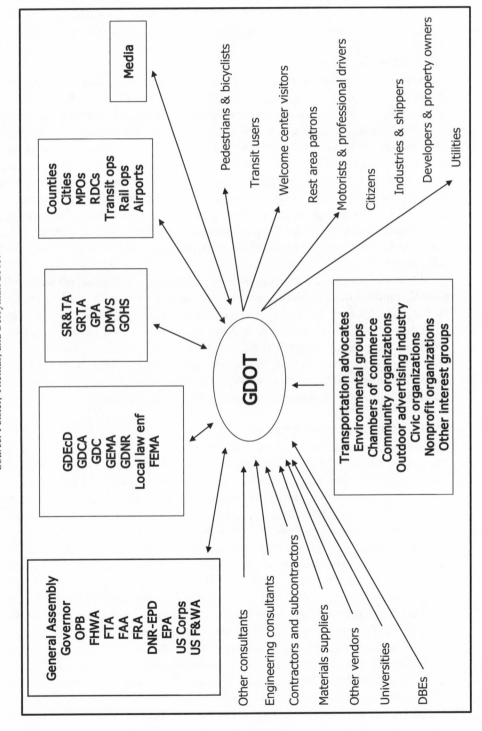

GDOT initially move forward with nine of the proposed opportunities for enhanced stakeholder feedback. Departmental leaders accepted the recommendations and asked us to conduct further research on external stakeholder groups plus GDOT employees as internal stakeholders.

The Stakeholder Surveys

We conducted a separate survey for each of nine stakeholder groups: (1) planning and design consultants; (2) highway contractors; (3) top county and municipal elected officials; (4) top county and municipal transportation administrators; (5) Georgia residents; (6) licensed drivers; (7) professional drivers (e.g., truck drivers); (8) members of the General Assembly (the state legislature); and (9) GDOT employees. We developed instruments for each survey working with GDOT steering committees composed of departmental staff whose responsibilities intersected with the particular stakeholder group and, for most of the surveys, advisory committees, convened as focus groups, of representatives of specific stakeholders. For example, advisory committees created by the Georgia Municipal Association and the Association of County Commissioners of Georgia assisted in developing the two local government surveys.

While the surveys have some questions in common, most questions were individually tailored to the specific groups. Common questions focused on performance grades for the GDOT, departmental priorities, and satisfaction with working relationships with the department. Tailored questions focused largely on GDOT programs of interest to a particular group and specific processes through which group members interacted with the department. With consultants, for example, these processes included consultant selection, contract negotiation, project management, consultant evaluation, payment, and the audit process.

The Focus of the Current Research

In another paper we use data from all of the surveys to develop a global, or 360-degree, assessment of the GDOT's performance (Poister, Thomas, and Berryman 2013), paralleling similar efforts in private-sector organizations (Rao and Rao 2005; Dalessio 1998). Here the interest in public values recommends focusing in depth on only a few of the surveys.

We choose to focus on three surveys—those for local government administrators, state legislators, and consultants—because we believe that the three together provide an instructive range of perspectives on public values questions. Local administrators provide the perspective of public officials who function as customers and partners relative to the GDOT (Thomas, Poister, and Ertas 2010). Legislators provide the perspective of overseers or principals since they must authorize GDOT programs and funding. Finally, consultants offer the perspective of third parties who are funded by GDOT to perform some of its functions.[1]

The survey of local administrators targeted the top transportation administrator in each of Georgia's 515 municipalities and 159 counties. "Top administrator" refers to the appointed official with each local government who was principally responsible for its transportation function, such as the head of a public works department or a transportation engineer in larger jurisdictions or the city or county manager or administrator in smaller jurisdictions. The survey was conducted during midsummer 2006, using a dual-mode, online and hard-copy method, with two rounds of reminders sent to initial nonrespondents. This procedure brought responses from 43 percent of the administrators, a good response rate for a survey of this kind and similar to Van Ryzin and Freeman's (1997) response rate of 46 percent for another stakeholder survey. The response rate would be even higher had it not been for a low response rate from municipalities with populations below ten thousand, jurisdictions that often have no involvement with the GDOT anyway.

The legislator survey was conducted in summer 2007, again administered both online and by hard copy via regular mail with two follow-up reminders to initial nonrespondents. This survey achieved a 47 percent response rate—again an excellent rate for this kind of survey; the rates were almost identical for the Georgia House and the Senate.

The consultant survey was administered online in early fall 2005 to all 579 consulting firms on the GDOT's list of certified consultants, followed by the usual reminders to nonrespondents. A total of 176 completed surveys were returned for a nominal response rate of 30 percent, but the response rate was much higher for firms that had actually worked with the GDOT in the preceding five years.

FINDINGS

Questions in all of the surveys were designed to obtain information on assessments of GDOT performance on desired outcomes, perceptions of the quality of the processes of working with the GDOT, and desired priorities for future GDOT work. In this chapter we focus on the first two of those elements to examine the specific public value dimensions in the surveys themselves and their fit to the Beck Jørgensen-Bozeman schema and the relationships between the various public value dimensions within the specific stakeholder groups. The actual levels of perceived GDOT achievement are discussed elsewhere (Poister, Thomas, and Berryman 2013). Table 11.1 displays sample questions from the legislator survey to illustrate how both the process and outcome dimensions were measured, where "outcomes" refer to intended end products or services and "processes" refer to steps toward the outcomes.

Can we assume that the survey questions reflect the actual public values of interest to the various stakeholders? One might wonder in the case of the questions about aspects of GDOT outcome performance because they were mostly either stipulated by the GDOT leadership team or based on measures with currency in the national transportation community (American Association of State Highway and Transportation Officials 2004; Transportation Research Board 2005). Similar questions were suggested by the focus groups, however, and their actual survey responses, as detailed below, imply that the questions resonated as public value dimensions for the stakeholder groups.

The process public value dimensions, by contrast, reflect suggestions made by the stakeholders themselves in the advisory focus groups we convened. In general, when a focus group member suggested a possible process dimension, we asked other group members for their opinions on its importance and then translated to survey questions any dimensions that appeared important for multiple group members. As a consequence, the process elements included in the surveys reflect what these stakeholders valued.

Table 11.1. Sample process and outcome questions: GDOT legislator survey

Examples of Questions on Program Processes

To what extent have you been satisfied with the response(s) of GDOT officials to your contacts with them in the last 12 months on each of the following dimensions?

	Very Satisfied	Satisfied	Unsure/ Neutral	Dissatisfied	Very Dissatisfied	Not Applicable
Helpfulness	O	O	O	O	O	O
Timeliness	O	O	O	O	O	O
Courtesy	O	O	O	O	O	O
Fairness	O	O	O	O	O	O
Overall Responsiveness	O	O	O	O	O	O

Examples of Questions on Performance Outcomes

How would you grade the state highways *in your area* in each of the following areas (where A is excellent, B = good, C = fair, D = poor, F = failing, and DK = Don't Know)? (Please circle the appropriate grade)

Highway condition and ride quality	A B C D F DK
Traffic flow and congestion	A B C D F DK
Safety	A B C D F DK

The Public Values of GDOT Stakeholders

Tables 11.2 and 11.3 show the public values included in the GDOT stakeholder surveys, separated into GDOT processes and GDOT outcomes. The two tables list the specific values cited by stakeholders, show the correspondence of each value to the Beck Jørgensen-Bozeman categories (as judged by the authors), and indicate which stakeholder survey(s) cited each value. Some of the evaluative dimensions refer to an index (e.g., cumulative scores of GDOT timeliness in responding to consultants at each of several points), and others to a single item (e.g., road condition and ride quality). Full explanation of the indices is available elsewhere (Poister, Thomas, and Berryman 2013).

As the first notable finding, the survey questions indicate that the three stakeholder groups suggested relatively similar evaluative dimensions for both GDOT processes and outcomes. On the process side, all three groups expressed interest in responsiveness, timeliness, fairness, and satisfaction with their GDOT working relationship. Two of the groups shared concerns for burden, clarity, and consistency in their GDOT contracts (consultants) or grants (local administrators). Legislators could not be expected to share these concerns because they do not come to GDOT as supplicants seeking contracts or grants. The groups also differ in which dimensions of helpfulness, courtesy, customer service, professional treatment, competence, and usefulness they cite as important, but these differences may mostly reflect semantics. That is, helpfulness and courtesy probably equate to customer service, and judgments about professional treatment and competence may well translate to quality of customer service.

Table 11.2. Stakeholder evaluative dimensions versus public values: GDOT processes

GDOT Stakeholder Evaluative Dimension*	Corresponding Public Value (Beck Jørgensen and Bozeman 2007)	L**	A	C
Burden (of paperwork, etc.)	Relationship between public administration and environment: user orientation		X	X
Clarity (of proposal guidelines)	Relationship between public administration and environment: user orientation		X	X
Consistency (of decisions)	Relationship between public administration and environment: user orientation		X	X
Process effectiveness	Relationship between public administration and environment: user orientation		X	X
Responsiveness (to requests)	Relationship between public administration and citizens: responsiveness	X	X	X
Timeliness (of responses)	Relationship between public administration and citizens: responsiveness	X	X	X
Fairness (of decisions)	Relationship between public administration and citizens: equity/fairness	X	X	X
Helpfulness	Relationship between public administration and citizens: user orientation	X		
Courtesy	Relationship between public administration and citizens: user orientation—friendliness	X		
Customer service	Relationship between public administration and environment: user orientation		X	
Professional treatment	Behavior of public-sector employees: accountability—professionalism			X
Communication quality	Relationship between public administration and citizens: dialogue	X	X	
Competence	Intraorganizational aspects of public administration: productivity—effectiveness			X
Usefulness (of programs)	Intraorganizational: productivity/ effectiveness		X	
Communication (to stakeholders)	Relationship between public administration and environment: openness/secrecy	X		X
Satisfaction with working relationship	*No corresponding public value*	X	X	X

Notes: *Dimensions may include multiple stakeholder survey questions. Wording of questions on some dimensions varied slightly between surveys. **L = legislators; A = local government administrators; C = consultants; X = applied to group; blank = did not apply.

Table 11.3. Stakeholder evaluative dimensions versus public values: GDOT outcomes

GDOT Stakeholder Evaluative Dimension*	Corresponding Public Value (Beck Jørgensen and Bozeman 2007)	L**	A	C
Pavement condition and/or road quality	Contribution to society: common good	X	X	X
Traffic flow and congestion	Contribution to society: common good	X	X	X
Highway safety	Contribution to society: common good	X	X	X
On-time project delivery	Contribution to society: common good	X		
Providing variety of transportation options	Contribution to society: common good	X	X	X
Performance in planning and designing highways	Contribution to society: common good			X
Preserving the environment in road building	Contribution to society: sustainability	X	X	X
Spending appropriately	Intraorganizational: productivity/parsimony	X		
Adequately involving the public	Relationship between public administration and environment: openness/secrecy— listening to public opinion	X		
Meeting the needs of the General Assembly	Relationship between public administrators and politicians: responsiveness	X		
Meeting Georgia's transportation needs	Contribution to society: common good	X	X	X

Notes: *Wording of questions on some dimensions varied slightly between surveys. **L = legislators; A = local government administrators; C = consultants; X = applied to group; blank = did not apply.

One evaluative dimension for GDOT processes—satisfaction with the GDOT working relationship—is conspicuous in its lack of correspondence to the Beck Jørgensen-Bozeman categories. Moore also appears to omit this dimension from his classification of public values (1995, 52–55). This is an important dimension, affecting all three groups and arguably providing a summary judgment on working with the GDOT for each. While perhaps capturing well the *effects* on the public of actions by public servants, the Beck Jørgensen-Bozeman inventory appears to overlook an important public value dimension for the *interaction* between public servants and their stakeholders.

On the outcome side, all three groups were asked about the six evaluative dimensions linked to the GDOT's contribution to society, including pavement condition and road quality, traffic flow and congestion, highway safety, providing a variety of transportation options, preserving the environment (in GDOT construction projects), and meeting Georgia's transportation needs. Legislators, as overseers to the GDOT, suggested and were asked about the additional dimensions of the appropriateness of the GDOT's spending and the adequacy of its public involvement processes.

Together the various evaluative dimensions touch on six of the seven Beck Jørgensen-Bozeman categories of public values, missing only "transformation of interest to decisions." That category probably applies better to the work of elected political bodies than to the work of an administrative agency such as the GDOT.

Constellations of Public Values

To assess how the different values relate to each other, we use factor analysis, a technique designed to show how variables in a data set cluster (Kim and Mueller 1978). With each of the three data sets (that is, the three sets of survey questions), we first examined the initial results and dropped any variables in which high uniqueness scores indicated that they were not well explained in the factor analysis. After completing a principal component factor analysis with the remaining variables, we conducted factor rotation to simplify the structure. We report the results for the orthogonal factor rotation because "the factors remain perfectly uncorrelated with one another and are inherently easier to interpret" (Kieffer 1998, 13).

Looking first at the legislator data, the results in table 11.4 show three principal factors that explain 68.9 percent of the variance for the full set of variables, with the high Cronbach alpha of .872 indicating high internal consistency of the variables. Factor 1 might be termed "process and bottom-line performance" since it includes both two bottom-line performance metrics (grades for meeting the General Assembly's needs and the state's transportation needs) and three metrics for the quality of GDOT processes (i.e., responsiveness to contacts, satisfaction with the working relationship, and grades for on-time project delivery). Notably, only one true GDOT outcome measure, the grade for road maintenance, is associated with this factor. When thinking about the GDOT's performance in meeting the needs of the General Assembly and the state, legislators appear to think mostly about the effectiveness of GDOT processes.

By contrast, outcome performance metrics dominate factor 2, which we accordingly label "performance outcomes." This factor consists of four variables for elements of outcome performance: grades for (1) highway condition, (2) traffic flow and congestion, and (3) highway safety—all in the legislator's home district—as well as for (4) performance in preserving the environment. This factor explains only slightly less of the variance (28.3 percent) than does the first factor (28.9 percent), implying that legislators give performance outcomes a high—though not the highest—priority.

Factor 3 might be termed "funding availability for alternative transportation." It consists of (1) perceptions of the adequacy of GDOT funding,[2] and (2) grades for providing a variety of transportation options, suggesting that legislators see providing transportation alternatives as linked to the level of available funding.

Using the same procedure with the data on local government administrators also resulted in three factors, as shown in table 11.5. As with the legislators, factor 1 appears to reflect "process and bottom-line performance." This factor contains a number of process elements—a general process effectiveness index,[3] responsiveness, consistency, timeliness, burden, clarity, and working relationship

Table 11.4. Orthogonal factor loadings: legislator data

	Factor Loadings		
Variable	Factor 1	Factor 2	Factor 3
Overall responsiveness	.847	—	—
Working relationship satisfaction	.857	—	—
Road maintenance grade	.602	.477	—
On-time project delivery grade	.619	—	.439
Meeting Georgia Assembly needs grade	.760	—	.449
Meeting Georgia's transportation needs grade	.612	—	.416
Highway condition grade (in home district)	—	.718	—
Traffic flow and congestion grade (in home district)	—	.736	—
Highway safety grade (in home district)	—	.857	—
Preserving the environment grade	—	.657	—
Adequacy of funding	—	—	.777
Providing variety of transportation options	—	—	.718
Percentage of variance explained	28.3	23.7	16.9
$n = 85$			
Cronbach's alpha (test scale) = .872			

Note: A dash (—) indicates loading < .4.

satisfaction—along with the single outcome measure of the bottom-line grade for meeting the state's transportation needs. Even more than was true with the legislators, local administrators appear to associate the GDOT's bottom-line performance with the quality of their own interaction with the department. Moreover, this factor accounts for more than half (44.8 percent) of the total variance explained by the three factors (70.2 percent).

We label factor 2 "road congestion and safety outcomes" because it consists solely of grades for (1) traffic flow and congestion and (2) highway safety in the administrator's home area, an understandable pairing since congestion can exacerbate road safety problems. As with the legislators, however, these outcome performance metrics are not linked as closely to bottom-line performance as are ratings of GDOT processes.

Factor 3 appears to reflect "funding availability for maintaining roads" since it is limited to the two variables of (1) funding adequacy (an index) and (2) grades for road quality. Like state legislators, local administrators associate funding adequacy with a specific performance outcome, but that outcome for local administrators is road quality, whereas for legislators it was transportation alternatives.

Following the same procedure with the consultants' data again resulted in three factors, which together account for 68.6 percent of the variance, as shown in table 11.6. Factor 1 captures "quality of program processes" by including the process dimensions of responsiveness, professionalism, competence, timeliness, clarity, and working relationship satisfaction. Factor 2 clearly reflects "GDOT outcome performance" by including (1) a general effectiveness index, (2) grades for performance in highway development, and (3) overall performance in meeting the state's needs. Finally, factor 3 might be termed "program process challenges" since it com-

Table 11.5. Orthogonal factor loadings: local administrator data

Variable	Factor Loadings		
	Factor 1	Factor 2	Factor 3
Process effectiveness (index)	.823	—	—
Burden (index)	.642	—	—
Clarity (index)	.833	—	—
Consistency (index)	.723	—	—
Responsiveness (index)	.835	—	—
Timeliness (index)	.837	—	—
Customer service (index)	.901	—	—
Working relationship satisfaction	-.815	—	—
Meeting Georgia's transportation needs grade	-.686	—	—
Traffic flow and congestion grade (in home area)	—	.851	—
Highway safety grade (in home area)	—	.851	—
Highway condition grade (in home area)	—	.459	.712
Funding adequacy (index)	—	—	.710
Percentage of variance explained	44.8	16.7	8.7
$n = 191$			
Cronbach's alpha (test scale) = .834			

Note: A dash (—) indicates loading < .4.

bines the process dimensions of burden, fairness, clarity, and (for a second time) working relationship satisfaction. This factor appears to be a variation on factor 1, but refers more to process challenges than to process in general.

Looking across the three factor analyses, several themes emerge. Most notably, the perceived quality of program interactions with the GDOT looms largest for all three groups. For legislators and administrators, those processes are so important that they link more closely to perceptions of the GDOT's bottom-line performance than does any true outcome performance measure (e.g., road quality or highway safety). Although program interactions do not link to bottom-line performance for consultants, two of the factors there reflect the quality of those interactions. In other words, all of these groups appear to give more importance to interactions with the GDOT than to actual performance outcomes, and those interactions are so important for two of the groups that they cluster with bottom-line grades for meeting the state's transportation needs.

Elements of outcome achievement emerge as only a secondary factor for all three groups. For legislators and administrators, this factor includes some combination of traffic flow and congestion, highway safety, and road quality and pavement condition in the respondent's home area, plus performance in preserving the environment. For consultants the factor consists of the outcome variables of a generic effectiveness measure,[4] the grade for performance in road development, and the overall grade for meeting the state's transportation needs.

Finally, funding adequacy as linked to an element of GDOT outcome performance emerges as central to a third factor for legislators and local administrators. (Consultants were not asked about funding adequacy.) For legislators, funding

Table 11.6. Orthogonal factor loadings: consultant data

Variable	Factor Loadings		
	Factor 1	Factor 2	Factor 3
Responsiveness (index)	.652	—	.441
Professional treatment (index)	.843	—	—
Competence (index)	.816	—	—
Timeliness (index)	.739	—	—
Process effectiveness (index)	—	-.985	—
Clarity (index)	.482	—	.506
Burden (index)	—	—	.877
Fairness (index)	—	—	.627
Performance in planning and designing highways grade	—	.713	—
Meeting transportation needs in General Assembly grade	—	.904	—
Working relationship satisfaction	−.435	—	−.494
Percentage of variance explained	26.9	23.6	18.1

$n = 78$
Cronbach's alpha (test scale) = .798

Note: A dash (—) indicates loading < .4.

adequacy linked to the GDOT's performance in providing transportation options; for local administrators, the link was to road quality and pavement condition.

Paths of Influence

Another valuable perspective comes from examining how the different public value assessments may link with each other in a possible causal sequence. Here we will summarize results as reported in two earlier papers on possible paths of influence for the local government administrators and the legislators (Thomas, Poister, and Ertas 2010; Thomas, Su, and Poister 2012).[5]

Analysis of the assessment data from the survey of local government administrators reveal that they see themselves relating to the GDOT in three distinct, if interrelated, roles:

1. They want to be treated like *customers*, receiving prompt and helpful service, when they approach the GDOT about specific programs for their jurisdictions.
2. They *partner* with the GDOT in the many programs that require joint work by the department and local governments in providing transportation services and infrastructure and, more generally, in creating public value.
3. They function as *principals* in monitoring the GDOT's performance based on their standing as appointed officials in a democratic and federal system of government.

Multinomial regression analyses identified factors that appear to underlie these perceptions. Feeling treated like a customer proved to be a function primarily of the perceived quality of interactions with the GDOT, as measured especially by perceptions of the quality of GDOT communications.

The perceived quality of partnering, as measured by satisfaction with the GDOT working relationships, proved to be principally a function of (1) a feeling of being treated as a customer, (2) the perceived timeliness of the GDOT's responses, and (3) the perceived quality of the GDOT's communications. A fourth significant predictor was the programmatic benefits these administrators reported their jurisdictions receiving from the GDOT relationship (measured by the number of GDOT programs they reported receiving in recent years). (All four predictors were statistically significant at the .01 level or better.) Working relationship satisfaction thus appears to reflect both the quality of interactions with the GDOT *and* direct substantive benefits received from the GDOT.

Perhaps the most interesting pattern emerged in trying to explain assessments of the GDOT's mission achievement, as measured by grades for meeting the state's transportation needs. As might be expected, perceptions of the quality of several specific transportation outcomes (i.e., grades for road quality, traffic flow and congestion, and highway safety) contributed substantially to this bottom-line assessment for local administrators, but their satisfaction with the GDOT working relationship also figured prominently. Table 11.7 summarizes the linkages for the three relationships.

We initially proposed a similar three-part model for legislator assessments of the GDOT's pursuit of public values, positing that legislators would focus separately on how effectively GDOT assists them in providing service to constituents (the customer perspective), assists the legislature as an institution (the partner perspective), and fulfills its mission of meeting the transportation needs of the State of Georgia (the principal perspective). Here the customer perspective is measured by legislators' satisfaction with their individual working relationships with the GDOT, the partner perspective by legislators' grades for the GDOT's performance in meeting the needs of the General Assembly, and the principal perspective by GDOT's performance in meeting Georgia's transportation needs.

Table 11.7. The flow of influence: local government administrators

Service interactions (index) →	Quality of customer service
GDOT timeliness (index) ↘	↓
Quality of GDOT communication ↘	↘
Programmatic benefits (index) →	Satisfaction with working relationship
	↓
Perceptions of transportation outcomes (index) →	Performance in meeting state's transportation needs

The data suggested a divided verdict on this model. As expected, the personal factors of perceived overall responsiveness to legislator requests and the specific perceived responsiveness of the GDOT's central office in Atlanta emerged as the principal statistically significant determinants of working-relationship satisfaction. Unexpectedly, the GDOT's perceived performance in meeting the needs of the General Assembly also proved to be principally a function of personal legislative criteria only—specifically, legislators' satisfaction with their personal working relationship with the GDOT, and the GDOT's perceived performance in delivering projects on schedule. The GDOT's perceived performance in keeping the legislature informed did not prove a significant predictor.

These findings suggest that most legislators relate to administrative departments principally in terms of what the department can do for them: Can you address this constituent request? Can you deliver projects for my district on time? They may be less concerned with what a department does for the legislature as a whole because, as a consequence of their specializing, only a minority of legislators engage in depth in the work of any particular department. In any event, it is largely personal legislative criteria that appear to shape both satisfaction with the working relationship with the GDOT and the grades for GDOT performance in meeting the legislature's needs.

Personal legislative criteria even affect assessments of bottom-line departmental performance. Grades for meeting the needs of the General Assembly, itself a reflection of personal legislative criteria, proved the strongest single predictor of grades for meeting the state's transportation needs. Here, though, perceptions of a number of other aspects of GDOT performance (i.e., road safety, road maintenance, and providing a variety of transportation options) also emerged as statistically significant, as did the perceived appropriateness and adequacy of the GDOT's funding. In assessing the department's overall performance, legislators appear to consider what the GDOT has done for them as individual legislators, how well it has provided various services to the state and its residents, how

Table 11.8. The flow of influence: legislators

Responsiveness to legislator requests	→	Working relationship satisfaction
		↓
On-time project delivery	→	Performance in meeting needs of General Assembly
		↓
Perceptions of transportation outcomes (index)	→	Performance in meeting state's transportation needs
Appropriateness of GDOT spending	↗	

appropriately it spends, and how adequately it is funded. Table 11.8 summarizes the various linkages.

Taken together, the findings for legislators and local administrators imply a substantial, sometimes primary, role for process criteria—that is, quality of interactions with the department—in assessments of the GDOT's bottom-line performance. Perceptions of outcome achievement, such as grades for road quality and highway safety, also exert influence on those assessments, but in every case they must share top billing with process criteria—the perceived quality of personal interactions with the GDOT.

CONCLUSIONS

The various findings suggest a number of conclusions about stakeholder perspectives on public values and about public values in general. At the most basic level, the findings imply support for most aspects of the Beck Jørgensen-Bozeman inventory and categorization of public values. Only one of the Beck Jørgensen-Bozeman categories did not emerge as important for any of these stakeholder groups, and that category, "transformation of interests to decisions," should not be expected to apply to an administrative body (the focus here). As well, only one of the public value dimensions of interest to the three groups of GDOT stakeholders did not fit in one of those categories.

The Significance of Partnering in a Service-Dominant World

At the same time, the one public value dimension missing from both the Beck Jørgensen-Bozeman and Moore listings, "working relationship satisfaction," represents a significant omission. Working relationship satisfaction speaks to the quality of *partnering* between the GDOT and its stakeholders, as when local governments join with the department in building local roads and bridges. That partnering has arguably become a crucial public value dimension as a consequence of a sea change in what the public realm is about. As Osborne, Radnor, and Nasi explain, "the business of government is, by and large, not about delivering pre-manufactured products. . . . On the contrary, the majority of 'public goods' (whether provided by government, the non-profit and third sector or the private sector) are in fact not 'public products' but rather 'public services.' . . . Social work, health care, education, economic and business support services, community development and regeneration, for example, are all services rather than concrete products" (2013, 136). That change is significant because, *"the role of the user is qualitatively different for manufactured products and services.* In the former they are 'simply' their purchasers and consumers. However, for services, *the user is also a co-producer of the service.* At a fundamental level, therefore, co-production is not an 'add-on' to services but a core feature of them" (139; emphasis in the original).

For the world of public values, this reality implies that the quality of partnering itself warrants inclusion in any exhaustive listing. This partnering goes beyond what public actors provide in terms of such public value process dimensions as "timeliness," "enthusiasm," "reliability," and the like to encompass the quality of the *joint* action of authoritative public actors and citizens as well as other stakeholders.

The Importance of Public Value Process Dimensions

In a service-dominant public realm, how things get done can be as important as whatever outcomes may eventually be achieved. For government, that assertion echoes the long-standing observation that process can be as important as outcomes in the evaluations of the work of government. Sometimes, as Fountain has observed, the process can even *become* the outcome since "customers find it difficult to distinguish clearly between the quality of an intangible service and the process by which the service was rendered" (2001, 4). Additional evidence comes from Van Ryzin (2011), who found in an analysis of a resident survey covering thirty-three nations that citizens' evaluations of bureaucratic processes proved more important in explaining citizen trust of bureaucrats than did citizens' evaluations of outcomes.

We might expect that elites, in contrast to citizens, would more clearly differentiate process elements from outcomes and, in so doing, give greater weight to the latter in their assessments of any public agency's performance. Elites by virtue of their training and experience might understand better that outcomes are the bottom line for government.

We might expect that, but it did not prove to be the case here. In particular, state legislators and local government administrators, two indisputably elite public groups in terms of training and experience, appeared to be influenced in assessing the GDOT's bottom-line performance more by their personal experiences with the department than by their perceptions of specific GDOT transportation outcomes. (Comparable data were not available for the consultants.) These elites showed no inclination to differentiate public value process dimensions from public value outcome dimensions in assessing the performance of public agencies.

To be clear, these findings and speculations apply only to the circumscribed world of three stakeholder groups for one state government agency. It would be valuable to test how well the propositions might fit stakeholder groups for other public agencies in other states and at other levels of government. Much remains to be learned about public values as seen from the perspective of government's stakeholders.

NOTES

1. We chose not to include the survey of Georgia residents in this research because it asked only about outcomes, not about any significant process components.
2. Although questions on the adequacy of the GDOT's funding were included in all three surveys, that adequacy does not appear to qualify as a public value. It is better viewed as a constraint on or facilitator of GDOT performance on various public values.
3. Process effectiveness is an index reflecting several evaluations of process that do not fit under any other rubric.
4. Effectiveness is an index based on several questions about the effectiveness of specific GDOT programs.
5. To be clear, the data in both studies is cross-sectional. The assertions of possible causal paths are based on theory.

PART III

MEASURING AND MANAGING PERFORMANCE

12

CREATING PUBLIC VALUE USING PERFORMANCE INFORMATION

ALEXANDER KROLL AND DONALD P. MOYNIHAN

Under the label of performance management, reforms promising to provide public value by tracking and encouraging goal achievement were adopted in most countries in the Organisation for Economic Co-operation and Development (Bouckaert and Halligan 2008; OECD 2009). The explicit values associated with these reforms are efficiency (minimizing costs for a given output) and effectiveness (selecting, designing, and managing programs and services so that they can achieve maximum impact). Reformers argued that public organizations were short on such values, that performance management systems could deliver them, and that this in turn would raise the legitimacy of governance (Osborne and Gaebler 1993).

This chapter examines the relationship between performance management and public value. First, we discuss how performance measurement processes— formulating a mission, setting a strategic goal, measuring performance, reporting to stakeholders—define and record public value. We point to the importance of non-mission-based goals and discuss the (sometimes questionable) link between performance management and values like accountability, transparency, and legitimacy. Second, we introduce the concept of performance information use, identifying different types—passive, political, perverse, and purposeful—and explaining how each type of use relates to public value. The third part of the chapter focuses in greater depth on purposeful performance information use, since this is the aspect of performance management most likely to foster the creation of public value. We review empirical evidence on the antecedents to this desirable behavior. We conclude by considering the lessons of performance management for public value.

PERFORMANCE MANAGEMENT PROCESSES AND PUBLIC VALUE(S)

How do we know if the actions of a public manager create public value? To judge by public-sector reform in recent decades, the answer has been to develop quantitative indicators of achievement. This section discusses how basic performance management processes relate to public value creation. Unless otherwise noted, we will use the term "public value" as a placeholder for what a society values and aims to create through its public institutions, which is a broad enough conceptualization to capture the sometimes competing interpretations of Moore (1995) and Bozeman (2007). What this value might be can differ from one society (or community) to another, and it is determined by democratic politics and representation. Occasionally we will refer to specific values (consistent with the Bozeman approach to public values), when considering the relationship of performance systems with a variety of normative standards. Table 12.1 offers a brief overview of the performance management concept and its features, which we will discuss below.

A stylized summary of the claims that proponents of performance management have made include the following (for a more detailed discussion, see Moynihan 2008; Pollitt and Bouckaert 2011; Van Dooren, Bouckaert, and Halligan 2010): Over time, public organizations became increasingly focused on rules at the expense of organizational goals, contributing to inefficiency and a growing loss of public trust—a loss of public value. Performance management reforms promise to redirect attention toward the mission and goals of organizations and in turn restore public faith in government. Whether or not these claims have been borne out is not the primary focus of this chapter. Performance management systems have been widely implemented, and here we address what we know about how they relate to public value. It is worth noting that the doctrine of performance management explicitly invokes certain values—most obviously efficiency and effectiveness but also transparency, accountability, and the legitimacy of the state.

In practice, mandates to implement performance management have boiled down to a few key processes: requiring public agencies to identify their mission, set strategic goals and performance targets, track measurable indicators of performance, and broadly disseminate this data (Hatry 2006). Clearly defining an organization's mission can help answer the question of what the public value is that a particular entity provides. Defining a mission and identifying strategic goals may be as important as rigorously measuring whether these goals have been actually achieved. (In some cases providing guidance and meaning through a mission and strategic outlook has been more important than actually collecting operational performance data.) Public organizations are often confronted with numerous ambiguous and often conflicting objectives, which is why deciding on a mission

Table 12.1. Performance information use for value creation

Key elements

- Stating a mission; setting strategic goals; setting performance targets
- Indicators-based data collection
- Analysis (trends and benchmarks) and reporting of performance information
- Use the data

When *not* to use it

- When its purpose is only symbolic
- When its only purpose is cost cutting and to direct blame
- When there are not enough resources to ensure capacity for analysis and thus a minimum of data quality
- When complex services are paired with high-powered incentives

narrative can help prioritize effort and resources, channel discussion and serve as a source of inspiration (Bryson 2004a).

Performance information can increase transparency by offering feedback on the outcomes of service provision; it can also increase accountability, showing the degree to which a governmental unit achieved its goals. Just measuring performance can be a first step toward the creation of public value, as it puts normative pressure on individuals and emphasizes that what they do is not without consequences but will be documented and evaluated (Pollitt 2010).

Creating Value, or Displacing Values?

Performance management processes have become central mechanisms by which public value is represented, recorded, and communicated to employees, stakeholders, and the public. While performance management is sometimes framed as a neutral tool, this underestimates the inherently political nature of defining a mission statement, setting goals, and measuring performance. Defining performance is a political act; choosing the most minor measure represents a categorization of the role and responsibility of the state.

One critique of performance management processes is that they tend to privilege certain values over others. The mission of the organization, however defined, is given priority over other public values. Though mission orientation can generally help to strengthen an organization's public value focus, it can also harm the achievement of non-mission-based values that might be less prominent but still desirable. In the context of UK local government, Boyne (2002) concludes that performance measures prioritized efficiency and effectiveness but largely excluded indicators of equity, responsiveness, or participation (see also Radin 2006). Piotrowski and Rosenbloom (2002) argue that the emphasis on performance measures has served to reduce efforts to provide other, more valuable, mechanisms to ensure transparency, such as Freedom of Information Act requests. Wichowsky and Moynihan (2008) offer the same argument in the context of what they call citizenship outcomes, such as due process and civic engagement. For example, they point out that the measurement of results for community development programs emphasized employment and safe and stable housing, neglecting measures like participation in governing boards, percentage of households reporting they feel a part of the community, or volunteer hours devoted to community action efforts. Rosenbloom (2007) argues that these problems can best be remedied by mandating the measurement of non-mission-based goals in what he calls constitutional scorecards.

Whereas from a managerial perspective a mission-based focus helps to deal with outcome complexity, ignoring non-mission-based goals has to be considered more critically from a public value perspective. It is perfectly understandable that managers seeking to create public value might argue that they cannot measure everything but must focus their attention on goal achievement. This view rests on the notion that the primary basis for public legitimacy is goal achievement and that other values matter less. Such an assumption is contestable. Van Ryzin (2011) offers a cross-national analysis of trust in government, showing that confidence in due process and equity of treatment is more important than perceptions of effectiveness.

Does Information Use Lead to Value Creation?

Though mission statements, measurement, and reporting are necessary conditions of public value creation, current research argues that the most critical issue is whether systematically and laboriously produced performance information is actually used in decision making (De Lancer Julnes and Holzer 2001; Kroll 2014; Moynihan 2008; Moynihan and Pandey 2010; Van Dooren and Van de Walle 2008). There is no automatic connection between measurement and improvements in agency performance or in outcomes. After all, if no one appears to be using performance data, it is difficult to believe it is doing much to facilitate public value.

There are a variety of different ways in which performance measures can be used (Moynihan 2009), and all of them have different relationships with public value. We focus the bulk of this chapter on the most obvious way, which is purposeful use of data to better inform decisions in ways that will improve programs and services and thus contribute to the creation of public value. But we consider three other potential uses of performance data that illustrate the more complex relationship between performance management and public value in table 12.2.

Passive Use

One response to performance mandates may be passive, where public managers use data only to comply with the procedural requirements but for little else. Requirements to regularly document progress in terms of goal achievement can create significant transaction costs but with little apparent benefit (Radin 2006). As employees see multiple waves of reforms making little difference, they may become cynical about the value of such efforts. Beyond transaction costs, producing more and more data may have negative consequences in other ways. It may systemize biases against non-mission-based values, as discussed above. It may also lead to information overload, increasing information asymmetries between bureaucrats and politicians at the expense of the latter (Kroll and Proeller 2013).

Political Use

One goal of using performance information is to create political legitimacy and support. Both stakeholder theory (Freeman 1984) and new institutional theory (Meyer and Scott 1992) portray organizations as engaged in an ongoing effort to acquire legitimacy from their environment. In order to receive the support of external stakeholders, organizations' actions have to be considered "desirable, proper, appropriate within some socially constructed system of norms, values, beliefs, and definitions" (Suchman 1995, 574). One way to prove that public administrators do what relevant stakeholders and politicians expect them to is to report information on goal achievement. Thus, performance reporting can fulfill the function of "promoting" (Behn 2003) or "advocating" (Moynihan 2008) public organizations, departments, or their programs. Moore (1995) argues that creating support, which is necessary to acquire resources and autonomy, is an essential management challenge in public value creation.

The existing work on political performance information use does not suggest that it is inherently helpful or damaging to public value but simply a reflection of how performance systems are increasingly integrated into contemporary political

Table 12.2. Performance information use and public value

Type of performance information use	Relationship to public value
Passive: using data to comply with reporting requirements	**Strengths** • Formulating a mission and performance goals can help to determine what the value is a particular public organization can create • Measuring goal achievement can increase transparency and accountability in terms of whether the intended value was created **Weaknesses** • Creates sense of cynicism about performance management reforms • Transaction costs of performance systems not justified if data is not being used • Danger of neglecting non-mission-based indicators (e.g., equity, due process)
Purposeful: using data to learn, innovate, and motivate in ways that improve performance	**Strengths** • Directs attention to mission achievement • Encourages innovation and improvements in performance • Directs attention to public value in budget and management decisions
Perverse: using data to improve measured performance via goal displacement and data manipulation	**Weaknesses** • May create appearance of success if formal targets are being reached, but weakens public value • Creates cynicism about underlying purpose of public programs
Political: using data to argue about appropriate goals and program achievement	**Strengths** • Facilitates debate about meaning of public value • May buffer organization from external demands • Can help to create legitimacy, acquire resources, and create autonomy necessary to creating value **Weaknesses** • Reporting is counterproductive if it is only symbolic and decoupled from organizational routines

processes. In some cases these processes place unrealistic and countervailing demands on public organizations; in other cases they can be used to protect and strengthen public organizations.

In the most positive terms, the political use of performance information may be seen as part of a pluralistic dialogue through which public value is actively negotiated, reflecting a managerial responsibility to communicate with stakeholders. The picture becomes more negative if advocacy becomes "spinning" (Hood 2006), a propaganda tool through which there is a significant gap between "talk" and "action." A growing number of studies have applied this theoretical approach to the case of performance reporting (Lawton, McKevitt, and Millar 2000; Rautiainen 2010; Taylor 2009; Van Dooren 2005; for a review, see Modell 2009). They find that performance reporting often serves an external purpose: it is used to meet the expectations of external stakeholders and to portray public organizations as modern and performance-driven even as internal management processes remain unaffected. This strategy fits with what Brunsson (2003) refers to as "organizational hypocrisy."

Organizations may also be especially concerned with ensuring that they are not seen as failing. A basic insight from psychology is that humans are more motivated by avoiding loss than achieving positive outcomes. This "negativity bias" reveals itself in performance reporting via directing attention to performance scores that are not meeting aspirational levels (Nielsen 2014a), disproportionate citizen dissatisfaction with missed targets (James 2011), bureaucratic explanations of failed performance (Charbonneau and Bellavance 2012), and setting artificially low performance targets (Hood 2006).

Organizational hypocrisy does offer some virtues. One of the best managerial strategies to protect organizational performance is to buffer the organization from significant changes (O'Toole and Meier 2003). Public organizations are not the only actors that might use data about public program performance—so too may stakeholders, clients, and elected officials both friendly and unfriendly to the organization. To the extent that public organizations can use performance information as a buffer against externally imposed change, political uses of performance data are beneficial and may also pave the way for purposeful utilization. For example, performance reporting set up only to satisfy politicians may become internally relevant for managerial purposes if agency leaders take this reform as an opportunity to foster double-loop learning, cultural change, improving internal communication and coordination, or leadership development (Moynihan 2008).

Perverse Use

Perverse use occurs when agents use performance data in ways clearly at odds with public value. Examples of dysfunctional uses of these data are gaming (creatively interpreting numbers), cheating (making up numbers), effort substitution (focusing on easy or highly rewarded targets at the expense of others), and cream skimming (excluding more difficult-to-serve populations). These responses become more likely under certain conditions. More complex tasks give rise to incomplete contracts that fail to specify all key aspects of performance and are more difficult to monitor. High-stakes rewards to achieve measured performance create an incentive for perverse behavior. The likelihood of perversity increases when agents lack traditional rule-based constraints or intrinsic values that might discourage misbehavior (Bevan and Hood 2006; James 2004; Radin 2006; Heinrich and Marschke 2010; Soss, Fording, and Schram 2011).

These conditions are most likely to occur in service delivery contexts that rely upon performance-based contracts. While a passive response evokes cynicism of performance reforms, perverse responses give rise to a more corrosive sense of cynicism about whether the basic purpose of a program is being fulfilled. Qualitative accounts of employees working under these conditions reveal a sense of helplessness and frustration among frontline employees who believe their skills are not being used to help clients (Dias and Maynard-Moody 2007; Soss, Fording, and Schram 2011).

It is critically important that the perversity of performance systems be addressed and minimized where possible. This is the Achilles' heel of the performance movement and serves as the most effective rebuttal to its success stories, such as the "stat" model that originated in New York City policing where it helped reduce crime, encouraged the reform of welfare systems to encourage work, or promoted the restructuring of education to emphasize better performance. In each of these examples, performance measurement systems have been a central part of the policy change that appears to have generated greater public value. But in each case, critics point to widespread manipulation of data by providers and the displacement of important goals. In the case of welfare reform there is ample evidence that performance systems did not encourage the provision of meaningful skills to those seeking work, there were systematic differences in treatment based on race, and that low-skilled clients were systematically pushed off the roles (Soss, Fording, and Schram 2011; Brodkin and Majmundar 2010). In education, the emphasis on test scores has opened a debate on whether other educational values are being ignored (Abernathy 2007), as well as giving rise to scandals where cheating on tests appears to have become endemic in entire school systems (Jacob and Levitt 2003). For example, in the city of Atlanta, evidence of systematic cheating led to the indictment of the school district superintendent, who had previously won national accolades for her achievements (Winerip 2013). In the case of policing, Compstat-like performance management systems were criticized for encouraging aggressive stop-and-frisk practices targeted toward minorities as well as a culture of data manipulation (Eterno 2012). These types of perverse behavior have been documented enough that they should be seen not as inherently unusual but as a systematic risk that elected officials need to consider in the design of performance systems.

ANTECEDENTS OF PURPOSEFUL PERFORMANCE INFORMATION USE

The purposeful use of performance data in decision making is the element most closely linked to the improvement of outputs and outcomes for the public, and therefore to public value (for examples and references, see Van Dooren and Van de Walle 2008). Understanding its dynamics and antecedents is important for professionals and researchers alike; it is crucial for the practice of public management in order to design systems and create a supportive environment that makes it easy for public managers to use performance data in a way that aligns with public value. It is also relevant for researchers who can optimize their models and sharpen existing explanations of whether the performance movement is having an impact (Moynihan and Pandey 2010; Van Dooren 2008).

The literature we will review will incorporate mainly recent studies, beginning with an early article by De Lancer Julnes and Holzer (2001). We are aware that the research on the use of information systems is much older (Bozeman and Bretschneider 1986), even more so when including studies from the private sector (Lucas 1975). However, for the sake of comparability and reliable inference we have decided to focus on studies whose measurement demonstrates a shared understanding of what "performance information" and "purposeful use" mean while limiting ourselves to studies that focus primarily on public officials. Table 12.3 provides an overview of the most important antecedents we identified, grouped in a series of categories for easy communication (though we acknowledge that many variables span multiple categories).

Environmental Factors

There is evidence that the involvement of external stakeholders—such as oversight bodies, politicians, citizens, or interest groups—in performance measurement practices matters not just for political use of performance data but also for purposeful use. Stakeholders can encourage managers to take performance information seriously, and they can also help in making sense of numbers or in identifying meaningful indicators (Askim, Johnsen, and Christophersen 2008; Berman and Wang 2000; Bourdeaux and Chikoto 2008; De Lancer Julnes and Holzer 2001; Moynihan and Hawes 2012; Yang and Hsieh 2007). Knowing that stakeholders care about performance data adds "political weight" (Ho 2006) and signals to managers that they should be on top of their department's data, performance trends, and explanations of outliers (Moynihan and Ingraham 2004).

Another important factor is the political environment. Notably, research indicates that competition and conflict foster the use of performance information rather than constrain it. In such an environment, performance data is more likely to become critical "ammunition" in contested political debates, and managers will need such data to justify their decisions to a heterogeneous field of competing stakeholders (Bourdeaux and Chikoto 2008; Moynihan and Hawes 2012). Askim, Johnsen, and Christophersen (2008) suggest that political competition creates pressure on the government in charge to improve, and that performance reports are an important source of feedback to determine where the major problems are or what the right benchmark is.

A final relevant environmental factor is the general political support that public service providers receive. Managers in organizations that have been assured of this support are more likely to engage in performance data use and more open to experimental learning based on this information because they do not fear immediate budget cuts, sanctions, or blame in cases where poor performance is reported or failure becomes transparent (Moynihan, Pandey, and Wright 2012a; Yang and Hsieh 2006).

Organizational Support

Leadership support is another crucial factor. Only if managers and employees are convinced that top-level leaders are committed to a reform will they make the effort to participate and devote their scarce resources accordingly (Boyne et al. 2004; Moynihan and Ingraham 2004; Moynihan and Lavertu 2012; Yang and Hsieh 2006). This might require that top-level leaders show symbolic commitment as well as make purposeful use of strategic performance data themselves. Dull (2009, 260) summarized the leadership effect quite well: "If they perceive a lack of credible leadership commitment to results-model reform, managers may see reform as a threat or a nonissue, gathering less information from fewer, less diverse sources, engaging

Table 12.3. Factors influencing performance information use, exemplary measures, and exemplary studies

Factor	Exemplary Measures	Exemplary Studies
Environmental		
Stakeholder involvement	"The extent of support for performance measures by elected officials and/or citizens." "Citizens help this organization evaluate performance."	Berman and Wang 2000; Bourdeaux and Chikoto 2008; Moynihan and Ingraham 2004; Ho 2006; Moynihan and Hawes 2012; Moynihan and Pandey 2010; Yang and Hsieh 2006.
Political competition/ conflict	"Party concentration in the municipal council indicated by 1-Herfindahl Index." "The stakeholders in this school district fulfill in general their agreements with one another [reversed]."	Askim, Johnsen, and Christophersen 2008; Bourdeaux and Chikoto 2008; Moynihan and Hawes 2012.
General political support	"Most elected officials trust our organization." "Most elected officials believe that our organization is effective."	Moynihan, Pandey, and Wright 2012a; Yang and Hsieh 2006.
Performance Management System Design		
Measurement of system maturity	"Performance indicators are easy to access, have stretching but achievable performance targets, and meet performance information needs." "Managers are involved in a PI-based benchmarking with other cities."	Ammons and Rivenbark 2008; Berman and Wang 2000; De Lancer Julnes and Holzer 2001; Ho 2006; Kroll and Proeller 2013; Melkers and Willoughby 2005; Moynihan and Pandey 2010; Taylor 2009; Yang and Hsieh 2006.
Employee involvement	"Employees were involved in evaluation prior to the review." "Most administrators support the use of performance measures."	Boyne et al. 2004; Folz, Abdelrazek, and Chung 2009; Kroll 2013; Melkers and Willoughby 2005.
Data quality/ usability	"Assessment of data's understandability, reliability, and overall quality." "Difficulty obtaining valid or reliable data [reversed]."	Ammons and Rivenbark 2008; Dull 2009; Kroll 2013.

(continued)

text continues on page 199

Table 12.3. (continued)

Factor	Exemplary Measures	Exemplary Studies
Learning forums/routines	"Work groups are actively involved in making work processes more effective." "The individual I report to periodically reviews with me the results or outcomes of the programs/operations/projects that I am responsible for."	Moynihan 2008; Moynihan and Landuyt 2009; Moynihan and Lavertu 2012.

Organizational Support

Leadership support	"Agency's top leadership demonstrates a strong commitment to achieving results." "Top managers emphasize and care about the process of performance management."	Boyne et al. 2004; Dull 2009; Moynihan and Ingraham 2004; Moynihan and Lavertu 2012; Yang and Hsieh 2006.
Support capacity	"The extent to which the organization has committed resources time, people, money to be used in measurement of program performance." "Most departments in our jurisdiction have adequate information technology for performance measurement."	Berman and Wang 2000; De Lancer Julnes and Holzer 2001; Moynihan and Hawes 2012; Yang and Hsieh 2006.

Generic Organizational

Innovative culture	"My department is a very dynamic and entrepreneurial place. People are willing to stick their necks out and take risks." "The glue that holds my department together is a commitment to innovation and development. There is an emphasis on being the best."	Folz, Abdelrazek, and Chung 2009; Johansson and Siverbo 2009; Moynihan 2008; Moynihan and Pandey 2010; Moynihan, Pandey, and Wright 2012b.
Goal orientation/clarity	"It is easy to explain the goals of this organization to outsiders." "This organization's mission is clear to those who work here."	Moynihan and Landuyt 2009; Moynihan, Pandey, and Wright 2012a, 2012b.

Table 12.3. (continued)

Factor	Exemplary Measures	Exemplary Studies
Individual		
Flexibility/decision discretion	"Agency managers/supervisors at my level have the decision-making authority they need to help the agency accomplish its strategic goals."	Moynihan and Lavertu 2012; Moynihan and Landuyt 2009; Moynihan and Pandey 2010; Nielsen 2014b.
	"Decision making and control are given to employees doing the actual work."	
Attitude toward PM	"I believe that steering with performance data is important."	Ammons and Rivenbark 2008; Ho 2006; Kroll 2013a; Taylor 2011.
	"Performance measurement has brought more advantages than disadvantages to my unit/agency."	
Prosocial motivation	"Making a difference in society means more to me than personal achievements."	Kroll and Vogel 2013; Moynihan and Pandey 2010; Moynihan, Pandey, and Wright 2012a.
	"I am prepared to make sacrifices for the good of society."	
Networking behavior	"Assessment of how frequently managers interact with different relevant stakeholders."	Kroll 2013b; Moynihan and Hawes 2012.
	"I maintain a regular exchange with colleagues from other cities who work in the same field."	

Note: PI = performance information; PM = performance management.

fewer people, and leaning on familiar ideas and practices." Support capacity is similarly important. There are quite a few studies that have found that an investment in the know-how and technology needed to analyze performance data and produce usable reports is a critical condition of purposeful use (Berman and Wang 2000; De Lancer Julnes and Holzer 2001; Moynihan and Hawes 2012; Yang and Hsieh 2006).

Performance Management System Design

A number of findings speak directly to how performance management systems are designed. One of the most prominent factors in performance data use is the sophistication of the measurement system. These systems can differ in terms of the variety, usefulness, and accessibility of data. Data use tends to be higher when measurement systems score high on these dimensions (Ammons and Rivenbark

2008; Berman and Wang 2000; De Lancer Julnes and Holzer 2001; Ho 2006; Kroll and Proeller 2013; Melkers and Willoughby 2005; Moynihan and Pandey 2010; Taylor 2009; Yang and Hsieh 2006). A similar positive effect was found when users evaluated the quality of data positively (Ammons and Rivenbark 2008; Dull 2009; Kroll 2015).

Performance systems also tend to facilitate greater information use if they involve line managers and employees in developing these systems (Boyne et al. 2004; Folz, Abdelrazek, and Chung 2009; Melkers and Willoughby 2005). Such involvement fosters support of performance management practices and buy-in to the system. One recent study further examined the positive effect of a social norm embracing performance measurement (Kroll 2015) and found that such a norm creates readiness for data use among managers (affects their intentions) and at the same time pressures managers to show this behavior even if this is not consistent with their intentions.

One challenge faced by performance systems is that they invariably create routines to collect and disseminate data but too rarely create learning routines to encourage the use of this data. Research has indicated that managers make purposeful use of performance data when their organizations have established mechanisms for discussing and collectively making sense of this information (Moynihan 2008; Moynihan and Landuyt 2009; Moynihan and Lavertu 2012). These "learning forums" create opportunities for managers and employees to reflect on their core processes and related outcomes and to provide communication channels to make solutions to problems on the individual level usable for the whole organization. A recent practical example of these routines comes in the GPRA Modernization Act of 2010, which mandated that all US federal agencies create quarterly data-driven meetings centered on their most important goals (Moynihan 2013).

Generic Organizational Factors

Another category of variables are organizational factors that are not directly linked to the adoption of measurement practices and can therefore be labeled generic. One highly relevant factor in this category is organizational culture. There is a good deal of support for the finding that an innovative culture has a positive effect on the use of performance information (Folz, Abdelrazek, and Chung 2009; Johansson and Siverbo 2009; Moynihan 2008; Moynihan and Pandey 2010; Moynihan, Pandey, and Wright 2012b). "Innovative" here means that the members of the organization are open to change and to learn from mistakes in order to improve programs and services for customers and target groups. Performance information is most likely to be valued as important additional feedback that can be used to improve and innovate. A similar effect was found for the existence of goal clarity in public administration (Moynihan and Landuyt 2009; Moynihan, Pandey, and Wright 2012a, 2012b). If organizations have clearly stated goals, it is also more likely that the achievement of these objectives will be regularly discussed and evaluated, thus adding weight to the organizations' performance information.

Individual Factors

On the individual level, managers' attitudes toward a performance-based steering philosophy are important. If they are not convinced that performance data will help them manage their entities more effectively, they will not devote effort toward using the information (Ammons and Rivenbark 2008; Ho 2006; Kroll 2015; Taylor 2011). This research suggests that managers matter, and that they can make a difference even in settings where performance measurement is difficult or reporting and evaluation routines are underdeveloped. It also implies that people's perceptions of performance management reforms are critical. Reforms are more likely to succeed when there is a convincing reform narrative and a participative implementation strategy.

Another individual variable is the managers' motivation. Performance systems have often been paired with monetary incentives. These incentives matter, but have been associated with perverse rather than purposeful behavior in many cases (Heinrich and Marschke 2010; Soss, Fording, and Schram 2011). There is growing evidence that purposeful performance information use can be better achieved by appealing to the prosocial motivation of helping others and making a difference in society (Kroll and Vogel 2013; Moynihan and Pandey 2010; Moynihan, Pandey, and Wright 2012a). This is because data use requires effort on the part of the managers (reading reports, making sense of data, initiating change) that is hard to observe—and therefore to enforce. Managers who have a strong prosocial orientation are found to take on this burden voluntarily. Moreover, performance reports often incorporate data on the impact that services and programs have on clients, which is important feedback for those who care about the difference they can make through their work. There is much practical work to be done to design performance systems to better relate performance indicators to the desire of employees to make a difference (Moynihan 2013).

Notably, sociodemographic differences (age, gender, education, position, experience, etc.) appear to matter little to data use; most of these variables were found to be inconclusive or insignificant (De Lancer Julnes and Holzer 2001; Dull 2009; Melkers and Willoughby 2005; Moynihan and Ingraham 2004; Moynihan and Pandey 2010; Taylor 2011). Networking behavior can be positively associated with purposeful use, however (Moynihan and Hawes 2012). Though the research on this variable is still scarce, there is evidence that managers who are active networkers and open to feedback from diverse sources also show great interest in performance reports (Kroll 2013).

A final variable in this category is the managers' discretion. This factor was found to have a positive effect (Moynihan and Lavertu 2012; Moynihan and Landuyt 2009; Moynihan and Pandey 2010). The reasoning behind this is that managers have a stronger incentive to use performance data if they are able to change processes autonomously and to determine how to achieve their goals. One study of Danish school administrators found that managerial authority was central to making performance management systems actually improve organizational performance (Nielsen 2014b).

CONCLUSION: LESSONS FOR PUBLIC VALUE

We conclude by drawing out the key lessons from our analysis on the relation between performance management and public value.

Performance systems have become a key way through which public value is represented. In contemporary governance, mission statements, strategic goals, and performance measures have become perhaps the dominant mechanism through which public managers are asked to define and be held accountable to the public value promises they make.

Creating performance information is a political act. In a democratic environment, asserting one particular goal or measure versus another represents a form of policymaking and should be recognized as such. Our literature review suggests that compared to other types of performance information use, there is perhaps least attention to political use. This is an oversight that needs to be remedied, since one thing in common among Moore's account of entrepreneurial public managers creating public value, Bozeman's considerations of choices between public values, and the creation and use of performance data is that they are all inherently political activities.

Performance management systems tend to privilege certain values and displace others. The virtue of performance systems is that they direct attention to mission achievement. But this can also be a danger if public managers only define public value in terms of the efficiency and effectiveness of their mission achievement. Attention to other traditional values, such as equity and due process, may be lost. In this one key dimension, the use of performance systems seems to illustrate the differences between Moore's and Bozeman's conceptions of public value(s). The entrepreneurial manager seeking to achieve greater performance may improve public value in the Moore conception of the term while undercutting other public values in the Bozeman understanding of the term. Even if performance systems aim at including non-mission-based outcomes and adding more scorecard dimensions (see, for example, Moore's chapter 8 in this volume), it is unlikely that they will be able to give a full account of the value a program or organization has created. By definition these systems are imperfect and lacking in complexity, but they can facilitate prioritization and learning if decision makers consider them as what they are—one information source among many.

The relationship between performance data and public value depends upon how the data is used. This chapter has suggested that performance management can help to strengthen values like accountability, transparency, and legitimacy, but there are also examples in which the adoption of such systems has fallen short of these values. Much depends upon how performance data is used. We have focused the greatest attention here on purposeful performance information use because of its strong potential impact in creating public value, but we should not assume that performance systems are always positively related to public value. A discussion of passive, political, and perverse forms of performance information use illustrates that in some cases performance systems may do little to facilitate, and may even damage, public value. In particular, the evidence of perverse outcomes is strong enough that they cannot be dismissed as an exception or unanticipated consequence of performance management.

The key benefits of performance systems lie in encouraging purposeful use of performance data. Overall, research on performance management seems to indicate that planning, measuring, and reporting are important elements that are able to create transparency, accountability, and legitimacy. However, to generate value for citizens in the sense that the quality and intended impact of public services increase, it is not enough to set up sophisticated measurement systems. Instead, managers need to make use of performance information to learn what works and what doesn't and initiate change when necessary. In particular, this means finding ways to encourage purposeful use.

Establishing purposeful use is not easy. While we advocate for purposeful performance information use, this is not an easy task. Different US federal reforms have had little effect on purposeful use but have instead encouraged passive use (Moynihan and Lavertu 2012). One challenge is that while it is easy to require the creation and dissemination of performance data, finding ways to facilitate use is both a novel task for governments and one for which they have little existing knowledge. This chapter has offered an overview of important antecedents of purposeful performance information use. Some of the factors have been tested more often than others, increasing our confidence about their influence. For example, measurement system maturity, stakeholder involvement, leadership support, support capacity, and an innovative culture have turned out to be highly relevant impact factors in a great number of studies, whereas others have shown positive effects that still deserve further examination. It is surprising that we know relatively little about the role of the data users themselves, particularly since sociodemographic differences were found to be of little relevance. Therefore, studying the extent to which individual factors—such as identities or learning styles—matter for data use is a promising endeavor for further research.

Set realistic expectations for performance management. It is also helpful to temper expectations about the potential impact of performance systems. Changing ingrained patterns of decision making is no small task, and efforts to foster purposeful performance information use will, at best, likely result in incremental changes, with data use orientated toward existing patterns and routines of decision making. Another limitation is that performance information is descriptive and subjective—that is, these data do not suggest why there may be a problem or how it can be solved. Interpretations can vary among individuals and are often controversial and role-induced.

13

PUTTING PUBLIC VALUE TO WORK

A FRAMEWORK FOR PUBLIC MANAGEMENT DECISION MAKING

ANTHONY M. CRESSWELL, MEGHAN COOK,
AND NATALIE HELBIG

This chapter presents a practical solution to the problems government managers face when attempting to use public value creation as a guide for decision making and investment. The current context of ideological polarization and often fractured and privatized government exacerbates these problems. As a result, decision makers need improved tools to support their pursuit of public value, particularly in situations complicated by competing public values.

To be useful and effective, tools to incorporate public value thinking in government decision making must address issues of political strategy, operational planning, and effective implementation of initiatives. They must provide means for taking into account the relevant diversity in public values as contested principles or preferences held by citizens and groups (Bozeman 2007; Davis and West 2009), and a more general idea of public value in terms of how government actions can provide specific desirable outcomes from the point of view of particular citizens or groups (Moore 1995; Moore and Khgram 2004). To translate public value thinking into practice, government decision makers need ways to take into account both the context of value diversity linked to the particulars of their decision problem—that is, the Bozeman perspective—and how those preferences are linked to the expected actions and outcomes of the decision from Moore's perspective. Without linking to specific actions and outcomes, the abstract notions of a *public* or of *public value* are not particularly useful. Indeed, finding an applicable understanding of what constitutes the public is problematic. As Bryson, Crosby, and Bloomberg note, "In practical terms, the public may already be known, may need to make itself known, or may need to be created" (2014, 451). The methods presented here offer one approach to that problem.

In addition, the tools should also accommodate the complex forms and nuances of public value without the resulting complexity overwhelming the decision-making process. Analytical and decision support tools must frame public value in a sufficiently specific and detailed way in order to guide assessment of realistic alternatives when examining actual government initiatives.

This chapter describes the public value assessment tool (PVAT),[1] which speaks to these needs. The PVAT uses the key concepts from the Center for Technology in Government's public value framework (Cresswell, Burke, and Pardo 2006) and draws on the CTG's twenty-two years of applied research on information and communication technologies and effective forms of cross-boundary collaboration to support government policymaking and service delivery. The PVAT helps create a formal and structured method for assessing public value and a way to make it a systematic part of the planning process. It also addresses several of the practical problems identified in recent theory and research about public value and value-oriented or normative approaches to government administration and reform (Benington and Moore 2011a; Cresswell 2010; Davis and West 2009; Frederickson 1990, 2010; Hui and Hayllar 2010; Beck Jørgensen and Vrangbæk 2011; Beck Jørgensen and Bozeman 2007).

The PVAT offers one solution that addresses a core problem in putting public value thinking into practice: the deep complexity of the concepts themselves and the range of possible value propositions and impacts. This problem arises in part as a result of disagreement on the many forms public value can take (Alford and Hughes 2008; Beck Jørgensen and Bozeman 2007; Rutgers 2008; Van der Wal and Van Hout 2009) and about the specific content and sources of public values (Beck Jørgensen and Bozeman 2007; Bozeman 2012).

The PVAT was made available to government users and analysts, originally as part of National Science Foundation Grant 52732. The tool outlines a series of steps that document the perceived public value for various initiatives across a set of seven public value dimensions and constructs an overall summary of public value propositions that can guide group deliberation and decision making, mainly among public managers but potentially also involving the public. As of December 2014, an electronic version of the PVAT has been downloaded over 650 times by public, private, nonprofit, and academic organizations throughout the world. The PVAT has also been adopted by one large US government agency for use in developing its open government plan for submission to the White House. This chapter briefly describes initial government responses to the use of the tool and the implications for public value assessment generally.

A PUBLIC VALUE FRAMEWORK

The framework described here is simple in concept but complex in application. It brings into focus two distinct but equally important types of public value: the delivery of benefits directly to citizens and other private entities, and enhancing the value of government itself as a public asset. These two types are grounded in both the philosophical foundations of the public value concept and its development in the public administration literature; it connects what happens in the government with the impacts on stakeholders in the public domain. The approach helps decision makers expand the typical view of stakeholders and their interests to do justice to the scope of government and how it affects individuals, groups, and other public and private organizations. A more detailed discussion of the mechanisms by which value is generated appear in the following sections.

Public Value Dimensions

The public value framework organizes public value descriptions into seven basic clusters, each identified as a high-level value dimension; each dimension has several subdimensions. The seven dimensions are stated at a high enough level of abstraction to make them applicable to virtually any government initiative. The subdimensions can be stated or adapted in more specific terms tailored to the characteristics of an initiative under consideration. The seven dimensions are as follows (Cresswell, Burke, and Pardo 2006; Center for Technology in Government 2011):

1. **Financial:** impacts on current or anticipated income; asset values; liabilities; entitlements; other aspects of wealth; or risks to any of the above.
2. **Political:** impacts on personal or corporate influence on government actions or policy; the stakeholder's role in political affairs; or influence in political parties or prospects for current or future public office.
3. **Social:** impacts on family or community relationships; social mobility; status; and identity.
4. **Strategic:** impacts on economic or political advantage or opportunities; goals; and resources for innovation or planning.
5. **Ideological:** impacts on beliefs; moral or ethical commitments; alignment of government actions, policies, or social outcomes with beliefs; or moral or ethical positions.
6. **Stewardship:** impacts on the public's view of government officials as faithful stewards or guardians of the value of the government itself in terms of public trust, integrity, and legitimacy.
7. **Quality of life:** impacts on individual and household health; security; satisfaction; and general well-being.

By naming the value impact dimensions in this way, we aim to reduce the complexity when thinking about the variety of public values. Similarly, Beck Jørgensen and Bozeman (2007), based on an analysis of over two hundred published articles, used cataloging to reduce the complexity associated with public value concepts; they identified nodal values that "appear to occupy a central position in a network of values" (371). Some of the values are expressed as competing ideas or opposite ends of a continuum, such as advocacy versus neutrality or competitiveness versus cooperativeness. One limitation of this approach to reducing complexity is that any attempt beyond simple groupings raises questions about the hierarchical aspects of values or interdependence among them.

The dimensions are also similar to those identified in more recent work. Benington (2009) describes four dimensions of public value: ecological, political, economic, and social and cultural. Using factor analysis of survey results, Meynhardt and Bartholomes (2011) found evidence of three basic value dimensions rooted in psychological theories of human needs and motivation: instrumental-utilitarian (institutional performance), moral-ethical (moral obligation), and political-social (political stability). While reducing complexity by cataloging concepts is effective, it leaves unanswered the question of who benefits.

The framework's dimensions also employ concepts in public finance and economics. In these literatures, "public" refers to publicly as opposed to privately held goods. Public goods are those that persons can enjoy in common; those enjoyed by any one person or group do not diminish those available to others (Samuelson 1954), such as security provided by government investments in military and law enforcement capabilities. Private returns, by contrast, can be captured exclusively by individuals, such as the benefits of government-provided health insurance for senior citizens or trash collection provided by local governments. Some government activities provide a mix of public and private goods in these terms. Public education, for example, provides a mix of benefits to individual students and their families along with the benefits to society as a whole resulting from a more productive economy, a better-informed electorate, and improved social behavior inculcated in schools (Weisbrod 1962). The public value framework described here includes public, private, and mixed returns as impacts of government activity. The public part of our public value approach also includes citizen beneficiaries (or private returns) whose interests are the foundation of the value propositions (Benington 2009).

Central to our public value framework is an expanded—and shifting—view of where impacts of government activity occur. Following Meynhardt and Metelmann's (2009) recasting of public value not as something that the public values but as the impact on values about the public, the CTG's public value framework allows room for both positive and negative value impacts. At a granular level, the value propositions refer to impacts on persons both inside and outside government, including ideological and tangible impacts. Thus the variety of possible value propositions for government initiatives will be quite large and complex, typically including a mix of positive and negative results.

To illustrate, consider who wins and who loses when a city's department of health puts restaurant health inspection results online. Restaurant patrons might avoid unhealthy eateries and reduce their risk of food-borne illness. Encouraged by favorable public response, the mayor might publish other kinds of data, such as hospital ratings, with similar positive impacts for some patients and for the mayor as well. Some restaurateurs might lose business or even fail, and restaurant business might decline overall, reducing tax revenues. Health inspector workload and stress might grow dramatically and require the city to increase the inspection staff and budget at the cost of some other program. Software developers might profit from creating mobile applications for access to these data resources. Other second-order effects might be even more diverse and tangled.

To account for this diversity of possible outcomes, our multidisciplinary approach links to the literature in economics and public finance, political science, sociology, management and organizational studies, philosophy, public administration, and psychology. It arranges values in clusters, not in hierarchies. Although the approach does not identify relations among the value dimensions or how they can interact in practice, it does lead analysts and decision makers to take potential interdependencies into account. A special advantage of the set of dimensions is that it encourages consideration of impacts beyond financial efficiency or specific program effectiveness.

Linking Value to Initiatives: Understanding the Value Chain

The value dimensions are just one part of the public value framework. In use, the framework begins with description of a specific policy or program initiative as the focus of attention; that initiative would not necessarily involve impacts on all public value dimensions. Therefore, use of the framework should identify the links between the initiative and its explicit or implied value chain and the subset of desired or expected impacts.

For that purpose the framework includes a generic way to view the potential value propositions for a government initiative. In figure 13.1, the smaller ellipse shown with broken lines includes what could be called a limited "internal" value proposition from the point of view of an agency or program. The costs are expressed in financial terms and the returns or impacts are in terms of agency-defined efficiencies or effectiveness gains. The larger ellipse includes possible broader "external" impacts to both government more generally and the environment.

The implicit benefits are typically not part of the expressed goals of the initiative. The policy or electoral benefit refer to the positive impacts of the initiative on the reputation, status, support, or career prospects of officials. Secondary performance gains are impacts on the performance of parts of government other than those involved directly in the initiative. For example, an initiative that improves the nutritional value of school lunches may lead to healthier children (the direct benefit) but may also lead to higher academic achievement levels. The benefit assessment includes *development risk*, whether or not the initiative can be successfully developed, and *benefit risk*, whether a successfully developed initiative actually produces the expected results.

Basic Public Value Generators

Each specific initiative will involve some mix of operational mechanisms or business processes that are intended to generate the desired impacts within the value chain. A simple initiative involving, say, a new benefit payment may have a simple value chain running from eligibility determination, through the payment transaction, to how the payments are used. An entirely new service program, such as a job training program for green industry, would likely have more complex business processes; those processes would consist of the purposeful sequences of activities and events that result in the delivery of the service and are believed to account for an increase or decrease in public value. For a given public value analysis, it would be the responsibility of the persons applying the framework to identify and analyze the appropriate business processes and expected value impacts.

That description and analysis can be quite challenging. To guide and assist in that task, the framework identifies what we call generic value generators. These generators, based on the case studies and literature foundations of the framework, serve to broaden the scope of what a public value analysis might include. The generators reflect the idea that value can take many forms, including but not at all limited to economic or financial impacts. Any government initiative has the potential to generate more than one kind of public value impact as described by the seven value dimensions listed above. These generators can serve as a heuristic device to assist in identifying a wide range of possible value mechanisms and

Figure 13.1 General public value propositions

Source: Adapted by Anthony M. Cresswell from Anthony M. Cresswell, G. Brian Burke, and Theresa A. Pardo (2006), *Advancing Return on Investment Analysis for Government IT: A Public Value Framework* (Albany, NY: Center for Technology in Government, 7).

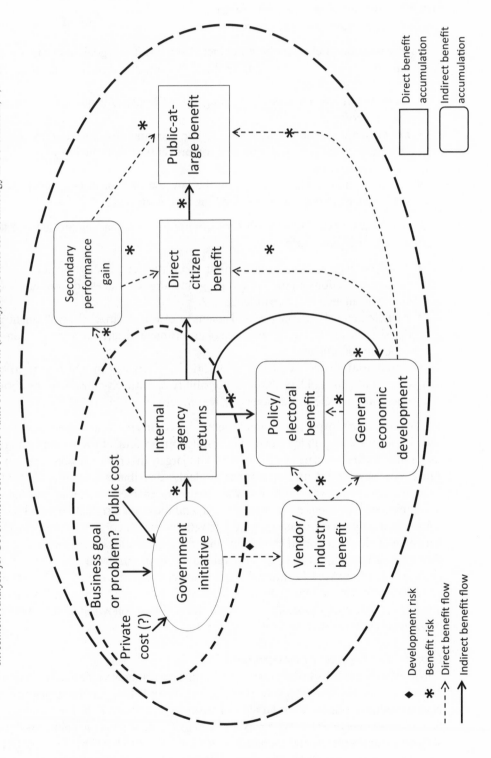

impacts and how they come about. Each generator can apply independently to virtually any kind of government initiative.

The generic value generators are:

- **Increases in efficiency:** obtaining increased outputs or goal attainment with the same resources, or obtaining the same outputs or goals with lower resource consumption.
- **Increases in effectiveness:** increasing the quality and/or quantity of the desired outcome.
- **Enablement:** providing the means for or allowing desirable activity that is otherwise infeasible or prohibited, or preventing or reducing undesirable events or outcomes.
- **Intrinsic enhancements:** changing the environment or circumstances of a stakeholder in ways that are valued for their own sake.

Adapting the framework to open government initiatives was accomplished by adding the following generators:

- **Transparency:** access to information about the actions of government officials or operation of government programs that enhances accountability or citizen influence on government.
- **Participation:** the frequency and intensity of direct citizens' involvement in decision making about or operation of government programs or in selection of or actions of officials.
- **Collaboration:** the frequency or duration of activities in which more than one set of stakeholders share responsibility or authority for decisions about operation, policies, or actions of government.

The restaurant inspection example above, based on an actual case in New York City, illustrates how public returns can result from all four of these value generators, some of which accrue in addition to—and largely independently of—efficiency gains. The New York City Department of Health distributes data in a more efficient and apparently more effective way; that data enables restaurant patrons to make improved decisions about where to eat, and they may also feel safer and more confident in city government. Judging from the initial reaction, however, the Department of Health reported complaints that the reinspections were too slow, such that a bad grade could not be quickly remedied. In addition, the New York City chapter of the New York Restaurant Association claimed that the grades hurt overall restaurant business. That claim was disputed by the mayor's office, which offered data on the reduction of incidences of food-borne illness following implementation of the inspection regime.

Links to the Business of Government

Public value is generated when an initiative links government goals and operations, as well as business processes, to public interests and then generates positive or negative value to stakeholders. Goals and business processes provide links between how the initiative interacts with stakeholders to generate value. A public value assessment framework should therefore include attention to how the initiative links to the relevant government goals, operations, and business processes.

This linking process is typically more complex than it may appear, requiring a comprehensive and reasonably detailed picture of the government goals and operations that make up the initiative. Such a picture identifies the relevant links between the stakeholders and the initiative's business processes. Many government initiatives have potential links across many agencies and processes. For example, the Washington State Digital Archives collects records from hundreds of state and local agencies and makes many of them available to the public online.[2] The Pennsylvania Integrated Enterprise System supports human resources management, budgeting, and other administrative functions for all state executive agencies.[3] To deal with this broad a scope of potential value impacts, the framework should accommodate a wide range of possible value outcomes across many agencies or processes. Using the framework can lead analysts to incorporate such a comprehensive view of where value impacts can originate.

An analysis of the business processes and potential impacts of initiatives can also use additional frameworks and models. The business reference models that have been developed for the US and Australian governments are good examples for government generally.[4] A business reference model describes the business operations of an organization independent of the organizational structure that performs them. Additional work has been done for the health sector (Brown, Kelly, and Querusio 2011). These reference models supplement the public value framework by assisting in making explicit the links between public value goals and an initiative's business processes. The business reference model approach is incorporated in the design of the PVAT for open government discussed in the next section.

The Stakeholder Analysis: Who Receives Value?

An analysis of value impacts requires identifying those with an interest in the value generating process—that is, the stakeholders. When the influence mapping is combined with identified stakeholder interests, the details of possible value impacts can be brought to light. Using the PVAT thus includes: (1) identifying the persons or groups (including organizations) whose interests are potentially affected, (2) identifying what their specific interests may be, and (3) assessing their role and potential influence in the delivery of public value. The first two aspects are necessary to identify specific value impacts and possible assessment strategies and thus are outlined briefly here. A more detailed discussion of stakeholder analysis can be found in the work of Williams and Lewis (2008) and Bryson (2004b).

The method in the framework is simple: it is based on identifying stakeholders and mapping them in a way that reflects their importance, and means of influence, and then estimating the way the initiative will impact their interests, as noted in figure 13.2.

Accurate mapping of this sort requires ample knowledge of the political and organizational context (Meyer and Höllerer 2010). All the requisite knowledge may not be found inside the agency, raising the prospect of involving external participants and environmental scanning as part of the analysis. External participation of interest groups can increase the difficulty of process management, which can impact outcomes (Bryson 2004b; Edelenbos and Klijn 2006; Hendricks 2006). The details for working through this process in the context of a particular initiative are described in the PVAT materials.

Figure 13.2 The stakeholder map: power versus interest
Source: Adapted from Ackermann and Eden (1998, 122; and 2011, 183).

Level of Interest

		Low	High
Power	Low	Minimal effect	Keep informed
	High	Keep satisfied	Key player

A PUBLIC VALUE ASSESSMENT TOOL: APPLYING IT TO OPEN GOVERNMENT INITIATIVES

The PVAT is a simplified approach to combining descriptions of an initiative's public value impacts, value chain, and stakeholder analysis into a convenient form to support deliberation and group decision making. The tool provides a method to deal with two central challenges of applying public value analysis to decisions about specific government initiatives: how to validly apply a general method to particular cases and how to reduce the level of effort required to feasible levels. To further facilitate the analysis, the PVAT was developed into an electronic tool that provides a way to electronically collect and present the results of a group-based approach and to identify the public value of a portfolio. A portfolio approach to planning and assessment for open government is crucial in the current climate of scarce resources and growing pressure for improved performance. Organizations face tough challenges in justifying, planning, implementing, and balancing their open government portfolios; decision makers do not have readily available, generally accepted ways to systematically identify and analyze information about the public value of government programs and services. The PVAT, however,

- sets forth a common language to discuss public value
- helps identify both explicit and implicit assumptions about value
- provides a documentation structure for data gathering
- summarizes individual public value assessments into a portfolio view
- serves as the foundation for group discussion and deliberation

Origins of the PVAT: Grounded in Practice

In late 2009 the CTG received an Early Concept Grant for Exploratory Research from the National Science Foundation to develop a resource for open government leaders. Undertaken in cooperation with the US General Services Administration, the approach for this work included a mix of best practices analysis and data gathering from federal agency representatives, nonprofit groups, and other state and local government officials and scholars interested or involved in open government efforts. In a December 2010 workshop held at the National Academy of Public Administration in Washington, DC, the CTG tested the conceptual design and elicited advice and feedback from open government teams from seven federal agencies: the US Office of Personnel Management, the US Department of Transportation, the US Department of Housing and Urban Development, the US Merit Systems Protection Board, the US Environmental Protection Agency, the US General Services Administration, and the White House Office of Science and Technology Policy. After the workshop, two agencies took the draft framework and used it in their current open government planning efforts; they provided valuable feedback about the mechanics of conducting open government assessments. Using the comments from these agencies, the CTG refined the tool.

The PVAT Process

The PVAT process involves six steps, and a detailed description of each step is shown in figure 13.3. In steps 1–5, each initiative is subjected to the public value analysis; step 6 combines those assessments into a portfolio view. With the current PVAT, analysis of as many as twenty efforts can be conducted in steps 1–5 and summarized in the step 6 portfolio view.

Steps 3 and 4 are the most challenging; they call for an assessment of both positive and negative public value for each primary stakeholder affected by that effort. Public value statements are described using the value types and descriptions above. Using these dimensions and descriptions, the participants record the expected public value impacts for each stakeholder for as many of the dimensions as they judge to be relevant.

Using the public value impacts for each stakeholder, the group identifies changes stakeholders will see in realizing that value. For instance, if certain stakeholders are going to see a positive economic value, what is the source of that value? Will there be a change in efficiency or a change in transparency that allows the stakeholders to do something they could not do before? In the PVAT, stakeholder changes are described using the public value generators, which include changes in efficiency, effectiveness, enablement, intrinsic enhancements, transparency, participation, and collaboration.

As noted previously, analysis of a portfolio from a public value perspective creates a richer picture of value and is meant to complement and enhance other forms of traditional strategic analysis such as return on investment and risk analysis. When organizations use the PVAT they can begin to compare and discuss their overall portfolio in terms of public value. As such, after a PVAT analysis, government leaders can ask the following questions of their own portfolio:

- What types of public value are we providing?
- Does our overall portfolio address our mission and deliver the best mix of public value returns to our stakeholders with available resources?
- Which initiatives will generate the most public value?
- What are the capabilities needed to implement an action plan?

Figure 13.3 Steps in the PVAT process

STEP 1	STEP 2	STEP 3	STEP 4	STEP 5	STEP 6
Describe Initiative	**Identify and Prioritize Stakeholders**	**Identify and Rate the Public Value**	**Identify Mechanisms of Change**	**Summarize the Public Value Assessments**	**Review Open Government Public Value Portfolio**
Initiative Description: • Title • Purpose • Supporting strategic goals • Program or policy area • Tactics	• Identify a full list of initiative stakeholders • Prioritize rating each stakeholder as A, B, or C	• Identify the type and level of public value the initiative is expected to create for each of the primary stakeholders Public value is expressed in terms of • Economic value • Social value • Political value • Strategic value • Quality-of-life value • Ideological value • Stewardship **value**	• For each stakeholder and each change mechanism describe how the expected value will be produced Change mechanisms include impacts on • Efficiency • Effectiveness • Intrinsic enhancement • Transparency • Collaboration • Participation	• Establish a summary assessment for the initiative for each public value type across all the primary stakeholders • All summary assessments are populated into the portfolio review workbook (step 6)	• Review public value assessments across all initiatives to inform decision making. • Does our open government portfolio, taken as a whole, optimize our resources and capabilities while meeting our mission and delivering maximum public value to all stakeholders?

Workbooks, steps 1–5

Portfolio review workbook

- What are the costs of implementing the efforts?
- Are we providing the desired mix of value types?
- How can we adjust our portfolio so that we offer the public value we intend?
- Are we addressing the interests of a comprehensive set of stakeholders, or only for a few?

Since the PVAT has been released, it was highlighted by the Australian government as one of the best ways to understand the value of information in Australia, and in the United States it was identified as a best practice by the US General Services Administration and shared on the US government's Howto.gov website.

This general interest and evidence of acceptance is not because the PVAT is a source of automated direction setting or decision making. The tool itself will not generate an answer to what is the best mix or balance of open government initiatives, but it will give government leaders a common language and framework through which to discuss the public value of their efforts and then use this information to inform and support their decision making and planning.

An Example of Use: The US Department of Transportation Case

Under President Barack Obama's Open Government Directive,[5] every federal agency was required to update its open government plan during 2012. In December 2011, the US Department of Transportation (DOT) staff sought the CTG's help in using the PVAT to support agency-wide open government planning. Over the next four months, the CTG worked with DOT staff to conduct the PVAT analysis, including a workshop to train DOT planners in the use of the PVAT. The project planners then used the PVAT to assess their open government projects and submitted their results to the agency-level open government team. The CTG worked with the open government team to prepare an agency-wide portfolio of projects based on the PVAT results; that portfolio was presented to the DOT Open Government Executive Steering Committee in March 2012 and ultimately became the agency's final open government plan.[6]

Analysis of the DOT Case

After using IdeaScale to solicit ideas from across the agency[7] DOT teams proposed eighteen different projects to include in the agency's open government action plan. To have their project included in the agency's open government plan, the department teams were required to conduct a PVAT analysis. Each team described its effort, identifying primary and secondary stakeholders as well as the public value and stakeholder interests.

After the team-level analysis, the workbooks went to the open government team to conduct the agency-level portfolio analysis. That team extracted a core list of stakeholders from the PVAT workbooks and common initiatives proposed across the agency. The team could then see what subset of the overall stakeholder list would be primary stakeholders in a new portfolio of projects. For this round of PVAT analysis the agency identified the following nine groups as primary stakeholders for their proposed efforts:

1. regional transit agencies
2. data developers

3. academic and research institutions
4. DOT internal departments
5. emergency responders
6. citizens who use online travel tools
7. veterans and veteran agencies
8. advocacy groups
9. regional transit agencies

The public value statements and stakeholder interests summarized by the DOT teams made up the core of the PVAT portfolio analysis, demonstrating how each proposed effort would likely provide value to the stakeholders, as well as highlighting public managers' associated logic models. The summary of one initiative, opening more regional transit data, indicated that negative economic value may accrue for some equipment vendors, whereas advocacy groups would likely see positive strategic value. Primary stakeholders such as regional transit authorities would likely see changes in operating effectiveness. The teams also identified the logic models associated with their reasoning as part of the summary document. For example, one model assumed that that opening data would lead to more informed decision making and that application developers would see an economic gain due to the data being available. The teams discussed these logic models as part of the public value planning process. The summary analysis exercise provided leaders an enterprise view of their overall portfolio.

Results of Using the PVAT in the DOT Case

The DOT released its open government plan on April 9, 2012.[8] In that plan it recapped where the agency made progress over the preceding two years, detailed its planning process for this update, and set forth a plan for the following three years. In the report the DOT presented how it used the PVAT to conduct the analysis and how the information guided its planning process. The public value assessment statements identified by DOT teams were the basis for the report, and there are references to the PVAT throughout. Such analysis helped to build the case for the projects that were selected to be part of the DOT's open government action plan. After describing the use of the PVAT, the *Open Government Report* states, "Using the PVAT process DOT developed both in-depth qualitative public value statements and overall activity summary judgments, both of which are essential inputs to overall agency decision making for Open Government Planning. The PVAT process was then used to help describe the value of the set of activities considered for adoption in DOT's Open Government Plan, as a portfolio."

There are other potential benefits of the PVAT approach—in particular, a more systematic, in-depth understanding of stakeholders and their interests. Discourse about public value is often mixed with strategic and tactical planning. Ordinary discussions of value are unlikely to include and document all types. PVAT results provide a structured and coordinated view of value impacts and risks, and establish a sound basis for implementation strategies; they can also be a valuable boundary object for group deliberations, and agencies can use some or all of this information for developing business cases, marketing materials, or action plans.

Challenges in Using the PVAT as Revealed by the DOT Case

The DOT's use of the PVAT revealed several challenges to successful use of public value approaches in practice: the need for sufficient time on task, the difficulty learning an unfamiliar terminology, the time it takes to manage group dynamics, and the challenges of integrating the tool and results with existing planning cycles and techniques.

Time on task needed to complete the right level of analysis. Undertaking a public value assessment in the detail required by the PVAT is a major task. The DOT limited the allotted time for its teams to conduct this analysis because of other competing priorities. Some teams reported the need for more time for analysis and discussion to obtain the right level of granularity in their statements.

Comfort and facility with the specialized language. Those conducting the assessment must understand the public value types and how to construct value statements based on those descriptions. In particular, creating qualitative statements often takes considerable time. Some participants needed more examples and explanation of public value before they could start the assessment. Some public value types are difficult to interpret. Several participants had substantial discussion about each value type before starting any assessments.

Crafting statements of value. Thinking about value with a three-pronged approach—specific project, specific stakeholder, and specific public value type—took practice. Making a judgment about value often took multiple tries, starting at a high level and then revising the judgment to be at a more granular and specific level. Some statements combined two or more values, requiring a second reviewer or members of the group to help craft separate value statements that could be assessed independently.

Making it a group effort, not an individual one. The PVAT was meant to support group planning and decision making. The two most frequently used strategies by the DOT department teams were (1) individuals doing the assessment alone, then coming together in groups to discuss and reconcile their statements and judgments, and (2) groups working together from the beginning through each PVAT section with one person documenting their statements. When time was short, the participants did more individual analyses, deferring discussion until the portfolio review; in such a case, the analysis for each effort did not go through a vetting process. The limitation of this approach is that the group must then either backtrack through all the work or simply accept each value statement as given.

Integrating public value information with traditional planning analyses. Once a full PVAT portfolio assessment is completed, including a summary of mostly qualitative public value statements, it is sometimes difficult for decision makers to connect this qualitative information with more quantitative return on investment and risk analysis data. Since a PVAT analysis is not meant to generate an *answer* but to instead provide a more comprehensive picture of value, it is sometimes not clear how to use that information. The DOT teams often wanted a single score or value; what they and the decision makers had was more overall knowledge about projected value, but, they did not have information on how it linked to the financial side of decision making. How to make those links can be informed by the PVAT results, but will still require judgment and other forms of analysis by decision makers.

IMPLICATIONS FOR RESEARCH AND PRACTICE

This chapter illustrates the promises and challenges of putting public value to work as a managerial decision support tool. Putting public value to work in a practical sense requires attention to implementation challenges, which can be formidable. Any move to institute public value thinking within a unit, division, or enterprise will require finding ways to overcome these challenges. The suggestions that follow address how research and practice can mutually inform one another.

There is little guidance in the empirical literature to assist officials in using forms of public value analysis, though a start has been made. Our work is in line with Moore's process perspective (1995) to examine more inductively how public value is construed in government decision making (Meynhardt and Metelmann 2009). Our examination here of a similar process shows how government actors adapt a given construction of public value, the PVAT, to fit particular program issues. Single cases such as this can provide fairly rich and useful descriptions of decision processes but cast only a very narrow beam of light onto the dimly lit range of government action. This is one line of research that can build grounded knowledge of public value analysis as a decision tool through the use of additional case studies. Absent theoretical consensus about public value in government processes, much can be learned from both approaches to the study of public value in use: inductive construction in process versus testing a priori frameworks.

Some studies empirically define, determine, and prioritize important public values. Other scholars criticize the basic premise of defining universal values and instead propose that values are enacted by individual citizens and groups (see, for example, West and Davis 2011). This work would take a different tack than ours and include such questions as: How does the public perceive the value propositions and dimensions? How does the public assess the performance of government in terms of these dimensions (Meynhardt and Bartholomes 2011)? How does the public interact with government to pursue these interests? The large body of existing interest group research (see, for example, Contandriopoulos 2011; Cooper, Nownes, and Roberts 2005; Dür and De Bièvre 2007; Hendricks 2006; Keiser and Miller 2010) already contains rich sources of material on these questions, but that material is not necessarily framed in a way that sheds direct light on these public value issues. Thorough reviews of this literature can add much to the discourse on public value.

It was clear from our limited work with a US federal agency that there is wide variation in how well agency decision makers know their stakeholders. If stakeholder interest is one basis for identifying public value, then government officials will need thorough and current knowledge of those interests. That suggests studies of current knowledge levels, how that knowledge is acquired and used, and how it is balanced against other decision criteria. Pursuit of these questions could be informed by the existing literature on representative bureaucracy (see, for example, Sawa and Selden 2003) in examining how administrators' objectives are balanced with stakeholder values and demands. It would also help expand the overall understanding of public value in practice to further examine how interests and stakeholder value propositions affect coalition formation and other interactions among stakeholders to influence policy and programs. Existing interest group research does speak to this question, but not from the point of view of public value creation (Contandriopoulos 2011; Edelenbos and Klijn 2006; Robbins 2010).

NOTES

1. The PVAT can be obtained at http://www.ctg.albany.edu/publications/online/pvat/?sub =online.
2. The Washington State Digital Archives can be found at http://www.digitalarchives.wa .gov.
3. The Pennsylvania Integrated Enterprise System can be found at http://www.ies.state.pa .us.
4. The federal enterprise reference models can be obtained at http://www.whitehouse.gov /omb/e-gov/fea;   http://www.finance.gov.au/policy-guides-procurement/australian -government-architecture-aga/aga-rm/2-reference-model-overview/.
5. The Open Government Directive can be found at http://www.whitehouse.gov/sites /default/files/omb/assets/memoranda_2010/m10-06.pdf.
6. For the final plan, see http://www.dot.gov/sites/dot.dev/files/docs/open-gov-v2_0.pdf.
7. IdeaScale was an online application used by federal government agencies working on the president's Open Government Directive; see https://ideascale.com/.
8. The DOT's open government plan can be obtained at http://www.dot.gov/sites/dot.gov /files/docs/DOT%20Open%20Government%20Plan%20v3.0.pdf.

14

SHARED RESPONSIBILITY FOR THE COMMON GOOD

MEASURING PUBLIC VALUE ACROSS INSTITUTIONAL BOUNDARIES

ENRICO GUARINI

Public management research has paid increasing attention to the public value paradigm. Despite the number of studies on the topic, we do not yet have a comprehensive empirical understanding of what happens when the public value paradigm is translated into performance measurement regimes and models.

A major issue here is how to integrate public value measurement across networks of business, civil society, and government within which public policies and services are implemented these days (Cleveland 2002; Linden 2002; Page 2004; Klijn 2005; Crosby and Bryson 2005, 2010; Osborne 2010). The changing economic climate in the wake of the financial crisis from 2007 onward can only add new twists to the debate. Measurement is a basic condition for discerning and assessing public value in these cross-sector environments.

Given their focus on government performance under the aegis of what has come to be called new public management, public value studies generally have not concerned themselves with the output of private-sector organizations. Business and nonprofits have been regarded as little more than "alternative providers" in efforts to diminish the state, or "service agents" for the delivery of government policy (Osborne and McLaughlin 2004).

On the other side, studies on corporate social responsibility (CSR) and social entrepreneurship have grown in parallel and have developed frameworks to properly consider the role of business and civil society in the provision of socially desirable outcomes.

Despite the shifting roles and responsibilities of business and governments in regard to societal problems, a need for increased governance of boundary-crossing partnerships also arises because of the range of interests and powers of the various actors involved (Bryson, Crosby, and Stone 2006). This functional issue cuts across the sectorial domains, and the question of public accountability becomes paramount.

Improving information and data flow among cross-sector networks is an essential and urgent prerequisite for discerning and assessing public value and public values as well as promoting collaborations and partnerships.

Performance measurement and reporting systems play an important role in achieving this goal. How should the existing performance measurement and reporting systems in place across governments, nonprofit organizations, and private firms be reshaped to operate within cross-sector environments?

Although scholars have focused on public value creation in strategic performance measurement (Moore 1995, 2003, 2013; Spano 2009), there have been relatively few attempts to embed public value issues into performance management within cross-sector networks. How citizen involvement in performance measurement and reporting is developed, implemented, and sustained at the local level has also been a limited area of research given its importance for improving democratic governance (Sanger 2008; Woolum 2011).

By looking for implications for public management, this chapter aims to offer a set of preliminary answers to the question of how governments themselves should shape policymaking, performance measurement, and reporting in order to integrate the contribution of civil society and private business to public value creation.

Presented in this chapter are the results from a case study of a regional government in Italy experiencing boundary-crossing public value measurement and reporting. The goal of the research was to collect information about how measurement efforts at the local level reflect public value creation in a networked setting, about the process that was used for community engagement, and about the extent to which the process to develop public value measurement and reporting is relevant for public and private leaders. As a conclusion, some implications for public management and governance are emphasized.

PUBLIC VALUE AND THE "SOCIAL" RESPONSIBILITY OF ORGANIZATIONS

Steering toward public value has become a management paradigm of increasing salience in recent years (Moore 1995, 2013; Benington and Moore 2011b; Stoker 2006; O'Flynn 2007; Alford 2008; Alford and O'Flynn 2009). According to this managerial approach (Moore 1995), value is created by public managers when governments achieve authorized outcomes that benefit the public.

Yet defining what the "value" created by an organization is and discerning the "public" or "private" nature of such value is a complex theoretical and practical issue. A classic problem is how the public interest is pursued (Bozeman 2002; Benington and Moore 2011b). While general economic, management, and policymaking theories have in the past been based on the clear separation—and often the juxtaposition—of market and state or between corporate goals and the rationale of public choices, current theories seek to integrate and make the two elements more compatible (Bozeman 2007; West and Davis 2011).

The last two decades have also witnessed a significant rethinking of what governance means and how the government role is evolving to encompass the notion of partnership and policy network for service delivery (Rhodes and Marsh 1992; Klijn, Koppenjan, and Termeer 1995; O'Toole 1997, 2000; Kickert, Klijn, and

Koppenjan 1997; Goldsmith and Eggers 2004; Stoker 2006; Agranoff 2006; Bryson et al. 2006; Osborne 2010).

As clearly emphasized by the CSR paradigm (Perrini 2006; Schwab 2008; Porter and Kramer 2011), both businesses and nonprofits can contribute to the pursuit of public value through their socially responsible actions, and by making services and policies more relevant, responsive, and effective. Clarifying the public values that might be achieved (or demolished) by private actors is a relevant issue in Bozeman and other colleagues' approach (Frederickson 1991; Bozeman 2007; Beck Jørgensen 2007; Beck Jørgensen and Bozeman 2007; Julnes 2012).

By pointing out the aspect of the "value for the society" in a democracy, Bozeman emphasizes the importance of discerning what the public values are when the market or the government is involved in the provision of goods and services in a policy area. Conversely, given the focus on government operational capacity, Moore's public value approach generally has not been explicitly concerned with the contribution of private-sector organizations to government achieving public value. Business and nonprofits have been considered by Moore mainly as "service agents" for the efficient and effective delivery of government strategy. Only recently, Moore's managerial approach is evolving toward integrating a broader range of public values in performance measurement tools (Moore, 2013).

Yet a unitary and integrative conceptual framework of these different approaches to public value is still needed. In this view, it is interesting to integrate current literature with the Italian theoretical tradition of *economia aziendale* developed since the mid-1920s (Zappa 1927) but still unknown in the international academic context.[1] The interdependence between economic performance and public value is central in the theoretical basis of economia aziendale. Within this tradition the concept of "public value" may be ascribed to any socioeconomic entity in society. The dimension of "value" refers to the organization's results. Any socioeconomic entity uses resources as inputs and adds—or subtracts—economic value to them. This value is inherently measured by the costs and benefits of the various resources used for the production of goods and services (the "proposed value"), but also what it should be worth for stakeholders and society (the "recognized value"). Here the dimension of "public" refers to stakeholder interest as well as to the closely related criteria to be used in order to assess an organization's results. "Private interest" refers to the individual needs of stakeholders, whereas "public interest" is related to collective preferences and to the pursuit of the well-being of society. So, according to economia aziendale, any socioeconomic entity has a "social" responsibility (i.e., a responsibility to society) to create public value. This value is achieved if the organization's results fulfill stakeholder expectations and contribute to the common good. One challenge presented by this holistic approach is that society and a wide range of stakeholders—including employees—have legitimacy and should be considered in the governance of organizations in all sectors. In operational terms, this means that societal expectations should be embedded in performance management regimes and stakeholders involved in discerning and assessing how public value and public values might be achieved. This proposition contrasts with the traditional model of public administration and points toward a future characterized by the more collaborative, consultative approach indicated by the modern conceptual framework of the new public governance. So, being both positive and normative, the Italian economia aziendale theoretical tradition seems to have attempted to integrate the managerial approach and the societal-oriented approach to public values since the mid-1920s.

While integrating societal expectations in business decisions has formed the object of several studies in recent years (Chrisman and Carroll 1984; Kaplan and Norton 1993; Griffin 2000; Carroll 2000; Gray 2001), the implications of socially responsible initiatives on public value are a relatively new field and much less investigated.

Is it enough to simply consider how individual governments or businesses are responsive to society, or must we consider how networks, taken as a whole, are responsible for creating public value? To whom should lead networked actors be accountable?

This point appears to be of great importance especially within transforming welfare state societies accustomed to a strong tradition of government intervention or within institutional settings characterized by the Napoleonic administrative tradition (Pollitt and Bouckaert 2000; Ongaro 2009; Borgonovi and Mussari 2011). In this context, trust, fairness, legitimacy, and confidence in government as a "guarantor of public values" (Beck Jørgensen and Bozeman 2007, 373–74) are critical to public value creation. The public values the fact that government has the necessary overview of public needs and should be accountable for final outcomes and social impact (i.e., high-order aspirations such as public health, poverty reduction, etc.), even if public services and activities are carried out by business or nonprofit organizations.

In managerial-driven performance measurement systems, public managers determine what measures to collect and how to report and distribute the information to external audiences. The internal focus of such systems is an important tool for program and service delivery management, but there is no guarantee that what is tracked is what matters to citizens and external stakeholders (Woolum 2011).

Although scholars have focused on public value, there have been relatively few attempts to redesign performance measurement and reporting in the light of new cross-sector environments. Taking into account the perspective of public managers achieving their organization's aims, and their responsibility toward societal public values, we are led to two research questions: How can public value be discerned within a complex network of business, government and nonprofit actors? What type of measurement and reporting system allows government to better integrate business and civil society in creating public value?

RESEARCH DESIGN AND METHODOLOGY

The above questions could be answered using a variety of approaches to social scientific inquiry. This chapter describes and assesses a participatory action research effort (McIntyre 2008) spanning 2004–9 that involved the regional government of Veneto in Italy. Given the research questions and the present author's dual role as active participant and researcher, this approach was considered the most appropriate in this case: the research process and assessment were contextual and their relevance was determined by the participating actors.

The Veneto case is the sole Italian instance of a boundary-crossing public value measurement and reporting system led by a government, and the reasons for considering the regional government as a relevant unit of analysis are several. First, the process of devolution of authority from the central government in Italy is ongoing, and the regions are asked to set their own policy and strategy on a great number of topics. While previously the regions were simply asked to implement national policies, they are today increasingly autonomous. Second, regions are levels of government that, like municipalities, are close to citizens. Regions act mainly as redistributors of resources, and as a result they are more likely to be sensible to public value and cross-sector collaborations because their performance is related to the effective collaboration of other local public authorities and private local actors.

The participatory action research process included three key steps:

1. The collaborative development of a boundary-crossing conceptual framework for measuring and assessing public value creation by multisector actors lying at the intersection of regional public programs.

Table 14.1. Data sources

Data Source	Key Issues	Informants	Analysis
Interviews with top managers and elected officials	Public value reporting aims Methodology Stakeholder engagement	10 top managers 30 middle managers 6 elected officials	Qualitative analysis of accountability issues
Informal meetings with key stakeholders	Visualizing public value Measuring public value Social responsibility for the common good	150 representatives from business, nonprofit organizations, civic institutions	Summary of meetings and events
Interaction with the community	Visualizing public value Citizenship for the common good Public value measurement and reporting	1,000 students met during high school meetings 30 high school representatives online forum 8 small municipalities testing boundary-crossing public value reporting	Qualitative analysis of key emergent issues

2. A framework that was translated into a quantitative scheme by the collection of data on outcomes and the flows of financial resources as they move across public and private actors in the implementation of public programs.
3. The analysis of implications for policymaking processes and socially responsible initiatives.

These analyses benefit from an array of data sources, as summarized in table 14.1.

THE CONTEXT OF THE CASE

Italy has four levels of government: central (the parliament and the cabinet), regional (20 regions), provincial (103 provinces), and municipal (8,102 municipalities). Each level is multifunctional in that it has jurisdiction over several issues and mandatory activities. Each region has a council and a president elected directly by the citizens, as well as a professional bureaucracy. Regions are allowed to raise autonomous taxes, but a large percentage of their revenue flow is still represented by transfers from the central government. Regions play a limited role in the production of services, and they act mainly as regulatory actors and redistributors of resources to local provinces and municipalities.

Veneto is located in the northeast of Italy and is among the wealthiest and most industrialized regions of the country; its capital and largest city is Venice. Once the heartland of the Venetian Republic, Veneto is characterized by a strong community identity and a long tradition of social responsibility in business and civic volunteerism.

BOUNDARY-CROSSING PUBLIC VALUE REPORTING

At the start of the term of office in 2003 the newly elected regional officials were strongly interested in public accountability and reporting. The regional government had for years produced information and public performance reporting, but it was often based on sector-specific mandatory obligations. About 280 mandatory sector-specific reports were published and, overall, reporting was extremely fragmented. The newly elected officials struggled to get information in a concise form so that they could easily undertake policymaking, evaluate results, and interact effectively with business and civil society.

The public value measurement and reporting project grew out of the integrative leadership of an elected member of the cabinet, along with the efforts of the chief budget officer and a group of local partners in other sectors, to remedy this shortcoming. The political commitment and sponsorship from the elected member of the cabinet was crucial for the implementation of the initiative. The project structure consisted of the whole regional cabinet as a policy board, and a ten-member steering committee comprising local civil society and business leaders who were formally appointed by the chief budget officer together with the political leader of the cabinet (who launched the project). A small group of regional managers based in Venice and leading experts participated at the committee meetings and supported their operations. A number of representatives from government, businesses, and nonprofits were also engaged throughout the project.

The public value reporting was developed during the political term 2004–9, after which the process ceased when a political changeover took place. The community engagement is still ongoing, but with a differently shaped framework envisioned by the newly elected political leaders. A web platform is now used just to share and discuss policy priorities for the economic development of the region.

The Process of Public Value Reporting

The regional government developed the public value reporting process by involving the local community. Actors, activities, and outcomes of the process are summarized in table 14.2. The steering committee led the process, which took place in three phases. In the first phase (2004–5), the committee members clarified their assumptions, developed some guiding principles for measurement and reporting, and produced the value chain framework presented in figure 14.1. In the second phase (2006–9), the committee analyzed qualitative and quantitative data in order to better understand the flow of resources, outputs, and outcomes in the value chain framework. Based on this further analysis, the committee analyzed the full set of public programs and developed more specific value chain frameworks. A preliminary set of performance indicators was also developed. The third phase (2007–9) was developed parallel to the second phase and involved a large number of local stakeholders in the processes of measurement and reporting. The goal was to assess public value using data in the value chain framework and the preliminary set of performance indicators as well as to collect additional data across sectors.

Two multistakeholder forums were organized (2007–9) with 150 representatives of business, civil society, and local government involved in the value chain framework. The political leader sponsoring the project took part in these forums but avoided influencing decisions. Community leaders were involved in two informal multistakeholder meetings in which a preliminary set of indicators set out by the regional government was proposed for discussion. The list of significant items differed among firms and other stakeholders but took into account all the public programs delivered by the regional government. Additional characterizations of social responsibility indicators were clearly called for in each program. Relevance for each stakeholder was the criterion used within the forums for deciding if an indicator was significant enough to be included in the public value reporting. The steering committee facilitated the dialogue about relevance, and the final decision was taken by mutual agreement.

Each representative was required to determine what indicators were likely to be of sufficient significance to be worth measuring in a systematic way and be included in the public value reporting. During this process, some indicators were dropped from the preliminary set and others were added. While some stakeholder groups were interested in some of the indicators but not others, all actors agreed to embed every endorsed measure in a common set.

Finally, participating actors developed three additional practices as a result of the shared process. First, a unique web platform, which benefited from a grant from the central government, was developed to find and share data relevant to boundary-crossing public value reporting; people used this platform as a virtual agora to find and offer ideas, resources, and best practices and to join discussion

Table 14.2. The process of public value reporting

Phase	Actor	Activity	Outcome
1 (2004–5)	Steering committee	• Clarification of assumptions	• Guiding principles for measurement and reporting
	Regional managers	• Development of principles for public value reporting	• Value chain framework (fig. 14.1)
2 (2006–9)	Steering committee	• Quantitative analysis of the full set of public programs	• Quantitative representation of value chain framework
	Regional managers		
		• Collection of performance data	• Development of more specific value chain frameworks
			• Preliminary set of PIs
3 (2007–9)	Steering committee	• Multi-stakeholder forums	• Community engagement
	Regional managers	• Web platform	
	Political leader	• Online discussion groups	• Assessment of public value
	Local stakeholders and community	• High schools educational project on citizenship	• Collection of additional data
	Local municipalities	• Separate boundary-crossing public value reporting	• Validated set of PIs

groups. Since its launch the website has received over 800,000 visits. More than 1,900 people have registered for its newsletter and 285 people have uploaded profiles enabling them to share resources. This web platform also supported the work of community leaders involved in the multistakeholder forums and facilitated the discussion about indicators of public value. Second, thirty high schools and over one thousand students engaged in a project of education on citizenship for the common good (2007–8). Issues such as social responsibility, public value reporting, and citizenship were discussed in an informal manner during face-to-face sessions held by regional officials at schools and online. Teachers and students were also engaged in individual research assignments. Third, a separate project on boundary-crossing public value reporting grew from the larger regional process of measuring public value, and it was activated by a network of eight small local municipalities. Here some members of the regional steering committee provided expertise in terms of both content and process.

The Measurement and Reporting Framework

During the initial six-month steering committee discussions in 2004, the present author facilitated a set of "visualizing public value" sessions that helped the group to identify a shared framework for the measurement and reporting of public value.

The framework had its roots in the theoretical model of the value chain (Porter 1985) and public policy studies (Hall and O'Toole 2004; Kisby 2007). The committee members agreed that, at the regional level, public value creation cannot be understood by looking at an individual level of government. Most important, there was consensus about the need for boundary-crossing measurement and reporting systems. It should be noted that this consensus was also facilitated by the fact that local leaders were involved with the steering committee of the project since its conception; this helped them to perceive the public value reporting as a multisector project and not just a government initiative. The following main assumptions were considered:

- The contribution of business and nonprofits to public needs should be integrated in regional planning and public priority setting.
- Rules and decisions are formalized by regional laws, so the legislation defines networked patterns of program implementation as well as the shape of those patterns (i.e., the content of programs, services, final recipients, actors involved, role of actors, process of consultation, appropriations, etc.).
- Private-sector organizations have a key role in creating value for the public as they act as intermediate implementation agents and/or as autonomous socially responsible actors.

For the purposes of the research, two lines of relationships were considered: the network with other levels of government (the "vertical" perspective), and the network with business and civil society (the "horizontal" perspective).

Public value at the program implementation level is embedded in a larger stream of dimensions, as is illustrated in figure 14.1. It should be emphasized that this discussion has been developed in a context—such as Italy—with a decentralized setting and the tradition of a welfare state. Central and supranational levels of government have programs and resources that create and deliver the input used by regions in Italy; these higher levels of government not only transfer funds but also can influence a region's performance in many other ways (e.g., by rule making). In addition, many programs pass through "implementation channels" on their way to the final recipients (e.g., a firm may receive special funds from the regional government in order to transfer money to—or to provide a service for—the final recipients). Channels may perform additional activities, add new resources, or arrange new programs that affect value for the final recipients. When private actors are involved, a social responsibility may be undertaken by firms or nonprofits and enforced by the regional government. Finally, public value may be created by the autonomous initiative of businesses and nonprofits.

In the second half of 2005, several meetings were held by the steering committee to conduct interviews with public managers and to analyze relevant government documents. Based on insights gained from document analysis and face-to-face interviews, a more extensive analysis was launched that drew on

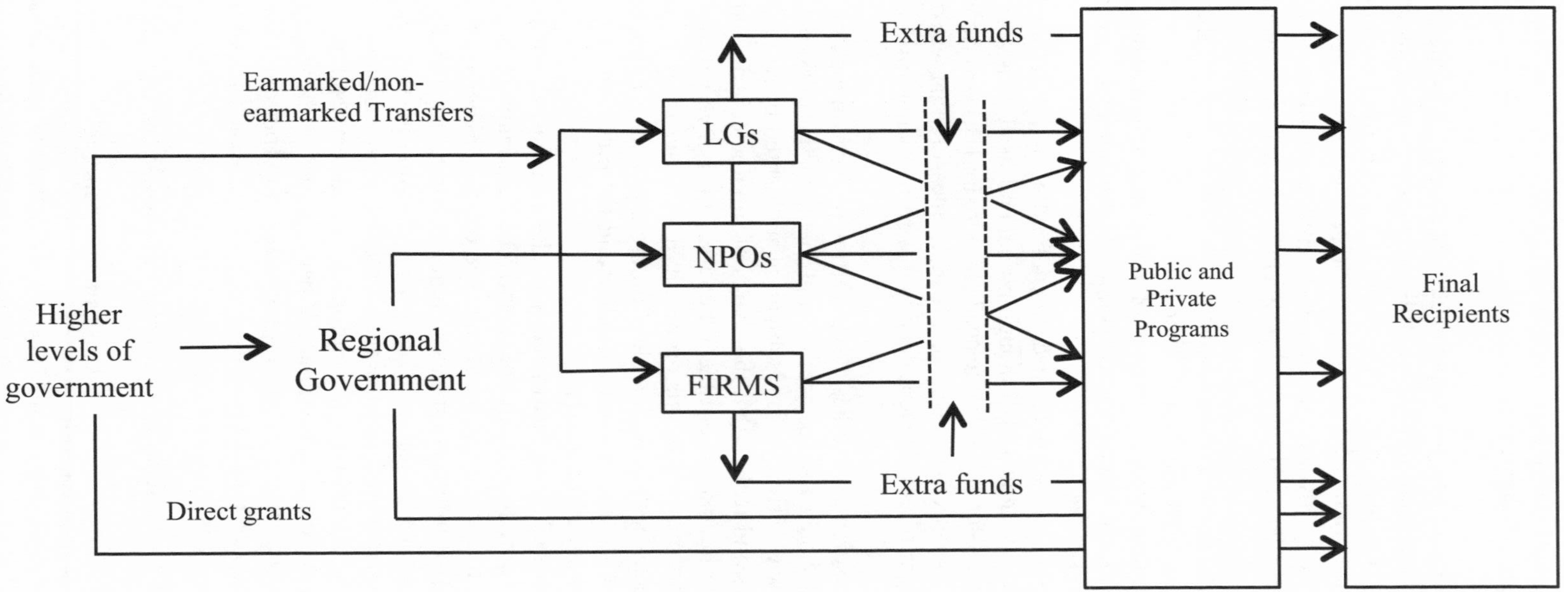

Figure 14.1 Program implementation and network of funding at the local level

qualitative and quantitative data. This activity was developed for four years (2006–9), progressively increasing the number of public programs phased into the analysis.

The work mapped the implementation structures explicitly required or encouraged by legislation itself. The full set of current laws passed by the regional council was reviewed, and all the public programs were considered. In each instance of a program two types of stakeholders were recorded—for example, the stakeholder to be involved in the implementation of the program (the "intermediate" stakeholder) and the final recipient of the program, as mentioned explicitly in the law.

Identifying the program implementation network enabled the group to identify how much money flowed to particular sectors for implementation of particular sets of policy mandates. The amount of money that flowed to final recipients, either directly or through businesses and nonprofit organizations, was considered to be a specific aspect of public value.

Here the relative share of government funding in a policy area was considered to have inherent value and, although not an end itself, was seen as instrumental to other values—for example, the need for more (or less) government financial support. In this perspective, a very simple proxy measure that was discussed was the relative weight of government spending within the network, as represented in figure 14.2.

This measurement implies that government decision making concerning public programs should also consider its implementation network: policymakers should consider how government funds might be augmented by social investments from other sectors and realize that the shares of funding contributed by the different sectors might fluctuate over time. Of course, this is a very rough financial indicator, but actors involved in this process have conceived it to be useful in order to stimulate discussion about the role of different providers of public services within a policy area, their social responsibility, and the public value failures that might occur (Bozeman 2002, 2007).

Expenditure data was extracted from the accounting system by allocating expenses according to type and recipient. The "destination" of expenses was first specified as to the dimension of the type of stakeholder involved in the implementation. This information was systematically recorded by the accounting system, but thus far was not used for decision making. Further on, expenditures by intermediate stakeholders were reallocated to final recipients. Data was coded by public officials involved in the program. Besides expenditure data and the network resource index, the nonfinancial performance of the value chain framework was also considered. Here, several measures of output and outcomes connected to the creation of public value were collected for each public program and ar-

Figure 14.2 The relative weight of government spending within the network

$$\text{Network resource index} = \frac{\text{Government spending}}{\text{Business and nonprofit organizations' social investments} + \text{government spending}}$$

ranged in a preliminary set of indicators to be included in the public value reporting. This task was conducted by regional managers under the supervision of the steering committee.

DISCLOSING PUBLIC VALUE AT THE LOCAL LEVEL

In order to understand the management implications of the case, this section offers two preliminary propositions. Although the case structure, processes, and participants in the Veneto case mesh well with Bryson and colleagues' (2006) framework for understanding cross-sector collaborations, the proposed evaluation here is on the theory of action informing the initiative as defined by community leaders (Weiss 1995; Sandfort and Bloomberg 2012).

The first proposition is that *social responsibility of business and civil society in public value creation at the local level is primarily shaped by government policy implementation processes.* Multiactor implementation arrays sketched through public policy are the main tracks along which the social responsibility of each participant—business, civil society, and government—should be acknowledged. Each of these arrays can contribute to public value creation. This evidence reinforces conclusions drawn from previous studies analyzing formal products of rule-making processes (Hall and O'Toole 2004).

The empirical data provide additional evidence of the ways the value chain framework helps to explain the paths of public value creation. About sixteen program recipient categories were identified. An example of visualization through the value chain can be seen in the initiatives creating programs for the unemployed, as shown in figure 14.3.

The implementation process appears to be increasingly directed toward providing services and financial transfers through business and nonprofit organizations. These issues reflect less the old principal-agent dimensions of devolution and more the community-building and networking dynamics of partnership development. The goal of the relationship then relies on service provision and community building by means of shared values, planning, and interagency networking; this approach involves moving from the old "auditor" model of compliance activity to the new "partner" model in which social responsibility issues can play a central role.

The second proposition is that *to be effective, the discourse on public value creation and accountability at the community level should be "visualized" by a cross-boundary measurement and reporting system.* The starting point for the multistakeholder forums (2007–9) was the value chain framework for reporting. The performance indicators were used in concert with the flow of resources in each public value chain to assess public value. The members of the group tested the usefulness of data and indicators for internal and external reporting purposes within their own organizations and met regularly with the steering committee to share experiences and exchange knowledge. Each stakeholder was also required to enrich the indicator set in order to publicly disclose more data on its own level of responsibility. An example of indicators that emerged from these forums, and which all stakeholders endorsed, is shown in table 14.3. Some common questions helped the process and some common issues emerged.

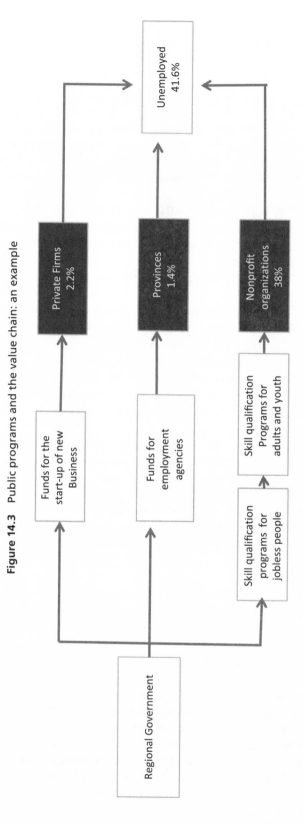

Figure 14.3 Public programs and the value chain: an example

Note: 41.6% identifies the share of regional government funding channeled to particular sectors for the provision of services to the unemployed. The residual 58.4% is channeled through different value chains providing services to the other program recipient categories.

Table 14.3. Public value indicators

Program	Measure	Indicator
Education and training	Quality of human capital	• % of population with higher education degrees
	Training	• % of population age 25–64 sharing lifelong training programs
		• Value of training and development provided to staff
	Quality of employment	• Employment rate suited to education program's aim
	Quality of postgraduate programs	• % of postgraduate students coming from other regions
Welfare	Employment rate	• % of eligible workers employed
	Community programs	• Company support as % of total of public and private resources
		• Regional government support as % of total of public and private resources
		• Perception measure by workers about the effectiveness of public and private programs
		• Impact evaluation of community programs
	Labor accident rate	• % of labor accidents
	Indigence rate	• % of population with low wage rates
		• Pay and conditions compared against local equivalent averages
	Effectiveness of employment offices	• % of applicants returned to work
	Equal opportunity	• % of women engaged in work
		• % of disabled workers
Research and Innovation	Research and development	• % of research investments by public and private sector organizations
		• % of engagements coherent with labor demand
		• Start-up of new businesses
		• % of partnerships and new business agreements
		• Perception measures of "the territory as a good business opportunity"

Usefulness of the Reporting

This type of network reporting was identified by different stakeholders of the forum to be a crucial issue and one that they could not easily ignore. The examination of the expenditure value chains reinforced output obtained from analyzing the implementation networks designed by legislation. All participating actors were very surprised about figures showing the share of funding of different sectors in the implementation process. The share of business and nonprofits in public programs had not been ascertained prior to this, and none of the representatives expected it to be so relevant.

Further, value channels shaped by the expenditure process tended to call for even more ambitious social responsibility of business and civil society than did the formal design of programs explained by laws. Stakeholders recognized that the proposed disclosure framework could result in a marked improvement in their planning and interaction with the regional government. Firms realized that collecting and submitting data as to the proposed reporting model could help them in interacting with political leaders and public managers from the regional government and better integrate their socially responsible initiatives with the implementation networks of government programs.

While data showed the significance of firms in public program implementation, the discussion of public value creation was, however, mainly focused on the responsibility of the regional government rather than the social responsibility of business. This seems to be related to the strong Italian tradition of government intervention in the market. Some firms asked the government to make achievement of the indicators a condition for creating public value, and others requested more government financial support for small businesses as a preliminary condition for increasing business responsibility in public-private partnerships. A key conclusion of the group was that citizens and final recipients had a more clear understanding of the paths along which public value is created or destroyed.

Evaluation of Public Value Indicators

As noted above, the process of stakeholder engagement conducted within the multistakeholder forums (2007–9) determined which indicators should have been included in the reporting set. An observation drawn from the forums' work is that stakeholders from business and civil society sectors were, in general terms, no better informed as to which indicators should be included in the public value reporting than was the regional government itself. Furthermore, some indicators of public value that stakeholders discussed primarily reflected the regional government's responsibility (e.g., increasing economic growth, raising the living standards of poor people, etc.) rather than the social responsibility of business and civil society. This happened because regional government managers felt more comfortable in leading the conversations around successful programs, whereas local stakeholders were much more interested in discussing priorities and principles on which regional policies should be based (apart from quantitative measures). This issue characterized also the wider initial dialogue that developed within the web platform. After the first round of meetings and web forums, however, the conversations were much more constructive and stakeholders contributed effectively to the validation of performance indicators. This circumstance helps clarify that the meaning of public value and public values is intimately connected with how they are visualized and addressed by public managers, political leaders, and other stakeholders.

In particular, stakeholders most valued effective reporting, improved decision making, accurate data, transparency, and the well-maintained web platform. They found that the process of measuring created value in and of itself: it generated trust and empowered participants through increased knowledge. This simply serves to highlight the importance of a regular stakeholder dialogue and further confirms the need to integrate Moore's managerial approach with Bozeman's society-oriented focus to public values and embed this combined approach into performance management regimes.

IMPLICATIONS FOR PUBLIC MANAGEMENT AND GOVERNANCE

Social responsibility of business and civil society is exciting for a local government because it offers additional, or alternative, cost-effective ways of achieving economic, social, and environmental benefits. Civic initiatives and responsible business practices must rest on principles integrated into government policy-making and must be managed throughout its operations. A boundary-crossing public value measurement and reporting system can be initiated with a preliminary database for each channel of value at the local level. Public value is not "financial" in essence, but in some circumstances to be operationalized it might require financial measurement, which is the primary routine in business and government. Nevertheless, the answer to the question of how public value can be visualized across institutional boundaries (i.e., integrating the managerial and the societal approaches) does not lie as much in the kind of measures that are needed but in the process of community engagement by which these measures are developed and reported. As confirmed by this case, to implement such a system a strong relationship with key political and professional constituencies within the organization and within the local network is needed. This requires public managers to work across boundaries and develop a new culture and new leadership skills to better fit within a public value frame. It should also be noted that sometimes active citizenship does not immediately fall into an explicit request to government for engagement. This case shows that public managers, while apparently acting in the background, were able to catalyze the social responsibility of local stakeholders. Public managers acted as "guarantors of operations" that helped create and guide the stakeholders' dialogue and helped maintain and enhance the overall effectiveness of the system. This point gives further evidence regarding Moore's arguments of public managers acting as entrepreneurs in creating public value. Political commitment or sponsorship is also crucial for effective public managers' entrepreneurship.

Yet, on the government side, further issues should be figured out:

- What responsibility are firms and nonprofits going to undertake as regards the considerable share of funding? Are additional private resources added to public funds?

- What community programs are arranged by firms and nonprofits, and how well may they be integrated with regional programs?
- How are public values achieved and protected?

Clearly the answers to such questions have important implications for the role of the regional government, especially within institutional contexts where corporate social responsibility should be developed and supported. More fundamentally, it requires an ability to select which governance structure or sector (business, government, or civil society) is most appropriate and in what conditions (O'Flynn 2007).

Part of this will involve enacting legislation in order to create a normative framework that will ensure that business practices deliver outcomes that meet the systemic challenges facing societies. On the other hand, the regional government should work with business to create the incentives that will encourage firms to take further action at the instrumental level for the mutual benefit of both business and society.

CONCLUSIONS

The voluntary social responsibility practices of businesses and nonprofits are not and cannot be an effective substitute for good governance of public values. Public-sector regulatory capacity plays a crucial role in facilitating, supporting, and empowering these practices. The absence of governance actions on the part of local governments may represent a significant barrier to the real effectiveness of responsible business practices (World Bank 2004) and, as such, a threat to the protection of public values. Cross-sector collaborations may create synergies between the complementary skills and social responsibilities of public, private, and civil society actors to achieve public value and public values. Social responsibility is based on the distribution of resources among various actors, the goals they pursue, and their perceptions of their resource dependencies.

The relevance of the public value reporting framework for the participating actors supports empirical evidence that legislation and the regional government expenditure process influence the design of value chains of public program implementation. Private firms and civil society have agreed that these public value channels represent the tracks along which shared responsibility can be exercised.

The value chain framework is helpful because it allows

- tracking the dimensions along which each actor creates public value for citizens
- identifying businesses and nonprofits involved by the regional government within a framework of policy implementation
- acknowledging socially responsible initiatives and their relative social impact in order to promote and facilitate private-sector responsibility

Improving this kind of information allows regional and local governments to effectively map existing societal expectations and jointly plan initiatives both with businesses and nonprofit organizations. Reporting data and performance in both directions is an essential prerequisite for promoting cross-sector collaboration.

The formulation of what constitutes public value can only be achieved through deliberation involving the key stakeholders and actions that depend on mixing in a reflexive manner a range of intervention options. Interested parties should develop agreed measures of public value and standards for reporting. Here the main responsibility lies with government.

The development of managerial tools in governments faced with the cross-boundary public value paradigm is at a very early stage. The case discussed in this chapter built a bridge across issues of strategy, performance measurement, and public policymaking and contributed a demonstration in practice of how the managerially focused perspective of creating public value might complement and be well integrated with societal expectations and discernment of public values. More theoretical and fundamental questions remain for the field. Future research includes, but is not limited to, understanding the structure of the decision-making process of the network enabled through the participatory mechanism, analyzing how power dynamics shape the discourse on performance information among the network actors, and examining the barriers to informing policy decisions based on social responsibility of private actors. When public managers are made aware of these questions, the propositions discussed in this chapter can ultimately facilitate systems thinking and strategic management in order to assess public value and to integrate social responsibility across institutional boundaries.

NOTE

1. The Italian management and accounting context is characterized by the strong and vibrant theoretical tradition known as economia aziendale that is rooted in the economics (*economia*) of socioeconomic units (family, business, government, and nonprofits) considered as long-term, multifaceted, but integrated entities (*aziende*). These entities are investigated from a unitary perspective of management, organization, and accounting. It should be emphasized that economia aziendale is a space- and time-specific label; spatially it is considered purely in an Italian context, and it is regarded within a time frame beginning in the mid-1920s with Gino Zappa (1927). An in-depth analysis of the Italian business economics tradition is given in Zan (1994), Viganò (1998), Capalbo and Clarke (2006), and Canziani (2007). Advances of economia aziendale in the study of public administration are summarized in Anessi-Pessina (2002).

Conclusions

John M. Bryson, Barbara C. Crosby, and Laura Bloomberg

In this book we have sought to make several contributions.[1] First, the chapters together demonstrate that the concepts of public value, public values, and the public sphere offer fruitful paths forward philosophically, theoretically, *and* practically beyond the older debates about the public interest or the common good. Developing a way forward is particularly important at a time when things public are increasingly called into question. Additionally, public value is at the heart of the emerging approach to public administration that involves governance across multiple sectors, many stakeholders, and multiple—often conflicting and contentious—takes on value questions, including those involving fundamental democratic values.

The book's second contribution is to bring together the conversations about public value, public values, and the public sphere that have generally proceeded separately within the public administration field. We have tried to demonstrate the power of jointly considering public managerial action and cross-sector work as important for creating public value; seeing public value and its legitimation and authorization from a variety of perspectives, including Moore's (1995, 2013), Bozeman's (2007), Bozeman and Johnson's (2014), and Meynhardt's (2009); and maintaining and enhancing the public sphere as the democratic space—psychological, social, political, institutional, and physical—within which public values and public value are held, created, or diminished. Aligning these streams helps advance the public value literature and the public administration field. The public value governance triangle (PVGT) is a graphic way of demonstrating the interconnectedness of these different streams of the public value literature (see figure 1.2).

Beyond the public administration field, conversations about public value, public values, and related topics have spawned operationalization efforts internationally in a variety of fields, including public economics, political science, nonprofit management, business management, evaluation, education, urban and regional planning, journalism, and law. While the discourse in these fields typically does not specifically mention public value, public values, or the public sphere, the ideas are nonetheless present. The chapters in this book thus make a third contribution by drawing on this broader conversation, thereby advancing the public administration discourse through cross-fertilization. Such an effort is particularly important at a time when public administration as a field is fairly isolated from other important disciplines (Wright 2011).

A fourth contribution is illustrating how to operationalize the concepts of public value and public values. Doing so seems especially important when scholars and practitioners alike recognize that many complex public challenges can only be solved through cross-sector collaborations (and other institutional and organizational designs) involving business, nonprofit, media, and/or community organizations in addition to government (e.g., Stoker 2006; Crosby and Bryson 2005, 2010). These collaborations, however, pose particular challenges to those who care about democratic governance and accountability. The public value literature can offer a way to help public managers and other stakeholders make informed decisions about when, where, and how collaborations should be initiated, maintained, restructured, or disbanded. Several chapters in this book offer examples of this kind of work.

In short, *Public Value and Public Administration* broadens and deepens previous theorizing in the public value literature and offers language, frameworks, methods, measurement approaches, and processes for deepening our understanding of the worth of what leaders, managers, citizens, and different kinds of organizations can achieve together. The book reveals the potential for, and benefits of, focusing public value within and across multiple sectors, not just governments and markets. As a result, the book makes a significant contribution to the emerging approach to public administration that likely will overtake both traditional public administration and what has been called new public management (Bryson, Crosby, and Bloomberg 2014, 2015).

What that emerging approach will be called is still an open question, though we prefer public value governance. In the next section we compare and contrast the central chapters in the book, and in the third section we propose an agenda for advancing practice and theory.

COMPARING AND CONTRASTING THE CONTRIBUTIONS

We compare and contrast the chapters' contributions in two different but partly overlapping ways. The first set of comparisons and contrasts clarifies the strand of the public value literature to which the chapter mainly contributes—that is, Moore's managerial action focus or Bozeman's policy or societal focus; whether the chapter contributes secondarily to the alternative view or to other parts of the literature; and how the chapter's author(s) propose(s) reconciling the managerial and public policy or societal views (see tables C.1.1–5). We also consider whether, in the chapters, the objects of value are subjective psychological states, or objective states of the world; relatedly, whether value is intrinsic, extrinsic, or relational; whether something is valuable for its own sake, or as a means to something else; whether there are hierarchies of values; who does the valuing; how the valuing is done; and against what criteria the object of value is measured.

The second set of comparisons helps clarify what the chapters contribute to the PVGT framework and therefore to a more integrated view of the public value literature as a whole (see tables C.2.1–5). We also lay the groundwork for a normative argument about how public managers might—indeed, *should*—approach their work as part of the emerging approach to public administration. The comparisons and contrasts proceed according to the book's central sections: helping managers create public value; measuring and assessing public value; and measuring and managing performance.

Part I: Helping Managers Focus on Creating Public Value

Creating public values requires practical conceptual frameworks and methods, tools, techniques, and skills. The chapters in part I all contribute primarily to the managerial focus on public value creation and in doing so touch on all three points of Moore's strategic triangle and the PVGT (see tables C.1.1–2 and C.2.1–2). In each chapter, elected officials and citizens are the final arbiters of public value, but public managers and the citizens themselves can expand the possibilities for public value creation. Leadership of many kinds has an important role to play in each of the chapters. All of the chapters in part I discuss ways of engaging various stakeholders, including elected officials, to articulate values and to make decisions. They vary greatly, however, in the ways they involve stakeholders, the numbers of stakeholders involved, and the extent to which analytic methods inform understanding and decision making. There clearly are many ways to involve stakeholders and to inform their articulations and valuations of public value and public values. An important way forward for the public values literature is to catalog these practices and their strengths and weaknesses for discerning, measuring, and assessing public value and public values.

In relation to the authorizing environment, one of the points of the strategic triangle, John Alford, Jean Hartley, and John Hughes argue in chapter 2 that public managers' *political astuteness* is a key skill. The authors urge public managers to use a variety of ways to develop a sense of "what a sustainable plurality of citizens wants regarding a given issue, and . . . to shape it into a value proposition—not to supplant politicians' views and policies but to supplement and enhance them or to provide an alternative perspective that politicians may find helpful." Managerial activities that require political astuteness include: reading collective aspirations, securing a mandate, enlisting capabilities to get things done, and knowing the limits of political astuteness. The politics-administration divide is thus honored, even if it is understood to be blurred in practice, for the sake of enhancing public value.

Public value for Alford, Hartley, and Hughes generally refers to objective states of the world that often can be measured; also relevant, however, are the subjective judgments of elected officials and managers (see table C.1.1). Public value is seen as extrinsic and also intrinsic to the functioning of an effective public organization and democratic polity. What is being valued may be either valuable in its own right or instrumental; the effective functioning of democratic governance is both. The only hierarchies of values would be those established by elected officials and the citizenry. Government decision makers (whether elected or appointed) and the citizenry do the valuing based on the elected officials' judgments, managerial discernment and advice, or various techniques for "reading" collective aspirations, including elections. Valuations are made against criteria established by elected officials and the citizenry, but the professional advice of managers is also relevant.

Political astuteness fits most clearly in the capabilities box of the PVGT and, within that, especially with the individual competencies needed to create public value (see table C.2.1). As noted, it is also an important part of gaining necessary legitimacy and authority to proceed with public value creation efforts. In addition, it is an important part of effectively using any of the practical approaches to addressing

Table C.1.1. Comparing attributes of value from part I, "Helping Managers Focus on Creating Public Value," chapters 2–4

Value Attribute	Chapter 2 Alford, Hartley, and Hughes	Chapter 3 Sandfort and Quick	Chapter 4 Richardson, Andersen, and Luna-Reyes
(1) To which approach in the public value literature does the chapter primarily contribute?	Creating public value	Creating public value	Creating public value
(2) To which approach does the chapter contribute secondarily?	Public values	Public values and public sphere	Public values
(3) How are the differing approaches reconciled?	Elected officials and managerial officials both engage in "reading" public values and in deciding how best to create public value; elected officials and the citizenry get the final say	Participants bring their own views about public values and what might create public value to the sessions; through facilitated dialogue and deliberation, proposals, plans, and recommendations can be developed that garner broad support	The process helps managers (or other participants) create public value by using sophisticated analysis, dialogue, and deliberation to help figure out how to achieve organizational, public policy, or societal goals
(4) Are the objects of value subjective psychological states, or objective states of the world?	Generally objective states of the world that often can be measured, but the subjective judgments of elected officials and managers are often relevant	Both subjective and objective; public value is a resource, including shared understandings and civic capacity, and also an outcome in the form of better solutions to public problems	Generally objective states of the world that can be measured

text continues on page 245

(5) Relatedly, is value intrinsic, extrinsic, or relational?	Public value is extrinsic and also intrinsic to the functioning of an effective public organization and democratic polity	Value is intrinsic in well designed and implemented civic engagement processes that allow participants to cocreate solutions to public problems; building relationships among participants helps generate public value; solutions developed would indicate extrinsic public value	Public value is extrinsic as reflected in the model, but also intrinsic in the relationships built among participants in the model-building group that allow model building to proceed
(6) Is what is being valued valuable for its own sake or as a means to something else?	What is being valued may be either valuable for its own sake or instrumental; the effective functioning of democratic governance is seen as being both	Public value as deliberative capacity is valuable for its own sake and as a means to producing effective and efficient solutions	Public value as represented by outputs of the model may be valuable for its own sake or instrumental; the same is true of relational value among group participants
(7) Are there hierarchies of values?	No, other than what might be established by elected officials and the citizenry	Developing deliberative capacity is privileged over other public values	No
(8) Who does the valuing?	Government decision makers and the citizenry	Participants in Art of Hosting events	The model-building participants
(9) How is the valuing done?	By elected officials, managerial discernment, or various techniques for reading collective aspirations	Via techniques such as relationship building, Open Space Technology, dialogue, documentation of meeting results, action steps	Via assessments of the usefulness of the model
(10) Against what criteria is the object of value measured?	Value delivery is measured against criteria established by elected officials and the citizenry, but advice from managers is also important	Outcomes are measured in the form of implementable solutions and increased sense of civic agency on the part of participants	Value delivery is measured against elements of Moore's triangle and values important to stakeholders

Table C.1.2. Comparing attributes of value from part I, "Helping Managers Focus on Creating Public Value," chapters 5–6

Value Attribute	Chapter 5 Alford	Chapter 6 Hartley
(1) To which approach in the public value literature does the chapter primarily contribute?	Creating public value	Creating public value, as defined mostly by Benington
(2) To which approach does the chapter contribute secondarily?	Public values	Public sphere
(3) How are the differing approaches reconciled?	The contingent decision rules provide a way for public managers to create public value that optimizes the net benefits of service delivery, relationships, and the government's strategic positioning	A framework is offered to help public managers understand how public value might be created through considering the different phases of innovation and the different kinds of public innovations involving public values
(4) Are the objects of value subjective psychological states, or objective states of the world?	Public value consists of efficient allocation of tax dollars, maintenance of key relationships, and strategic positioning	Public value is dividends added to the public realm via activities, services, relationships, and investment
(5) Relatedly, is value intrinsic, extrinsic, or relational?	Value is all three; service benefits and costs are extrinsic; relational benefits and costs refer, of course, to relational value; and strategic benefits and costs are intrinsic to government	Value is extrinsic in that it includes what the public values, and intrinsic as it includes what adds value to the public sphere (e.g., rules supporting fairness)
(6) Is what is being valued valuable for its own sake or as a means to something else?	A focus on the three dimensions of public value is a means to providing public services that maximize benefits	Both
(7) Are there hierarchies of values?	No	No
(8) Who does the valuing?	Public managers	Managers, networks, citizens, elected politicians
(9) How is the valuing done?	Via decision framework	Managerial and political judgment

Table C.1.2. (continued)

Value Attribute	Chapter 5 Alford	Chapter 6 Hartley
(10) Against what criteria is the object of value measured?	Quantitative and qualitative benefit-cost analysis regarding use of tax dollars, relationships, and strategic positioning	Varies according to stage of innovation; organizational performance metrics plus sustenance of the public sphere

public value and public values concerns and to clarifying exactly what public value is to mean in a given situation.

In chapter 3, Jodi Sandfort and Kathryn Quick describe the Art of Hosting (AoH) process, which consists of *a suite of complementary facilitated methods, tools, and techniques of engaging stakeholders in face-to-face interactions, dialogue, and deliberation.* AoH can help groups develop shared understanding of a public concern and develop ideas and plans for responding to it. The approach thus represents a far deeper and more integrative way of engaging stakeholders than the Georgia Department of Transportation's survey approach described in chapter 11, but cannot handle the larger numbers of people involved in the GDOT approach.

Sandfort and Quick flag the importance of training hosts (or facilitators) in the techniques, theories, and design frameworks that can be used to conduct particular deliberative processes. The cases that the authors studied indicate that the method has potential for creating public value by prompting "better-informed actions" on public policy issues and programs, and simultaneously for developing the longer-term deliberative capacity of participants, a clear contribution to the public sphere. Their research highlights the importance of honoring the centrality of relationship building among participants if public value is to be created. The research also indicates that the particulars of an engagement design can have significant consequences for creating public value; not all designs are equally effective. The approach thus attends mostly to the public value and operational capacity points of the PVGT, though the authors also make use of Bozeman's normative consensus approach to defining public values.

In AoH events, public value is both objective and subjective. Deliberative civic capacity that includes shared understandings and problem solving ability is seen as a public value in and of itself but also as a means to producing effective and efficient solutions. Shared understandings, civic capacity, and new solutions may be viewed as joining individuals' views on values with policy or society values. Value can be seen as intrinsic in well-designed and implemented civic engagement processes that allow participants to cocreate solutions to public problems. Value is also relational in the form of shared understandings and heightened civic capacity. Value is extrinsic in the form of new solutions to public problems. There is a hierarchy of values in that deliberative capacity is given a privileged position. Participants in AoH events do the valuing via the suite of AoH methods, tools, and techniques.

Table C.2.1. Comparing contributions from part I, "Helping Managers Focus on Creating Public Value," chapters 2–4

Contributions to Elements of the Public Value Governance Triangle	Chapter 2 Alford, Hartley, and Hughes	Chapter 3 Sandfort and Quick	Chapter 4 Richardson, Andersen, and Luna-Reyes
Legitimacy and authority	Elected officials and the citizenry are the final arbiters of public value, but managers can help expand the possibilities for public value creation via their political astuteness while still loyally serving the government.	Citizens are viewed as important sources of legitimacy and authority. The chapter's emphasis is on helping citizens move beyond being consumers or recipients of policy decisions to being active partners in both defining public issues and developing strategies to address them.	Elected officials and the citizenry are the final arbiters of public value, but managers can help expand the possibilities for public value creation via the use of system dynamics group model building (SDGMB).
Public value	The authors use Moore's conception of public value as revealed through the use of the strategic triangle; Bozeman's normative consensus approach is seen as not strategic enough. The authors are silent on the use of Bozeman and Johnson's public value criteria.	The authors include Bozeman's conception of public value as including the rights, benefits, and prerogatives to which citizens are entitled, and also Moore's about achieving what elected officials and citizens decide. Dialogue, deliberation, and deliberative capacity are seen as public values.	The authors see SDGMB primarily as an analytic method to help managers create public value in Moore's sense and to help avoid public value failure in Bozeman's conception. They also believe the approach and the models it produces can be used to promote conversations and dialogue about normative public values in Bozeman's sense to a wider audience.
Capabilities to create public value	Creation of public value can be facilitated (or undermined) by political astuteness on the part of public managers.	Building deliberative capacity advances democratic participation in governance and provides assistance in producing effective and efficient policy solutions. Procedural legitimacy and justice are emphasized; procedural rationality and substantive rationality receive less emphasis.	Creation of public value can be facilitated by the use of SDGMB, which provides a tool to build causal hypotheses related to instrumental, sometimes competing values, and uses simulation as a form of empirical testing of such hypotheses. Looking at the results of simulations over time contributes to understanding the impact of policies in the short and long terms, helping to increase public value success and reduce public value failure.

Competence in SDGMB and analysis is required. Procedural legitimacy and justice are emphasized, as are procedural and substantive rationality. |

text continues on page 251

Practical Approaches to Addressing Public Value and Public Values Concerns			
Policy analysis, design, and evaluation	Political astuteness can help promote better policy analysis, design, and evaluation.	Dialogue and deliberation are seen as important ways of improving policy analysis, design, and evaluation. Democratic participation in pursuing these tasks is seen as important.	SDGMB can help public managers and elected officials engage stakeholders, build on their mental models to help them understand complex systems, define problems, articulate viable solutions, and link them to desired public values and outcomes.
Leadership	Public managers are seen as leaders, though ones subservient to their political masters.	Leadership is important for sponsoring, designing, and facilitating deliberative processes.	Leadership is important for sponsoring, designing, and facilitating SDGMB exercises. Technical expertise (a kind of leadership) is also needed on the part of facilitators. Leadership is also necessary to implement results of the exercises.
Dialogue and deliberation	Political astuteness may be exercised or enhanced through dialogue and deliberation, though this is not a focus of the chapter.	Dialogue and deliberation embody democratic participation, but also help participants learn how to influence collective actions through engagements with others.	Dialogue and deliberation are important features of SDGMB activities, both in terms of building the model and figuring out what responses might be required as a result of analyzing the model.
Institutional and organizational design, including designing and implementing cross-sector collaborations	Better institutional and organizational designs may result from political astuteness, though this is not a focus of the chapter.	The cases involved designs for three endeavors: the Local Government Innovation project, a realignment of HIV/AIDS field services, and the Resilient Region project. The extent to which the dialogue and deliberation processes produced public value depended on session designs, facilitation, and follow-through.	The case illustration in the chapter involved responses to welfare reform in three New York State counties. The public managers in the counties varied in the use they made of the SDGMB analyses. In two counties the senior managers made significant use of the analyses to redesign systems, while in the third the manager did not.

(continued)

Table C.2.1. (continued)

Practical Approaches to Addressing Public Value and Public Values Concerns		
Formal and informal processes of democracy	Political astuteness is an integral part of the formal and informal processes of democracy. Public managers (1) sometimes need to cross the line into political territory to get the job done and (2) need to be sensitive about how far they should go; political astuteness is necessary on both counts.	Dialogue and deliberation processes may be used as part of the formal and informal processes of democracy. They are especially helpful for issue articulation, a search for possible solutions, and choice of a solution.	SDGMB can be used directly or indirectly to inform formal and informal processes of democracy, though this is not a focus of the chapter.
Strategic management, including performance management regimes and models	Political astuteness is also an integral part of effective strategic management, though this is not a focus of the chapter.	Dialogue and deliberation are, typically, directly or indirectly a part of effective strategic management processes, as in the three cases cited.	SDGMB was used to enhance the strategic management of two of the counties, especially through the use of performance indicators derived from the models.

Table C.2.2. Comparing contributions from part I, "Helping Managers Focus on Creating Public Value," chapters 5–6

Contributions to Elements of the Public Value Governance Triangle	Chapter 5 Alford	Chapter 6 Hartley
Legitimacy and authority	Elected officials and the citizenry are the final arbiters of public value, but managers can help expand the possibilities for public value creation via the use of the contingency framework for weighing public service provision alternatives.	Elected officials and the citizenry are the final arbiters of public value, but elected officials, public managers, and others can help expand the possibilities for public value creation via innovation.
Public value	The author's focus is on managerial decision making and thus his approach fits best with Moore's conception. Public value consists of efficient allocation of tax dollars, maintenance of key relationships, and appropriate strategic positioning of the government.	The author relies primarily on Benington's approach, in which public value has two major dimensions: what the public values (which may be different from what it wants or needs), and what adds value to the public sphere. It includes not only goods, services, and obligations, which are valued by the public collectively and which contribute to the public sphere, but also the rules and governance arrangements that shape how society conducts itself, including fairness, justice, and efficiency.
Capabilities to create public value	Public value may be created by many kinds of organizations, not just governments. Depending on how it is pursued, externalizing service provision can create or diminish public value, benefit or diminish government's position, and add or subtract from government's competence. An important government competence involves the use of public power.	Capabilities to innovate may be found in managers, networks, users, and elected politicians. Public value thus may be created not just by governments, but governments often have a special role to play. Government's capacity to innovate is therefore a public value.

(continued)

Table C.2.2. (continued)

Practical Approaches to Addressing Public Value and Public Values Concerns		
Policy analysis, design, and evaluation	The author offers a contingency framework for helping think through decisions about if and how to externalize provision of public services.	Policy analysis, design, and evaluation are or should be important parts of any innovation process.
Leadership	Leadership is required to use the contingency framework and to act based on what the framework indicates.	Leadership is required for successful innovation and may be provided by elected officials, public managers, and others involved in the process.
Dialogue and deliberation	The framework may be used as an aid to dialogue and deliberation about if and how to externalize service provision.	Dialogue and deliberation are likely to be part of any innovation process, but they are not a focus of the chapter.
Institutional and organizational design, including designing and implementing cross-sector collaborations	The differing choices outlined in the framework imply differing designs for service delivery.	In both the public and private sectors, innovations may be in products, services, processes, strategies, and positioning. Public-sector innovations also include new or changed policies, governance arrangements, or rhetoric.
Formal and informal processes of democracy	The framework might be used to directly or indirectly inform both formal and informal processes of democracy, though this is not a focus of the chapter.	Some innovations come about as a consequence of the formal and informal processes of democracy. Innovations in governance and the processes of democracy are also possible.
Strategic management, including performance management regimes and models	The framework is intended to be an aid to strategic management decision making.	Strategic management systems and processes may deliberately encourage innovation. Innovations may also occur in strategic management processes.

Dialogue and deliberation are key practices for addressing public value and public values concerns. In the emerging approach to public administration, the importance of both are hard to overestimate (Stoker 2006; Bryson et al. 2014, 2015), in part because of their contributions to procedural and substantive rationality and to procedural legitimacy and procedural justice. The skills necessary to design and participate in effective dialogue and deliberation processes would fit in the capabilities box of the PVGT, but dialogue and deliberation also play important roles in legitimating and authorizing actions to create public value and in determining what public value should mean. Beyond that, dialogue and deliberation are typically an important component of the other practical approaches for addressing public value and public values concerns. Dialogue and deliberation have long been recognized as a part of public administration in practice, but scholars have not done sustained research on how they contribute to public value creation in practice.

In chapter 4, George Richardson, David Andersen, and Luis Luna-Reyes describe *system dynamics group model building* (SDGMB), which can help groups of stakeholders "build on their mental models to help them understand complex systems, define problems, articulate viable solutions, and link them to desired public values and outcomes." The approach thus helps individuals and groups use analysis, dialogue, and deliberation to link their conceptions of public value to policy-level or societal public values. Showing how the approach can help do that is the chapter's main contribution to the public value literature. SDGMB is somewhat similar to AoH because it also helps groups build their capacity to solve public problems and thereby create public value. The approach differs from AoH in that much greater analytic power is brought to bear and fewer participants are involved.

A strength of SDGMB is that it has been used and evaluated for twenty years and has a proven track record. The authors note several keys to using it effectively: a reliance on team facilitation, careful planning of sessions, scripted tasks for whole-group sessions, and additional model building work between sessions. The method is more likely to produce public value when the sponsoring team is open to new problem-solving approaches and appreciates the use of empirical data in decision making.

In system dynamics models, the objects being valued are generally seen as objective states of the world that can be measured, although subjective psychological states are also at work. In SDGMB, value is extrinsic as reflected in the model but also intrinsic in the relationships built among participants in the model-building exercise. Public value, as represented by model outputs, may be valuable for its own sake or instrumental; the same is true of relational value among group participants. There are no predetermined hierarchies of values. Finally, valuing is done by the model-building participants based on criteria they establish and the usefulness of the model and what it shows.

The skills necessary to design and participate in effective SDGMB sessions would fit in the capabilities box of the PVGT. These capabilities can help support effective policy analysis, design, and evaluation, which in turn can support the other practical approaches to addressing public value and public values concerns. Ideally, policy analysis, design, and evaluation will inform legitimating and authorizing actions to create public value and help determine what public value should mean. The approach thus can touch on all three points of the PVGT. SDGMB has not been used much in the public administration field, but it should be given its capacity to handle complex systems and feedback issues. Research on SDGMB—and other policy analysis, design, and evaluation methods—should take into account all three points of the PVGT and the other practical approaches to addressing value concerns.

In chapter 5, John Alford offers a set of *contingent decision rules* that can be helpful for public managers seeking to optimize public value when deciding whether all or part of a public service should be contracted out or otherwise "externalized" (see table C.1.2). The rules include attention to the purpose of the service and to an array of benefits and costs. There are, of course, the direct service benefits and costs, to which Alford adds relationship benefits and costs due to the particular type of arrangements chosen. For example, managing a service in-house would have a different profile of relationship benefits and costs than would a "full service" contract, use of volunteers, or broad community engagement. Finally, there are what Alford calls "strategic benefits and costs" resulting from the decision's effects on the government organization's positioning or capabilities. The rules are presented as part of a contingent decision framework meant to aid judgment in the context of political realities. Alford's framework thus attends to all three points of Moore's strategic triangle and of the PVGT (see table C.2.2). More generally, a contingent perspective on public value represents an important way forward for the public value literature beyond the specific contingent choice framework Alford presents.

For Alford, public value consists of efficient allocation of tax dollars, maintenance of key relationships, and strategic positioning of the government. Value can be extrinsic (in terms of service benefits and costs to taxpayers and service recipients); relational; and intrinsic (in terms of strategic benefits and costs to government organizations). A focus on the three dimensions of public value is instrumental—that is, as a means to providing public services that maximize net benefits. There is no hierarchy of values; public managers do the valuing using the decision framework, but are likely to need sign-offs from elected officials as well. Alford provides a quantitative and qualitative cost-benefit analysis regarding use of tax dollars, relationships, and strategic positioning. The approach is thus mostly utilitarian.

In relation to the PVGT, Alford's framework has several implications. First, public value may be created by many kinds of organizations (not just governments), but different kinds of organizations have different capacities to create public value. Depending on how externalization of services is pursued it can create or diminish public value narrowly conceived, government's key relationships and position, or competence. An important government competence in this regard is the ability to use public power. Alford's contingency framework is most obviously a kind of policy analysis, design, and evaluation tool, but can be used to inform any of the other practical approaches. The kind of contingent thinking Alford advocates can—and should—be applied to many other topics beside service externalization.

In chapter 6, the final chapter in part I, Jean Hartley argues that public managers attempting to carry out *innovations that create public value* should think through the distinctive aspects of innovation in and by public organizations. Focusing on each phase of the innovation process, she suggests how public managers can foster public value by moving well beyond the common business approaches to innovation. Hartley acknowledges that the kinds of innovation—such as products, services, processes, and strategic positioning—can be similar in both government and business sectors. Beyond those areas, however, public service organizations innovate in policy development, governance, and public rhetoric.

For Hartley, following Benington (2011), public value is the "dividend" added to the public realm via activities, services, relationships, and investments. Public value is extrinsic in that it includes what the public values, and also intrinsic in that it includes what adds value to the public sphere (e.g., rules supporting fairness). Public value thus has value for its own sake and can also be instrumental to achieving other ends. Many kinds of persons and groups do the valuing, including managers, networks of various kinds, citizens, and elected politicians. Valuations are made based primarily on managerial and political judgment against criteria that vary according to the stage of innovation, organizational performance metrics, and inputs from the public realm. Political astuteness is an important part of any successful public innovation process. Hartley thus also shows a concern with the three points of Moore's strategic triangle and the PVGT.

Explicitly connecting the innovation literature to the public value literature is the chapter's most important contribution. In terms of the PVGT, Hartley argues that innovative capabilities for creating public value may be found in managers, networks, users, and elected politicians. Public value thus may be created not just by governments, though governments often have a special role to play. Hartley argues that government's capacity to innovate is thus a public value. Innovations—seen as "stepwise" changes—typically must receive legitimacy and authorization from elected officials. Innovations may add to what the public values and to the public sphere, but they also may not, which typically is more problematic in government than in business. Policy analysis, design, and evaluation are or should be important parts of any innovation process, and leadership is required for success. Some innovations come about as a consequence of the formal and informal processes of democracy, and innovations in the processes of democracy are also possible. Finally, strategic management may stimulate innovation, and innovations in strategic management processes are also possible. Clearly, additional research is merited on how innovation can help create public value and assure achievement of important public values.

Part II: Measuring and Assessing Public Value

Knowing what public value has been or might be created requires approaches to measuring and assessing it. The purposes of discerning, assessing, and measuring public value are many. For example, policymakers, citizens, and public managers may simply want to know whether they are getting value for money—that is, whether the short- and long-term, tangible and intangible results of public endeavors are worth the expenditure of tax dollars and public employees' time. Alternatively, identifying and measuring public value can also help policymakers choose wisely among policy alternatives at key decision points, foster citizen engagement in public work, and strengthen the public sphere.

The chapters in part II show that progress is being made in both the public value creation and public values streams on developing practical approaches to measuring and assessing public value (see tables C.1.3–4 and C.2.3–4). Clive

Table C.1.3. Comparing attributes of value from part II, "Measuring and Assessing Public Value," chapters 7–9

Value Attribute	Chapter 7 Belfield	Chapter 8 Moore	Chapter 9 Welch, Rimes, and Bozeman
(1) To which approach in the public value literature does the chapter primarily contribute?	Creating public value	Creating public value	Public values
(2) To which approach does the chapter contribute secondarily?		Public values and public sphere	Creating public value and public sphere
(3) How are the differing approaches reconciled?	Provides an overview of cost-benefit analysis to determine what net public value has been created	Public value account provides a way for assessing net public benefit produced by an aggregation of costs and benefits broadly conceived; by collective determinations concerning the welfare of others, duties to others, and conceptions of a good and just society	Public value mapping (PVM) provides a way for assessing public value and market successes and failures and can be used as a tool by public managers, elected officials, and others to assess what public value has been created against specific public value criteria
(4) Are the objects of value subjective psychological states, or objective states of the world?	Objective states of the world that can be measured	Objective states of the world linked to both individually and collectively valued aspirations of the good and the just	Objective states of the world that can be measured
(5) Relatedly, is value intrinsic, extrinsic, or relational?	Extrinsic, in the form of public goods and externalities that can be monetized	Public value is intrinsic, extrinsic, and relational	Public value is extrinsic and also intrinsic to the functioning of an effective democratic polity

text continues on page 257

(6) Is what is being valued valuable for its own sake or as a means to something else?	Objects being valued hold value for their own sake, or as instruments (e.g., policies) for achieving something else	An evaluand may be deemed to hold inherent value or may be seen as a means to something else; this will be reflected in the criteria used to judge it	An evaluand may be deemed to hold inherent value or may be seen as a means to something else; this will be reflected in the specific criteria and values used to judge it
(7) Are there hierarchies of values?	Values can be measured, and some hold greater inherent benefit for the public	Yes; public organizational effectiveness, efficiency, accountability, justness, and fairness in the context of democratic governance are prime values	Not necessarily, although PVM can be used to identify linkages among values that may be hierarchical
(8) Who does the valuing?	Technical experts	Ultimately, elected officials and the citizenry are the arbiters of public value, but public managers also play an important part	Makers of the public value map identify important values by assessing a variety of documents and other sources; users of the results also value, although information from other sources can be incorporated
(9) How is the valuing done?	Through cost-benefit analysis	Via the public value account and public value scorecard	Via public value mapping
(10) Against what criteria is the object of value measured?	The costs of producing value(s) are weighed against the benefits of the value(s) created.	The costs of using collectively owned assets and associated costs, in relation to the achievement of collectively valued social outcomes	Public value success and failure assessments and market success and failure assessments

Table C.1.4. Comparing attributes of value from part II, "Measuring and Assessing Public Value," chapters 10–11

Value Attribute	Chapter 10 Meynhardt	Chapter 11 Thomas, Poister, and Su
(1) To which approach in the public value literature does the chapter primarily contribute?	Creating public value	Public values
(2) To which approach does the chapter contribute secondarily?	Public values and public sphere	Creating public value
(3) How are the differing approaches reconciled?	Public value arises from intersubjective valuing; a public value concerns individuals' relationship with their community or society; a public value scorecard may be used to help users create public value or to assess public value successes and failures, as measured against basic human needs	The focus is on values stakeholders use to judge managerial performance in creating public value
(4) Are the objects of value subjective psychological states, or objective states of the world?	Public value begins with subjective valuations based on meeting basic human needs; aggregating individual judgments or else interaction among valuing subjects leads to collective valuation, a more objective phenomenon	Public value differs by stakeholder group; group evaluations are reasonably objective as compilations of individual subjective value judgments
(5) Relatedly, is value intrinsic, extrinsic, or relational?	Value exists in the relations between the person, group, organization or institution and what is being valued	Value is extrinsic—measured by aggregating responses of individuals by groups doing the valuing, but also relational in that one of the values that emerges is the quality of relationships between public servants and other stakeholders

Table C.1.4. (continued)

Value Attribute	Chapter 10 Meynhardt	Chapter 11 Thomas, Poister, and Su
(6) Is what is being valued valuable for its own sake or as a means to something else?	Public values are a means of meeting basic human needs	Certain outcomes, such as high-quality roads, are valuable for their own sake; others help accomplish the mission of the transportation department
(7) Are there hierarchies of values?	No	No
(8) Who does the valuing?	Individuals	Stakeholders
(9) How is the valuing done?	Via psychological processes and interaction among people, groups, etc.	Via stakeholder surveys and compilation
(10) Against what criteria is the object of value measured?	Criteria related to sets of human needs (e.g., instrumental-utilitarian and moral-ethical)	Outcome measures (e.g., safety, road condition, etc.) and process measures

Belfield, Mark Moore, and Timo Meynhardt contribute primarily to the creating public value stream, while Jennie Welch, Heather Rimes, and Barry Bozeman, and John Thomas, Theodore Poister, and Min Su contribute primarily to the public values streams.

The tools and techniques for discerning, measuring, and assessing public value clearly matter, and these authors have pointed the way toward practical applications as well as additional fruitful scholarly work and practical applications. The chapters also demonstrate some of the difficulties in using indicators, accounts, and scorecards. For example, while the chapters offer some overlap on the dimensions of public value, they do not agree on a common list. Methods also vary based on the context and purpose. Belfield relies on cost-benefit analysis; Moore and Meynhardt describe public value accounts, but the entry lines in the accounts are not the same; Welch, Rimes, and Bozeman rely on public value mapping, not accounting; and Thomas, Poister, and Su use focus groups and surveys.

The approaches also vary in terms of required staff capacity, technical expertise, and training. Managers may have to make trade-offs between the attractiveness of the method and available resources to make the method work well. For example, crude calculations based on Belfield's cost-benefit analysis and Moore's scorecard might be made on the back of an envelope. Use of public value mapping, Meynhardt's scorecard, and Thomas, Poister, and Su's survey would require larger investments of time and effort. Clearly, additional development of all of these approaches can be beneficial, including careful studies of how best to use the approaches and their effectiveness. Note that each of the techniques emphasizes

Table C.2.3. Comparing contributions from part II, "Measuring and Assessing Public Value," chapters 7–9

Contributions to Elements of the Public Value Governance Triangle	Chapter 7 Belfield	Chapter 8 Moore	Chapter 9 Welch, Rimes, and Bozeman
Legitimacy and authority	Cost-benefit analysis (CBA) does not address questions of legitimacy and authority.	In a democracy, the arbiter of value is a collective public and its elected officials. The interests of that public include limiting the use of authority and ensuring the justice and fairness with which government operates, as well as its efficiency and effectiveness. A democratic government cannot act legitimately, responsively, or efficiently and effectively without a process that can call a public into existence that can understand and act on its own interests.	Issues of legitimacy and authority are not addressed directly. Makers of a public value map (PVM) would identify important values by assessing a variety of documents and other sources.
Public value	CBA is a method of assessing initiatives that quantifies the value of their impacts and consequences in monetary terms. It is meant to help improve collective decision making through clarifying how to make efficient allocations of society's resources when markets fail. If something of public value is not being created, most economists conclude the market is ipso facto allocatively inefficient. The approach is utilitarian.	Moore's approach to public value predominates. The public value account (PVA) provides a way for assessing net public benefit produced by an aggregation of costs and benefits, broadly conceived, and by collective determinations concerning the welfare of others, duties to others, and conceptions of a good and just society. The approach is utilitarian and deontological and can be used positively and normatively. The PVA is incorporated as the "bottom line" into a public value scorecard (PVS) used primarily by public managers.	Bozeman's normative consensus approach to public value prevails, along with Bozeman's (2007; Bozeman and Johnson 2014) conception of public value success and failure. The approach is both utilitarian and deontological and can be used positively and normatively. Nonetheless, public managers might find a PVM useful as part of the process of creating public value.

text continues on page 263

Capabilities to create public value	The author believes most criticisms of CBA on theoretical grounds are over-drawn and, moreover, that credible alternatives are typically not offered. Instead he argues that the more limiting factors are the practical challenges to use of CBA. Competence in economics and CBA are required. Procedural and substantive rationality are emphasized, but if the results of a CBA are to be utilized, procedural legitimacy and justice would also need to be given attention.	The PVS is designed to help public managers focus on what is necessary to help them create public value as measured by the PVA. The capabilities necessary to produce and analyze the PVA and PVS are necessary. Procedural and substantive rationality are emphasized, but if the results of a PVA and PVS are to be used, procedural legitimacy and justice would also need attention.	Use of the PVM requires the ability to identify public values, assess public value successes and failures, map values, and consider what to do about public value and market successes and failures. The PVM is designed to help policy makers, public managers, and others focus on what is necessary in the creation of public value as indicated by the PVM. Procedural and substantive rationality are emphasized, but if the results of a PVM exercise are to be used, procedural legitimacy and justice would also need attention.
Practical Approaches to Addressing Public Value and Public Values Concerns			
Policy analysis, design, and evaluation	CBA is a standard technique useful for policy analysis, design, and evaluation.	The PVA and PVS can be useful for policy analysis, design, and evaluation purposes.	The PVM can be useful for policy analysis, design, and evaluation purposes.
Leadership	Intellectual leadership is necessary for good use of CBA on technical grounds. Broader leadership is required if the results are to be an aid to decision making.	Leadership is required if the PVA and PVS are to be used as aids to decision making and ongoing management.	Leadership is required if the PVM is to be used as an aid to decision making and ongoing management.

(continued)

Table C.2.3. (continued)

Contributions to Elements of the Public Value Governance Triangle	Chapter 7 Belfield	Chapter 8 Moore	Chapter 9 Welch, Rimes, and Bozeman
Dialogue and deliberation	CBA can inform dialogue and deliberation. Dialogue and deliberation would also be needed to address several of the practical challenges to the use of CBA.	The PVA and PVS can inform dialogue and deliberation. Dialogue and deliberation would likely also be needed to create an effective PVA and PVS.	PVM can inform dialogue and deliberation. Dialogue and deliberation would likely be needed to create an effective PVM and interpret what it shows.
Institutional and organizational design, including designing and implementing cross-sector collaborations	CBA can be used to assess institutional and organizational designs, as in several of the author's examples.	The PVA and PVS can be used to assess institutional and organizational designs.	PVM can be used to assess institutional and organizational designs.
Formal and informal processes of democracy	CBA can inform the formal and informal processes of democracy, though the author argues that it does not nearly to the extent that it should.	The PVA and PVS can inform the formal and informal processes of democracy.	PVM can inform the formal and informal processes of democracy.
Strategic management, including performance management regimes and models	CBA can inform strategic management, though the author argues that it does not nearly to the extent that it should.	The PVA and PVS are intended primarily as aids to public strategic management that attend to all three points of Moore's strategic triangle.	PVM can serve as an aid to public strategic management.

Table C.2.4. Comparing contributions from part II, "Measuring and Assessing Public Value," chapters 10–11

Contributions to Elements of the Public Value Governance Triangle	Chapter 10 Meynhardt	Chapter 11 Thomas, Poister, and Su
Legitimacy and authority	The author is essentially silent on issues of legitimacy and authority.	The authors acknowledge the importance of all three points of Moore's strategic triangle. They develop a survey to assess what legislators and local government administrators, as sources of legitimacy and authority, think of the performance of the Georgia Department of Transportation (GDOT), the quality of working with the GDOT, and what the GDOT's priorities should be.
Public value	A public value concerns a shared or collectively held value about the quality of a relationship involving the public. Public value is *for* the public when it concerns relationships with the public, and *from* the public when it is drawn from experience of the public. The approach is primarily utilitarian, but also deontological, and resonates with Benington's approach to individuals' experience of the public sphere.	Public value is seen as what elected officials, public managers, and the GDOT's partners see as serving the public. The approach is thus most closely connected to Moore's conception of public value. The authors also make use of Beck Jørgensen and Bozeman's (2007) public values inventory and add a new category: satisfaction with the quality of working relationships with a government agency. The approach is mostly utilitarian, but also partly deontological; it can be used positively and normatively.
Capabilities to create public value	The capabilities needed to create public value are those necessary to provide positively valued experiences in relation to the five dimensions of Meynhardt's public value scorecard (PVSC).	The capabilities needed to create public value are those necessary to provide positively valued experiences according to the GDOT surveys.

(continued)

Table C.2.4. (continued)

Contributions to Elements of the Public Value Governance Triangle	Chapter 10 Meynhardt	Chapter 11 Thomas, Poister, and Su
	The capabilities necessary to produce and analyze the PVSC are necessary.	The capabilities to produce and analyze the GDOT surveys are necessary.
	Procedural and substantive rationality are emphasized, but if the results of a PVSC are to be utilized, procedural legitimacy and justice would also need attention.	Procedural and substantive rationality are emphasized, but if the results of a GDOT survey are to be utilized, procedural legitimacy and justice would also need attention.
Public Values in the Creation of Public Value as Articulated through the Following Practical Integrative Approaches		
Policy analysis, design, and evaluation	The PVSC can be useful for policy analysis, design, and evaluation.	The GDOT survey can be useful for policy analysis, design, and evaluation.
Leadership	Leadership is required if the PVSC is to be used as an aid to decision making and ongoing management.	Leadership is required to create a survey like the GDOT's and to ensure that the results of the GDOT survey are used as aids to decision making and ongoing management.
Dialogue and deliberation	The PVSC can inform dialogue and deliberation. Dialogue and deliberation would likely also be needed to create an effective PVSC and interpret it.	The GDOT survey can inform dialogue and deliberation. Dialogue and deliberation are also needed to create an effective GDOT survey.
Institutional and organizational design, including designing and implementing cross-sector collaborations	The PVSC can be used to assess institutional and organizational designs.	The GDOT surveys can be used to assess institutional and organizational designs for the GDOT.

Table C.2.4. (continued)

Public Values in the Creation of Public Value as Articulated through the Following Practical Integrative Approaches		
Formal and informal processes of democracy	The PVSC can inform the formal and informal processes of democracy.	Results of the GDOT surveys can inform the formal and informal processes of democracy.
Strategic management, including performance management regimes and models	The PVSC can serve as an aid to public strategic management.	The GDOT surveys were designed to serve as an aid to public strategic management.

procedural and substantive rationality, but if they are to be used effectively procedural legitimacy and procedural justice must be attended to as well.

In chapter 7, Clive Belfield focuses on *cost-benefit analysis* (CBA), an archetypal method for valuing public value. Indeed, CBA is an important benchmark for understanding the net worth of any public value created, although Alford (chapter 5), Moore (chapter 8), Welch, Rimes, and Bozeman (chapter 9), and Meynhardt (chapter 10) caution that the full array of valuing tasks and challenges goes beyond the conceptual and practical limits of CBA. Moore (1995) was the first to introduce CBA to the public value literature, but Belfield is the first economist to explore connections of CBA to that literature. He argues that most criticisms of CBA on theoretical grounds are overdrawn; moreover, the critics often do not offer credible alternatives that can adequately account for monetary costs and benefits and the efficient allocation of societal resources.

Belfield's chapter outlines the breadth of some of the challenges involved in discerning, measuring, and assessing public value and public values using CBA. He argues that rigorous CBA is one of the most useful—and underutilized—methods for public value assessment, and provides an overview of how it can be used in specific situations to determine what net public value has been created, typically in monetary terms. He offers examples that show how CBA can help policymakers avoid costly mistakes and cope more effectively with some of the most challenging public problems, such as climate change. The approach therefore is utilitarian (see table C.1.3). Belfield sees value as representing objective states of the world that can be measured. Values are defined fairly narrowly as public goods and externalities that can be monetized. There is a hierarchy of values in that some hold greater benefit for the public. Technical experts do the valuing via CBA, which weighs the costs of producing value(s) against the benefits of the value(s) created.

In terms of the PVGT, the ability to do useful CBA clearly requires competence in the process and in economics (see table C.2.3). The technique emphasizes procedural and substantive rationality, but if the results of a CBA are to be utilized, leadership, procedural legitimacy, and procedural justice must be attended to as well. The technique is important generally for policy analysis, design, and evaluation and can provide useful information as part of the other practical approaches. CBA does not address questions of legitimacy and authority; public value is assessed in utilitarian and monetary terms.

In chapter 8, Mark Moore presents a *public value account* (PVA) and *public value scorecard* (PVS) for assessing the performance of government agencies. He offered both in his 2013 book *Recognizing Public Value*, but here they are presented for the first time in juxtaposition to other approaches to measuring and assessing public value. The PVA provides a way for assessing net public benefit produced by an aggregation of costs and benefits broadly conceived, but also by collective determinations concerning the welfare of others, duties to others, and conceptions of a good and just society. The account therefore provides a quantitative and qualitative way of linking the managerial focus on public value and some specific public values. His account is a much broader approach than CBA and includes both utilitarian and deontological concerns. The scorecard includes the PVA, but also attends to the legitimacy and authority and capability points of Moore's strategic triangle; it is a source of performance measures.

In Moore's view, the development of a specific PVA, a PVS, and performance measures is an iterative process that requires attention to philosophical, technical, managerial, and political dimensions. Philosophical reflection is needed to decide what is valuable about an agency's actions. On the technical side, measures should "accurately capture the degree to which valued effects are occurring." In relation to the managerial dimension, managers must be able to use performance measures in ways that can help their organizations learn and adapt in order to carry out their missions effectively. Finally, Moore emphasizes that the political dimension is crucial for practical reasons and because "the only appropriate arbiters of public value in democratic political systems are citizens, taxpayers, and their elected representatives."

For Moore, public value generally implies objective states of the world that can be measured. Public value is extrinsic, but also intrinsic to the effective functioning of a democracy. Public value thus may be deemed to hold inherent value or may be seen as instrumental to something else. Moore does argue that there is a hierarchy of values in which prime values include organizational effectiveness, efficiency, accountability, justness, and fairness in the context of democratic governance. Given the primacy of democracy, elected officials and the citizenry are the ultimate valuers, but public managers also play an important role. Moore's approach is also directly related to the maintenance and enhancement of the public sphere.

Not surprisingly, Moore's PVA and PVS, which focus on government agencies, fit neatly into the broader multisector PVGT. Public value is measured by the PVA. Legitimacy and authority are clearly located in the final analysis with elected officials and citizens and registered, along with necessary capabilities needed to create public value, in the PVS. Leadership, especially by public managers, clearly is central to the use of the PVA and PVS, as are the competencies to produce and use them. The PVA and PVS can provide useful information as part of employing the other practical approaches to addressing public value and public values concerns. Note, however, that some critics continue to see a somewhat antidemocratic bias in Moore's recent work (2013) given his lack of a concise definition of public value, frustrations at times with democratic decision making, and focus on helping managers navigate challenging environments without necessarily having clear guidance from governing collectives (Rutgers and Overeem 2014). Our own view is that these cautions are worth noting, but we also fully acknowledge Moore's commitment to democracy and his deep appreciation of how challenging it can be to do the right thing as a public manager in a flawed democracy. The PVA and PVS certainly merit further scholarly and practitioner attention.

In chapter 9, Jennie Welch, Heather Rimes, and Barry Bozeman explain the usefulness of the *public value mapping* (PVM) tool, which allows users to identify public values connected to a particular public issue or problem and then assess to what extent the values are being enacted successfully. The PVM tool has also been presented elsewhere, but in this book is lined up for the first time opposite other approaches to public value measurement and assessment. It helps public managers, elected officials, and others consider interrelationships among values and links public value successes and failures with market successes and failures in an issue or problem area. The tool thus can help assess what public value has been, or might be, created in specific situations as measured against specific market-related and public value criteria. PVM has been used to evaluate policies in many areas, and the authors suggest several additional ways of applying the tool and of collecting data on its efficacy as well as making stronger connections between the tool and social innovation theory.

Welch, Rimes, and Bozeman conceptualize value as objective states of the world that can be measured. Public value is extrinsic but also intrinsic to the functioning of an effective democratic polity. The authors see evaluands as capable of holding inherent value or instrumental value. The users of the PVM are the ones who identify the public values based on documents and other sources capturing the values of citizens and other stakeholders. The valuing is done via the PVM tool in terms of market and public value successes and failures.

Regarding the PVGT, PVM fits mostly in the capabilities and public value boxes. It provides a useful way of assessing what public value has been or might be created, but the competence to use the tool clearly is necessary. PVM also can be useful in all of the key practices for addressing public value and public values concerns. Issues of legitimacy and authority are not addressed directly. Makers and users of a public value map would identify important values by analyzing a variety of documents and other sources. PVM can apply to both utilitarian and deontological concerns.

Timo Meynhardt offers in chapter 10 a *public value scorecard* based on different dimensions than Moore's and one that is derived from his own well-grounded theory of public valuing that draws on well-known psychological theory and emphasizes the satisfaction of basic human needs. Meynhardt's scorecard allows individuals or groups from any sector to rate an actual or proposed policy, program, or product according to the dimensions and then use the results to aid decision making and monitor change. This scorecard has been used in different formats by a number of government and business organizations, and the author can provide a manual that supports its use. Like Moore, Meynhardt also hopes to refine the scorecard to reveal interdependencies. As with the tools in the previous two chapters, Meynhardt's PVSC has been presented elsewhere, but never in juxtaposition to other major approaches to public value measurement and assessment.

For Meynhardt, public value begins with subjective valuations based on meeting basic human needs; aggregation of individual judgments or else interaction among valuing subjects leads to collective valuations, a more objective phenomenon (see table C.1.4). Value exists in the relations between the person, group, organization, or institution and what is being valued. For Meynhardt, public value and public values are means of meeting basic human needs; there is no hierarchy of values. Individuals do the valuing via psychological processes and interactions among people and groups. These valuations are made against sets of human needs: utilitarian-instrumental, moral-ethical, political-social, and hedonistic-aesthetic. Like Moore's approach, Meynhardt's is both utilitarian and deontological, but it is far different from Moore's in that it is more focused on individual, psychologically based valuations and not tied to democratic governance.

In a way similar to PVM, Meynhardt's PVSC fits mostly in the capabilities and public value boxes of the PVGT (see table C.2.4). The scorecard provides a useful way of helping assess what public value has been or might be created, but the competence to use the tool clearly is necessary. The scorecard also can offer useful information for all of the practical approaches for addressing public value and public values concerns. Meynhardt is essentially silent on issues of legitimacy and authority.

In chapter 11, John Thomas, Theodore Poister, and Min Su describe the creation of a number of *stakeholder surveys of public values* for the Georgia Department of Transportation (GDOT). Their chapter is the first to bring stakeholder surveys in such detail into the public value literature. The authors relied on a combination of stakeholder advisory groups and department leaders in shaping the survey questions. The focus is on values that stakeholders use to judge managerial performance in creating public value. The surveys were administered to different stakeholder groups, resulting in group-based, reasonably objective evaluations compiled from individual subjective value judgments. The construction of the surveys revealed that different stakeholder groups had used similar value dimensions to judge the GDOT's performance. All but one of the dimensions fit Beck Jørgensen and Bozeman's (2007) public values categories. The authors propose adding to that list a dimension related to the quality of interaction, or "working relationship satisfaction." They found that stakeholder groups, including state legislators, were at least as interested in process as they were in outcomes, a finding Van Ryzin (2011) has found to be generally true across nations. The surveys mainly revealed support for utilitarian values, but deontological values were also important. The GDOT uses survey results to inform decisions about what it should do, how, and why.

Public value in the GDOT survey is extrinsic, but also relational in that one of the values is the quality of relationships between public servants and other stakeholders. Stakeholder valuations represent both output and outcome measures (e.g., road conditions and safety) and process measures (e.g., working relationships). Both help the GDOT understand what it means to create public value in transportation. Values are not placed in a hierarchy.

Again, as with public value mapping and Meynhardt's scorecard, the GDOT stakeholder survey technique fits mostly in the capabilities and public value boxes of the PVGT. The surveys provide a valuable way of assessing what public value has been or might be created. The competence to use the tool clearly is necessary. The surveys also can offer useful information for all of the practical approaches for addressing public value and public values concerns. Legitimacy and authority come from elected officials as well as agency and stakeholder support. Further research on the uses of surveys for public value creation clearly can be worthwhile; much of that work might involve recasting existing research into a public value frame.

Part III: Measuring and Managing Performance

Knowing how to create public value and how to measure and assess it are both preliminary steps toward measuring and managing performance. The chapters in part III focus on measuring and managing performance. All contribute primarily to the public value stream but also to the public values stream in that the approaches are all about how to create public value as assessed against a variety of values (see tables C.1.5 and C.2.5). In other words, when compared to the chapters in the previous two sections, the set of chapters in this section do a better job of integrating the two major streams in the public value literature.

In chapter 12, Alexander Kroll and Donald Moynihan offer a significant and insightful review of the literature on *performance measurement and management for purposes of creating public value*. They warn public managers that performance management systems can create public value but that they also typically privilege some public values and displace others. The authors usefully highlight the potential for data manipulation, injustice, and other unintended or perverse behaviors that can emerge from the push to show measurable results in public programs. Kroll and Moynihan urge public managers to engage in "purposeful performance information use," by which they mean "use of data to better inform decisions in ways that will improve programs and services and thus contribute to the creation of public value." Purposeful use of performance information relies on involvement of external stakeholders, political debate, support of policymakers and top administrators, staff support, and a supportive organizational culture. The performance measurement system should aim for data collection and reporting that are from multiple sources, useful, and accessible. The authors suggest that managers who have a strong "prosocial orientation" and more discretion are more likely to engage in purposeful performance information use.

For Kroll and Moynihan, public value refers to objective states of the world that can generally be measured (see table C.1.5). Public value is seen as generally extrinsic to the performance measurement system. It may hold inherent value or may be seen as a means to something else; this will be reflected in the criteria used to judge it, as reflected in performance information. There is no predetermined hierarchy of values. Performance information users do the valuing via the assessment of the information collected according to specific procedures.

Table C.1.5. Comparing attributes of value from part III, "Measuring and Managing Performance," chapters 12–14

Value Attribute	Chapter 12 Kroll and Moynihan	Chapter 13 Cresswell, Cook, and Helbig	Chapter 14 Guarini
(1) To which approach in the public value literature does the chapter primarily contribute?	Creating public value	Creating public value	Creating public value
(2) To which approach does the chapter contribute secondarily?	Public values	Public values	Public values
(3) How are the differing approaches reconciled?	Public managers are responsible for achieving public value, which encompasses normative standards societies want applied to public concerns	Public value can be described via dimensions that have some similarity to others' categories of public values	Public value is created when investments by government, nonprofits, and business perform well against indicators validated in multistakeholder forums
(4) Are the objects of value subjective psychological states, or objective states of the world?	Objective states of the world that can be measured	Public value can be characterized along dimensions that have both subjective and objective elements: financial, political, social, strategic, ideological, stewardship, and quality of life	Objective states of the world that can be measured
(5) Relatedly, is value intrinsic, extrinsic, or relational?	Public value is extrinsic	Both intrinsic and extrinsic values are considered	Public value is relational in that it is created and expanded in a loosely causal "chain of value creating activities"

text continues on page 273

(6) Is what is being valued valuable for its own sake or as a means to something else?	An evaluand may be deemed to hold inherent value or may be seen as a means to something else; this will be reflected in the criteria used to judge it as reflected in performance information	Some elements are valuable in their own right (e.g, personal health); others are a means to something else (e.g, income)	Both
(7) Are there hierarchies of values?	No	While multiple dimensions of value are explored, they are not presented as a hierarchy	There are temporal chains of value creation, but not a hierarchy of values
(8) Who does the valuing?	Performance information users	Public managers with stakeholder input	Public managers and cross-sector partners
(9) How is the valuing done?	Via the assessment of performance information collected according to specific procedures	By use of the public value assessment tool (PVAT)	Through implementation of a public value reporting framework that examines the relative impact of multisector stakeholder contributions
(10) Against what criteria is the object of value measured?	Against specific performance measures	Value delivery is measured against the standards set in the PVAT	Public value creation between and among multisector players is measured via a predesigned "network resource index" and a common set of outcome measures

Table C.2.5. Comparing and contrasting contributions from part III, "Measuring and Managing Performance," chapters 12–14

Contributions to Elements of the Public Value Governance Triangle	Chapter 12 Kroll and Moynihan	Chapter 13 Cresswell, Cook, and Helbig	Chapter 14 Guarini
Legitimacy and authority	Elected officials and the citizenry are the final arbiters of public value, but managers can help expand the possibilities for public value creation via the way they use performance information and performance management systems. Defining performance is seen as a political act.	Elected officials and the citizenry are the final arbiters of public value, but managers can help expand the possibilities for public value creation via the way they use the public value assessment tool (PVAT).	Elected officials have a crucial role to play as legitimizers, authorizers, and guarantors of important public values, but businesses, nonprofits, and citizens also have a role to play in legitimating and authorizing cross-sector creation of public value.
Public value	The authors include both Moore's approach to public value and Bozeman's broader approach to public values. Moore's is more focused on organizational mission, while Bozeman's attends to non-mission-related values as well.	The authors, like Moore, approach the creation of public value primarily from the standpoint of a government, but the PVAT includes a broader range of values than Moore explicitly does, and in that way is more in line with Bozeman's approach. Utilitarian and deonotological values are included.	The Veneto case makes use of Moore's notion of creating public value, but in a cross-sector, multijurisdictional context. The definition of what constitutes public value fits primarily with Bozeman's idea of a normative consensus among involved and affected stakeholders. The measures are mostly utilitarian.
Capabilities to create public value	Creating performance information systems that are used purposefully requires a range of individual, organizational, performance management system design, and environmental supports.	Using the PVAT effectively requires training, skill, facilitation, and analytic support. The authors emphasize seven generic value generators: increases in efficiency,	Developing a cross-sector, multijurisdictional performance information system that is used purposefully requires a range of convening, facilitation, value chain mapping, data collection and analysis, and leadership skills.

	Procedural and substantive rationality and procedural legitimacy and justice would need to be given adequate attention if performance information is to be used purposefully.	increases in effectiveness, enablement, intrinsic enhancements, transparency, participation, and collaboration. Procedural and substantive rationality and procedural legitimacy and justice would need to be given adequate attention if the PVAT is to be used effectively.	Procedural and substantive rationality and procedural legitimacy and justice are important components of creating cross-sector, multijurisdictional public value tracking and reporting systems.
Practical Approaches to Addressing Public Value and Public Values Concerns			
Policy analysis, design, and evaluation	Performance information is increasingly a component of policy analysis, design, and evaluation.	The PVAT can be useful for policy analysis, design, and evaluation.	The cross-sector regional performance information system can be useful for policy analysis, design, and evaluation.
Leadership	Political and managerial support are important for stimulating purposeful performance information use and for building useful performance management systems.	Leaders' support is required if the PVAT is to be used as an aid to decision making and ongoing management.	Political and managerial leadership across sectors is required for effective development and purposeful use of a regional, cross-sector performance information system.
Dialogue and deliberation	Purposeful use of performance information is facilitated by establishing mechanisms for collectively discussing and making sense of performance measures, data, and information.	The PVAT can inform dialogue and deliberation. Dialogue and deliberation are desirable as a part of developing the information that goes into the PVAT and to assessing any information that it produces.	A regional, cross-sector performance information system can inform dialogue and deliberation on relevant issues. Dialogue and deliberation are also necessary for development and effective use of such a system.

(continued)

Table C.2.5. (continued)

Practical Approaches to Addressing Public Value and Public Values Concerns		
Institutional and organizational design, including designing and implementing cross-sector collaborations	Performance management systems tend to privilege certain values and displace others. They tend to focus mostly on organizational mission-related values, and to ignore non-mission-related public values.	The PVAT can be used to assess institutional and organizational designs.	A regional, cross-sector performance information system can be used to help assess the actual or possible effectiveness of existing or potential institutional and organizational designs. Supportive legislation would be required to institutionalize the Veneto system.
Formal and informal processes of democracy	Performance information and systems are increasingly integrated into contemporary political processes.	The PVAT can inform the formal and informal processes of democracy.	A regional, cross-sector performance information system can be used to inform the formal and informal processes of democracy. The Veneto initiative was conceived in part as an exercise in civic engagement.
Strategic management, including performance management regimes and models	The key benefits of performance management systems lie in encouraging purposeful use of performance data. But establishing purposeful use is not easy; passive use is more likely.	The PVAT can serve as an aid to public strategic management.	A regional cross-sector performance information system is an important component of a regional cross-sector strategic management system. Government has a central role to play, but other sectors are also important.

Kroll and Moynihan's chapter touches on all four boxes in the PVGT, as well as each of the practical approaches to addressing public value and public values concerns (see table C.2.5). If performance information is to be used, it must be seen as legitimate and authorized by appropriate bodies and stakeholders. Note as well that managers can expand the possibilities for public value information by the way they use performance information and performance management systems. Performance information can—and no doubt should—help users make assessments in terms of public value and public values, typically via dialogue and deliberation. A range of competencies is needed if performance information systems are to be used purposefully. Similarly, procedural and substantive rationality and procedural legitimacy and justice should receive adequate attention. Performance management regimes and models are important strategic management components and can help inform policy analysis, design, and evaluation; institutional and organization design; and formal and informal processes of democracy. Leadership by elected officials and public managers is important for stimulating purposeful performance information use and for building performance management systems.

In chapter 13, Anthony Cresswell, Meghan Cook, and Natalie Helbig present a *public value assessment tool* (PVAT) that allows users to assess multiple types of public value from the perspective of various stakeholder groups. The tool (available online) can help public managers articulate and understand various "value propositions" and how they might be viewed by various stakeholders. It can thus help managers create public value and optimize resources and capabilities while meeting their organizations' mission and, ideally, delivering maximum public value to all stakeholders. The tool was developed in the context of the federal government's interest in open government initiatives. While conceived as a contribution to the public value literature, the tool has not received much scholarly attention.

For Cresswell, Cook, and Helbig, public value can be characterized along value dimensions that have both subjective and objective elements; they identify financial, political, social, strategic, ideological, stewardship, and quality of life dimensions. Stakeholders may disagree about the merits of particular programs or projects judged against these dimensions. Like Moore, the authors talk about creating value propositions and the importance of stakeholders' judgments of their merits. Value can be both intrinsic in terms of valuing government as a public asset and extrinsic in terms of outputs and outcomes. Also like Moore and most other authors in the public value literature, the authors of chapter 13 believe that some things are valuable in their own right (e.g., personal health), while others are more instrumental (e.g., income). Utilitarian and deontological values are considered. The authors present several value dimensions, but do not place them in a hierarchy. Public managers do the valuing with stakeholder input. The valuing is informed via the PVAT against the dimensions and standards embedded in use of the tool.

In terms of the PVGT, chapter 13, like Kroll and Moynihan's chapter 12, touches on all the boxes. If the PVAT is to be used effectively, it must be legitimate and authorized by appropriate bodies and stakeholders. As with performance information more generally, managers can expand the possibilities for public values creation by the way they use the PVAT. The tool is used to make assessments in terms of public value and public values and how to produce them. Effective use of it requires training, skill, and facilitation and analytic support. The PVAT emphasizes the importance of seven generic value generators: increases in efficiency and effectiveness, enablement, intrinsic enhancements, transparency, participation, and collaboration. As with performance information more generally, procedural and substantive rationality and procedural legitimacy and justice must receive adequate attention. The PVAT is essentially a policy analysis, design, and evaluation tool, but can be used to inform the other practical approaches. Leadership by elected officials and public managers is important for stimulating PVAT use. Further research on the tool and its usefulness should be pursued.

In chapter 14, Enrico Guarini describes a simple *value-chain framework for monitoring the cross-sector creation or destruction of public value*. The framework was developed in a participatory fashion for the Veneto region of northern Italy. Guarini's chapter demonstrates the potential viability and usefulness of developing an approach to discerning, measuring, and assessing public values across an entire region in which multiple sectors and levels have something to contribute. The cross-sector, cross-level application of public value thinking on a regional scale is the chapter's singular contribution.

In the Veneto framework, value is seen as objective and measureable. Public value is relational in the sense that it is created and expanded via value chains. There is no clear hierarchy of values, but there are instrumental and more end-state values in evidence via these value chains. Public managers and cross-sector partners do the valuing through implementation of a public value reporting framework that includes an examination of the relative impact of multisector stakeholder contributions. Public value creation is measured via a predesigned network resource index. The measures are mostly utilitarian.

In the United States, a number of states and regions have been engaged in somewhat similar efforts. For example, there is the federally sponsored Partnership for Sustainable Communities (http://www.sustainablecommunities.gov/miss ion/about-us); Virginia Performs in the State of Virginia (http://vaperforms.virginia .gov/); and the 2035 Comprehensive Plan and the process that created it in Portland, Oregon (https://www.portlandoregon.gov/bps/article/497622). Each of these is a public value governance effort; each works at building the legitimacy and authority to pursue the effort, invests in needed capabilities, and endeavors to create public value via the various approaches to addressing public value concerns. These and other experiments like the one studied by Guarini warrant careful scrutiny to determine the extent to which they actually do produce public value and, if so, how.

A BEGINNING AGENDA FOR ADVANCING PRACTICE, RESEARCH, AND THEORY

The chapters in this book bring together some of the very best theorizing, conceptual frameworks, approaches, methods, and techniques designed to help public managers and others create public value, advance public values, and enhance the public sphere. The chapters can help public managers, public officials, nonprofit and business leaders, and citizens create, measure, and assess public value and measure and manage performance. The chapters also indicate, however, that doing so may well not be easy in a world where public value and public values are typically contested. We thus close with some thoughts about a beginning agenda for advancing practice, research, and theory.

Advancing Practice

Practice has often been ahead of theory when it comes to generating knowledge about public value and public values. Moore (1995), for example, developed his strategic triangle approach to creating public value based on deep engagement with practitioners. Subsequent research, though sparse, has supported Moore's conceptualization (e.g., O'Toole, Meir, and Crotty 2005; Meynhardt and Metelmann 2009) and it is now quite popular among practitioners and many scholars (e.g., Rhodes and Wanna 2007; Alford and O'Flynn 2009; Williams and Shearer 2011). We therefore have relied on the strategic triangle as the base for the public value governance triangle (PVGT) and advocate it as a way of conceptualizing the move from Moore's narrower focus on managers of government agencies to the broader idea of managing for the creation of public value in a cross-sector, multilevel world—one in which the challenges of governance have moved beyond government. In other words, we believe that the PVGT is more suited for the emerging approach to public administration.

We are making a normative argument (as Moore did with his strategic triangle) that public management practice may be advanced by keeping the PVGT in mind. The conceptual framework of the PVGT can help advance the practice of, and also research on, the emerging approach to public administration in which public value and public values are emphasized, government has a special role as a guarantor of public values, public management broadly conceived is also emphasized, and citizenship and democratic and collaborative governance are emphasized (Bryson et al. 2014, 2015).

A special advantage of the PVGT is that it shows how the differing strands of the public value literature can be related to one another, if not necessarily reconciled in all cases. The PVGT includes a range of definitions of public value and public values that goes beyond Moore's to include Bozeman's, Bozeman and Johnson's, Meynhardt's, and Benington's, and can include others' definitions as well. Legitimacy and authority are considered in a multisector, multilevel context that goes beyond government. The triangle includes capabilities for creating public value that are also considered in a multisector, multilevel way that goes beyond government while also recognizing that government has a special role to play as guarantor of public values. The PVGT also highlights six particularly important practical approaches to dealing with public value and public values in a multisector, multilevel context: policy analysis, design, and evaluation; leadership; dialogue and deliberation; institutional and organizational design; the formal and informal processes of democracy; and strategic management, including performance measurement and management. All of the elements listed above sit within the public sphere.

If one accepts the usefulness of the PVGT, a number of implications flow from considering its interconnected elements. One of the most significant practical and theoretical implications of the PVGT is that Moore and Bozeman are both right, but incomplete without each other's views. The two views until now have been treated as quite separate from each other, but surely management action, especially by public managers, matters for the creation of public value. Just as surely, normative consensus on public values, and public value criteria for assessing societal and policy-related values, also matter for the creation of public value. Scholars might treat the two as quite distinct, and might need to for specific research purposes, but practicing managers cannot—or should not—proceed without considering both the substance and consequences of managerial action and societal and policy values. We therefore next consider the specific elements of the PVGT and what they imply for practice.

Public Value

The public value box incorporates the major definitions of public value and public values; it can also include other definitions. The public value literature provides a broader sense of public values than is typically found in traditional public administration and new public management. As the emerging approach to public administration unfolds, insights from the public value literature should be explicitly incorporated in practice because public value issues are so fundamental. For example, as noted earlier, too many performance measurement and management regimes and models focus principally on efficiency and effectiveness directly related to the mission (Radin 2006, 2012; Talbot 2010), and disregard what David Rosenbloom (2007) terms non-mission-based values, such as equity, due process, freedom of information, and citizenship development. Too many performance measurement and management schemes thus may actually weaken public value creation, as Kroll and Moynihan point out in chapter 12.

Practitioners thus should work to ensure that performance measurement and management approaches do include non-mission-based values and, at the very least, do not diminish democratic engagement and citizenship behavior. Rosenbloom's (2007) idea of a constitutional scorecard can help draw attention to non-mission-related values. Moore's public value account and PVS also help broaden the scope of value considerations beyond efficiency and effectiveness, as does Meynhardt's very different PVSC. Welch, Rimes, and Bozeman's public value mapping model also can help users understand more clearly where public value and market successes and failures occur. Similarly, public participation processes can be designed to enhance democratic behavior and citizenship (Nabatchi 2012; Bryson et al. 2013), if they are designed appropriately, as Sandfort and Quick note in chapter 3. Finally, policy analysis should include a broad array of values beyond its traditional focus on efficiency, effectiveness, and sometimes equity (Radin 2013). Many of the chapters in the book may be viewed as offering ways of enhancing policy analysis.

Highlighting the public value created, and public values served, by specific organizations, programs, projects, and services may well increase support for government generally and for government initiatives specifically. Practitioners and scholars thus should consider following Australia's lead, for example, and draw attention to the expected and actual public value created by policies, programs, projects, and other efforts (Kernaghan 2003). Relatedly, the "joined-up government," "whole-of-government," and collaborative governance initiatives that developed in many countries in response to the fragmentation caused by new public management were in part about better coordination, but were also about recovery and pursuit of public values beyond efficiency and effectiveness (Christensen and Lægreid 2007).

In the United States today, seeking agreement on values is often very difficult or even quixotic, and support for government can be weak. Nonetheless, Lawrence Jacobs (2014) asserts that the American people are "pragmatically liberal" and will support public programs when their benefits are made clear. As evidence, he offers the examples of Social Security, Medicare, the GI Bill, and a host of other programs. Thus, bringing public value and public values into the discussion can have very salutary benefits, although the conversations may well be difficult in a polity harboring deep divisions.

Note that when stakeholders consider public values, process values can matter as much as, or more than, output and outcomes values (Van Ryzin 2011). Most of the public values considered in the public value literature are output and outcome values. We have pointed out that procedural rationality, justice, and legitimacy matter greatly as capabilities, and these are the kinds of values that Van Ryzin found in his cross-national research as so important to the public's perceptions of the worth of public action.

Legitimacy and Authority

In terms of the legitimacy and authority box, the PVGT points to at least two important implications for practice. The first concerns how legislation, policies, or other authoritative guidance should be formulated, while the other concerns how to think about accountability within the emerging approach to public administration. Too often authoritative guidance is crafted without thinking about either the full range of public values that should be considered or how such guidance can be implemented effectively. These shortcomings might be averted if policy designers took adequate account of the intended public value and public values to be pursued from the standpoint of stakeholders meant to be affected, and of the capabilities needed to produce the desired effects. Public managers well versed in political astuteness might help craft the mandates likely to produce actual public value, as indicated by Alford, Hartley and Hughes in chapter 2. Of course, managers can abuse the discretion they might have (Rhodes and Wanna 2007); yes, public managers can overreach, but they also have a great deal to contribute to closing what is often referred to as "the implementation gap" (Pressman and Wildavsky 1973: Elmore 1979). They can help policy designers craft authoritative guidance that includes worthwhile goals and can garner the necessary coalition of support and other needed resources. They can do so, in particular, by appropriately using the key practices for addressing public values and public values concerns.

Accountability is an especially thorny problem with which the emerging approach to public administration must deal (Koliba, Zia, and Mills 2011). Recall that in the emerging approach, cross-sector efforts are increasingly common. Government becomes one actor among many having a responsibility for the creation of public value, although government has a special role as a guarantor of public values. In such a situation a "democratic deficit" is a very real danger (Papadopoulos 2007; Willems and van Dooren 2011).

Stephen Page and colleagues (2015) offer a practical framework for reducing the democratic deficit in cross-sector collaboration; they argue that such collaborations confront three challenges: responding to and addressing the concerns of citizens and their elected representatives, following established rules and procedures to prevent unfairness or the abuse of public power or resources, and producing results that benefit the public (Peters and Pierre 2010; Willems and van Dooren 2011). Page and colleagues (2015) argue that challenges reflect demands for democratic accountability (or responsiveness), procedural accountability (or responsibility), and performance accountability (or results). These differing accountability demands frequently produce tensions for collaborations (Behn 2001; Koppell 2005).

In order to address the differing accountability demands, Page and colleagues (2015) recommend a multifaceted public value framework for assessing accountability. Their framework addresses the legitimacy and authority, public value, and capabilities boxes of the PVGT and includes

- Vertical democratic accountability, meaning the extent to which decisions are legal and responsive to authorizers.
- Horizontal democratic accountability, or the extent to which decisions respond to collaboration partners and other stakeholders.
- Procedural rationality and procedural justice, in the same senses in which they are discussed in this book.
- Operational control, or the extent to which collaboration uses requirements, budgets, and schedules to oversee projects and activities.
- Effective and efficient performance.
- Equity of payment and benefits distributions.
- Problem-solving capacity, or new behaviors or norms that increase the potential to address complex problems.

This framework, and other means of addressing the same accountability issues, deserve further research aimed at revealing the best ways of assuring accountability in the emerging approach to public administration.

Capabilities

The chapters in this book have presented a number of practical capabilities that can be used to help produce public value. Managers can produce public value via political astuteness (chapter 2); methods, tools, and techniques for engaging stakeholders in face-to-face interactions, dialogue, and deliberation (chapter 3); system dynamics group model building (chapter 4); contingent public value–related decision rules (chapter 5); and innovation (chapter 6). Measuring and assessing public value can be achieved via cost-benefit analysis (chapter 7); Moore's public value account and PVS (chapter 8), public value mapping (chapter 9); Meynhardt's PVSC (chapter 10); and public value-related stakeholder surveys (chapter 11). Finally, measuring and managing performance can make use of performance measurement and management (chapter 12); the public value assessment tool (chapter 13); and value chain frameworks for monitoring and managing the creation or destruction of public value on a broad cross-sector, area-wide scale (chapter 14). Clearly this is just a representative sample of capabilities that can be used to create public value. Others should be explored, researched, and tested as well.

We want to highlight one capability in particular here: Given the complex networked and collaborative arrangements that practitioners now often find themselves in, they have a heightened need to cultivate what Benington and Moore call a "restless, value-seeking imagination" (2011a, 3) in a democratic context; public affairs scholars and educators should help them in this effort. That imagination also should incorporate attention to government's special role in assuring concern for important values and standing firm against efforts to diminish them (Dahl and Soss 2014). The need for imagination is obviously not new to public administration, where creativity, innovation, and strategic thinking and acting have always found a place (Osborne and Brown 2013; Bryson 2011; see also Hartley, chapter 6 of the present volume). Such imagination often involves bridging the politics-administration divide (Gulick 1933; Appleby 1945), but also knowing when to defer to elected officials, as Alford, Hartley, and Hughes point out in chapter 2. In all these cases, public administrators have a special obligation to turn their imaginations to enhancing democratic governance and citizenship.

The Key Practices for Addressing Public Value and Public Values Concerns

Further experimentation with all of the practical approaches seems merited as well. We have pointed out more than once that most of the chapters in this volume can make contributions to policy analysis, design, and evaluation. For example, Belfield (in chapter 7) points out that the old policy analysis warhorse, cost-benefit analysis, can make a bigger contribution than it has to date. Other chapters in the book show how the range of policy analysis techniques can be broadened to consider a far broader range of public values than efficiency. All of the tools can foster imaginative responses and attention to the array of public values, in line with Radin's (2012) hopes.

As tables C.2.1–5 demonstrate, leadership is an important part—often even a requirement—for effective use of the approaches and skills this book's authors recommend as means for creating public value. In terms of the emerging approach to public administration, "integrative leadership" (Crosby and Bryson 2010), "relational leadership" (Uhl-Bien and Ospina 2012), and "collaborative leadership" (Chrislip 2002) appear to be particularly useful ways of engaging elected leaders, citizens, and other stakeholders in the work of creating public value in cross-sector, multilevel circumstances.

As noted previously, dialogue and deliberation are central features of the emerging approach to public administration (e.g., Stoker 2006; Bryson et al. 2014, 2015). In chapter 3, Sandfort and Quick show how dialogue and deliberation can be used to help create public value. On a far larger scale are the efforts of such organizations as the Policy Consensus Initiative (http://policyconsensus.org/) and the widespread use of alternative dispute resolution methods that help produce public value. The emerging approach to public administration would benefit if organizations like the Policy Consensus Initiative could ensure that their initiatives attend to a broad range of public values; cataloging the results of these initiatives in public value terms would also be beneficial.

Addressing values concerns must take account of the features of effective deliberation, including the deliberative pathways that might be available. These features include speakers and audiences; information gathering, analysis, and synthesis; the development and framing of choices; judgment; intellect and emotion;

reasonable objectivity, but also partiality and passion; at times transparency and publicity, and at other times secrecy, so that people can develop and consider the full range of options, including the "unthinkable" or "unspeakable"; and at all times listening and respecting what others say, at least until final choices are made (Garsten 2006, 127–29, 131, 191–94). This honorable tradition of deliberation goes back at least to Aristotle and Cicero, both of whom analyzed and promoted its virtues.

To succeed, deliberative processes and practices also require supportive institutional and organizational arrangements. In addition, the deliberative tradition requires a willingness on the part of would-be deliberators to resist rushing to judgment; tolerate uncertainty, ambiguity, and equivocality; consider different views, new information, and various analyses; and be persuaded—but also be willing to end deliberations at some point and go with the group's considered judgment. The deliberative tradition does not presume there is a "correct" solution or "one best answer" to addressing major challenges, only that there is wisdom to be found via the process (Stone 2011). The chapters in this book offer some important ways of thinking, some tools and techniques, and some specific content categories that may become part of dialogical and deliberative processes. In a polity as sharply divided as that of the United States, concerted efforts at improving these processes are likely to be highly beneficial.

As noted in chapter 1, institutional and organizational design processes intentionally shape institutions so they embody particular public values and make it more likely that other particular values are realized in practice. Ernest Alexander (2015), for example, shows how institutional and organizational design are at work at varied scales from the European Union, to area-wide regional planning in Australia and the United States, to the way the US Congress designed the closing of military bases in the aftermath of the Cold War. Most of the chapters in this book focus on ways of assessing the prospective or retrospective effects of differing institutional and organizational designs. Institutional and organizational design in practice should focus directly on clarifying what public value is to be created and which public values are to be served (Moulton 2009).

The formal and informal processes of democracy also obviously have an important role to play in addressing public value–related concerns. Most of the chapters in the book grant that elected officials and the citizenry are the ultimate arbiters of public value, and most offer approaches to informing the formal and informal processes of democracy. Some chapters also show how innovations in governance may improve democracy—for example, Hartley on innovation (chapter 6) and Guarini on regional collaborative governance in the Veneto region of Italy (chapter 14). It is also important for practitioners to keep in mind Adam Dahl and Joe Soss's (2014) admonitions that public value is not just an output or outcome, and that democracy is not just instrumental but is an end in and of itself. Otherwise, public value advocates may mimic the very neoliberal or new public management rationality that Moore's original conception of creating public value was meant to challenge. Further, at least in the US polity, pursuit of public value can be particularly challenging given sharply divided public opinion on many issues, intense partisan politics, the power of organized and especially wealthy interests, the many veto points built into governance arrangements, and growing inequality (Jacobs 2014). Indeed, dialogue and deliberation and new institutional and organizational designs in a governance system already skewed toward the wealthy may further aggravate an already flawed system and reduce what many would see as public value.

Finally, strategic management, including performance measurement and management, can help public managers and others create, measure, and assess public value and public values, as pointed out by Beryl Radin (2006, 2012), Moynihan (2008), Kroll and Moynihan (this volume, chapter 12), and Bryson (2011), among others. Strategic management involves values and produces value, while values also provide a frame of reference for assessing strategic management practices (Van Dooren, Bouckaert, and Halligan 2010). As we noted in the introduction, Colin Talbot (2010, 205–15) argues that a good theory of performance in the public domain should attend to public values, performance regimes, and specific performance models. The chapters in this book collectively contribute to knowledge about all three elements. The most important point for practice is to assure that public strategic management systems in a democracy attend to a far broader range of values than just efficiency and effectiveness.

The Public Sphere

All six ways of addressing public value and public values concerns presume the presence of a workable public sphere. It is within that sphere that Moore's, Bozeman's, and others' approaches to public value will be related, if not fully integrated. The public sphere is the space within which public values exist and public value might be created.

In chapter 1 we quoted Benington, who sees the public sphere as "a democratic space" that includes the "web of values, places, organizations, rules, knowledge, and other cultural resources held in common by people through their everyday commitments and behaviors, and held in trust by government and public institutions" (2011, 32). In other words, the public sphere is a psychological, social, political, institutional, and physical space that "provides a society with some sense of belonging, meaning, purpose and continuity, and which enables people to thrive and strive amid uncertainty" (43). Benington believes that the public is not given, but made—it has to be continuously created and constructed; he also agrees that public value is necessarily contested and is often established through a continuous process of dialogue.

As noted in chapter 1, Bozeman and Japera Johnson (2014) have recently incorporated the creation, maintenance, and enhancement of the public sphere into their public values criteria. In doing so they have argued that Benington's conception actually includes two components. The first is the public value of "open public communication and deliberation about public values and about collective action pertaining to public values." The second is the importance of "public value enabling institutions," or "the space, physical or virtual, in which the realization of the public sphere value occurs" (see table 1.1). Public value mapping and broader efforts on the part of public managers should highlight when the public sphere is or might be enhanced and when and how it is not.

Advancing Research and Theory

We offer several suggestions for advancing research and theory. An important step is to keep the public value, public values, and public sphere conversations joined. The time has come to link the many approaches to creating public value more explicitly, to make sure the broad array of public values is considered, and to explicitly consider the maintenance and enhancement of the public sphere. Public administration has always been concerned with public value creation, public values in general, and the public sphere, so the call here is really nothing new, but the call now is for the researchers contributing to these often disparate streams to recognize the larger project with which they are involved and to which they contribute. The field as a whole will benefit. We have offered the public value governance triangle (PVGT) as a conceptual framework for indicating how the different strands of the public value literature may be related.

Another important step is to clarify further the definitions, conceptualizations, and measurements of public value and the public sphere. The chapters in this book give a sense of the breadth of approaches taken to date. While public administration scholars and practitioners may ultimately agree on these public value–related matters, they are unlikely to reach full consensus (Davis and West 2009). That is not necessarily a bad thing. In order to make progress, however, scholars should engage in further conceptual refinement, the continued development of suitable typologies and measures, and rigorous empirical testing. Research should attend to both subjectively held public values and more objective states of the world; whether a specific public value is intrinsic, extrinsic, or relational; whether something is a prime or instrumental public value; whether there are hierarchies of public values; who does the valuing; how the valuing is done; and against what criteria the object of value is measured.

The PVGT highlights six practical ways of reconciling or accommodating Moore's more managerial focus on creating public value with Bozeman's more policy-oriented or societal focus on public values; the six are analysis, leadership, dialogue and deliberation, institutional and organizational design, formal and informal processes of democracy, and performance management regimes and models. Much more research is needed into how these practices can actually help reconcile the approaches and produce real public value.

An important theoretical question is how to match methods of discerning, measuring, or assessing public value and public values to specific contexts. For example, what are the contextual opportunities and constraints on the use of various stakeholder engagement approaches in articulating values and making decisions? In what kinds of situations are the different approaches to indicators and scorecards most beneficial? How should the many skills in creating public value be appropriately adapted to different contexts? Context matters generally, and it matters greatly for creating public value and pursuing particular public values (Pollitt 2013). The result of this research endeavor is likely to be the development of more contingency approaches and decision rules, as advocated by Alford in chapter 5.

One way to approach the question of contextual suitability and effects would be deploying and testing the same approach or tool in different contexts. For example, Thomas, Poister, and Su suggest in chapter 11 that their survey process be replicated with stakeholder groups for other public agencies in other states and other levels of government. Testing conceptual frameworks like that of Alford, Hartley, and Hughes (chapter 2) in non-Westminster systems would also be very useful. Comparative case study analyses of public-sector or cross-sector innovations that highlight connection with public value and public values would be desirable as well (Borins 1998, 2014). Kroll and Moynihan (chapter 12) suggest research into how public employees and others actually use data about the performance of public programs. Doing so with particular attention to public value and public values would be extremely helpful; knowing contingency-related causes and effects of such use would be valuable. In short, major research questions revolve around the evaluation of the various approaches' and methods' effectiveness in particular kinds of situations and around recommendations for refining them in practice.

More research attention should also be devoted to the barriers to creating public value and realizing important public values in practice. That topic has been outside the scope of the chapters in this book, but is obviously extremely important (Bryson et al. 2014, 2015). A good deal of public administration research has focused on the barriers to achieving efficiency and effectiveness, but not to achieving the full range of public values. Here we are asking that researchers remedy this shortcoming and consider what might be done to overcome the barriers.

Finally, as noted earlier, this volume's authors do not attend much to the sources of value change, although several assert that various methods—such as mapping, modeling, analysis, and scorecards—can build shared understanding and often lead to changed minds as a consequence of participation, dialogue, and deliberation. Research is thus needed on the sources of change in public values and value assessments.

Summing Up

We believe that the language of "public value" represents an important rhetorical innovation; since Moore (1995) first coined the term, it has become a prominent feature of public administration discourse (Williams and Shearer 2011; Van der Wal, Nabatchi, and De Graaf 2013). That rhetorical turn helps provide a contemporary language for discussing what kind of society a free people do or should want to build, how it can be legitimated and authorized, how it can be created (including the help of public managers), and how these same free people can know whether and to what extent it has been created. The same language can be used to explore what the proper role of government—and of public managers—might be in specific circumstances in a multisector, multilevel, "no one wholly in charge" democratic society. In the chapters in this book, government and public managers play many roles, often including the role as guarantors of important public values.

We hope readers more fully appreciate the *idea* of public value and also understand more clearly the many ways of *appreciating, measuring,* and *assessing* both *public values and public value.* This book illustrates how the various strands of the public value literature—including Moore's and Bozeman's—may be related. The volume doesn't reveal consensus, but it provides important intellectual order to the field and helps clarify many key issues.

In short, our hope is that this book has demonstrated the purposes and power of the public value literature and especially of joining the too-often-disconnected streams in the field. The language, approaches, tools, techniques, and processes in that literature offer a valuable way forward for leaders, managers, and others across sectors—as well as citizens—who care about creating what the public values and what is good for the public as assessed against a variety of public values. This book alerts readers to the broad array of existing contributions to the field and proposes additional work of both theoretical and practical significance aimed at making the world and its public sphere more vibrant and effective in improving all of our lives together, now and in the future.

NOTE

1. Parts of this discussion draw on Bryson, Crosby, and Bloomberg (2014, 2015) and Bryson (2011, 8–9).

REFERENCES

Aberbach, Joel D., Robert D. Putnam, and Bert A. Rockman. 1981. *Bureaucrats and Politicians in Western Democracies*. Cambridge, MA: Harvard University Press.

Abernathy, Scott F. 2007. *No Child Left Behind and the Public Schools*. Ann Arbor: University of Michigan Press.

Abrahamson, Eric. 1991. "Managerial Fads and Fashion: The Diffusion and Rejection of Innovations." *Academy of Management Review* 16: 588–612.

Ackermann, Fran, and Colin Eden. 1998. *Making Strategy*. Thousand Oaks, CA: Sage.

———. 2011. "Strategic Management of Stakeholders: Theory and Practice." *Long Range Planning* 44: 179–96.

Ackermann, Fran, David F. Andersen, Colin Eden, and George P. Richardson. 2010. "Using a Group Decision Support System to Add Value to Group Model Building." *System Dynamics Review* 26 (4): 335–46.

———. 2011. "ScriptsMap: A Tool for Designing Multi-method Policy-making Workshops." *Omega* 39 (4): 427–34.

Agranoff, Robert. 2006. "Inside Collaborative Networks: Ten Lessons for Public Managers." *Public Administration Review* 66 (s1): 56–65.

Agranoff, Robert, and Michael McGuire. 2003. *Collaborative Public Management: New Strategies for Local Governments*. Washington, DC: Georgetown University Press.

Ahearn, Kathleen K., Gerald R. Ferris, Wayne A. Hochwarter, Ceasar Douglas, and Anthony P. Ammeter. 2004. "Leader Political Skill and Team Performance." *Journal of Management* 30 (3): 309–27.

Alänge, Sverker, Staffan Jacobsson, and Annika Jarnehammar. 1998. "Some Aspects of an Analytical Framework for Studying the Diffusion of Organizational Innovations." *Technology Analysis and Strategic Management* 10 (1): 3–21.

Albury, David. 2005. "Fostering Innovation in Public Services." *Public Money and Management* 2: 51–56.

Alexander, Ernest R. 2002. "The Public Interest in Planning: From Legitimation to Substantive Plan Evaluation." *Planning Theory* 1: 226–49.

———. 2015. "Effectuating Public Values by Institutional Design." In *Creating Public Value in Practice*, edited by John M. Bryson, Barbara C. Crosby, and Laura Bloomberg, 108–23. Boca Raton, FL: CRC.

Alford, John. 2008. "The Limits to Traditional Public Administration, or Rescuing Public Value from Misrepresentation." *Australian Journal of Public Administration* 67 (3): 357–66.

———. 2009. *Engaging Public Sector Clients: From Service Delivery to Co-production*. Basingstoke, England: Palgrave Macmillan.

Alford, John, and Owen Hughes. 2008. "Public Value Pragmatism as the Next Phase of Public Management." *American Review of Public Administration* 38 (2): 130–48.

Alford, John, and Janine O'Flynn. 2009. "Making Sense of Public Value: Concepts, Critiques, and Emergent Meanings." *International Journal of Public Administration* 32 (3–4): 171–91.

Allen, Tom L. 2002. "Public Accountability and Government Reporting." In *Models of Public Budgeting and Financial Reform*, edited by James L. Chan and Chen Xiaoyoue. Special issue, *OECD Journal on Budgeting* 2 (s1): 11–36.

Allison, Graham T. 2012. "Public and Private Management: Are They Fundamentally Alike in All Unimportant Respects?" In *Public Management: Public and Private Perspectives*, edited by James L. Perry and Kenneth L. Kraemer, 121–25. Mountain View, CA: Mayfield.

Altshuler, Alan A., and Robert D. Behn. 1997. *Innovation in American Government: Challenges, Opportunities, and Dilemmas*. Washington, DC: Brookings Institution Press.

Altshuler, A., and M. Zegans. 1997. "Innovation and Public Management: Notes from the State House and City Hall." In *Innovation in American Government*, edited by A. Altshuler and R. Behn, 49. Washington, DC: Brookings Institution Press.

American Association of State Highway and Transportation Officials. 2004. *Strategic Performance Measures for State DOTs: A Handbook for CEOs and Executives*. Washington, DC: AASHTO.

Ammons, David, and William Rivenbark. 2008. "Factors Influencing the Use of Performance Data to Improve Municipal Services: Evidence from the North Carolina Benchmarking Project." *Public Administration Review* 68 (2): 304–31.

Andersen, David F., and George P. Richardson. 1997. "Scripts for Group Model Building." *System Dynamics Review* 13 (2): 107–29.

Andersen, David F., George P. Richardson, John Rohrbaugh, Aldo A. Zagonel, and Tsuey-Ping Lee. 2000. "The Impact of US Welfare Reform on States and Counties: Group Facilitated System Dynamics Modeling, Policy Analysis and Implementation." GDN2000, INFORMS Section on Group Decision and Negotiation. University of Strathclyde. Glasgow, Scotland.

Andersen, Lotte Bøgh, Torben Beck Jørgensen, Anne Mette Kjeldsen, Lene Holm Pedersen, and Karsten Vrangbæk. 2012. "Public Value Dimensions: Developing and Testing a Multi-Dimensional Classification." *International Journal of Public Administration* 35 (11): 715–28.

Anessi-Pessina, Eugenio. 2002. *Principles of Public Management*. Milan: Egea.

Apple, M. 2006. "Interrupting the Right: On Doing Critical Educational Work in Conservative Times." In *Educational Research in the Public Interest: Social Justice, Action, and Policy*, edited by G. Ladson-Billings and W. F. Tate, 27–45. New York: Teachers College Press.

Appleby, Paul. 1945. *Big Democracy*. New York: Knopf.

Armsen, Wencke, Stefan Moeller, Rainer Lampe, and Emanuele Gatti. 2013. "Gesundheitsdienstleistungen in der öffentlichen Wahrnehmung. Die Messung des gesellschaftlichen Nutzens privatisierter Gesundheitsdienstleistungen." *Organisationsentwicklung—Zeitschrift für Unternehmensentwicklung und Change Management* 4: 20–26.

Arnstein, Sherri R. 1969. "A Ladder of Citizen Participation." *Journal of American Institute of Planners* 35: 216–24.

Askim, Jostein, Åge Johnsen, and Knut-Andreas Christophersen. 2008. "Factors behind Organizational Learning from Benchmarking: Experiences from Norwegian Municipal Benchmarking Networks." *Journal of Public Administration Research and Theory* 18 (2): 297–320.

Atkins, Stuart, Allan Katcher, and Elias Porter. 1967. *LIFO: Life Orientations and Strength Excess Profile*. Los Angeles: Atkins-Katcher.

Au, W., B. Bigelow, and S. Karp. 2007. "Introduction: Creating Classrooms for Equity and Social Justice." In *Rethinking Our Classrooms*, vol. 1, edited by W. Au, B. Bigelow, and S. Karp. http://www.rethinkingschools.org/ProdDetails.asp?ID=9780942961355.

Baldwin, Christina. 1998. *Calling the Circle: The First and Future Culture*. New York: Bantam.

Baldwin, Christina, and Ann Linnea. 2010. *The Circle Way: A Leader in Every Chair*. San Francisco: Berrett-Koehler.

Baran, Peter. 1991. "Werte." In *Europäische Enzyklopädie zu Philosophie und Wissenschaften* vol. 4, edited by Hans-Jörg Sandkühler, 805–15. Hamburg: Felix Meiner Verlag.

Bardach, Eugene. 2011. *A Practical Guide for Policy Analysis: The Eightfold Path to More Effective Problem Solving.* 4th ed. Washington, DC: CQ Press.

Baron, Helen. 1996. "Strengths and Limitations of Ipsative Measurement." *Journal of Occupational and Organizational Psychology* 69: 49–56.

Barton, G. 2012. "The G4S Debacle in London is a Wake-up Call on Outsourcing Security." *The Conversation,* July 18. http://theconversation.edu.au/the-g4s-debacle-in-london-is-a-wake-up-call-on-outsourcing-security.

Bason, C. 2010. *Leading Public Sector Innovation.* Bristol, England: Policy Press.

Bator, F. M. 1958. "The Anatomy of Market Failure." *Quarterly Journal of Economics* 72 (3): 351–79.

Beck Jørgensen, Torben. 1996. "Rescuing Public Services: On the Tasks of Public Organizations." In *Quality, Innovation and Measurement in the Public Sector,* edited by H. Hill, H. Klages, and E. Loffler, 161–82. Frankfurt: Lang.

———. 2007. "Public Values, Their Nature, Stability and Change: The Case of Denmark." *Public Administration Quarterly* 30 (4): 365–98.

Beck Jørgensen, Torben, and Barry Bozeman. 2002. "Public Values Lost? Comparing Cases on Contracting Out from Denmark and the United States." *Public Management Review* 4 (1): 63–81.

———. 2007. "Public Values: An Inventory." *Administration and Society* 39 (3): 354–81.

Beck Jørgensen, Torben, and Karsten Vrangbæk. 2011. "Value Dynamics: Towards a Framework for Analyzing Public Value Changes." *International Journal of Public Administration* 34 (8): 486–96.

Behn, Robert D. 2001. *Rethinking Democratic Accountability.* Washington, DC: Brookings Institution Press.

———. 2003. "Why Measure Performance?" *Public Administration Review* 63 (5): 586–607.

———. 2008. "Designing Performance Stat: Or What Are the Key Strategic Decisions That a Jurisdiction or Organization Must Make When Adopting the Performance-Stat/CitiStat Class of Performance Strategies?" *Public Performance and Management Review* 32 (2): 206–35.

Belfield, Clive, and Henry Levin. 2007. *The Price We Pay: The Economic and Social Costs of Inadequate Education.* Washington, DC: Brookings Institution Press.

Belussi, F., and F. Arcangeli. 1998. "A Typology of Networks." *Research Policy* 27: 415–28.

Benhabib, Seyla, ed. 1996. *Democracy and Difference: Contesting the Boundaries of the Political.* Princeton, NJ: Princeton University Press.

Benington, John. 2009. "Creating the Public in Order to Create Public Value?" *International Journal of Public Administration* 32 (3–4): 232–49.

———. 2011. "From Private Choice to Public Value?" In *Public Value: Theory and Practice,* edited by John Benington and Mark H. Moore, 3–29. Basingstoke, England: Palgrave Macmillan.

Benington, John, and Mark H. Moore. 2011a. "Public Value in Complex and Changing Times." In *Public Value: Theory and Practice,* edited by John Benington and Mark H. Moore, 1–20. Basingstoke, England: Palgrave Macmillan.

———. 2011b. *Public Value: Theory and Practice.* Basingstoke, England: Palgrave Macmillan.

Bennett, J., and M. Johnson. 1981. *Better Government at Half the Price.* Ottawa, IL: Caroline House.

Beringer, Lorenz, and Sebastian Bernard. 2013. "Stern des Südens—Fußballverein oder weltweites Entertainment? Der Public Value des FC Bayern München."

Organisationsentwicklung—Zeitschrift für Unternehmensentwicklung und Change Management 4: 13–19.

Berman, Evan, and XioHu Wang. 2000. "Performance Measurement in U.S. Counties: Capacity for Reform." *Public Administration Review* 60 (5): 409–20.

Berry, F. 1994. "Sizing Up State Policy Innovation Research." *Policy Studies Journal* 22 (3): 442–56.

Best, Allan, Pamela I. Clark, Scott J. Leischow, and William M. K. Trochim, eds. 2007. *Greater Than the Sum: Systems Thinking in Tobacco Control.* NCI Tobacco Control Monograph Series 18. Bethesda, MD: National Institutes of Health. http://cancercontrol.cancer.gov/brp/tcrb/monographs/18/m18_complete.pdf.

Bessant, J. 2005. "Enabling Continuous and Discontinuous Innovation: Learning from the Private Sector." *Public Money and Management* 25 (1): 35–42.

Bevan, Gwyn, and Christopher Hood. 2006. "What's Measured Is What Matters: Targets and Gaming in the English Public Health Care System." *Public Administration* 84 (3): 517–38.

Birkinshaw, J., J. Bessant, and R. Delbridge. 2007. "Finding, Forming and Performing: Creating Networks for Discontinuous Innovation." *California Management Review* 49 (3): 67–83.

Birkinshaw, J., G. Hamel, and M. Mol. 2008. "Management Innovation." *Academy of Management Journal* 33 (4): 825–45.

Black, Laura J. 2013. "When Visuals Are Boundary Objects In System Dynamics Work." *System Dynamics Review* 29 (2): 70–86.

Black, Laura J., and David F. Andersen. 2012. "Using Visual Representations as Boundary Objects to Resolve Conflict in Collaborative Model-Building Approaches." *Systems Research and Behavioral Science* 29 (2): 194–208.

Blader, S. L., and T. R. Tyler. 2003. "A Four-component Model of Procedural Justice: Defining the Meaning of a 'Fair' Process." *Personality and Social Psychology Review* 29: 747–58.

Block, Peter. 2009. *Community: The Structure of Belonging.* San Francisco: Berrett-Koehler.

Boardman, Adrian, David Greenberg, Adrian Vining, and David Weimer. 2006. *Cost-Benefit Analysis: Concepts and Practice.* New York: Prentice Hall.

Bolman, Lee, and Terrence Deal. 2008. *Reframing Organizations: Artistry, Choice and Leadership.* 4th ed. San Francisco: Jossey-Bass.

Borgonovi, Elio, and Riccardo Mussari. 2011. "Pubblico e Privato: Armonizzare gli Opposti." *Azienda Pubblica* 2: 103–18.

Borins, Sanford. 1998. *Innovating with Integrity.* Washington, DC: Georgetown University Press.

———. 2008. *Innovations in Government: Research, Recognition and Replications.* Washington, DC: Brookings Institution Press.

———. 2012. "Making Narrative Count: A Narratological Approach to Public Management Innovation." *Journal of Public Administration Research and Theory* 22 (1): 143–64.

———. 2014. *The Persistence of Innovation in Government.* Washington, DC: Brookings Institution Press.

Bouckaert, Geert, and John Halligan. 2008. *Managing Performance: International Comparisons.* London: Routledge.

Bourdeaux, Carolyn, and Grace Chikoto. 2008. "Legislative Influences on Performance Management Reform." *Public Administration Review* 68 (2): 253–65.

Bovaird, Tony. 2007. "Beyond Engagement and Participation: User and Community Co-production of Public Services." *Public Administration Review* 67 (5): 846–60.

Box, Richard C. 2014. *Public Service Values.* New York: Routledge.

Boyne, George. 2002. "Concepts and Indicators of Local Authority Performance: An Evaluation of the Statutory Frameworks in England and Wales." *Public Money and Management* 22 (2): 17–24.

Boyne, George, Julian Gould-Williams, Jennifer Law, and Richard Walker. 2004. "Toward the Self-Evaluating Organization? An Empirical Test of the Wildavsky Model." *Public Administration Review* 64 (4): 463–73.

Boyte, Harry. 1989. *Commonwealth: A Return to Citizen Politics.* New York: Free Press.

———. 2005. "Reframing Democracy: Governance, Civic Agency, and Politics." *Public Administration Review* 65 (5): 536–46.

———. 2011. "Constructive Politics as Public Work: Organizing the Literature." *Political Theory* 39 (5): 630–60.

———. 2012. "Public Work versus Polarizing Politics: Contributions of the New Civic Field." Paper presented at the Creating Public Value Conference, Minneapolis, September 20–22.

Bozeman, Barry. 1987. *All Organizations Are Public.* San Francisco: Jossey-Bass.

———. 2002. "Public-Value Failure: When Efficient Markets May Not Do." *Public Administration Review* 62 (2): 145–61.

———. 2003. *Public Value Mapping of Science Outcomes: Theory and Method.* Washington, DC: Center for Science, Policy, and Outcomes.

———. 2007. *Public Values and Public Interest: Counterbalancing Economic Individualism.* Washington, DC: Georgetown University Press.

Bozeman, Barry, and Stuart Bretschneider. 1986. "Public Management Information Systems: Theory and Prescription." *Public Administration Review* 46: 475–87.

Bozeman, Barry, and J. Johnson. 2014. "The Political Economy of Public Values: A Case for the Public Sphere and Progressive Opportunity." *American Review of Public Administration.* DOI: 10.1177/0275074014532826.

Bozeman, Barry, and G. Kingsley. 1998. "Risk Culture in Public and Private Organizations." *Public Administration Review* 58: 109–18.

Bozeman, Barry, and S. Moulton. 2011. "Integrative Publicness: A Framework for Public Management Strategy and Performance." *Journal of Public Administration Research and Theory* 21 (s3): 363–80.

Bozeman, Barry, and J. Rogers. 2002. "Churn Model of Scientific Knowledge Value: Internet Researchers as a Knowledge Value Collective." *Research Policy* 31: 769–94.

Bozeman, B., and D. Sarewitz. 2005. "Public Values and Public Failure in U.S. Science Policy." *Science and Public Policy* 32 (2): 119–36.

———. 2011. "Public Value Mapping and Science Policy Evaluation." *Minerva: A Review of Science, Learning and Policy* 49 (1): 1–23.

Bozeman, B., D. Sarewitz, S. Feinson, G. Foladori, M. Gaughan, A. Gupta, B. Sampat, and G. Zachary. 2003. *Knowledge Flows and Knowledge Collectives: Understanding the Role of Science and Technology Policies in Development.* Global Inclusion Program. New York: Rockefeller Foundation.

Briggs, Xavier de Souza. 2008. *Democracy as Problem Solving: Civic Capacity in Communities Across the Globe.* Cambridge, MA: MIT Press.

Brodkin, Evelyn Z., and Malay Majmundar. 2010. "Administrative Exclusion: Organizations and the Hidden Costs of Welfare Claiming." *Journal of Public Administration Research and Theory* 20 (4): 827–48.

Brown, Juanita, and David Isaacs. 2005. *The World Café: Shaping Our Futures through Conversations That Matter.* San Francisco: Berrett-Koehler.

Brown, Paul C., John Kelly, and David Querusio. 2011. "Toward a Health Care Business-Process Reference Model." *IT Professional* 13 (3): 38–47.

Brown, P. G. 1992. "The Failure of Market Failures." *Journal of Socio-Economics* 21 (1): 1–24.

Brown, Trevor L., Matthew Potoski, and David M. Van Slyke. 2006. "Managing Public Service Contracts: Aligning Values, Institutions, and Markets." *Public Administration Review* 66 (3): 53–67.

Brudney, J. 1990. "The Availability of Volunteers: Implications for Local Governments." *Administration and Society* 21 (4): 413–24.

Brunsson, Nils. 2003. *The Organization of Hypocrisy: Talk, Decisions and Actions in Organizations*. Copenhagen: Business School Press.

Bryson, John M. 2004a. *Strategic Planning for Public and Nonprofit Organizations: A Guide to Strengthening and Sustaining Organizational Achievement*. 3rd ed. San Francisco: Jossey-Bass.

———. 2004b. "What to Do When Stakeholders Matter: Stakeholder Identification and Analysis Techniques." *Public Management Review* 6 (1): 21–53.

———. 2011. *Strategic Planning for Public and Nonprofit Organizations*. 4th ed. San Francisco: Jossey-Bass.

Bryson, John M., Fran Ackermann, Colin Eden, and Charles B. Finn. 2004. *Visible Thinking: Unlocking Causal Mapping for Practical Business Results*. 1st ed. Chichester, England: Wiley.

Bryson, John M., Barbara C. Crosby, and Laura Bloomberg. 2014. "Public Value Governance: Moving Beyond Traditional Public Administration and the New Public Management." *Public Administration Review* 74 (4): 445–56.

———, eds. 2015. *Creating Public Value in Practice: Advancing the Common Good in a Multi-Sector, Shared-Power, No-One-Wholly-in-Charge World*. Boca Raton, FL: CRC.

Bryson, John M., Barbara C. Crosby, and Melissa M. Stone. 2006. "The Design and Implementation of Cross-Sector Collaborations: Propositions from the Literature." *Public Administration Review* 66 (s1): 44–55.

Bryson, John M., Gary L. Cunningham, and Karen J. Lokkesmoe. 2002. "What to Do When Stakeholders Matter: The Case of Problem Formulation for the African American Men Project of Hennepin County, Minnesota." *Public Administration Review* 62 (5): 568–84.

Bryson, John M., and Michael Q. Patton. 2010. "Analyzing and Engaging Stakeholders." In *Handbook of Practical Program Evaluation*, 3rd ed., edited by Joseph Wholey, Harry Hatry, and Kathryn E. Newcomer, 30–54. Hoboken, NJ: Wiley.

Bryson, John M., Kathryn Quick, Carissa Schively Slotterback, and Barbara C. Crosby. 2013. "Designing Public Participation Processes." *Public Administration Review* 73 (1): 23–34.

Buchanan, D. 2008. "You Stab My Back, I'll Stab Yours: Management Experience and Perceptions of Organization Political Behaviour." *British Journal of Management* 19: 49–64.

Buchanan, D., L. Fitzgerald, and D. Ketley. 2006. *The Sustainability and Spread of Organizational Change*. Abingdon, England: Routledge.

Burns, James McGregor. 1978. *Leadership*. New York: Harper.

Burns, T., and G. Stalker. 1961. *The Management of Innovation*. London: Tavistock.

Campbell, C., and G. Wilson. 1995. *The End of Whitehall*. Cambridge, MA: Blackwell.

Campbell, D. 2012. "Public Managers in Integrated Services Collaboratives: What Works Is Workarounds." *Public Administration Review* 72 (5): 721–30.

Canziani, Arnaldo. 2007. "Economia Aziendale and Betriebswirtschaftlehre as Autonomous Sciences of the Firm." In *The Firm as an Entity: Implications for Economics, Accounting and the Law*, edited by Yuri Biondi, Arnaldo Canziani, and Thierry Kirat, 107–30. New York: Routledge.

Capalbo, Francesco, and Frank Clarke. 2006. "The Italian Economia Aziendale and Chambers' CoCoA." *Abacus* 42 (1): 66–86.

Carlile, Paul. 2002. "A Pragmatic View of Knowledge and Boundaries: Boundary Objects in New Product Development." *Organization Science* 13 (4): 442–55.

Carlson, J. 2005. *The Economics of Fire Protection: From the Great Fire of London to Rural/Metro*. 9th IEA Discussion Paper. London: Institute of Economic Affairs.

Carroll, Archie B. 2000. "A Commentary and an Overview of Key Questions of Corporate Social Performance Measurement." *Business and Society* 39 (4): 466–78.

Center for Technology in Government. 2011. *Open Government and Public Value: Conceptualizing a Portfolio Assessment Tool.* Albany, NY: Center for Technology in Government. http://www.ctg.albany.edu/publications/online/pvat/PVAT_Conceptua lizingtheTool.pdf.

Charbonneau, Etienne, and François Bellavance. 2012. "Blame Avoidance in Public Reporting." *Public Performance and Management Review* 35 (3): 399–421.

Chen, Chung-an. 2009. "Antecedents of Contracting-Back-In: A View beyond the Economic Paradigm." *Administration and Society* 41 (1): 101–26.

Chesbrough, H. 2003. *Open Innovation.* Boston: Harvard Business School Press.

Chettiar, Ian, Michael Livermore, and Jason Schwartz. 2009. *The Price of Neglect: The Hidden Environmental and Public Health Costs of Bad Economics.* Monograph. New York: Institute for Policy Integrity, New York University.

Chrislip, David D. 2002. *The Collaborative Leadership Fieldbook.* San Francisco: Jossey-Bass.

Chrisman, James J., and Archie B. Carroll. 1984. "Corporate Responsibility: Reconciling Economic and Social Goals." *Sloan Management Review* 25 (2): 59–65.

Christensen, T., and P. Lægreid. 2007. "The Whole-of-Government Approach to Public Sector Reform." *Public Administration Review* 67 (6): 1059–66.

Clark, J. 2006. "Social Justice, Education, and Schooling: Some Philosophical Issues." *British Journal of Educational Studies* 54 (3): 272–87.

Clarke, J., and D. McCool. 1996. *Staking Out the Terrain: Power and Performance among Natural Resource Agencies.* Albany: State University of New York Press.

Cleveland, Harlan. 2002. *Nobody in Charge: Essays on the Future of Leadership.* New York: Wiley.

Clune, William. 2002. "Methodological Strength and Policy Usefulness of Cost-Effectiveness Research." In *Cost-Effectiveness and Educational Policy,* edited by Henry M. Levin and Patrick J. McEwan, 98–121. Larchmont, NY: Eye on Education.

Cochran-Smith, Marilyn. 2004. *Walking the Road: Race, Diversity, and Social Justice in Teacher Education.* New York: Teachers College Press.

Coleman, Clive, and Jenny Moynihan. 1996. *Understanding Crime Data: Haunted by the Dark Figure.* Crime and Justice 120. Maidenhead, England: Buckingham Open University Press.

Commission on Wartime Contracting in Iraq and Afghanistan. 2011. *At What Risk? Correcting Over-Reliance on Contractors in Contingency Operations.* Second Interim Report to Congress. Washington, DC: Commission on Wartime Contracting in Iraq and Afghanistan.

Considine, Mark, and Jenny M. Lewis. 2003. "Bureaucracy, Network, or Enterprise? Comparing the Models of Governance in Australia, Britain, the Netherlands, and New Zealand." *Public Administration Review* 63 (2): 131–40.

Contandriopoulos, Damien. 2011. "On the Nature and Strategies of Organized Interests in Health Care Policy Making." *Administration and Society* 43 (1): 45–65.

Cooke, Maeve. 2000. "Five Arguments for Deliberative Democracy." *Political Studies* 48 (5): 947–69.

Cooper, Christopher A., Anthony J. Nownes, and Steven Roberts. 2005. "Perceptions of Power: Interest Groups in Local Politics." *State and Local Government Review* 1 (3): 206–17.

Cooper, Terry L., Thomas A. Bryer, and Jack W. Meek. 2006. "Citizen-Centered Collaborative Public Management." *Public Administration Review* 66 (s1): 76–88.

Cooperrider, David L., and Suresh Srivastva. 1987. "Appreciative Inquiry in Organizational Life." In *Research in Organizational Change and Development,* edited by William A. Pasmore and Richard W. Woodman, 129–69. Greenwich, CT: JAI.

Cooperrider, David L., and D. Whitney. 2000. *Appreciative Inquiry: A Positive Revolution in Change*. San Francisco: Berrett-Koehler.

Creighton, James L. 2005. *The Public Participation Handbook: Making Better Decisions through Citizen Involvement*. San Francisco: Jossey-Bass.

Crenson, Matthew, and Benjamin Ginsberg. 2002. *Downsizing Democracy: How America Sidelined Its Citizens and Privatized Its Public*. Baltimore: Johns Hopkins University Press.

Cresswell, Anthony M. 2010. "Public Value and Government ICT Investment." Paper presented at the Second International Conference on eGovernment and eGovernance, Antalya, Turkey, March 11–12.

Cresswell, Anthony M., G. Brian Burke, and Theresa A. Pardo. 2006. *Advancing Return on Investment Analysis for Government IT: A Public Value Framework*. Albany, NY: Center for Technology in Government.

Crick, B. 1993. *In Defense of Politics*. Chicago: University of Chicago Press.

Crosby, Barbara C., and John M. Bryson. 2005. *Leadership for the Common Good: Tackling Public Problems in a Shared-Power World*. 2nd ed. San Francisco: Jossey-Bass.

———. 2010. "Integrative Leadership and the Creation and Maintenance of Cross-Sector Collaborations." *Leadership Quarterly* 21 (2): 211–30.

Crouch, C. 2011. "Privates, Publics and Values." In *Public Value: Theory and Practice*, edited by J. Benington and M. Moore, 52–73. Basingstoke, England: Palgrave Macmillan.

Dahl, Adam, and Joe Soss. 2014. "Neoliberalism for the Common Good? Public Value Governance and the Downsizing of Democracy." *Public Administration Review* 74 (4): 496–504.

Dalessio, A. T. 1998. "Using Multisource Feedback for Employee Development and Personnel Decisions." In *Performance Appraisal: State of the Art in Practice*, edited by J. W. Smither, 278–330. San Francisco: Jossey-Bass.

Daley, Dorothy M. 2009. "Interdisciplinary Problems and Agency Boundaries: Exploring Effective Cross-Agency Collaboration." *Journal of Public Administration Research and Theory* 19: 477–93.

Damanpour, Fariborz. 1992. "Organizational Size and Innovation." *Organization Studies* 13: 375–402.

Damanpour, Fariborz, and Shanthi Gopalakrishnan. 1998. "Theories of Organizational Structure and Innovation Adoption: The Role of Environmental Change." *Journal of Engineering and Technology Management* 15 (1): 1–24.

Dao, J. 2013. "Criticism of Veterans Affairs Secretary Mounts over Backlog in Claims." *New York Times*, May 18. http://www.nytimes.com/2013/05/19/us/shinseki-faces-mounting-criticism-over-backlog-of-benefit-claims.html?pagewanted=all.

Davidson, J. 2010. "Problems with Security at Federal Buildings Continue, GAO Report Finds." *Washington Post*, April 14. http://www.washingtonpost.com/wpdyn/content/article/2010/04/13/AR2010041304428.html.

Davis, P., and K. West. 2009. "What Do Public Values Mean for Public Action? Putting Public Values in Their Plural Place." *American Review of Public Administration* 39 (6): 602–18.

Dawes, Sharon S., Anthony M. Cresswell, and Theresa A. Pardo. 2009. "From 'Need to Know' to 'Need to Share': Tangled Problems, Information Boundaries, and the Building of Public Sector Knowledge Networks." *Public Administration Review* 69 (3): 392–402.

Dean, J. W., and M. P. Sharfman. 1993. "The Relationship between Procedural Rationality and Political Behavior in Strategic Decision Making." *Decision Sciences* 24 (6): 1069–83.

De Lancer Julnes, Patria, and Marc Holzer. 2001. "Promoting the Utilization of Performance Measures in Public Organizations: An Empirical Study of Factors Affecting Adoption and Implementation." *Public Administration Review* 61 (6): 693–708.

Denhardt, Janet V., and Robert B. Denhardt. 2011. *The New Public Service: Serving, Not Steering.* 3rd ed. Armonk, NY: M. E. Sharpe.

Denis, J. L., Y. Hebert, A. Langley, D. Lozeau, and L. Trottier. 2002. "Explaining Diffusion Patterns for Complex Health Care Innovations." *Health Care Management Review* 27: 60–73.

Desanctis, Gerardine, and R. Brent Gallupe. 1987. "A Foundation for the Study of Group Decision Support Systems." *Management Science* 33 (5): 589–609.

DeWalt, Kathleen M., and Billie R. DeWalt. 2002. *Participant Observation: A Guide for Fieldworkers.* Lanham, MD: Rowman and Littlefield/Altamira.

Dewey, John. 1927. *The Public and Its Problems.* New York: Holt.

Dias, Janice J., and Steven Maynard-Moody. 2007. "For-Profit Welfare: Contracts, Conflicts and the Performance Paradox." *Journal of Public Administration Research and Theory* 17 (1): 189–211.

DiMaggio, P. J., and W. W. Powell. 1983. "The Iron Cage Revisited: Institutional Isomorphism and Collective Rationality in Organizational Fields." *American Sociological Review* 48 (2): 147–60.

Donahue, J. 1989. *The Privatization Decision: Public Ends, Private Means.* New York: Basic Books.

Donahue, John D., and Mark H. Moore, eds. 2012. *Ports in a Storm: Public Management in a Turbulent World.* Washington, DC: Brookings Institution Press.

Dryzek, John S. 2002. *Deliberative Democracy and Beyond: Liberals, Critics, Contestations.* New York: Oxford University Press.

Dull, Matthew. 2009. "Results-Model Reform Leadership: Questions of Credible Commitment." *Journal of Public Administration Research and Theory* 19 (2): 255–84.

Dür, Andreas, and Dirk de Bièvre. 2007. "The Question of Interest Group Influence." *Journal of Public Policy* 27 (1): 1–12.

Earl, L., and S. Katz. 2007. "Leadership in Networked Learning Communities: Defining the Terrain." *School Leadership and Management* 27 (3): 239–58.

Edelenbos, Jurian, and Erik-Hans Klijn. 2006. "Managing Stakeholder Involvement in Decision Making: A Comparative Analysis of Six Interactive Processes in the Netherlands." *Journal of Public Administration Research and Theory* 16: 417–46.

Eden, Colin, and Fran Ackermann. 1998. *Making Strategy: The Journey of Strategic Management.* 1st ed. London: SAGE Publications Ltd.

Eden, Colin, Fran Ackermann, John M. Bryson, George P. Richardson, David F. Andersen, and Charles B. Finn. 2009. "Integrating Modes of Policy Analysis and Strategic Management Practice: Requisite Elements and Dilemmas." *Journal of the Operational Research Society* 60 (1): 2–13.

Eden, Colin, Sue Jones, and David Sims. 1983. *Messing About in Problems: An Informal Structured Approach to Their Identification and Management.* Headington Hill Hall: Pergamon Press.

Eggers, William D. 2008. "The Changing Nature of Government: Network Governance." In *Collaborative Governance: A New Era of Public Policy in Australia?,* edited by J. O'Flynn and J. Wanna, 23–28. Canberra, Australia: ANU E-Press

Elliot, R., and S. Tevavichulada. 1999. "Computer Literacy and Human Resource Management: A Public/Private Sector Comparison." *Public Personnel Management* 28: 259–74.

Epstein, Seymour. 1989. "Values from the Perspective of Cognitive-Experiential Self-Theory." In *Social and Moral Values,* edited by N. Eisenberg, 3–22. Hillsdale, NJ: Erlbaum.

———. 1993. "Emotion and Self-Theory." In *Handbook of Emotions,* edited by M. Lewis and J. M. Haviland-Jones, 313–26. New York: Guilford.

———. 2003. "Cognitive-Experiential Self-Theory of Personality." In *Handbook of Psychology,* vol. 5, *Personality and Social Psychology,* edited by Th. Millon, M. L. Lerner, and I. B. Weiner, 159–84. New York: Wiley.

Escobar, Oscar. 2011. *Public Dialogue and Deliberation: A Communication Perspective for Public Engagement Practitioners.* Edinburgh, Scotland: University of Edinburgh.

Eterno, John A. 2012. "Policing by the Numbers." *New York Times,* June 18.

Ewalt, Jo Ann G., and Edward T. Jennings. 2004. "Administration, Governance, and Policy Tools in Welfare Policy Implementation." *Public Administration Review* 64 (4): 449–62.

Feeney, Mary K., and B. Bozeman. 2007. "Public Values and Public Failure: Implications of the 2004–2005 Flu Vaccine Case." *Public Integrity* 9 (2): 175–90.

Feldman, Martha S. 2004. "Resources in Emerging Structures and Processes of Change." *Organization Science* 15 (3): 295–309.

Feldman, Martha S., and Brian T. Pentland. 2008. "Routine Dynamics." In *The Sage Handbook of New Approaches in Management and Organization,* edited by Daved Barry and Hans Hansen, 302–15. Los Angeles: Sage.

Feldman, Martha S., and Kathryn S. Quick. 2009. "Generating Resources and Energizing Frameworks through Inclusive Public Management." *International Public Management Journal* 12 (2): 137–71.

Ferris, G., and D. Treadway. 2012. *Politics in Organizations: Theory and Research Considerations.* New York: Routledge.

Ferris, G., D. Treadway, R. Kolodinsky, W. Hochwarter, C. Kacmar, C. Douglas, and D. Frink. 2005. "Development and Validation of the Political Skill Inventory." *Journal of Management* 31 (1): 126–52.

Festinger, Leon. 1957. *A Theory of Cognitive Dissonance.* Stanford, CA: Stanford University Press.

Fiedler, D. 2012. "Segregating Children Is Wrong." *Korea Herald,* March 13. http://www.koreaherald.com/view.php?ud=20120312000347.

Fischer, Frank, and John Forester. 1993. *The Argumentative Turn in Policy Analysis and Planning.* Durham, NC: Duke University Press.

Fisher, E., C. Slade, D. Anderson, and B. Bozeman. 2010. "The Public Value of Nanotechnology?" *Scientometrics* 85 (1): 29–39.

Fisher, Thomas. 2014. "Public Value and the Integrative Mind: How Multiple Sectors Can Collaborate in City Building." *Public Administration Review* 74 (4): 457–64.

Flynn, Norman. 2007. *Public Sector Management.* London: Sage.

Flyvberg, Bent. 1998. *Rationality and Power.* Chicago: University of Chicago Press.

Folz, David, Reem Abdelrazek, and Yeonsoo Chung. 2009. "The Adoption, Use, and Impacts of Performance Measures in Medium-Size Cities." *Public Performance and Management Review* 33 (1): 63–87.

Forester, John. 1998. "Rationality, Dialogue and Learning: What Community and Environmental Mediators Can Teach Us about the Practice of Civil Society." In *Cities for Citizens: Planning and the Rise of Civil Society,* edited by Mike Douglass and John Friedmann, 213–26. New York: Wiley.

Forrer, John J., James Edwin Kee, and Eric Boyer. 2014. *Governing Cross-Sector Collaboration.* San Francisco: Jossey-Bass.

Fountain, Jane E. 2001. "Paradoxes of Public Sector Customer Service." *Governance* 14 (1): 55–73.

Frankena, William K. 1973. *Ethics.* Upper Saddle River, NJ: Prentice Hall.

Frederickson, H. George. 1990. "Public Administration and Social Equity." *Public Administration Review* 50 (2): 228–37.

———. 1991. "Toward a Theory of the Public for Public Administration." *Administration and Society* 22 (4): 395–417.

———. 2010. "Searching for Virtue in the Public Life: Revisiting the Vulgar Ethics Thesis." *Public Integrity* 12 (3): 239–46.

Freeman, R. Edward. 1984. *Strategic Management: A Stakeholder Approach*. Boston: Pitman.

Friedman, Milton. 1962. *Capitalism and Freedom*. Chicago: University of Chicago Press.

Fung, Archon, ed. 2003. *Deepening Democracy: Institutional Innovations in Empowered Participatory Governance*. Brooklyn, NY: Verso.

———. 2004. *Empowered Participation: Reinventing Urban Democracy*. Princeton, NJ: Princeton University Press.

———. 2006. "Varieties of Participation in Complex Governance." *Public Administration Review* 66 (s1): 66–75.

Gallie, W. B. 1956. "Essentially Contested Concepts." *Proceedings of the Aristotelian Society* 56: 167–98.

Gallouj, F. 2002. *Innovation in the Service Economy*. Cheltenham, England: Edward Elgar.

Gandz, J., and V. Murray. 1980. "The Experience of Workplace Politics." *Academy of Management Journal* 23: 237–51.

Garsten, Bryan. 2006. *Saving Persuasion: A Defense of Rhetoric and Judgment*. Cambridge, MA: Harvard University Press.

Gastil, John, and James P. Dillard. 2006. "Increasing Political Sophistication through Public Deliberation." *Political Communication* 16 (1): 3–23.

Gaughan, M. 2003. *Public Value Mapping Breast Cancer Case Studies*. Washington, DC: Center for Science Policy and Outcomes.

Gaus, G. F. 1990. *Value and Justification: The Foundations of Liberal Theory*. New York: Cambridge University Press.

Gen, Sheldon, and Gordon Kingsley. 2007. "Effects of Contracting Out Engineering Services Over Time in a State Department of Transportation." *Public Works Management and Policy* 13 (1): 331–43.

Glaser, Barney, and Anselm Strauss. 1967. *The Discovery of Grounded Theory: Strategies for Qualitative Research*. New York: Transaction Publishers.

Goldsmith, Stephen, and William D. Eggers. 2004. *Governing by Network: The New Shape of the Public Sector*. Washington, DC: Brookings Institution Press.

Gomez, Peter, and Gilbert Probst. 1999. *Die Praxis des ganzheitlichen Problemlösens: Vernetzt denken, unternehmerisch handeln, persönlich überzeugen*. 3rd ed. Bern, Switzerland: Haupt Verlag.

Graumann, Carl F., and Robert Willig. 1983. "Wert, Wertung, Werthaltung." In *Enzyklopädie der Psychologie: Theorien und Formen der Motivation*, vol. 1, edited by Hans Thomae, 312–96. Göttingen, West Germany: Hogrefe.

Gray, Rob. 2001. "Thirty Years of Social Accounting, Reporting and Auditing: What (If Anything) Have We Learnt?" *Business Ethics: A European Review* 10 (1): 9–15.

Greenhalgh, T., G. Robert, F. Macfarlane, P. Bate, O. Kyriakidou, and R. Peacock. 2004. "Diffusion of Innovations in Service Organisations: Systematic Literature Review and Recommendations for Future Research." *Milbank Quarterly* 82: 581–629.

Griffen, T., David F. Andersen, George P. Richardson, and Charles B. Finn. 2000. "Using Group Model Building to Support Strategic Reform of the Real Property Tax System in New York State: A Case Study." Paper presented at the International Conference of the System Dynamics Society, Bergen, Norway, August 6–10.

Griffin, Jennifer J. 2000. "Corporate Social Performance: Research Direction for the 21st Century." *Business and Society* 39 (4): 479–92.

Gulick, Luther. 1933. "Politics, Administration, and the New Deal." *Annals of the American Academy of Political and Social Science* 169 (1): 55–66.

Gunn, John. 1969. *Politics and the Public Interest in the Seventeenth Century*. Toronto: University of Toronto Press.

Gupta, Akhil. 2003. *Public Value Mapping in a Developing Country Context: A Methodology to Promote Socially Beneficial Public Biotechnology Research and Uptake in India*. Washington, DC: Center for Science Policy and Outcomes.

Gupta, Akhil, and James Ferguson, eds. 1997. *Anthropological Locations: Boundaries and Grounds of a Field Science*. Berkeley: University of California Press.

Gutmann, Amy, and Dennis Thompson. 2004. *Why Deliberative Democracy?* Princeton, NJ: Princeton University Press.

Habermas, Jürgen. 1988. *Der philosophische Diskurs der Moderne. Zwölf Vorlesungen*. Frankfurt am Main: Suhrkamp Verlag.

Hage, J., and M. Aiken. 1967. "Program Change and Organizational Properties." *American Journal of Sociology* 72 (2): 503–19.

Hahn, Robert, and Peter Passell. 2010. "The Economics of Allowing More U.S. Drilling." *Energy Economics* 32: 638–50.

Hahn, Robert, and Paul Tetlock. 2008. "Has Economic Analysis Improved Regulatory Decisions?" *Journal of Economic Perspectives* 22: 67–84.

Haken, Hermann. 1977. *Synergetics: Nonequilibrium Phase Transition and Self-Organization in Physics, Chemistry and Biology*. Berlin: Springer Verlag.

Haken, Hermann, and Günter Schiepek. 2005. *Synergetik in der Psychologie: Selbstorganisation verstehen und gestalten*. Göttingen, Germany: Hogrefe.

Hall, Thad E., and Laurence J. O'Toole. 2004. "Shaping Formal Networks through the Regulatory Process." *Administration and Society* 36 (2): 186–207.

Hallinger, P., and R. H. Heck. 2010. "Collaborative Leadership and School Improvement: Understanding the Impact on School Capacity and Student Learning." *School Leadership and Management* 30 (2): 95–110.

Hargadon, A. 2002. "Brokering Knowledge: Linking Learning and Innovation." *Research in Organizational Behavior* 24: 41–86.

Harrington, Winston, Richard Morgenstern, and Peter Nelson. 2000. "On the Accuracy of Regulatory Cost Estimates." *Journal of Economic Perspectives* 19: 297–322.

Harrison, Teresa, Theresa A. Pardo, Anthony M. Cresswell, and Meghan Cook. 2011. "Delivering Public Value Through Open Government." Center for Technology in Government. http://www.ctg.albany.edu/publications/issuebriefs/opengov_pubvalue.

Hartley, Jean. 2005. "Innovation in Governance and Public Services: Past and Present." *Public Money and Management* 25 (1): 27–34.

———. 2011. "Public Value through Innovation and Improvement." In *Public Value: Theory and Practice*, edited by J. Benington and M. Moore, 171–84. Basingstoke, England: Palgrave Macmillan.

———. 2013. "Public and Private Features of Innovation." In *Handbook of Innovation in Public Services*, edited by S. Osborne and L. Brown, 44–59. London: Sage.

Hartley, Jean, J. Alford, Owen Hughes, and Sophie Yates. 2013. *Leading with Political Astuteness: A Study of Public Managers in Australia, New Zealand and the United Kingdom*. https://www.anzsog.edu.au/media/upload/publication/124_124_LWPA-report-Hartley-Alford-Hughes-Yates.pdf.

Hartley, Jean, and John Benington. 2006. "Copy and Paste, or Graft and Transplant? Knowledge Sharing in Inter-Organizational Networks." *Public Money and Management* 26 (2): 101–8.

Hartley, Jean, and James Downe. 2007. "The Shining Lights? Public Service Awards as an Approach to Service Improvement." *Public Administration* 85 (2): 329–53.

Hartley, Jean, and Colin Fletcher. 2008. "Leadership with Political Awareness: Leadership across Diverse Interests inside and outside the Organization." In *Leadership Perspectives: Knowledge into Action*, edited by K. James and J. Collins, 163–74. London: Palgrave.

Hartley, Jean, Colin Fletcher, and Christoph Ungemach. 2011. "Political Astuteness in Organizational Leadership." Paper presented to the Academy of Management Conference, Chicago, August 7–11.

Hartley, Jean, and Stella Manzie. 2013. *Dancing on Ice: Leadership with Political Astuteness by Senior Public Servants in the UK.* Milton Keynes, England: Open University Business School.

Hartley Jean, and Lyndsay Rashman. 2007. "How Is Knowledge Transferred between Organizations Involved in Change?" In *Managing Change in the Public Services,* edited by M. Wallace, M. Fertig, and E. Schneller, 173–92. Oxford: Blackwell.

———. 2010. "The Role of Leadership in Knowledge Creation and Transfer for Organizational Learning and Improvement." In *From Knowing to Doing: Connecting Knowledge and Performance in Public Services,* edited by Kieran Walshe, Gill Harvey, Eileen Spencer, Chris Skelcher, and Pauline Jas, 145–72. Cambridge: Cambridge University Press.

Hartley, Jean, and Chris Skelcher. 2008. "The Agenda for Public Service Improvement." In *Managing to Improve Public Services,* edited by J. Hartley, C. Donaldson, C. Skelcher, and M. Wallace, 3–23. Cambridge: Cambridge University Press.

Hartley J., E. Sørensen, and J. Torfing. 2013. "Collaborative Innovation: A Viable Alternative to Market-Competition and Organizational Entrepreneurship." *Public Administration Review* 73 (6): 821–30.

Hatry, Harry P. 2006. *Performance Measurement: Getting Results.* Washington, DC: Urban Institute Press.

Hatry, Harry P., John E. Marcotte, Therese van Houten, and Carol H. Weiss. 1998. *Customer Surveys for Agency Managers: What Managers Need to Know.* Washington, DC: Urban Institute Press.

Hays, Sean, and David Guston. (n.d.) *The Public Value of Social Policy Research: An Application of the Public Value Mapping Method at the National Institute of Justice.* Tempe: Arizona State University Consortium for Science Policy and Outcomes.

Head, Brian, and John Alford. 2013. "Wicked Problems: Implications for Public Policy and Management." *Administration and Society.* DOI: 10.1177/00953999713481601.

Hefetz, A., and M. Warner. 2004. "Privatization and Its Reverse: Explaining the Dynamics of the Government Contracting Process." *Journal of Public Administration Research and Theory* 14 (2): 171–90.

Heifetz, Ronald. 1994. *Leadership without Easy Answers.* Cambridge, MA: Harvard University Press.

Heifetz, Ronald, and Marty Linsky. 2002. *Leadership on the Line: Staying Alive through the Dangers of Leading.* Cambridge, MA: Harvard Business School Press.

Heinrich, Carolyn H., and Gerald R. Marschke. 2010. "Incentives and Their Dynamics in Public Sector Performance Management Systems." *Journal of Policy Analysis and Management* 29 (1): 183–208.

Hendricks, Carolyn M. 2006. "When the Forum Meets Interest Politics: Strategic Uses of Public Deliberation." *Politics and Society* 34 (4): 571–602.

Henig, J., C. Hamnett, and H. Feigenbaum. 1988. "The Politics of Privatization: A Comparative Perspective." *Governance* 14: 442–68.

Heyde, Johannes E. 1926. *Wert. Eine philosophische Grundlegung.* Erfurt, Germany: Verlag Kurt Stenger.

Hill, Carolyn J., and Laurence E. Lynn Jr. 2005. "Is Hierarchical Governance in Decline? Evidence from Empirical Research." *Journal of Public Administration Research and Theory* 15: 173–95.

Ho, Alfred. 2006. "Accounting for the Value of Performance Measurement from the Perspective of Midwestern Mayors." *Journal of Public Administration Research and Theory* 16 (2): 217–37.

Holman, Peg. 2010. *Engaging Emergence: Turning Upheaval into Opportunity.* San Francisco: Berrett-Koehler.

Holman, Peg, T. Devane, and S. Cady. 2007. *The Change Handbook: The Definitive Resource on Today's Best Methods for Engaging Whole Systems.* 2nd ed. San Francisco: Berrett-Koehler.

Hood, Christopher. 1991. "A Public Management for All Seasons." *Public Administration* 69 (1): 3–19.

———. 2005. "The Idea of Joined-Up Government: A Historical Perspective." In *Joined-Up Government,* edited by V. Bogdanor, 19–42. Oxford: Oxford University Press.

———. 2006. "Gaming in Targetworld: The Targets Approach to Managing British Public Services." *Public Administration Review* 66 (4): 515–21.

Hood, Christopher, Oliver James, George Jones, Colin Scott, and Tony Travers. 1999. "Regulation inside Government: Where the New Public Management Meets the Audit Explosion." *Public Money and Management* 18 (2): 61–68.

Hovmand, Peter S., David F. Andersen, A. Etiënne, J. A. Rouwette, George P. Richardson, Krista Rux, and Annaliese Calhoun. 2012. "Group Model-Building 'Scripts' as a Collaborative Planning Tool." *Systems Research and Behavioral Science* 29 (2): 179–93.

Howarth, R. B., and R. B. Norgaard. 1990. "Intergenerational Resource Rights, Efficiency, and Social Optimality." *Land Economics* 66 (1): 1.

Howick, Susan, Fran Ackermann, and David F. Andersen. 2006. "Linking Event Thinking with Structural Thinking: Methods to Improve Client Value in Projects." *System Dynamics Review* 22 (2): 113–40.

Hughes, Owen 2012. *Public Management and Administration.* 4th ed. Basingstoke, England: Palgrave Macmillan.

Hui, Glenn, and Mark Richard Hayllar. 2010. "Creating Public Value in E-government: A Public-Private-Citizen Collaboration Framework in Web 2.0." *Australian Journal of Public Administration* 69 (s1): S120–31.

Huxham, Chris, and Siv Vangen. 2005. *Managing to Collaborate: The Theory and Practice of Collaborative Advantage.* London: Routledge.

Huz, Steven, David F. Andersen, George P. Richardson, and Roger Boothroyd. 1997. "A Framework for Evaluating Systems Thinking Interventions: An Experimental Approach to Mental Health System Change." *System Dynamics Review* 13 (2): 149–69.

Inkpen, A., and M. Crossan. 1995. "Believing Is Seeing: Joint Ventures and Organization Learning." *Journal of Management Studies* 32 (5): 595–618.

Innes, Judith E., and David E. Booher. 2010. *Planning with Complexity: An Introduction to Collaborative Rationality for Public Policy.* New York: Routledge.

Iwin, Alexander A. 1975. *Grundlagen der Logik von Wertungen.* Berlin: Akademie-Verlag.

Jacob, Brian A., and Steven Levitt. 2003. "Rotten Apples: An Investigation of the Prevalence and Predictors of Teacher Cheating." *Quarterly Journal of Economics* 118 (3): 843–77.

Jacobs, Lawrence R. 2014. "The Contested Politics of Public Value." *Public Administration Review* 74 (4): 480–94.

Jacobs, Lawrence R., Fay Lomax Cook, and Michael Delli Carpini. 2009. *Talking Together: Public Deliberation and Political Participation in America.* Chicago: University of Chicago Press.

James, Oliver. 2004. "The UK Core Executive's Use of Public Service Agreements as a Tool of Governance." *Public Administration* 82 (2): 397–419.

Johansson, Tobias, and Sven Siverbo. 2009. "Explaining the Utilization of Relative Performance Evaluation in Local Government: A Multi-theoretical Study Using Data from Sweden." *Financial Accountability and Management* 25 (2): 197–224.

Julnes, George. 2012. "Developing Policies to Support Valuing in the Public Interest: Informing Policies for Judging Value in Evaluation." *New Directions for Evaluation* 133: 109–29.

Kalambokidis, Laura. 2014. "Creating Public Value with Tax and Spending Policies: The View from Public Economics." *Public Administration Review* 74: 519–26.

Kaner, Sam. 2007. *Facilitator's Guide to Participatory Decision-Making*. 2nd ed. San Francisco: Jossey-Bass.

Kanter, Rosabeth Moss. 1984. *The Change Masters*. London: Unwin.

Kaplan, Robert S., and David P. Norton. 1993. "Putting the Balanced Scorecard to Work." *Harvard Business Review* 71: 134–41.

———. 1996. *The Balanced Scorecard: Translating Strategy into Action*. Cambridge, MA: Harvard Business Review Press.

Keating, M. 1999. "The Public Service: Independence, Responsibility and Responsiveness." *Australian Journal of Public Administration* 58 (1): 39–47.

Keiser, Lael R., and Susan M. Miller. 2010. "The Impact of Organized Interests on Eligibility Determination: The Case of Veterans' Disability Compensation." *Journal of Public Administration Research and Theory* 20 (2): 505–31.

Kernaghan, Kenneth. 2003. "Integrating Values into Public Service: The Values Statement as Centerpiece." *Public Administration Review* 63 (6): 711–19.

Kettl, Donald. 1993. *Sharing Power: Public Governance and Private Markets*. Washington, DC: Brookings Institution Press.

———. 2002. *The Transformation of Governance: Public Administration for Twenty-First Century America*. Baltimore: Johns Hopkins University Press.

———. 2008. *The Next Government of the United States: Why Our Institutions Fail Us and How to Fix Them*. New York: Norton.

Kickert, Walter J. M., Erik-Hans Klijn, and Jopp F. M. Koppenjan. 1997. *Managing Complex Networks: Strategies for the Public Sector*. London: Sage.

Kieffer, K. M. 1998. "Orthogonal versus Oblique Factor Rotation: A Review of the Literature Regarding the Pros and Cons." Paper presented at the Annual Meeting of the Mid-South Educational Research Association, New Orleans, November 1998.

Kim, Hyunjung. 2009. "In Search of a Mental Model-like Concept for Group-level Modeling." *System Dynamics Review* 25 (3): 207–23.

Kim, Hyunjung, Roderick H. MacDonald, and David F. Andersen. 2013. "Simulation and Managerial Decision Making: A Double-Loop Learning Framework." *Public Administration Review* 73 (2): 291–300.

Kim, J. O., and C. W. Mueller. 1978. *Introduction to Factor Analysis: What It Is and How to Do It*. Thousand Oaks, CA: Sage.

Kingdon, John. 2011. *Agendas, Alternatives, and Public Policies*. 2nd ed. London: Longman.

Kirlin, John J. 1996. "What Government Must Do Well: Creating Value for Society." *Journal of Public Administration Research and Theory* 6 (1): 161–85.

Kisby, Ben. 2007. "Analysing Policy Networks: Towards an Ideational Approach." *Policy Studies* 28 (1): 71–101.

Klijn, Erik-Hans. 2005. "Networks and Interorganizational Management." In *The Oxford Handbook of Public Management*, edited by Evan Ferlie, Laurence E. Lynn Jr., and Christopher Pollit, 257–81. Oxford: Oxford University Press.

Klijn, Erik-Hans, Joop F. M. Koppenjan, and Katrien Termeer. 1995. "Managing Networks in the Public Sector: A Theoretical Study of Management Strategies in Policy Networks." *Public Administration* 73 (3): 437–54.

Koch, Per, and Johan Hauknes. 2005. *On Innovation in the Public Sector*. Oslo: NIFU STEP.

Kofman, Fred, and Peter M. Senge. 1993. "Communities of Commitment: The Heart of Learning Organizations." *Organizational Dynamics* 22 (2): 24–29.

Koliba, Christopher, Asim Zia, and Russell M. Mills. 2011. "Accountability in Governance Networks: An Assessment of Public, Private, and Nonprofit Emergency Management Practices Following Hurricane Katrina." *Public Administration Review* 71 (2): 210–20.

Koppell, Jonathan. 2005. "Pathologies of Accountability: ICANN and the Challenge of 'Multiple Accountabilities Disorder.'" *Public Administration Review* 65 (1): 94–108.

Krause, G. 1996. "The Institutional Dynamics of Policy Administration: Bureaucratic Influence over Securities Regulation." *American Journal of Political Science* 40 (4): 1083–1121.

Kroll, Alexander. 2013. "The Other Type of Performance Information: Non-Routine Feedback, Its Relevance and Use." *Public Administration Review* 73 (2): 265–76.

———. 2014. "Why Performance Information Use Varies among Public Managers: Testing Manager-Related Explanations." *International Public Management Journal* 17 (2): 174–201.

———. 2015. "Explaining the Use of Performance Information by Public Managers: A Planned-Behavior Approach." *American Review of Public Administration* 45 (2): 201–15.

Kroll, Alexander, and Isabella Proeller. 2013. "Controlling the Control System: Performance Information in the German Childcare Administration." *International Journal of Public Sector Management* 26 (1): 74–85.

Kroll, Alexander, and Dominik Vogel. 2013. "The PSM-Leadership Fit: A Model of Performance Information Use." *Public Administration*. DOI 10.1111/padm.12014.

Lane, Robert. 1991. *The Market Experience.* Cambridge: Cambridge University Press.

Lawton, Alan, David McKevitt, and Michelle Millar. 2000. "Coping with Ambiguity: Reconciling External Legitimacy and Organizational Implementation in Performance Measurement." *Public Money and Management* 20 (3): 13–20.

Leach, William D., and Paul A. Sabatier. 2005. "To Trust an Adversary: Integrating Rational and Psychological Models of Collaborative Policy Making." *American Political Science Review* 99 (4): 491–503.

Lee, Tsuey-Ping. 2001. "The Dynamics of New York State Social Welfare Reform Finance at the County Level: A Feedback View of System Behavior." Paper presented at the International Conference of the System Dynamics Society, Atlanta, Georgia, July 23–27.

Lee, Tsuey-Ping, Aldo A. Zagonel, David F. Andersen, John Rohrbaugh, and George P. Richardson. 1998. "A Judgment Approach to Estimating Parameters in Group Model-building: A Case Study of Social Welfare Reform at Dutchess County." Paper presented at the International Conference of the System Dynamics Society, Québec City, Canada, July 20–23.

Levin, Henry M. (2001). "Waiting for Godot: Cost-Effectiveness Analysis in Education." In *New Directions for Evaluation*, edited by R. Light, 55–68. San Francisco: Jossey-Bass.

Levin, Henry, and Patrick McEwan, eds. 2002. *Cost-Effectiveness and Educational Policy.* Larchmont, NY: Eye on Education.

Lewis, Michael, Jeannette M. Haviland-Jones, and Lisa Feldman Barrett. 2008. *Handbook of Emotions.* 3rd ed. New York: Guilford.

Linden, Russell M. 2002. *Working across Boundaries: Making Collaboration Work in Government and Nonprofit Organizations.* San Francisco: Jossey-Bass.

Lipsky, Michael. 1980. *Street-Level Bureaucracy: Dilemmas of the Individual in Public Services.* New York: Russell Sage Foundation.

Logar, N. 2011. "Chemistry, Green Chemistry, and the Instrumental Valuation of Sustainability." *Minerva: A Review of Science, Learning and Policy* 49 (1): 113–36.

Lucas, Henry. 1975. "Performance and the Use of an Information System." *Management Science* 21 (8): 908–19.

Luna-Reyes, Luis F., Ignacio J. Martinez-Moyano, Theresa A. Pardo, Anthony M. Cresswell, David F. Andersen, and George P. Richardson. 2006. "Anatomy of a Group Model-building Intervention: Building Dynamic Theory from Case Study Research." *System Dynamics Review* 22 (4): 291–320.

Lynn, Laurence. 1997. "Innovation and the Public Interest: Insights from the Private Sector." In *Innovation in American Government*, edited by A. Altshuler and R. Behn, 83–103. Washington, DC: Brookings Institution Press.

———. 2013. "Innovation and Reform in Public Administration: One Subject or Two?" In *Handbook of Innovation in Public Services*, edited by S. Osborne and L. Brown. London: Sage.

Lyons, W. E., David Lowery, and Ruth Hoogland DeHoog. 1992. *The Politics of Dissatisfaction: Citizens, Services, and Urban Institutions*. Armonk, NY: M. E. Sharpe.

Majone, Giandomenico. 1998. "Europe's 'Democratic Deficit': The Question of Standards." *European Law Journal* 4 (1): 5–28.

Mansbridge, Jane J. 1999. "On the Idea That Political Participation Makes Better Citizens." In *Citizen Competence and Democratic Institutions*, edited by Stephen L. Elkin and Karol E. Soltan, 291–326. University Park: Pennsylvania State University Press.

Marcus, George E. 1995. "Ethnography in/of the World System: The Emergence of Multi-Sited Ethnography." *Annual Review of Anthropology* 24: 95–117.

Maricle, G. 2011. "Prediction as an Impediment to Preparedness: Lessons from the U.S. Hurricane and Earthquake Research Enterprises." *Minerva: A Review of Science, Learning and Policy* 49 (1): 87–111.

Marquand, D. 2004. *Decline of the Public*. Cambridge: Polity.

Marsh, Kevin, Aaron Chalfin, and John Roman. 2008. "What Does Cost-Benefit Analysis Add to Decision-Making? Evidence from the Criminal Justice System Literature." *Journal of Experimental Criminology* 4: 117–35.

Martinez-Moyano, Ignacio J., Stephen H. Conrad, and David F. Andersen. 2011. "Modeling Behavioral Considerations Related to Information Security." *Computers and Security* 30 (6–7): 397–409.

Mashaw, Jerry L. 1983. *Bureaucratic Justice: Managing Social Security Disability Claims*. New Haven, CT: Yale University Press.

Matsuyama, K. 2000. "Endogenous Inequality." *Review of Economic Studies* 67: 743–59.

McCartt, Anne T., and John Rohrbaugh. 1995. "Managerial Openness to Change and the Introduction of GDSS: Explaining Initial Success and Failure in Decision Conferencing." *Organization Science* 6 (5): 569–84.

McIntyre, Alice. 2008. *Participatory Action Research: Qualitative Research Methods*. Thousand Oaks, CA: Sage.

Meade, Adam W. 2004. "Psychometric Problems and Issues Involved with Creating and Using Ipsative Measures for Selection." *Journal of Occupational and Organizational Psychology* 77: 531–52.

Melkers, Julia, and Katherine Willoughby. 2005. "Models of Performance-Measurement Use in Local Governments." *Public Administration Review* 65 (2): 180–90.

Mendelberg, Tali. 2002. "The Deliberative Citizen: Theory and Evidence." In *Political Decision Making, Deliberation, and Participation: Research in Micropolitics*, vol. 6, edited by Michael Delli Carpini, Leonie Huddy, and Robert Y. Shapiro, 151–93. Greenwich, CT: JAI.

Meyer, John, and Richard Scott. 1992. "Centralization and the Legitimacy Problems of Local Government." In *Organizational Environments: Ritual and Rationality*, edited by John Meyer and Richard Scott, 199–215. Newbury Park, CA: Sage.

Meyer, R. 2011. "The Public Values Failures of Climate Science in the U.S." *Minerva: A Review of Science, Learning and Policy* 49 (1): 47–70.

Meyer, Renate E., and Markus A. Höllerer. 2010. "Meaning Structures in a Contested Issue Field: A Topographic Map of Shareholder Value in Austria." *Academy of Management Journal* 53 (6): 1241–62.

Meynhardt, Timo. 2004. *Wertwissen. Was Organisationen wirklich bewegt.* Münster, Germany: Waxmann.

———. 2009. "Public Value Inside: What Is Public Value Creation?" *International Journal of Public Administration* 32: 192–219.

Meynhardt, Timo, and Steffen Bartholomes. 2011. "(De)composing Public Value: In Search of Basic Dimensions and Common Ground." *International Public Management Journal* 14 (3): 284–308.

Meynhardt, Timo, and Peter Gomez. 2013. "Manual Public Value Scorecard." Unpublished manuscript.

Meynhardt, Timo, Peter Gomez, and Markus Schweizer. 2014. "The Public Value Scorecard: What Makes an Organization Valuable to Society?" *Performance* 6 (1): 1–8.

Meynhardt, Timo, Jürgen Maier, and Eric Schulze. 2010. "Zeit für eine Gemeinwohlstrategie: Steigerung des Public Values am Beispiel des Goethe-Instituts." *Organisationsentwicklung—Zeitschrift für Unternehmensentwicklung und Change Management* 4: 50–57.

Meynhardt, Timo, and Jörg Metelmann. 2009. "Pushing the Envelope: Creating Public Value in the Labor Market: An Empirical Study on the Role of Middle Managers." *International Journal of Public Administration* 32 (3–4): 274–312.

Meynhardt, Timo, and Camillo von Müller. 2013. "'Wir wollen Werte schaffen für die Gesellschaft'—Der Public Value im Spannungsfeld zwischen Aktienwert und Gemeinwohl. Eine Fallstudie am Beispiel der Deutsche Börse AG." *Zeitschrift für öffentliche und gemeinwirtschaftliche Unternehmen* 2–3: 119–49.

Meynhardt, Timo, Pepe Strathoff, Lorenz Beringer, and Sebastian Bernard. In press. *FC Bayern München: A Football Club Defines Its Societal Role between Local Rootedness and Global Ambitions.* Cranfield, England: European Case Clearing House.

Miles, I. 2000. "Innovation in Services." In *The Oxford Handbook of Innovation,* edited by J. Fagerberg, D. Mowery, and R. Nelson, 433–58. Oxford: Oxford University Press.

Miller, Thomas I., Michelle Miller Kobayashi, and Shannon Elissa Hayden. 2008. *Citizen Surveys for Local Government: A Comprehensive Guide to Making Them Matter.* 3rd ed. Washington, DC: ICMA Press.

Milter, Richard G., and John Rohrbaugh. 1985. "Microcomputers and Strategic Decision Making." *Public Productivity Review* 9 (2/3): 175–89.

Mishan, E. J. 1980. "How Valid Are Economic Evaluations of Allocative Changes?" *Journal of Economic Issues* 14 (1): 143.

Mitnick, Barry. 1976. "A Typology of Conceptions of the Public Interest." *Administration and Society* 8: 5–28.

Modell, Sven. 2009. "Institutional Research on Performance Measurement and Management in the Public Sector Accounting Literature: A Review and Assessment." *Financial Accountability and Management* 25 (3): 277–303.

Mookherjee, D., and D. Ray. 2002. "Is Equality Stable?" *American Economic Review* 92: 253–59.

Moore, Mark H. 1994. "Policing: Deregulating or Redefining Accountability?" In *Deregulating the Public Service: Can Government Be Improved?*, edited by John DiIulio Jr., 198–235. Washington, DC: Brookings Institution Press.

———. 1995. *Creating Public Value: Strategic Management in Government.* Cambridge, MA: Harvard University Press.

———. 2000. "Managing for Value: Organizational Strategy in For-Profit, Nonprofit, and Governmental Organizations." *Nonprofit and Voluntary Sector Quarterly* 29 (s1): 183–208.

———. 2003. *The Public Value Scorecard: A Rejoinder and an Alternative to "Strategic Performance Measurement and Management in Non-Profit Organizations" by Robert Kaplan.* Hauser Center for Nonprofit Organizations Working Paper No. 18. Cambridge, Massachusetts.

———. 2005. "Break-Through Innovations and Continuous Improvement: Two Different Models of Innovative Processes in the Public Sector." *Public Money and Management* 25 (1): 43–50.

———. 2013. *Recognizing Public Value.* Cambridge, MA: Harvard University Press.

———. 2014. "Public Value Accounting: Establishing a Philosophical Basis." *Public Administration Review* 74 (4): 465–77.

Moore, Mark H., Adrian Boardman, Adrian Vining, David Weimer, and David Greenberg. 2004. "Just Give Me a Number! Practical Values for the Social Discount Rate." *Journal of Policy Analysis and Management* 23: 789–812.

Moore, Mark H., and Archon Fung. 2012. "Calling Publics into Existence: The Political Arts of Public Management." In *Ports in a Storm: Public Management in a Turbulent World,* edited by John D. Donahue and Mark H. Moore, 203–33. Washington, DC: Brookings Institution Press.

Moore, Mark H., and Margaret Jane Gates. 1986. *Inspectors General: Junkyard Dogs or Man's Best Friend?* New York: Russell Sage Foundation.

Moore, Mark H., and J. Hartley. 2008. "Innovations in Governance." *Public Management Review* 10 (1): 3–20.

Moore, Mark H., and Sanjeev Khgram. 2004. *On Creating Public Value: What Business Might Learn from Government about Strategic Management.* Corporate Social Responsibility Initiative Working Paper No. 3. Cambridge, Massachusetts: John F. Kennedy School of Government, Harvard University.

Moran, M. 2003. *The British Regulatory State: High Modernism and Hyper-Innovation.* Oxford: Oxford University Press.

Moulton, Stephanie. 2009. "Putting Together the Publicness Puzzle: A Framework for Realized Publicness." *Public Administration Review* 69 (5): 889–900.

Moynihan, Donald P. 2008. *The Dynamics of Performance Management: Constructing Information and Reform.* Washington, DC: Georgetown University Press.

———. 2009. "Through a Glass, Darkly: Understanding the Effects of Performance Regimes." *Public Performance and Management Review* 32 (4): 592–603.

———. 2013. *The New Federal Performance System: Implementing the New GPRA Modernization Act.* Washington, DC: IBM Center for the Business of Government.

Moynihan, Donald P., and Daniel Hawes. 2012. "Responsiveness to Reform Values: The Influence of the Environment on Performance Information Use." *Public Administration Review* 72 (s1): 95–105.

Moynihan, Donald P., and Patricia Ingraham. 2004. "Integrative Leadership in the Public Sector: A Model of Performance-Information Use." *Administration and Society* 36 (4): 427–53.

Moynihan, Donald P., and Noel Landuyt. 2009. "How Do Public Organizations Learn? Bridging Cultural and Structural Perspectives." *Public Administration Review* 69 (6): 1097–1105.

Moynihan, Donald P., and Stephane Lavertu. 2012. "Does Involvement in Performance Management Routines Encourage Performance Information Use? Evaluating GPRA and PART." *Public Administration Review* 72 (4): 592–602.

Moynihan, Donald P., and Sanjay Pandey. 2010. "The Big Question for Performance Management: Why Do Managers Use Performance Information?" *Journal of Public Administration Research and Theory* 20 (4): 849–66.

Moynihan, Donald P., Sanjay K. Pandey, and Bradley E. Wright. 2012a. "Prosocial Values and Performance Management Theory: The Link between Perceived Social Impact and Performance Information Use." *Governance* 25 (3): 463–83.

———. 2012b. "Setting the Table: How Transformational Leadership Fosters Performance Information Use." *Journal of Public Administration Research and Theory* 22 (1): 143–64.

Mulgan, Geoff, and David Albury. 2003. *Innovations in the Public Sector.* London: Cabinet Office.

Müller, Johanna, Markus Menz, and Timo Meynhardt. 2013. *Haniel (A): Corporate Strategy and Corporate Responsibility.* Cranfield, England: European Case Clearing House.

———. In press. *Haniel (B): Implementing the CR Strategy.* Cranfield, England: European Case Clearing House.

Nabatchi, Tina. 2012. "Putting the 'Public' Back in Public Values Research: Designing Participation to Identify and Respond to Public Values." *Public Administration Review* 72 (5): 699–708.

Nabatchi, Tina, John Gastil, Michael Weiksner, and Matt Leighninger, eds. 2012. *Democracy in Motion: Evaluating the Practice and Impact of Deliberative Civic Engagement.* New York: Oxford University Press.

Nabatchi, Tina, and Matt Leighninger. 2015. *Public Participation for 21st Century Democracy.* San Francisco: Jossey-Bass.

National Audit Office. 2007. *The Budget for the London 2012 Olympic and Paralympic Games: Report by the Comptroller and Auditor General.* London: National Audit Office.

Newman, J., J. Raine, and C. Skelcher. 2001. "Transforming Local Government: Innovation and Modernisation." *Public Money and Management* 21 (2): 61–68.

Nicholson-Crotty, J., and S. Miller. 2011. "Bureaucratic Effectiveness and Influence in the Legislature." *Journal of Public Administration Research and Theory* 22 (2): 347–71.

Nielsen, Poul A. 2014a. "Learning from Performance Feedback: Performance Information, Aspiration Levels, and Managerial Priorities." *Public Administration* 92 (1): 142–60.

———. 2014b. "Performance Management, Managerial Authority, and Public Service Performance." *Journal of Public Administration Research and Theory* 24 (2): 431–58.

Niskanen, William. 1971. *Bureaucracy and Representative Government.* Chicago: Rand McNally.

Nonaka, Ikujiro. 1994. "A Dynamic Theory of Organizational Knowledge Creation." *Organization Science* 5: 14–37.

Nordhaus, William D. 2007. "A Review of the *Stern Review on the Economics of Climate Change.*" *Journal of Economic Literature* 45 (3): 686–702.

Norman, R. 2011. "Redefining 'Public Value' in New Zealand's Performance Management System: Managing for Outcomes While Accounting for Outputs." In *Public Value: Theory and Practice,* edited by John Benington and Mark H. Moore, 52–66. Basingstoke, England: Palgrave Macmillan.

North, Douglass C. 1990. *Institutions, Institutional Change and Economic Performance.* Cambridge: Cambridge University Press.

Norton, B. G., and M. A. Toman. 1997. "Sustainability: Ecological and Economic Perspectives." *Land Economics* 73 (4): 553.

Ochsenbauer, Christian, and Konstanze Ziemke-Jerrentrup. 2013. "Dem Wert einen Preis geben. Der Beitrag öffentlicher Bäder zum Gemeinwohl und der 'Public Value Award.'" *Organisationsentwicklung—Zeitschrift für Unternehmensentwicklung und Change Management* 4: 40–47.

OECD [Organisation for Economic Co-operation and Development]. 2009. *Measuring Government Activity.* Paris: Organisation for Economic Co-operation and Development.

O'Flynn, Janine. 2007. "From New Public Management to Public Value: Paradigmatic Change and Managerial Implications." *Australian Journal of Public Administration* 66 (3): 353–66.

Oliver, James. 2011. "Managing Citizens' Expectations of Public Service Performance: Evidence from Observation and Experimentation in Local Government." *Public Administration* 89 (4): 1419–35.

Ongaro, Edoardo. 2009. *Public Management Reform and Modernization: Trajectories of Administrative Change in Italy, France, Greece, Portugal and Spain*. Cheltenham, England: Edward Elgar.

Osborne, David, and Ted Gaebler. 1993. *Reinventing Government: How the Entrepreneurial Spirit Is Transforming the Public Sector*. Reading, MA: Addison-Wesley.

Osborne, David, and Peter Hutchinson. 2004. *The Price of Government: Getting the Results We Need in an Age of Permanent Fiscal Crisis*. New York: Basic Books.

Osborne, Stephen P. 2010. *The New Public Governance? New Perspectives on the Theory and Practice of Public Governance*. London: Routledge.

Osborne, Stephen P., and Kerry Brown. 2005. *Managing Change and Innovation in Public Service Organizations*. London: Routledge.

Osborne, Stephen P., and Louise Brown. 2011. "Innovation, Public Policy and Public Services Delivery: The Word That Would Be King?" *Public Administration* 89 (4): 1335–50.

———. 2013. *Handbook of Innovation in Public Services*. Northampton, MA: Edward Elgar.

Osborne, Stephen P., and Kate McLaughlin. 2004. "The Cross-Cutting Review of the Voluntary Sector: Where Next for Local Government–Voluntary Sector Relationships?" *Regional Studies* 38 (5): 573–82.

Osborne, Stephen P., Zoe Radnor, and Greta Nasi. 2013. "A New Theory for Public Service Management? Toward a (Public) Service-Dominant Approach." *American Review of Public Administration* 43 (2): 135–58.

O'Toole, Laurence J. Jr. 1997. "Treating Networks Seriously: Practical and Research-Based Agendas in Public Administration." *Public Administration Review* 57 (1): 45–52.

———. 2000. "Research on Policy Implementation: Assessment and Prospect." *Journal of Public Administration Research and Theory* 10 (2): 263–88.

O'Toole, Laurence J. Jr., and Kenneth J. Meier. 2003. "Plus ça Change: Public Management, Personnel Stability, and Organizational Performance." *Journal of Public Administration Research and Theory* 13 (1): 43–64.

O'Toole, Laurence, Kenneth Meir, and Sean Nicholson-Crotty. 2005. "Managing Upward, Downward, and Outward: Networks, Hierarchical Relationships and Performance." *Public Management Review* 7 (1): 45–68.

Owen, Harrison. 1997. *Open Space Technology: A User's Guide*. San Francisco: Berrett-Koehler.

Padula, Marinella. 2011. *The Victorian Bushfire Reconstruction and Recovery Authority (A): The Challenge*. Case 2011-123.1. Melbourne: Case Program Australia and New Zealand School of Government.

Page, E. 2012. *Policy without Politicians: Bureaucratic Influence in Comparative Perspective*. Oxford: Oxford University Press.

Page, Stephen. 2004. "Measuring Accountability for Results in Interagency Collaborations." *Public Administration Review* 64 (5): 591–606.

Page, Stephen B., Melissa M. Stone, John M. Bryson, and Barbara C. Crosby. 2015. "Public Value Creation by Cross-Sector Collaborations: A Framework and Challenges of Assessment." *Public Administration*. Article first published online on March 25, 2015. DOI: 10.1111/padm.12161

Page, T. 1977. *Conservation and Economic Efficiency: An Approach to Materials Policy*. Baltimore: Johns Hopkins University Press.

Papadopoulos, Y. 2007. "Problems of Democratic Accountability in Network and Multilevel Governance." *European Law Journal* 13 (4): 469–86.

Parks, R., P. Baker., L. Kiser, R. Oakerson, E. Ostrom, V. Ostrom, S. Percy, M. Vandivort, G. Whitaker, and R. Wilson. 1981. "Consumers as Co-producers of Public Services: Some Economic and Institutional Considerations." *Policy Studies Journal* 9 (7): 1001–11.

Perrini, Francesco. 2006. *The New Social Entrepreneurship: What Awaits Social Entrepreneurship Ventures?* Cheltenham, England: Edward Elgar.

Perry, James. 2000. "Bringing Society In: Toward a Theory of Public Service Motivation." *Journal of Public Administration Research and Theory* 10 (2): 471–88.

Perry, J., Annie Hondeghem, and Lois R. Wise. 2010. "Revisiting the Motivational Bases of Public Service: Twenty Years of Research and an Agenda for the Future." *Public Administration Review* 70 (5): 681–90.

Perry, James, and Lois Wise. 1990. "The Motivational Bases of Public Service." *Public Administration Review* 50: 367–73.

Peters, B. Guy. 1987. "Politicians and Bureaucrats in the Politics of Policy Making." In *Bureaucracy and Public Choice*, edited by J. E. Lane, 256–82. London: Sage.

———. 2001. *The Politics of Bureaucracy.* London: Routledge.

Peters, B. Guy, and Jon Pierre. 2010. "Public–Private Partnerships and the Democratic Deficit: Is Performance-Based Legitimacy the Answer?" In *Democracy and Public–Private Partnerships in Global Governance*, edited by M. Bexell and U. Morth, 41–54. Basingstoke: Palgrave MacMillan.

Piotrowski, Suzanne J., and David Rosenbloom. 2002. "Nonmission-Based Values in Results Oriented Public Management." *Public Administration Review* 62: 643–57.

Poister, Theodore H., and Gregory Streib. 1999. "Performance Measurement in Municipal Government: Assessing the State of the Practice." *Public Administration Review* 59 (4): 325–35.

Poister, Theodore H., and John Clayton Thomas. 2009. "The Case of GDOT's Consultant and Contractor Surveys: An Approach to Strengthening Relationships with Government's Business Partners." *Public Performance and Management Review* 33: 122–40.

Poister, Theodore H., John Clayton Thomas, and Anita Faust Berryman. 2013. "Reaching Out to Stakeholders: The Georgia DOT 360 Degree Assessment Model." *Public Performance and Management Review* 37: 302–28.

Pollitt, Christopher. 2010. "Performance Blight and the Tyranny of Light? Accountability in Advanced Performance Measurement Regimes." In *Accountable Governance: Problems and Promises*, edited by Melvin J. Dubnick and H. George Frederickson, 81–98. Armonk, NY: M. E. Sharpe.

———. 2013. *Context in Public Policy and Management: The Missing Link.* Northampton, MA: Edward Elgar.

Pollitt, Christopher, and Geert Bouckaert. 2000. *Public Management Reform: A Comparative Analysis.* Oxford: Oxford University Press.

———. 2004. *Public Management Reform: A Comparative Analysis.* 2nd ed. Oxford: Oxford University Press.

———. 2011. *Public Management Reform: A Comparative Analysis—New Public Management, Governance, and the Neo-Weberian State.* Oxford: Oxford University Press.

Porter, Michael E. 1985. *Competitive Advantage: Creating and Sustaining Superior Performance.* New York: Free Press.

Porter, Michael E., and Mark R. Kramer. 2011. "Creating Shared Value." *Harvard Business Review* 89 (1–2): 62–77.

Posner, Richard. 2000. "Cost-Benefit Analysis: Definition, Justification, and Comment on Conference Papers." *Journal of Legal Studies* 29: 1153–77.

Prager, J. 1994. "Contracting Out Government Services: Lessons from the Private Sector." *Public Administration Review* 54 (2): 176–84.

Quick, Kathryn, and Martha Feldman. 2011. "Distinguishing Participation and Inclusion." *Journal of Planning Education and Research* 31 (3): 272–90.

Quick, Kathryn, and Jodi Sandfort. 2014. "Learning to Facilitate Deliberation: Practicing the Art of Hosting." *Critical Policy Studies.* DOI: 10.1080/19460171.2014.912959.

Quinn, Robert E., John Rohrbaugh, and Michael R. McGrath. 1985. "Automated Decision Conferencing: How It Works." *Personnel* 62 (6): 49–55.

Radin, Beryl. 2006. *Challenging the Performance Movement: Accountability, Complexity, and Democratic Values.* Washington, DC: Georgetown University Press.

———. 2012. *Federal Management Reform in a World of Contradictions.* Washington, DC: Georgetown University Press.

———. 2013. *Beyond Machiavelli: Policy Analysis Reaches Midlife.* Washington, DC: Georgetown University Press.

Rainey, Hal. 1982. "Reward Preference among Public and Private Managers: In Search of the Service Ethic." *American Review of Public Administration* 16 (4): 288–302.

———. 1983. "Public Agencies and Private Firms: Incentive Structures, Goals and Individual Roles." *Administration and Society* 15: 207–42.

———. 2009. *Understanding and Managing Public Organizations.* San Francisco: Jossey-Bass.

Rainey, Hal, and Young Han Chun. 2005. "Public and Private Management Compared." In *Oxford Handbook of Public Management,* edited by E. Ferlie, L. Lynn, and C. Pollitt, 72–102. Oxford: Oxford University Press.

Rao, T. V., and R. Rao. 2005. *The Power of 360 Degree Feedback: Maximizing Managerial and Leadership Effectiveness.* New Delhi: Response.

Rashman, Lyndsay, James Downe, and Jean Hartley. 2005. "Knowledge Creation and Transfer in the Beacon Scheme: Improving Services through Sharing Good Practice." *Local Government Studies* 31 (5): 683–700.

Rautiainen, Antti. 2010. "Contending Legitimations: Performance Measurement Coupling and Decoupling in Two Finnish Cities." *Accounting, Auditing and Accountability Journal* 23 (3): 373–91.

Reagan-Cirincione, Patricia, Sandor P. Schuman, George P. Richardson, and Stanley A. Dorf. 1991. "Decision Modeling: Tools for Strategic Thinking." *Interfaces* 21 (6): 52–65.

Reich, Robert B. 1990. "Policy Making in a Democracy." In *The Power of Public Ideas,* edited by Robert B. Reich, 123–56. Cambridge, MA: Harvard University Press.

Rescher, Nicholas. 1982. *Introduction to Value Theory.* Washington, DC: University Press of America.

Revesz, Richard, and Michael Livermore. 2008. *Retaking Rationality: How Cost-Benefit Analysis Can Better Protect the Environment and Our Health.* New York: Oxford University Press.

Rhodes, R. A. W., and David Marsh. 1992. "New Directions in the Study of Policy Networks." *European Journal of Political Research* 21 (1–2): 181–205.

Rhodes, R. A. W., and John Wanna. 2007. "Limits to Public Value, or Rescuing Responsible Government from the Platonic Guardians." *Australian Journal of Public Administration* 66 (4): 406–21.

Riahi-Belkaoui, Ahmei. 2005. *Accounting Theory.* 5th ed. Atlanta: Thompson.

Richardson, George P., and David F. Andersen. 1995. "Teamwork in Group Model Building." *System Dynamics Review* 11 (2): 113–37.

Richardson, George P., David F. Andersen, and Yi-jung Wu. 2002. "Misattribution in Welfare Dynamics: The Puzzling Dynamics of Recidivism." Paper presented at the International Conference of the System Dynamics Society, Palermo, Italy, July 28–August 1.

Rickards, T. 1996. "The Management of Innovation: Recasting the Role of Creativity." *European Journal of Work and Organizational Psychology* 5 (1): 13–27.

Rumberger, Russell W. 2011. *Dropping Out: Why Students Drop Out of School and What Can Be Done About It.* Cambridge, MA: Harvard University Press.

Rittel, Horst W. J., and Melvin M. Webber. 1973. "Dilemmas in a General Theory of Planning." *Policy Sciences* 4 (2): 155–69.

Rivlin, Alice M. 2012. "Rescuing the Budget Process." *Public Budgeting and Finance* 32 (3): 53–56.

Robbins, Suzanne. M. 2010. "Play Nice or Pick a Fight? Cooperation as an Interest Group Strategy at Implementation." *Policy Studies Journal* 38 (3): 515–35.

Roberts, Nancy. 2004. "Public Deliberation in an Age of Direct Citizen Participation." *American Review of Public Administration* 34 (4): 315–53.

Rogers, Everett. 2003. *Diffusion of Innovations.* 5th ed. New York: Free Press.

Rogers, Jane, Robert Johnson, Aldo A. Zagonel, John Rohrbaugh, David F. Andersen, George P. Richardson, and Tsuey-Ping Lee. 1997. "Group Model-Building to Support Welfare Reform in Rockland County."

Rogers, Juan D., and Barry Bozeman. 2001. "'Knowledge Value Alliances': An Alternative to the R&D Project Focus in Evaluation." *Science, Technology, and Human Values* 26 (1): 23–55.

Rohrbaugh, John. 1992. "Cognitive Challenges and Collective Accomplishments." In *Computer Augmented Teamwork: A Guided Tour,* edited by Robert P. Bostrom and Susan T. Kinney, 299–324. New York: Van Nostrand Reinhold.

———. 2000. "The Use of System Dynamics in Decision Conferencing." In *Handbook of Public Information Systems,* edited by G. David Garson. New York: Marcel Dekker.

Rohrbaugh, John, and Robert Johnson. 1998. "Welfare Reform Flies in New York." *Government Technology,* May 31, 1998.

Rosenberg, Shawn W. 2007. "Rethinking Democratic Deliberation: The Limits and Potential of Citizen Participation." *Polity* 39 (3): 335–60.

Rosenbloom, David H. 2007. "Reinventing Administrative Prescriptions: The Case for Democratic-Constitutional Impact Statements and Scorecards." *Public Administration Review* 67: 28–39.

Rosenbloom, David H., and Howard E. McCurdy, eds. 2006. *Revisiting Waldo's Administrative State: Constancy and Change in Public Administration.* Washington, DC: Georgetown University Press.

Rouwette, Etiënne A. J. A. 2003. *Group Model Building as Mutual Persuasion.* Nijmegen: Wolf Legal Publishers.

Rouwette, Etiënne A. J. A., Jac A. M. Vennix, and Theo Van Mullekom. 2002. "Group Model Building Effectiveness: A Review of Assessment Studies." *System Dynamics Review* 18 (1): 5–45.

Rumsfeld, Donald. 1995. *Thoughts from the Business World on Downsizing Government.* Chicago: Heartland Institute.

Rutgers, Mark R. 2008. "Sorting Out Public Values? On the Contingency of Value Classifications in Public Administration." *Administrative Theory and Praxis* 30 (1): 92–113.

Rutgers, Mark R., and Patrick Overeem. 2014. "Public Values in Public Administration." *Journal of Public Administration Research and Theory* 24 (3): 806–12.

Ryan, B. 2012. "Co-production: Option or Obligation?" *Australian Journal of Public Administration* 71 (3): 314–24.

Salamon, Lester, and Wojciech Sokolowski. 2001. *Volunteering in Cross-National Perspective: Evidence from 24 Countries.* Working Papers of the Johns Hopkins Comparative Nonprofit Sector Project. Baltimore: Johns Hopkins University.

Samuelson, Paul A. 1954. "The Pure Theory of Public Expenditure." *Review of Economics and Statistics* 36 (4): 387–89.

Sandel, Michael. 2009. *Justice: What's the Right Thing to Do?* New York: Farrar, Straus and Giroux.

Sandfort, Jodi. 2013. "Analyzing the Practice of Nonprofit Advocacy: Comparing Two Human Services Networks." In *Nonprofit Advocacy*, edited by Robert Peckham and Steven Smith, 72–76. Baltimore: Johns Hopkins University Press.

Sandfort, Jodi, and Laura Bloomberg. 2012. "In Commons: Supporting Community-Based Leadership." *Community Development* 43 (1): 12–30.

Sandfort, Jodi, Nicholas Stuber, and Kathryn Quick. 2012. *Practicing the Art of Hosting: Exploring What Art of Hosting and Harvesting Workshop Participants Understand and Do.* Minneapolis: Center for Integrative Leadership, University of Minnesota.

Sanger, Mary B. 2008. "From Measurement to Management: Breaking Through the Barriers to State and Local Performance." *Public Administration Review* 68: 70–85.

Savas, E. S. 1987. *Privatization: The Key to Better Government.* Chatham, NJ: Chatham House.

Savitz, Andrew. 2006. *The Triple Bottom Line: How Today's Best-Run Companies Are Achieving Economic, Social, and Environmental Success—And How You Can Too.* San Francisco: Jossey-Bass.

Sawa, Jessica E., and Sally Coleman Selden. 2003. "Administrative Discretion and Active Representation: An Expansion of the Theory of Representative Bureaucracy." *Public Administration Review* 63 (6): 700–709.

Schroeder, Mark. 2012. *Value Theory.* Stanford Encyclopedia of Philosophy. http://plato.stanford.edu/entries/value-theory.

Schulte, D. William. 2001. *The Strategy-Focused Organization: How Balanced Scorecard Companies Thrive in the New Business Environment.* Cambridge, MA: Harvard Business School Press.

Schulze, Eric. 2010. *Der Beitrag zum Gemeinwohl: Public Values definieren und legitimieren: eine Untersuchung am Beispiel des Goethe-Instituts.* Borsdorf, Germany: Edition Winterwork.

Schuman, Sandor. 1995. "Valuing and Using Data in Group Decision Making: An Examination of Decision Conferences and the Effect of Decision Makers' Perceptions of Data and Empirical Process Outcomes." Unpublished Dissertation, University of Albany, Rockefeller College of Public Affairs and Policy, Department of Public Administration, Albany, New York.

Schuman, Sandor, and John Rohrbaugh. 1991. "Decision Conferencing for Systems Planning." *Information and Management* 21 (3): 147–59.

Schumpeter, Joseph. 1950. *Capitalism, Socialism and Democracy.* New York: Harper and Row.

Schwab, Klaus. 2008. "Global Corporate Citizenship: Working with Government and Civil Society." *Foreign Affairs* 87 (1): 107–18.

Schwartz, Jason. 2010. *52 Experiments with Regulatory Review: The Political and Economic Inputs into State Rulemaking.* New York: Institute for Policy Integrity, New York University.

Schwarz, Roger. 2002. *The Skilled Facilitator: A Comprehensive Resource for Consultants, Facilitators, Managers, Trainers, and Coaches.* San Francisco: Jossey-Bass.

Scott, W. Richard. 2007. *Institutions and Organizations.* 3rd ed. London: Sage.

Scott, W. Richard, and Søren Christensen. 1995. *The Institutional Construction of Organizations: International and Longitudinal Studies.* Thousand Oaks, CA: Sage Publishing.

Selznick, Philip. 1994. *The Moral Commonwealth: Social Theory and the Promise of Community.* Berkeley: University of California Press.

Sen, Amartya. 1970. *Collective Choice and Social Welfare.* San Francisco: Holden-Day.

———. 1992. *Inequality Reexamined.* New York: Russell Sage Foundation.

———. 1997. "Inequality, Unemployment, and Contemporary Europe." *International Labor Review* 136: 155–71.

Sen, Amartya, and Bernard Williams. 1982. *Utilitarianism and Beyond.* New York: Cambridge University Press.

Shaffer, Marvin. 2010. *Multiple Account BCA: A Practical Guide.* Toronto: University of Toronto Press.

Shipman, Stephanie. 2010. "The Role of Context in Valuing Federal Programs." In *Promoting Valuation in the Public Interest: Informing Policies for Judging Value in Evaluation,* edited by George Julnes, 323–46. Hoboken, NJ: Wiley.

Silvester, J. 2008. "The Good, the Bad and the Ugly: Politics and Politicians at Work." In *International Review of Industrial and Organizational Psychology,* vol. 23, edited by G. Hodgkinson and J. Ford. DOI: 10.1002/9780470773277.ch4.

Simon, Herbert. 1996. *The Sciences of the Artificial.* 3rd ed. Cambridge, MA: MIT Press.

Sirianni, Carmen, and Lewis Friedland. 2001. *Civic Innovation in America: Community Empowerment, Public Policy, and the Movement for Civic Renewal.* Berkeley: University of California Press.

Slade, C. P. 2011. "Public Value Mapping of Equity in Emerging Nanomedicine." *Minerva: A Review of Science, Learning and Policy* 49 (1): 71–86.

Sloan, Frank, Jan Ostermann, Gabriel Picone, Christopher Conover, and Donald Taylor. 2004. *The Price of Smoking.* Cambridge, MA: MIT Press.

Smith, S., and M. Lipsky. 1993. *Nonprofits for Hire: The Welfare State in the Age of Contracting.* Cambridge, MA: Harvard University Press.

Sorauf, Frank. 1957. "The Public Interest Reconsidered." *The Journal of Politics* 19 (4): 616–39.

Soss, Joe, Richard Fording, and Sanford F. Schram. 2011. "The Organization of Discipline: From Performance Management to Perversity and Punishment." *Journal of Public Administration, Research and Theory* 21 (2): 203–32.

Spano, Alessandro. 2009. "Public Value Creation and Management Control Systems." *International Journal of Public Administration* 32: 328–48.

Sparrow, Malcolm K. 1994. *Imposing Duties: Government's Changing Approach to Compliance.* Westport, CT: Praeger.

Steiner, Peter O. 1970. "The Public Sector and the Public Interest." In *Public Expenditures and Policy Analysis,* edited by R. H. Haveman and J. Margolis. Chicago: Markham.

Stiglitz, Joseph E. 2013. *The Price of Inequality: How Today's Divided Society Endangers Our Future.* New York: Norton.

Stiglitz, Joseph E., and Linda J. Bilmes. 2008. *The Three Trillion Dollar War: The True Cost of the Iraq Conflict.* New York: Norton.

Stoker, Gerry. 2006. "Public Value Management: A New Narrative for Networked Governance?" *American Review of Public Administration* 36 (1): 41–57.

Stokey, Edith, and Richard Zeckhauser. 1974. *A Primer for Policy Analysis.* New York: Norton.

Stone, Deborah. 2011. *Policy Paradox: The Art of Political Decision Making.* New York: Norton.

Success Works. 2011. *Evaluation of the Art of Hosting and Harvesting Conversations That Matter: Success Works Conferences 2009–2011.* Carlton, Victoria, Australia: Success Works.

Suchman, Mark. 1995. "Managing Legitimacy: Strategic and Institutional Approaches." *Academy of Management Review* 20 (3): 571–610.

Susskind, Lawrence, and Patrick Field. 1996. *Dealing with an Angry Public: The Mutual Gains Approach to Resolving Disputes.* New York: Free Press.

Svara, J. 2001. "The Myth of the Dichotomy: Complementarity of Politics and Administration in the Past and Future of Public Administration." *Public Administration Review* 61 (2): 176–83.

Talbot, Colin. 2006. "Paradoxes and Prospects of 'Public Value.'" Paper presented at the Tenth International Research Symposium on Public Management, Glasgow, April 10–12.

———. 2009. "Public Value—The Next 'Big Thing' in Public Management?" *International Journal of Public Administration* 32 (3): 167–70.

———. 2010. *Theories of Performance*. New York: Oxford University Press.

Taylor, Jeanette. 2009. "Strengthening the Link between Performance Measurement and Decision Making." *Public Administration* 87 (4): 853–71.

———. 2011. "Factors Influencing the Use of Performance Information for Decision Making in Australian State Agencies." *Public Administration* 89 (4): 1316–34.

't Hart, P., and A. Wille. 2006. "Ministers and Top Officials in the Dutch Core Executive: Living Together, Growing Apart?" *Public Administration* 84 (1): 121–46.

Thomas, John Clayton. 2012. *Citizen, Customer, Partner: Engaging the Public in Public Management*. Armonk, NY: M. E. Sharpe.

Thomas, John Clayton, and Theodore H. Poister. 2009. "Thinking About Stakeholders of Public Agencies: The Georgia Department of Transportation Stakeholder Audit." *Public Organization Review* 9: 67–82.

Thomas, John Clayton, Theodore H. Poister, and Nevbahar Ertas. 2010. "Customer, Partner, Principal: Local Government Perspectives on State Agency Performance in Georgia." *Journal of Public Administration Research and Theory* 20 (October): 779–99.

Thomas, John Clayton, Min Su, and Theodore H. Poister. 2012. "How Do Legislators Assess Administrative Performance? Georgia's Department of Transportation in the Eyes of the State's General Assembly." Unpublished paper.

Thompson, Victor. 1965. "Bureaucracy and Innovation." *Administrative Science Quarterly* 10: 1–20.

Tidd, J., and J. Bessant. 2009. *Managing Innovation*. Chichester, England: Wiley.

Tönnies, Ferdinand. 2001. *Community and Civil Society*. Edited by Jose Harris. Cambridge: Cambridge University Press.

Toppe, C. M., A. D. Kirsch, and J. Michel. 2002. *Giving and Volunteering in the United States 2001: Findings from a National Survey*. Washington, DC: Independent Sector.

Transportation Research Board. 2005. *Performance Measures to Improve Transportation Systems: Summary of the Second National Conference*. Washington, DC: Transportation Research Board.

Tushman, Michael L., and Phillip Anderson. 1986. "Technological Discontinuities and Organizational Environments." *Administrative Sciences Quarterly* 31 (3): 439–65.

Tyler, Tom R. 2006. *Why Citizens Obey the Law*. Princeton, NJ: Princeton University Press.

Uhl-Bien, Mary, and Sonia M. Ospina. 2012. *Advancing Relational Leadership Research: A Dialogue Among Perspectives*. Charlotte, NC: Information Age Publishing.

US Department of Agriculture. 2013. "Wetlands." http://www.nrcs.usda.gov/wps/portal/nrcs/main/national/water/wetlands/.

US Government Accountability Office. 2013. "Effects of Budget Uncertainty from Continuing Resolutions on Agency Operations." http://gao.gov/assets/660/652999.pdf.

Valdivia, W. 2011. "The Stakes in Bayh-Dole: Public Values beyond the Pace of Innovation." *Minerva: A Review of Science, Learning and Policy* 49 (1): 25.

"Value." (n.d.) Merriam-Webster.com. http://www.merriam-webster.com/dictionary/Value.

Van de Ven, A. 1986. "Central Problems in the Management of Innovation." *Management Science* 32: 590–607.

Van der Wal, Zeger, Tina Nabatchi, and Gjalt de Graaf. 2013. "From Galaxies to Universe: A Cross-Disciplinary Review and Analysis of Public Values Publications from 1969 to 2012." *American Review of Public Administration*. DOI: 10.1177/0275074013488822.

Van der Wal, Zeger, and E. Th. J. van Hout. 2009. "Is Public Value Pluralism Paramount? The Intrinsic Multiplicity and Hybridity of Public Values." *International Journal of Public Administration* 32 (3–4): 220–31.

Van Deth, J. W., and E. Scarbrough. 1995. *The Impact of Values.* New York: Oxford University Press.

Van Dooren, Wouter. 2005. "What Makes Organisations Measure? Hypotheses on the Causes and Conditions for Performance Measurement." *Financial Accountability and Management* 21 (3): 363–83.

———. 2008. "Nothing New under the Sun? Change and Continuity in Twentieth Century Performance Movements." In *Performance Information in the Public Sector: How It Is Used*, edited by Wouter Van Dooren and Steven Van de Walle, 11–23. Basingstoke, England: Palgrave Macmillan.

Van Dooren, Wouter, Geert Bouckaert, and John Halligan. 2010. *Performance Management in the Public Sector.* London: Routledge.

Van Dooren, Wouter, and Steven Van de Walle, eds. 2008. *Performance Information in the Public Sector: How It Is Used.* Basingstoke, England: Palgrave Macmillan.

Van Ryzin, Gregg G. 2011. "Outcomes, Process, and Trust of Civil Servants." *Journal of Public Administration Research and Theory* 21 (4): 745–60.

Van Ryzin, Gregg G., and E. Wayne Freeman. 1997. "Viewing Organizations as Customers of Government Services." *Public Productivity and Management Review* 20: 419–31.

Van Wart, M. 1998. *Changing Public Sector Values.* New York: Garland.

Vennix, Jac A. M. 1996. *Group Model Building: Facilitating Team Learning Using System Dynamics.* 1st ed. Chichester: Wiley.

Vennix, Jac A. M., David F. Andersen, George P. Richardson, and John Rohrbaugh. 1994. "Model Building for Group Decision Support: Issues and Alternatives in Knowledge Elicitation." In *Modeling for Learning Organizations*, edited by John Morecroft and John D. Sterman. Portland, OR: Productivity Press.

Veterans Benefits Administration. 2013. "Department of Veterans Affairs Strategic Plan to Eliminate the Compensation Claims Backlog." http://benefits.va.gov/transformation /docs/va_strategic_plan_to_eliminate_the_compensation_claims_backlog.pdf.

Vickers, G. 1995. *The Art of Judgment: A Study of Policy Making.* Thousand Oaks, CA: Sage.

Viganò, Enrico. 1998. "Accounting and Business Economics Traditions in Italy." *European Accounting Review* 7 (3): 381–403.

Viscusi, William. 2010. "The Heterogeneity of the Value of Statistical Life: Introduction and Overview." *Journal of Risk and Uncertainty* 40: 1–13.

Von Hippel, Eric. 1998. *The Sources of Innovation.* New York: Oxford University Press.

———. 2005. *Democratizing Innovation.* Cambridge, MA: MIT Press.

Von Hippel, Eric, and Georg von Krogh. 2003. "Open-Source Software and the 'Private-Collective' Innovation Model: Issues for Organizational Science." *Organization Science* 14 (2): 209–23.

Voss, J.-P. 2007. "Innovation Processes in Governance: The Development of 'Emissions Trading' as a New Policy." *Science and Public Policy* 34 (5): 329–44.

Waldo, Dwight. 1984. *The Administrative State: A Study of the Political Theory of American Public Administration.* 2nd ed. New York: Holmes and Meier.

Walker, Richard M., and Barry Bozeman, eds. 2011. *Journal of Public Administration Research and Theory, Special Issue on Publicness and Organizational Performance* 20 (s3).

Walker, Richard M., Fariborz Damanpour, and Carlos Devece. 2011. "Management Innovation and Organizational Performance: The Mediating Effect of Performance Management." *Journal of Public Administration Research and Theory* 21 (2): 367–86.

Weber, Edward P., and Anne M. Khademian. 2008. "Wicked Problems, Knowledge Challenges, and Collaborative Capacity Builders in Network Settings." *Public Administration Review* 68 (2): 334–49.

Weber, Max. (1922) 1978. *Economy and Society*. Translated by Ephraim Fischoff. Berkeley: University of California Press.

Weimer, David and Aiden Vining. 2010. *Policy Analysis: Concepts and Practice*. 5th ed. New York: Routledge.

Weisbrod, Burton J. 1962. "Investment in Human Beings." *Journal of Political Economy* 70 (5, pt. 2): 106–23.

Weise, Frank-Jürgen, and Roland Deinzer. 2013. "Den sozialen Auftrag fest im Blick. Die gesellschaftliche Wertschöpfung der Bundesagentur für Arbeit." *Organisationsentwicklung - Zeitschrift für Unternehmensentwicklung und Change Management* 4: 30–36.

Weiss, Carol H. W. 1995. "Nothing as Practical as Good Theory: Exploring Theory-Based Evaluation for Comprehensive Community Initiatives for Children and Families." *Approaches to Evaluating Community Initiatives* 65: 123–42.

Willems, T., and W. van Dooren. 2011. "How Collaborative Arrangements Lead to an Accountability Paradox." *International Review of Administrative Sciences* 77 (3): 505–30.

WDA [Weltverband Deutscher Auslandsschulen]. 2014. *Wertvoll für die Welt. Wertvoll für Deutschland. Studie zum Public Value der Deutschen Auslandsschulen*. Berlin: Weltverband Deutscher Auslandsschulen.

West, Karen, and Paul Davis. 2011. "What Is the Public Value of Government Action? Towards a (New) Pragmatic Approach to Values Questions in Public Endeavours." *Public Administration* 89 (2): 226–41.

Wheatley, Margaret. 2006. *Leadership and the New Science: Discovering Order in a Chaotic World*. 3rd ed. San Francisco: Berrett-Koehler.

———. 2009. *Turning to One Another: Simple Conversations to Restore Hope to the Future*. 2nd ed. San Francisco: Berrett-Koehler.

Wheatley, Margaret, and Deborah Frieze. 2011. *Walk Out, Walk On: A Learning Journey into Communities Daring to Live the Future Now*. New York: BK Currents.

White, S. 2005. "Cooperation Costs, Governance Choice and Alliance Evolution." *Journal of Management Studies* 42 (7): 1383–1412.

Wholey, Joseph, Harry Hatry, and Kathryn E. Newcomer, eds. 2010. *Handbook of Practical Program Evaluation*. 3rd ed. Hoboken, NJ: Wiley.

Wichowsky, Amber, and Donald Moynihan. 2008. "Measuring How Administration Shapes Citizenship: A Policy Feedback Perspective on Performance Management." *Public Administration Review* 68 (5): 908–20.

Wildavsky, Aaron. 1979. *Speaking Truth to Power*. Boston: Little, Brown.

Wilde, S. 1991. *Life under the Bells*. Australia: Longman Cheshire.

Williams, Iestyn, and Heather Shearer. 2011. "Appraising Public Value: Past, Present and Futures." *Public Administration* 89: 1367–84.

Williams, Wil, and Duncan Lewis. 2008. "Strategic Management Tools and Public Sector Management." *Public Management Review* 10 (5): 653–71.

Williamson, Abby, and Archon Fung. 2004. "Public Deliberation: Where Are We and Where Can We Go?" *National Civic Review* 93 (4): 3–15.

Williamson, O. E. 1975. *Markets and Hierarchies: Analysis and Antitrust Implications*. New York: Free Press.

Wilson, James Q. 1989. *Bureaucracy*. New York: Basic Books.

Wilson, Woodrow. 1887. "The Study of Administration." *Political Science Quarterly* 2: 197–222.

Winerip, Michael. 2013. "Ex-Schools Chief in Atlanta Is Indicted in Testing Scandal." *New York Times*, March 29.

Wolf, Charles. 1988. *Markets or Governments: Choosing between Imperfect Alternatives*. Cambridge, MA: MIT Press.

Woolum, Janet. 2011. "Citizen Involvement in Performance Measurement and Reporting: A Comparative Case Study from Local Government." *Public Performance and Management Review* 25 (1): 79–102.

World Bank. 2004. *Public Sector Roles in Strengthening Corporate Social Responsibility: Taking Stock*. New York: World Bank.

Wright, Bradley E. 2011. "Public Administration as an Interdisciplinary Field: Assessing Its Relationship with Other Fields of Law, Management and Political Science." *Public Administration Review* 71 (1): 96–101.

Wulczyn, Fred H., David F. Andersen, George P. Richardson, and Eric A. Wuestman. 1991. "Caseload and Fiscal Implications of the Foster Care Baby Boom." Executive summary report. Albany, NY: New York State Department of Social Services.

Yang, Kaifeng, and Jun Hsieh. 2007. "Managerial Effectiveness of Government Performance Measurement: Testing a Middle-Range Model." *Public Administration Review* 67 (5): 861–79.

Young, Iris Marion. 2000. *Inclusion and Democracy*. New York: Oxford University Press.

Zagonel, Aldo A. 2002. "Model Conceptualization in Group Model Building: A Review of the Literature Exploring the Tension Between Representing Reality and Negotiating a Social Order." Paper presented at the International Conference of the System Dynamics Society, Palermo, Italy, July 28–August 1.

———. 2003. "Using Group Model-building to Inform Welfare Reform Policy Making in New York State: A Critical Look." Paper presented at the International Conference of the System Dynamics Society, New York City, July 20–24.

Zagonel, Aldo A., John Rohrbaugh, George P. Richardson, and David F. Andersen. 2004. "Using Simulation Models to Address 'What If' Questions About Welfare Reform." *Journal of Policy Analysis and Management* 23 (4): 890–901.

Zahra, S., and G. George. 2002. "Absorptive Capacity: A Review, Reconceptualisation and Extension." *Academy of Management Review* 27: 185–203.

Zan, Luca. 1994. "Towards a History of Accounting Histories: Perspectives from the Italian Tradition." *European Accounting Review* 3 (2): 255–307.

Zappa, Gino. 1927. *Tendenze nuove negli studi di Ragioneria*. Milan: Instituto Editoriale Scientifico.

CONTRIBUTORS

John Alford is a professor of public-sector management at the Melbourne Business School, University of Melbourne, and at the Australia and New Zealand School of Government. Two of his books have won international awards: *Engaging Public Sector Clients: From Service Delivery to Co-production* (2009) was the winner of the American Society for Public Administration's SPAR Award for best public administration book of 2011, while *Rethinking Public Service Delivery: Managing with External Providers* (2012; coauthored with Janine O'Flynn) won the Academy of Management's Public and Nonprofit Division award for best public management book of 2014.

David F. Andersen is a distinguished service professor of public administration and informatics at the University at Albany. He specializes in government information strategy and management, as well as the application of system dynamics to support organizational policy and strategy making. Anderson has consulted for numerous local, state, and federal agencies, often using group model building techniques.

Clive Belfield is an associate professor of economics at Queens College, City University of New York. He is also codirector of the Center for Benefit-Cost Studies in Education, Teachers College, Columbia University. His fields of expertise are the economics of education, cost-benefit analysis, and cost-effectiveness analysis. Belfield's most recent book is *The Price We Pay: The Economic and Social Consequences of Inadequate Education* (2007; coauthored with Henry Levin).

Laura Bloomberg is the associate dean of the Hubert H. Humphrey School of Public Affairs at the University of Minnesota. Her research and teaching focus on US education policy and administration, cross-sector leadership, and program evaluation. Bloomberg has previously held positions as an urban high school principal and as executive director of the University of Minnesota's Center for Integrative Leadership. She has authored several papers on cross-sector leadership and education policy.

Barry Bozeman is Arizona Centennial Professor of Technology Policy and Public Management at Arizona State University and director of the Center for Organization Research and Design. He previously served on the faculties of the University of Georgia and Syracuse University's Maxwell School of Citizenship and Public Affairs. Bozeman's research focuses on public policy, public management, science and technology policy, and innovation.

John M. Bryson is McKnight Presidential Professor of Planning and Public Affairs at the Hubert H. Humphrey School of Public Affairs at the University of Minnesota. He works in the areas of leadership, strategic management, and the design of organizational and community change processes. Bryson is the author of *Strategic Planning for Public and Nonprofit Organizations* (4th ed., 2011), and coauthor with Barbara C. Crosby of *Leadership for the Common Good: Tackling Public Problems in a Shared-Power World* (2nd ed., 2005). He is a Fellow of the National Academy of Public Administration. Bryson has consulted with a wide variety of governing bodies, government agencies, nonprofit organizations, and corporations in Europe and North America.

Meghan Cook is program director at the Center for Technology in Government at the University at Albany and has led large multidisciplinary and multisector applied research programs over the last eighteen years to foster public-sector innovation, enhance capability, and improve information management strategies. Cook has authored numerous articles, papers, and book chapters for both academic and practitioner audiences and has served on advisory boards, including the US Office of Personnel Management's Open Government Flagship Initiative Committee. As a speaker and facilitator in high demand, she has led over one hundred thought-leadership programs for governments all over the world, including Brazil's Digital Democracy Summit, the European Commission's ePractice Series, Mexico's Annual Government Innovation Forum, and Moscow's International Conference on Open Government.

Anthony M. Cresswell has a teaching and research career that spans over four decades and focuses on public policy, management, and technology innovation. He is an emeritus faculty member of the University at Albany, having served since 1979 on the faculties of the departments of Educational Administration and Information Science and as deputy director and interim director of the Center for Technology in Government, conducting applied research on information technology innovation in the public sector. Prior to his positions at the University at Albany, Cresswell served on the faculties of Northwestern University and Carnegie-Mellon University and as a faculty adviser in the US Office of Management and Budget.

Barbara C. Crosby is an associate professor at the Hubert H. Humphrey School of Public Affairs and former academic codirector of the Center for Integrative Leadership at the University of Minnesota. She is a Fellow of the Leadership Trust in the United Kingdom, and in 2002–3 she was a visiting fellow at the University of Strathclyde, Glasgow, Scotland. Crosby was coordinator of the Humphrey Fellowship Program at the University of Minnesota from 1990 to 1993 and director of the Humphrey School's Reflective Leadership Center from 1999 to 2002. She has taught and written extensively about leadership and public policy, integrative leadership, cross-sector collaboration, women in leadership, media and public policy, and strategic planning. Crosby is the author of *Leadership for Global Citizenship* (1999) and coauthor with John M. Bryson of *Leadership for the Common Good: Tackling Public Problems in a Shared-Power World* (2nd ed., 2005).

Enrico Guarini is an assistant professor of business administration and management at the University of Milano-Bicocca and professor of public management and policy at the SDA Bocconi School of Management, Italy. He is also cochair of the special interest group on local governance at the International Research Society for Public Management. Guarini's research interests include public management, public financial management and accountability, local government, and governance.

Jean Hartley is a professor of public leadership at the Open University Business School in the United Kingdom. She researches public leadership (by politicians, managers and professionals, and civil society agents) as well as innovation and organizational change in public organizations. Hartley has written six books and numerous articles on leadership, innovation, and organizational change.

Natalie Helbig is an affiliate faculty member in the Department of Informatics and teaches courses in public administration at the University at Albany. She is director of Health Data NY at the New York State Department of Health's Office of Quality and Patient Safety, and prior to holding that position was assistant research director at the Center for Technology in Government, where she led research efforts for over a decade. Helbig's research examines the use of performance information and the dynamics of opening government data.

Owen Hughes is the dean of students at the Royal Melbourne Institute of Technology. He is the author of *Public Management and Administration* (4th ed., 2012).

Alexander Kroll is an assistant professor of public administration at Florida International University. His research interest is in performance management and organizational behavior in public administration.

Luis F. Luna-Reyes is an associate professor of informatics at the University at Albany and also a member of the Mexican National Research System. His research focuses on electronic government and on modeling collaboration processes in the development of information technologies across functional and organizational boundaries.

Timo Meynhardt serves as the managing director of the Center for Leadership and Values in Society at the University of St. Gallen, Switzerland. He also holds the chair for management at Leuphana University, Germany. Meynhardt was trained as a psychologist and worked as a practice expert with McKinsey & Company.

Mark H. Moore is the Hauser Professor of Nonprofit Organizations at Harvard University's Kennedy School of Government, and the Herbert Simon Professor of Organization, Management, and Education at the Harvard Graduate School of Education. He has served as the founding faculty director of the Kennedy School's Hauser Center on Nonprofit Organizations and as the founding chairman of the Kennedy School's Committee on Executive Programs. His publications include

Creating Public Value: Strategic Management in Government (1995) and *Recognizing Public Value* (2013).

Donald P. Moynihan is a professor of public affairs at the University of Wisconsin–Madison. His work has examined how public organizations function, including the effects of efforts to improve their performance. Moynihan is a member of the National Academy of Public Administration, and his work has won a number of awards, including the Kershaw Award, given every two years for distinguished research on public policy and administration.

Theodore H. Poister is a professor of public management at the Andrew Young School of Policy Studies at Georgia State University, where his research focuses on strategic planning, performance management, and stakeholder engagement in the public sector. He has published widely on these topics in public management journals and is coauthor, with Maria P. Aristigueta and Jeremy L. Hall, of *Managing and Measuring Performance in Public and Nonprofit Organizations* (2nd ed., 2014). Poister has worked with numerous federal, state, and local government agencies on applied research and consulting projects and conducts professional development programs on performance management and applied statistical analysis for the Evaluators' Institute at George Washington University and for individual government agencies.

Kathryn S. Quick is an assistant professor at the Humphrey School of Public Affairs at the University of Minnesota. Her research and teaching focus on practices and processes for engaging diverse stakeholders in addressing complex public problems. Quick's research settings involve a range of policy content areas, the common thread being qualitative analysis of how they are enacted and their consequences for policy outcomes, democratic capacity building, and resilience.

George P. Richardson is professor emeritus of public administration, public policy, and informatics at the University at Albany. He is the author of more than fifty articles on theory and applications of system dynamics modeling. Two of his books were honored with the System Dynamics Society's Jay W. Forrester Award: *Introduction to System Dynamics Modeling with DYNAMO* (1981) and *Feedback Thought in Social Science and Systems Theory* (2nd ed., 1999).

Heather Rimes is a doctoral student and research assistant in the Department of Public Administration and Policy at the University of Georgia. Her research interests include science and technology policy, organizational theory and behavior, public values, and the policy process.

Jodi Sandfort is an associate professor at the University of Minnesota's Humphrey School of Public Affairs and chair of the school's Management and Leadership Area. Her research, teaching, and practice all focus on improving the implementation of social policy, particularly those policies designed to support low-income children and their families.

Min Su is a doctoral candidate at the Andrew Young School of Policy Studies at Georgia State University. Her fields of specialization include public and nonprofit financial management, urban governance, and citizen participation and collaboration. Her recent research investigates how financial slack influences local government management.

John C. Thomas is a professor of public management and policy in the Andrew Young School of Policy Studies at Georgia State University. He has published four books and more than sixty articles focusing principally on how citizens connect with their governments and how those connections can be improved. Thomas also serves as coeditor, with Guy Adams, of the *American Review of Public Administration.*

Jennie Welch is currently employed by the Georgia Leadership Institute for School Improvement, a nonprofit organization dedicated to developing world-class leaders who advance student achievement and organizational effectiveness. Her most recent research collaborations have examined the qualities of effective consulting organizations in partnerships with school districts; the dispositions of highly effective school leaders; and the identification and assessment of public values in the K–12 and higher education sectors.

Index

The letter *t* following a page number denotes a table; the letter *f* following a page number denotes a figure.